Katherine Mansfield (1888–1923) was born Kathleen Beauchamp in Wellington, New Zealand. She was educated at Queen's College, London, eventually settling in Britain in 1908. Her first volume of stories, *In a German Pension*, was published in 1911. In 1912 she met John Middleton Murry (1889–1957), then an Oxford undergraduate and editor of the modernist periodical *Rhythm*, and at her invitation he moved into her London flat. They became lovers (marrying in 1918), and together they edited the periodical until its collapse in 1913. Their relationship was stormy, alternating between intense love and virtual estrangement, and it was frequently punctuated by separations. At the request of Murry's friend, D.H. Lawrence, they spent some time living near the Lawrences in Cornwall, but relations became strained and Lawrence later portrayed Katherine and Murry as Gudrun and Gerald in his novel, *Women in Love*. In 1917 Katherine contracted tuberculosis and spent the remaining years of her life moving between London and France. During this period she was accompanied always by her lifelong friend Ida Baker (L.M.), or by Murry, who from 1919 to 1921 was editor of the *Athenaeum*, in which he published such fine writers as Virginia Woolf, T.S. Eliot, Paul Valéry and Katherine herself. A further collection of Katherine's stories, *Bliss*, was published in December 1920. But her health was deteriorating, and the following year she travelled to Switzerland, where she lived near her cousin, the novelist Elizabeth von Arnim. Finally, Katherine turned to the philosophy of Gurdjieff, entering the Gurdjieff Institute in Fontainebleau in 1922, the year she published *The Garden Party*. On 31 December she wrote to Murry, asking him to visit her; he arrived on 9 January, and she died that evening.

A year after Katherine's death, Murry founded the *Adelphi*, and though he married again three times, remained dedicated to the publication of Katherine Mansfield's works. Two collections of stories, *The Doves' Nest* (1923) and *Something Childish* (1924), and the short novel *The Aloe* (1924), were edited and posthumously published by him, along with letters and reminiscences. In addition to these and his numerous critical works, Murry's autobiography, *Between Two Worlds*, was published in 1935.

Cherry Hankin was born in Nelson, New Zealand. After completing university and teacher's training college, she lived in London and Montreal before enrolling for a Ph.D in English at the University of California in Berkeley. She returned to New Zealand on a Berkeley Advanced Graduate Travelling Fellowship to study the then unpublished papers of Katherine Mansfield held by the Turnbull Library in Wellington. After completing her Ph.D dissertation, a psychological study of Mansfield and her writing, she joined the Department of English at the University of Canterbury, where she specialises in teaching and writing about New Zealand and twentieth-century British fiction. She has published extensively on both Katherine Mansfield and John Middleton Murry, her major works including *Katherine Mansfield and Her Confessional Stories* (1983) and *Letters of John Middleton Murry to Katherine Mansfield* (1983). She has recently introduced five centennial editions of Mansfield's stories, and is working on a new study of the relationship between Murry and D.H. Lawrence.

Letters Between
KATHERINE MANSFIELD
and
JOHN MIDDLETON MURRY

SELECTED AND EDITED BY

Cherry A. Hankin

NEW AMSTERDAM
New York

First published in the United States of America in 1991 by

NEW AMSTERDAM BOOKS
171 Madison Avenue
New York, NY 10016

by arrangement with Virago Press Limited, London.

First printing.

Library of Congress Cataloging-in-Publication Data

Mansfield, Katherine, 1888–1923
    Letters between Katherine Mansfield and John Middleton Murry/selected
and edited by Cherry A. Hankin.
      p. cm
    Includes index
    ISBN 0-941533-76-X (acid-free paper)
    1. Mansfield, Katherine, 1888–1923—Correspondence. 2. Murry, John
Middleton, 1889–1957—Correspondence. 3. Authors, New Zealand—20th
century—Correspondence. 4. Authors, English—20th century—
Correspondence. I. Murry, John Middleton, 1889–1957. II. Hankin, C.A.
III. Title.
PR9639.3.M258Z494 1991
823'.912—dc20   90-40417
[B]   CIP

10 9 8 7 6 5 4 3 2 1

This book is printed on acid-free paper.

Contents

By the same author

Katherine Mansfield and her Confessional Stories
The Letters of John Middleton Murry to Katherine Mansfield (ed.
C.A. Hankin)

Introduction

Katherine Mansfield was born Kathleen Mansfield Beauchamp in Wellington, New Zealand, on 14 October 1888. Her rather delicate mother, who had already produced two daughters, Vera and Charlotte, subsequently gave birth to Gwendoline (who lived only three months), Jeanne, and Leslie, the Beauchamps' only son. Kathleen's father, Harold (later Sir Harold) Beauchamp, was a prosperous businessman whose intelligence and acumen brought him both financial and social success as well as public recognition.

In 1903 the Beauchamp girls were sent to England to be educated, as was the custom among well-to-do New Zealanders in the first part of this century. During her formative years at the enlightened Queen's College in London, Kathleen immersed herself in the musical, literary and artistic life of the metropolis. She also entered into what was to be one of the most important relationships of her life – with Ida Baker, the adoring school-friend whom she renamed Leslie Moore, or 'L.M.'. When she returned to colonial New Zealand in 1906, Kathleen had become a rebellious young woman, already determined to achieve fame as a writer. By July 1908 she had prevailed upon Harold Beauchamp to send her back to London with an allowance of £100 a year.

The years between 1908 and 1912, when Katherine Mansfield (as she now called herself) met John Middleton Murry, must have confirmed her parents' worst fears. In the course of trying out the bohemian lifestyle of an artist, Katherine indulged in a variety of love affairs, married George Bowden, a singing teacher much older than herself whom she promptly left, became pregnant by another man, and suffered a miscarriage in Wörishofen, Bavaria. It was Mrs Beauchamp who, hearing of the impulsive marriage and separation, hastened half-way across the world and, suspecting a lesbian involvement with L.M., dispatched her daughter to Bavaria to be 'cured'. On her return to New Zealand, she cut Katherine out of her will. Katherine Mansfield's relations with her respectable parents had never been easy. For the rest of her life she felt herself the outsider of the family, and, jealous of the favours bestowed on her

1

sisters, longed to win back the love of her parents – especially the love of her father – which she sensed she had forfeited.

One way to do that was to prove herself as a writer. In December 1911 Katherine Mansfield announced herself to the literary world with *In a German Pension*, her first collection of short stories. This remarkably accomplished volume brought her to the attention of John Middleton Murry, an Oxford undergraduate who was also flexing his muscles in the literary circles of London. He had recently launched the avant-garde magazine, *Rhythm*, and from the outset the association of the aspiring writer and the aspiring editor was mutually advantageous. By the spring of 1912, Katherine Mansfield had chosen Murry for her partner. Whatever she might do or say thereafter, their lives were to be inextricably intertwined until her tragically early death from tuberculosis in 1923.

By the time she died, Katherine Mansfield had secured herself a position in the literary world (on both sides of the Atlantic) through the publication of *Bliss and Other Stories* in 1920 and *The Garden Party and Other Stories* in 1922. Two further collections, edited by Murry, were published posthumously: *The Doves' Nest and Other Stories* in 1923 and *Something Childish and Other Stories* in 1924. Subsequently Murry edited and published her *Journal*, her *Letters*, her reviews for the *Athenaeum* and finally, in 1951, her *Letters to John Middleton Murry*.

So much survives from such a short life because Katherine Mansfield was a compulsive writer. When she was not filling notebooks with observations about people, places and her own feelings, and reshaping these into stories, she was writing letters – especially letters to Murry. The correspondence of Katherine Mansfield and John Middleton Murry is a story in its own right, one more compelling, more poignant, than any she ever invented. In a sense it is the novel she never wrote. Like the French diarist, Marie Bashkirtseff who, dying of tuberculosis, determined to 'tell all, yes, all ... Else what were the use of it?', Katherine recorded for Murry when they were apart the minutest details of her life. Especially she recorded the intensity of her feelings. Murry was spared little.

This selection of less than a third of Katherine Mansfield's letters to the man she began living with in 1912 and married in 1918, accompanied by rather fewer of his replies, focuses on the story of their chequered and often difficult love relationship. Pouring out daily letters, Katherine was insatiable for letters in return: 'I must you know I must have love, because I cannot live without love you know ...' says the heroine of an early story fragment who might have well have been herself. Chide and harangue Murry though she might, Katherine Mansfield depended upon the daily exchange of letters with him for the continual reassurance that she was loved. Indeed, if one theme runs through these letters, it is her overwhelming, devouring need for the sustaining power of love.

Before 1918, however, when she received the dreaded diagnosis of tuberculosis, Katherine could afford to be insouciant, in her letters as in her life. In 1913, while Murry was slogging it out in London, she chose to live near their friends, the Cannans, in Cholesbury. He commuted home at weekends. Later, in 1915, she had no compunction about leaving him for a brief interlude with his French friend, Francis Carco. Even after that affair had ended, she enjoyed the independence of going alone to write in Carco's Paris apartment. The first real flowering of Murry and Katherine's love seems to have occurred in December 1915, after the tragic death of her only brother. Then, when she summoned him, Murry joyfully hastened to Katherine's side at the Villa Pauline in Bandol. Nevertheless, during 1916 and 1917 the couple went, for a time, their separate ways.

Theirs was hardly a conventional association. The allowance Katherine received from her father, though never enough for her needs, enabled her to stand alone financially. Only in later years did she call on Murry to contribute to her support. Always the stronger personality, Katherine rejected the traditional female role and liked to think of herself and Murry as two boys together. He, though decisive in his own field as an editor, was essentially a passive man, happy for Katherine to take the initiative. After 1918, however, their relationship altered. Katherine's illness meant that she had to spend increasingly long periods apart from him in a warmer climate. As she became physically more incapacitated, her need for his letters to assuage her loneliness and keep her in touch with the outside world intensified. So did her emotional dependence upon Murry, whom she now required to become less like the acquiescent follower of earlier years, more like the strong, protective Harold Beauchamp whose type she had earlier avoided.

The changing demands of their relationship took Murry, at first, unawares. In spite of their earlier, voluntary separations, neither was really prepared for the emotional stresses of lives that had to be lived at a distance. Part of the problem was that these separate existences were necessarily different. Until the end of the war, Murry was under enormous pressure from his work at the War

Office; physically and mentally he was incapable of giving Katherine the companionship she sought. The best he could do was to write letters, little though there might be to tell, rejoice when there were signs of improvement in her health, and enthusiastically praise her stories. When she decided in 1918 not to enter a sanatorium, Murry acquiesced: it was neither his custom nor in his character to tell his wife what to do.

From July 1918 until September 1919, in spite of Katherine's illness, husband and wife kept up the pretence of leading a normal life at 2 Portland Villas in London. In the spring of 1919 Murry was appointed editor of the newly reconstituted *Athenaeum*, and he quickly set about making it the pre-eminent literary paper of its day. Katherine Mansfield involved herself in the success of the enterprise from the beginning, regularly reviewing fiction for the *Athenaeum* and sharing in editorial decisions. By August 1919, however, it became clear that her health could not stand another English winter. Reluctantly, she and L.M. established themselves in the Casetta Deerholm at Ospedaletti on the Italian Riviera.

In her letters Katherine insisted that Murry should not give up the *Athenaeum* in order to share her exile. But the cheerfulness that always heralded her arrival in a different place soon gave way to black feelings of hopelessness, despair and finally rage. Deep down Katherine Mansfield's impotent rage was against life itself. In her isolation, she vented her unhappiness upon the two people who loved her most: Murry and Ida Baker. L.M.'s tolerance of her friend's criticism is legendary. Less well known is the patience and genuine love with which Murry responded to his wife's outbursts. These continued throughout 1920 when she moved from Ospedaletti to Menton. It is little wonder that in his misery he did not reject the flattering overtures of an admirer, Princess Elizabeth Bibesco.

Katherine Mansfield's battle with illness exacted a terrible emotional toll on Murry as well as on Katherine. She alternated between hope that she might be saved and despair at the thought of her impending death. But while she could express her feelings openly, Murry could not. He must enthusiastically support her belief in the promises of each new doctor, yet always keep silent about the prospect of her death. Inevitably a barrier was erected between them. The year 1920 was a watershed. Katherine's letters show her coming to terms with her own mortality and in the process achieving a kind of spiritual independence. Murry, for his part, decided to give up the *Athenaeum* and so sacrifice his editorial career at its very height, in order to be with Katherine.

Only a few letters were exchanged in 1921 when the couple spent most of the time together at the Chalet des Sapins in Switzerland. But the harmony of that year, during which Katherine Mansfield wrote some of her greatest stories, and Murry composed and delivered his famous lectures on 'The Problem of Style', was broken in December. Katherine determined to try a new X-ray treatment for tuberculosis being given by Dr Manoukhine in Paris. After a brief exchange of letters, Murry joined her in a Paris hotel for the duration of the treatment. This was the last time that they really lived together. When Katherine returned to London in August 1922, she stayed with her friend Dorothy Brett; Murry retreated to the Selsfield home of his friend, Vivian Locke Ellis.

Up until 1922, Katherine and Murry had remained intellectually close, reading and discussing the same books and sharing their writing. The quasi-mystical books that captured Katherine Mansfield's attention in the last year of her life – books such as *Cosmic Anatomy* by 'M.B. Oxon' and *Tertium Organum* by P.D. Ouspensky – Murry could not share. Each had come to the end of their ability to sustain the other. And yet, even after Katherine made her last, lonely journey to the Gurdjieff Institute at Fontainebleau, they continued to correspond. Hardly any of Murry's last letters to Katherine survive; but those that do suggest his willingness once again to abandon his own path and follow hers.

Though the life story of Katherine Mansfield is well known, the juxtaposition here for the first time of the letters exchanged between her and John Middleton Murry sheds a slightly different light on their relationship. Such was Murry's loyalty to Katherine that he made virtually no attempt to defend himself against the charges she levelled at him. As a result, posterity has judged him far more harshly than ever Katherine Mansfield did. Her principal accusations against him (as against her father) were that he withheld money and love. Neither complaint was just. It was Katherine who had chosen to assert her independence of the wifely role by keeping her financial affairs separate. Murry, brought up in relative poverty, was no spendthrift; but neither was he completely ungenerous with a wife whose needs were expensive. What this exchange of letters assuredly refutes is the suggestion that he was unloving and uncaring. Murry's expressions of love may lack the lyricism of Katherine Mansfield's, but they are genuine. Indeed, given the alternation of her declarations of love and her icy criticism, one is tempted to question *her* feelings rather than his. Of

Linda Burnell's attitude to her husband in 'Prelude', Katherine wrote: 'She could have done her feelings up in little packets and given them to Stanley.' In her letters to Murry, Katherine Mansfield sometimes did just that. What she always relied on was that he would understand.

'I'm a writer first and a woman after,' Katherine told her husband in December 1920. She was a writer, moreover, whose art actively drew strength from her own personal suffering. From childhood onwards pain, especially emotional pain, seemed almost a necessary stimulant to her creativity. 'Out of my great sorrows I make my little songs', declares the heroine in 'The Modern Soul'. 'That is Heine or myself' – or Katherine Mansfield. Indeed, part of Katherine Mansfield's continuing fascination as a personality is surely the defiant way in which she virtually courted hardship, daring life to do its worst. Loving her as they did, both L.M. and Murry were caught up in the vicissitudes of Katherine's life. L.M.'s ambiguous role as her 'wife' was to provide practical help; Murry's was to provide the mental companionship, the essential support of one writer for another – and of an editor for an author. For all her protestations of physical love for Murry, it was probably this intellectual fellowship which mattered most to Katherine Mansfield and which sustained their relationship in spite of lengthy separations.

The other sustaining factor was the assurance, indeed the knowledge, that Murry in his own undemonstrative way loved and needed her. Evidence of quarrels and misunderstandings abounds in these letters; but so does the evidence of mutual love. In the luminous quality of their prose, Katherine Mansfield's love letters to Murry rank with her finest fiction. Lady Ottoline Morrell once commented that Katherine was never 'entirely "off-duty", so to speak, from being a writer'. One could, uncharitably, suggest that even when she wrote to Murry, Katherine Mansfield was consciously playing a role. Certainly, drafts in her notebooks indicate that some letters were rehearsed. But if Katherine did at times assume the mask that she advised Murry to wear for self-protection, it was one calculated to woo and cajole, to maintain the allegiance of an attractive young man with the weapon she best wielded: the magic of words.

Katherine Mansfield's power over Murry is also her power over us. Her genius as a writer is such that we cannot but share her joy in the beauty of nature, her fascination with the foibles of human character, her disappointment at the deceptions practised by one person on another. Imaginatively, we enter into her world, experience her need of letters (and of love), feel her fear of death as our own. Just as she 'became' the duck when she was writing 'Prelude', so we 'become' Katherine Mansfield when we read her letters. Yet although she could appraise her own physical suffering and her own spiritual progress with admirable objectivity, she was also capable of writing subjectively, irrationally, even cruelly. To be caught up by the magnetism of Katherine Mansfield's personality as it reveals itself in her letters is not necessarily to surrender our own fair-minded estimation of the man to whom she wrote: 'I feel no other lovers have walked the earth more joyfully – in spite of all.'

John Middleton Murry's letters have been selected from *The Letters of John Middleton Murry to Katherine Mansfield*, edited by C.A. Hankin (1983). Katherine Mansfield's letters, which were published by Murry in 1951 and which have been included in the first two volumes (1903–1919) of *The Collected Letters of Katherine Mansfield* edited by Vincent O'Sullivan and Margaret Scott, have been corrected against the originals held in the Alexander Turnbull Library in Wellington. Murry excised very little from his edition of the letters. Hitherto unpublished passages, containing criticisms of L.M., Virginia Woolf, Dorothy Brett and the Schiffs, however, appear here for the first time, as do Katherine Mansfield's comments in 1922 about the break-up of the marriage of Murry's friend, J.W. Sullivan. Previously unpublished letters are one written in May 1921 about her father, and the will she left for Murry in August 1922.

The punctuation of Katherine Mansfield and to a lesser extent Murry was, to say the least, erratic. She frequently left out commas, question marks, apostrophes and full stops. Most of the 'mistakes' which reflect the writers' moods have been reproduced here. Minor changes made to the punctuation include the addition of apostrophes and the standardisation of words such as 'French' and 'German' which were sometimes written without capitals. Katherine Mansfield's occasional deliberate misspelling of certain words, however, has been adhered to. Names given only as initials have been inserted in square brackets. In the interests of space, endnotes have deliberately been kept brief and to a minimum.

Grateful acknowledgement is made to John Middleton Murry's son, Colin Murry, for so generously agreeing to the publication of this correspondence. Thanks are also due to Oxford University Press and to Constable Publishers who graciously gave permission for material in which they hold copyright to be reproduced, to the manuscripts section of the Alexander Turnbull Library for its ready co-operation, and to the University of Canterbury for research assistance. I am indebted to Roma Woodnutt of the Society of Authors and to Ursula Owen of Virago Press for their continuing support. Especially I owe a debt of gratitude to Carole Acheson and Kate Trevella for their willing help in the preparation of the manuscript.

January 1912–June 1913

Katherine Mansfield and John Middleton Murry met at the house of a mutual acquaintance in December 1911. Both were relative newcomers to the London literary scene. Katherine had begun contributing stories to the *New Age*, edited by A.R. Orage, in 1910; and her first collected volume, *In a German Pension*, had just been published. Murry, although still an Oxford undergraduate, had embarked upon a career of literary journalism with the launching of the avant-garde magazine, *Rhythm*. Murry was twenty-two and Katherine ten months older. In spite of differences in their backgrounds (she was the daughter of a well-to-do New Zealand businessman, he the son of a hard-worked minor English civil servant), they immediately hit it off. Murry had already accepted her story, 'The Woman at the Store', for *Rhythm*: his letters to her in 1912 show that as well as being attracted to Katherine as a woman, he thought of her from the outset as his intellectual equal.

With the encouragement of Katherine, Murry decided to come down from Oxford, and by March 1912 he was living at his parents' house in Wandsworth. In April, to his surprise, she invited him to become her lodger at 69 Clovelly Mansions in London. In due course he also became her lover. From Clovelly Mansions the couple moved, in September 1912, to Runcton Cottage near Chichester. This 'honeymoon' period in their lives ended abruptly, however, when the publisher of *Rhythm* absconded, leaving heavy printing debts in Murry's name. From now on, much of Katherine Mansfield's allowance from her father went to pay off the debt.

Afterwards, they both lived for a time in the cramped flat at 57 Chancery Lane that was also *Rhythm*'s office. Then in March 1913, at the urging of Gilbert Cannan, they rented 'The Gables', a cottage near him in Cholesbury. Murry, attempting to keep *Rhythm* afloat as the revamped *Blue Review*, travelled back and forth between London and Cholesbury. Katherine Mansfield's first extant letters to him date from this period.

55, Holywell,
Oxford
January 27 1912

Dear Miss Katharine [sic] Mansfield,
    I don't know very much about the man Neuberg – but what I do I'll try to tell you. He is or rather was one of Aleister Crowley's push in the advanced spiritualist – obscene yet divine – stunt; and so far as I know he was Crowley's ἐραστής [lover]. Crowley's part being always pathic. He looks it. Then for some reason they quarrelled – over some money matter, and at present Neuberg is, I am told, holding over Crowley's head some books that he had privately published, and which are for England the ne plus ultra of dirt. I've never seen them; but they must be most amusing. One is called *The Daisy Chain* the other *Snowdrops from a Curate's Garden*. I believe he looks a very bedraggled weed but I never saw him, since when I knew Crowley in Paris he had some other fellow, Kennedy.
    I'm sorry I can't tell you more. Today is a good day in this bloodiest of bloody places – cold and fine; intellectually I feel just fit for this obvious meteorology. Next series of *Rhythm*, I want a number of Criticisms, preferably appreciation with a sting in it, of a half-dozen of the 'big' moderns in England. Each will go in two monthly numbers – about 4000 words in all. Will you do one of them? The half dozen I suggest are Wells, Shaw, Bennett, Galsworthy, Masefield, Frank Harris. It's rather early on to worry; but I'm trying to get out a prospectus of the new volume beforehand – and very much want to fix this up.
    Sorry to talk mere shop, but if you knew the ghastly life I lead here one half the day sweating over some cursed Aristotle, the rest dodging my creditors, and answering my letters, you would see it's difficult to be other than dull. Your idea about the sailor man was good – I don't believe they taste nice though

        Yours
        J.M.M.

13 Nicosia Rd,
Wandsworth Common S.W.
[before Tuesday 26 March 1912]

Dear K.M.

Here's fun for you. There's a batch of my verses for you. No wonder I can't do any work if my mind's been like that all the month. Chaos is nothing to it.

It's the first time I've resurrected any of the stuff from my drawer. It is a mixture. Lots of it I abominate. One or two I like.

I was thinking of looking in on Tuesday with a batch of MSS submitted to *Rhythm*. If you get as bored as I do nowadays it'll do you good. I think about three p.m. If you're not there it can't be helped.

I searched for some of my short stories but I must have left them all in London I mean Oxford, for I can't see anything at all in my box. If ever my few properties arrive from there you shall have them. I'm frightened about the devil's distraining on them in my absence. Also, I shall probably shift from Wandsworth in April I don't know where. Je m'étouffe here. I shall come into London if I can get a job

Yours
J.M.M.

It's bloody cold. I can't hold my pen.

13 Nicosia Road,
Wandsworth Common S.W.
26 March [1912]

Dear M.K.M.

Will you suggest the day for the visit to the pictures? They're all the same to me. I'm lunching with W.L.G[eorge] I believe on Thursday. I feel very much as though I want to get drunk now. I was delighted to see you, but you mustn't run away into the country yet. I'm still chuckling over the *Rhythm* set. I'm so awfully out of it.

Yours
J.M.M.

Thirteen. Nicosia Road,
Wandsworth Common
[March 28 1912]

Dear K.M.

Friday will be fine – I mean will do fine. Have you seen this *New Age* and *Present Day Criticism*? They really have done it this time. Good old Horace. You mustn't go on imagining all these places. I'm simply dying for sea washed windy hills – and it can't be done for ages. There's something I want to talk to you about. Will you remind me, as I'm sure to forget. I'll come in the afternoon time.

I've been staining my floor all day – everything's in a damnable mess.

J.M.M.

13 Nicosia Road,
Wandsworth Common
[March 30 1912]

Dear K.M.,

Sorry I was so boring – can't be helped. Forgot all about what I wanted to say – which was I want you to have a look at a couple of things sent me for *Rhythm*, both under strong recommendation from people I believe in. One I think is rotten, the other quite good. Tell me what you think of them, as I imagine your judgement is nearer what mine would be, were I in a normal state. Let's fix up a day next week to lunch out tea out, dine out with Johnny F[ergusson]. I'm going to try to touch Holbrook Jackson for a cheque tomorrow. Be charitable to a convalescent.

Your d-d house has got on my brain. I've just drawn a wonderful picture of it in words and told a friend of mine that I'm going to live there – you can run out naked in the long grass and roll, roll, right under the pine trees, and little winds creep about and pink your body all warm, and right over the wall on the right hand side is a deep place, all white nettle and convolvulus, and you don't dare jump down because there must be creepy things in the water, so you wriggle back under the tummocky grass right back to the Cherry Tree; and then you cry just out of pure joy because you know the world is made for you and you can do anything with it: and day after day you do nothing because you can do everything and you lie on your back under the pine tree and look right up the long tunnels and little stars just twinkle down, twiddling round and round the long barrel till they drop in your face, and they sing and you shout – My God it's awful: and all at the cherry-tree, Heronsgate. Heron's gate – my god those herons just coming on a wisp of wind and flickering over the pine tops.

It's all because my gas lamp makes a hard steel mark on the roof below and I hate this bloody place. You'll be able to write masterpieces and won't, because the windy blood is all round your heart; and I shan't be able to, and shall write absolute muck and think for an hour that it's good, and wake in the morning to know what a fool I've been. I'm simply bloody tonight. I found the daughter of the publican uncle, (It was a publican.) *waiting* to see me in my room. She talked to me about pure love as opposed to the other variety, and morals, and her 'boy' who is a stockbroker's clerk, secretary to a Y.M.C.A. 'Her dad was in low line of business – but she was going to marry a cultured man for love and not for money.' It all came out of a nightmare book from 7.30 to 9 when I tucked her into a taxi and ran all round Wandsworth Common blaspheming – and forgot to borrow a quid.

But I'm going to take you seriously. When you're swinging on Heron's Gate you must ask me down to the tramp room I am a goodish tramp – and I shall forget everything for a bit. Or if you want an expert stainer, stain all day for his food call on me at once. And don't forget all about it

Yours
J.M.M.

If Macqueen ever does worry you for God's sake tell him Fergusson's in Thurso N.B. and I'm in gaol for drunk and disorderly.

['The Gables',
Cholesbury, Bucks]
[April 1913]

Dear Jack.
This is just 'good morning' – to you.
It has been a warm bright day here – very quiet. Immediately you had gone the house fell fast asleep, and it refuses to wake up or so much as smile in a dream until next Friday. I feel that I have been

here a long time – and that it's New Zealand. I'm very happy, darling. But when you come into my thoughts I refuse you, quickly, quickly. It would take me a long time away from you before I could bear to think of you. You see, when I am not with you every little bit of you puts out a flaming sword –

The Blue Review,
57 Chancery Lane
London, W.C.
[?6 May 1913]
Tuesday 5 in the Afternoon

Tiger Darling,
    It's been raining all day; and I feel wet and miserable in soul, but not really downhearted. The bed felt terribly empty & big last night – we ought to have tiny little beds when we're apart don't you think so. I haven't done much work – it's all too clammy. You don't bear thinking about except that I see you in the corner of the kitchen with a big fire. You darling. I don't think I could have had a sweeter memory of you than that I carried away last week. It was fragrant and child-like enough to last me unfaded till Friday when I march up the hill again.
    I went to tea with Waterlow yesterday to meet those Woolff [sic] people. I don't think much of them. They belong to a perfectly impotent Cambridge set. Gordon has just rung me up to say Beatrice is in London and could he meet me to-night. So I'm going to Selwood Terrace after I've been to the *Daily News*. I'm getting all untidy again now you're not here; but I've kept your room beautiful. Boulestin has just been round. I like him very much, I think. He's working hard for us.
    We'll have a glorious time on Friday

Jack

['The Gables',
Cholesbury, Bucks]
[early May 1913]

Jack dear.
    Yes Friday *will* be fun. I am beginning to 'pretend' that you are a sailor – trading with all sorts of savages from Monday until Friday – & that the *Blue Review* is your schooner & Secker the Fish Eyed

Pilot. Couldn't you write a long-complicated-extremely-insulting-symbolical-serial round that idea with minute, obscene descriptions of the savage tribes ...? Thank you for Pa's letter. He was cheerful and poetic, a trifle puffed up but very loving. I feel towards my Pa man like a little girl. I want to jump and stamp on his chest and cry 'you've *got* to love me'. When he says he does, I feel quite confident that God is on my side.

It is raining again today, and last night the wind howled and I gloomed and shivered – and heard locks being filed and ladders balanced against windows & footsteps padding up-stairs – – – all the old properties jigged in the old way – I'm a lion all day, darling, but with the last point of daylight I begin to turn into a lamb and by midnight – mon Dieu! by midnight the whole world has turned into a butcher!

Yes, I like Boulestin very much. There's something very sympathetic about him.

Goodbye for today, darling

Tig.

57 Chancery Lane,
[London, W.C.]
[before 12 May 1913]

Dear Tig,

I'm writing this early because I want you to get it first thing in the morning. I know I shall feel lonely in the evening and I don't want to write to you if I'm feeling sad. I think this separation is beastly – you're so very far away that I can't talk to you. And do you know I thought you were more lovely and lovable than ever this last weekend. O Tig, you were so sweet, and so like a little child that I feel like crying when I write it. I adore you, darling.

But it's no use. I shall be alright if I set to work.

I took the key away – what will you have done without it? But don't be frightened, darling, it'll be alright. I'm sending you the only letters that were not newspapers

Your darling
Jack.

['The Gables',
Cholesbury, Bucks]
[? 12 May 1913]

Jack dearest.

... the postman knocked into my dream with your letter and the back door key. I had locked myself in 3 times 3 with Mrs Gom's key but I am glad you sent me ours.

I have begun the story and mean to finish it this evening: it feels pretty good, to me. Walpole's letter was a little too strenuous. (what is a beautiful picture?) But I prefer that to Gilbert's one remark 'Davies steeped in Bunyan'. Oh, dear! I'm afraid Walpole is having his birthday cake far too soon – like all our young men (except Jack & Tig.) What a surprise for them when we sit down at the heads of their tables – all among their cake crumbs and groaning little tummies – you, with a laurel wreath on your darling head, & me trailing a perfectly becoming cloud of glory.

Pride is a charming, sheltering tree: but don't think I'm nesting in it. I'm only standing underneath with my eyes turned up for a moment's grace.

Last night Mrs Gom and I had a glass of dandelion wine, and over it I heard how Mrs Brown's petticoat had dropped off in the hurdle race 'King Edward's Coronation time.' Such goings on!

Goodbye for today. I love you. 'Not tomorrow, not the next day, but the next.' Tell me what train you are coming by. I cannot quite believe that you are coming back here. I feel – – quite alone and as if I were writing to someone in the air – so strange.

The Blue Review,
57 Chancery Lane
London, W.C.
May 12 1913

Dear Tig,

Banks & Gaudier have just been. Of course I'm not worth a twopenny damn now. I've been crying out of sheer nervous reaction. The old lies shrieked at me + some Gaudier lies & venom. I can't do any work now. I'm just good for nothing. I don't know, but this Banks business simply does for me, darling. – I'm crying again now – O God. It'll be all over – all right when you get this; but somehow it's upset all my notions of what's right and just in the world. Am I a villain? why can't somebody stand up and say I'm not. I can bear anything almost. I'd be as poor as anything willingly but this kind of thing I cannot stand. God, is it all a joke. Or am I simply lying to myself when I say that we have struggled & fought for *Rhythm*?

Oh, I shall be alright. If you see Gilbert tell him as he loves me and thinks me straight to crush that woman when he sees her – or I shall kill her. I'm not crying any more. Before they came, I was happy & thinking how glorious the weather is now I'm a bit skew. But it won't last much longer now I've had a good cry.

Letters.

Tig, I love you – but, suddenly this beast has fouled everything

Jack.

['The Gables',
Cholesbury, Bucks]
[13 May 1913]

Dear Jack.

Floryan is taking this for me. Will you phone Ida [Baker] to come to Chancery Lane and see about his box, because some things of his are in the top of my box and he had better have them all. The story is really, rather what I'd thought. He has had false promises and believed them: it's no good discussing it. He promises to pay you back in little sums of £1 and £2.

About Banks and Gaudier – I can't write. Gilbert will deal with Banks as she deserves. I am worried and anxious about you all the time. Gilbert will silence Banks. Mary says he's seldom angry & when he is he's dreadful – that's true. He'll believe nothing but truth of you. He is devoted to you. He said 'I wish Jack would always come to me' ... Mary said 'Oh I'd like to put my arms round him and hug him'. Do not answer the door after office hours. During office hours don't answer yourself. Come tomorrow. My letter from G[eorge Bowden] says divorce papers will be served in a day or two. No damages & no costs for us to pay.

I've seen the farm & we all agree it's perfect.

All these things to comfort you a little. But come here and I will tell you all. I wait for you until tomorrow. Phone Ida to come at 7 & Floryan will then call for his box. If impossible for her then make some arrangement. I am going to telegraph you now.

Yours Tig.

The Blue Review
57 Chancery Lane
London, W.C.
[14 May 1913]

Darling Tig,

I've been working very hard to-day; for my week's books are very difficult. I've just come away from them to write this.

Floryan turned up this morning. I hardly spoke to him; & I couldn't say what I wanted to (1) because I *can't* be stern to people (2) because my German always goes to pot, when I feel strongly about anything. He wanted your address because he said he wanted to speak to you.

Floryan has just come; and Ida is coming round in ¾ of an hour. Darling, I'm so glad about Gilbert & so grateful. It's been like a great weight crushing me. I'm alright in other ways darling. I'm coming at 6.15 tomorrow

Jack.

['The Gables',
Cholesbury, Bucks]
[14 May 1913]
Wednesday

Dear Jack.

No letter from you today. I am sending you the Banks drawings this evening. Enough string came with my parcel from Ida to make it possible. If you want any meat (and if – oh, well no – not necessarily) bring some down with you, please dear. *Meat* and *tea*. That is all we want. It is a very grey day again, here, half raining – and a loud roaring noise in the trees. This morning a robin flew into my room. I caught it. It did not seem at all frightened but lay still and very warm. I carried it to the window & I cannot tell you what a strange joyful feeling – when the little bird flew out of my hands. I am sorry you did not write to me. I count on your letters in the morning & always wake up early and listen for the postman. Without them the day is very silent.

Do you want to drive – tomorrow? Let me know in time.

Goodbye for today, my darling.

Tig.

57 [Chancery Lane,
London, W.C.]
[19 May 1913]

Dear Tig.

I was a beast this morning. Forgive me. You know I don't mean
this things [sic]; and breakfast makes me horrible. I don't deserve to
have a darling like you when I'm like that.

I send you a letter which you must keep. It only is definite proof
of what a liar & Scoundrel Floryan is, and how he'll get us into
trouble everywhere. Just write to the woman & tell her exactly how
things really stood, will you not?

Also, a letter from Johnny [Fergusson] which shows the darling
he is. I am writing to him tonight.

Abercrombie was here when I arrived. He is a very attractive
man, with a curious lined, spectacled, quizzical face. I think if I saw
more of him I shd. get on with him famously.

Also, a letter from Albert, which is a very welcome surprise.

I send you all my love darling; tho' I'm hurrying to the
Westminster

    Your loving
    Jack.

['The Gables',
Cholesbury, Bucks]
[19 May 1913]

Dear Jack.

I've nursed the epilogue to no purpose. Every time I pick it up
and hear 'you'll keep it to six,' I *can't* cut it. To my knowledge there
aren't any superfluous words: I mean every line of it. I don't 'just
ramble on' you know, but this thing happened to just fit 6½ pages
– you can't cut it without making an ugly mess somewhere. I'm a
powerful stickler for form in this style of work. I hate the sort of
licence that English people give themselves – – to spread over and
flop and roll about. I feel as fastidious as though I wrote with acid.
All of which will seem, I suppose unconvincing and exaggeration. I
can only express my sincerest distress (which I do truly feel) and
send you the epilogue back. If you & Wilfrid feel more qualified for
the job – – oh, do by all means – But I'd rather it wasn't there at all

than sitting in the *Blue Review* with a broken nose and one ear as though it had jumped into an editorial dog fight. It's a queer day, with flickers of sun. The epilogue has worried me no end – and I can still hear – tossing about – the aftermath of that thunder. 'It's not fair. Swinnerton can do it ... you've got to cut it' ... etc etc. Can't you cut a slice off the D. Brown. I really am more interesting than he is – modest though I be ...

Tig

Don't think of this letter. I'm frightfully depressed today. I love you, darling. Do not let us forget that we love each other. Your sad beyond words   Tig.

> 57 Chancery Lane,
> [London, W.C.]
> [?20 May 1913]

Tig Darling,
   I'm all late & lonely tonight; not so much that the loneliness worries me as that I keep on accusing myself for being a beast on Monday at breakfast. But do forgive me; I didn't mean it. I've read both your story & your chronicle again. They are both top-notch & it would be impossible to cut them, at any rate I couldn't do it, and I don't think that anyone would have the stupidity to do so. They go in intact.
   Ransome was here yesterday & to-day trying to inveigle me into the country with him. I was adamant. Wilfrid's going however next week-end, so we shall be alone – which is first rate. W.H. Davies also was here.
   I don't think that there'll be any difficulty about placing stories of 1000 words if they aren't too 'shocking' in the sedate Saturday *Westminster*. The Royde-Smith, quite unprovoked, was expressing a great admiration for yr. work. Wilfrid thinks your story *great*, & you know what I think. You're alright.
   Books this week for the *Westminster* are particularly heavy; but I'll be down on Thursday at the old time. By God, I do wish I was there now.
   Hake was there yesterday. We talked from 9 to 12 at night; and I gave him supper. His mind is simply improving like anything. He's read all sorts of things that matter lately and too many that I haven't.

Darling, don't worry about me. I'm alright, except that now my stomach's empty. It's half past ten – people worry me so that I can't write before – and I haven't had supper. I'm going out to Sam Isaacs if I can find the outdoor key.

> My love darling
> Jack.

Visitors today Curle Swinnerton Davies Boulestin Ransome Spring-Rice   all at difft. times

> ['The Gables',
> Cholesbury, Bucks]
> [20 May 1913]
> Tuesday.

My dearest.

I am sorry for my anxiety of yesterday. It was not to be silenced at all except by your wire. Don't know what came over me – but I don't feel very well – and I suppose that was the reason. Nothing much – headache – Your letter – thank you. And the news was good. Johnny is a darling – Floryan a rather dangerous fraud – Albert – 'very sweet' – I'm glad you saw Abercrombie. Gilbert called here yesterday & I gave him his proof. He brought back your baccy pouch & some French books. Mrs. Gom is here today & my room is very clean & bright with a fire. It's dull – grey – inclined to rain. I am sending you some reviews.

Take care of yourself – I'm better today – except that I'm all burning up inside with a raging fire – – but, my God, it's good to be here –

On Thursday we'll see each other. Take my love.

> Tig.

P.S. I don't know whether you will roar at me, darling for doing these books in this way. But they lent themselves to it & I thought if you read the review you would see that it's almost silly to notice them singly & that they gain like this. If wrong – return the thing & I'll do you 2 little ones ... X

[57 Chancery Lane,
London, W.C.]
[21 May 1913]

Dear Tig,

It's funny writing at 5 in the afternoon; but I'm determined that you shall have this letter early in the morning.

I got the review this morning. I didn't roar. Thanks very much, darling; it'll do fine.

Gordon turned up at lunch-time; & took Wilfrid & me out to lunch in Grays Inn. It was very good. He's flourishing & coming down on Friday in the afternoon.

I'm going to supper with Rupert to-night because he's going off to America in the morning; it's all very silly but a free meal is fascinating. This extra day without you is rotten. London feels so very grey – and I get so forced back upon myself and the work that here I sit writing my column on Wednesday afternoon. The *B.R.* has gone to press to-day. I think it's very good. Wilfrid saw it off at Secker's – I suppose I knew he wood. I've been swanking about the great masterpieces you've been writing in the country; and I've got a howling respect for you. No I haven't. I think you're a nut – but I adore you even more than I respect you.

But, darling, what has been the matter with you? I can't quite tell from you're letter whether you're ill or not. My god, I hope not.

I'll bring your German dictionary tomorrow; and also a book about the backwoods of Australia for review (by Eleanor Mordaunt). It looks to me that it might be good – and anyhow you'll do a good review of it. I'll order Colette Willy's books for you and Ch. Phillippe for me when I go to the bank tomorrow; because I've only got 4/1 left. I had supper at Sam Isaacs last night 1/3 because there was nothing to eat at home.

> Anyhow I'm coming home tomorrow.
> Jack

	['The Gables',
	Cholesbury, Bucks]
3 reviews tomorrow.	[? May–June 1913]

Am I such a tyrant – Jack dear – or do you say it mainly to tease me? I suppose I'm a bad manager & the house seems to take up so much time if it isn't looked after with some sort of method. I mean

... when I have to clean up twice over or wash up extra unnecessary things I get frightfully impatient and want to be working. So often, this week, I've heard you and Gordon talking while I washed dishes. Well, someone's got to wash dishes & get food. Otherwise – 'there's nothing in the house but eggs to eat.' Yes, I hate hate HATE doing these things that you accept just as all men accept of their women. I can only play the servant with very bad grace indeed. It's all very well for females who have nothing else to do ... & then you say I am a tyrant & wonder because I get tired at night! The trouble with women like me is – they can't keep their nerves out of the job in hand – & Monday after you & Gordon & Lesley [L.M.] have gone I walk about with a mind full of ghosts of saucepans & primus stoveses & 'will there be enough to go round' ... & you calling (whatever I am doing) *Tig* – isn't there going to be tea. It's five o'clock. As though I were a dilatory housemaid! I loathe myself, today. I detest this woman who 'superintends' you and rushes about, slamming doors & slopping water – all untidy with her blouse out & her nails grimed. I am disgusted & repelled by the creature who shouts at you 'you might at least empty the pail & wash out the tea leaves!' Yes, no wonder you 'come over silent'.

Oh, Jack, I wish a miracle would happen – that you would take me in your arms & kiss my hands & my face & every bit of me & say 'it's alright – you darling thing. I quite understand.'

All the fault of money, I suppose.

But I love you & I feel humiliated & proud at the same time. That you *don't* see – that you *don't* understand and yet love me puzzles me – – –

Will you meet me on Wednesday evening at the Café Royale at about 10.30. If you can't be there let me know by Wednesday morning ... I'll come back & sleep at '57' if I may even though I *don't* live there.

Jack – Jack – Jack.

    Your wife
    Tig.

57 Chancery Lane
[London, W.C.]
[June 1913]
2.30 pm

Dear Tig,

Unless I write at this absurdly early hour I know that I shạn't catch the post. I am sending you a P.O. for 35/-. It wd have been £2; only I don't like to get more than £4 out of the bank, wh. less £1 Wilfrid & 10/- Wm. wd. only leave me 10/- for stamps & my fare down; so I've kept 15/-. I wish to heaven I didn't have to come back for anything at all.

I hate my room here so. It's almost impossible to do anything in it. There's something very unsympathetic about it after my blue room at Cholesbury, though I can't exactly say what it is. I'm pulling at my finger & I just remembered you – Tiger, ne fais pas ça, s'il vous plait – and I've left off *pro tem*. But I want to be back again at the Gables.

We caught the train with a quarter of an hour to spare and ate oranges on the station. Why am I so rude to Lesley Moore? I don't know; but I can't help it. But I love you – you're me –

Jack.

Will you send my glasses in the box so that I can take them back?

['The Gables',
Cholesbury, Bucks]
[June 1913]

Jack dearest –

I sent your glasses yesterday – packed – I hope – carefully enough. Thank you for the money: I'm going to start again keeping a strict account of every penny I spend & then we can see where the screw is loose or the shoe pinches – or whatever it is.

Last night as I got into bed the bed refused to have me & down I flew with my feet up in the air. I was terrified but I couldn't help laughing – & once started I kept on – It seemed no end of a joke to be all alone in what R.[ichard] C.[urle] would call the 'profound stillness of the June night' & to be served that age old trick!

'Mrs Walter' is here today and we're having clean pinnies from

head to foot. Such relief that I've written my reviews again &
started my epilogue. I went in to see Baby Gom this morning. He
was sucking. Such a pretty sight as a rule. But Mrs Gom's sharp
worn face above him somehow filled me with horror.

You poor darling! Having to write to me at such 'impossible
hours'. Well, assert yourself & 'be hanged if you will.' I'd rather
wait for the afternoon post or until you feel 'I want to talk to Tig' –
So treat me like that in future. I'll phone you when I get to London
tomorrow, but I know Wednesday is your busy day & I don't want
on any account to disturb you.

Things have straightened out in my mind & I'm rather ashamed
that I told you – what I did yesterday. It sings in my ears rather like
the wail of the little girl left behind on the fence – – – more anger
than anything else. I kiss your eyes and your soft furry ears and
your darling, frightening mouth –

I am your
Tig.

Café Royal 10.30. if I don't hear from you tomorrow.

February 1914

By July 1913 the *Blue Review* had collapsed, and in December Katherine and Murry began, as they optimistically thought, a new life in Paris. But circumstances conspired against them. Murry was unable to make a living there by literary journalism, and he was dogged by *Rhythm*'s debts. Forced back to London in February to face bankruptcy charges, he bowed to the inevitable; and Katherine, waiting anxiously for news in their Paris flat, agreed that he should accept the *Westminster Gazette*'s offer of work as a full-time reviewer and art critic. Wearily, they sold their furniture, packed up their possessions and moved back to London. Another interlude in their lives together had ended.

31 rue de Tournon (6ème),
[Paris]
[8 February 1914]

Sunday morning

Your letter this morning was a lovely surprise. I had not hoped to hear from you until tomorrow at earliest. Thank you, darling.

Everything is quite alright, here. Your room feels cold and it smells faintly of orange flower water or furniture polish – a little of both. I spent a great part of the day reading Theocritus and late last night, happening upon our only Saint Beuve I found the first essay was all about him. What I admire so much in your criticism – your *courteous* manner: Saint Beuve has it to perfection.

Do not worry about me. I'm not in the least frightened, but if Campbell abuses me too heartily tell him 'I am not one of a malignant nature but have a quiet temper.'

It's a spring day. The femme de ménage is cleaning the windows and I've had a bath –

Take every care of yourself
Tig.

[9 Selwood Terrace,
South Kensington, S.W.]
[8 February 1914]
Sunday

Dear Tig,
I have been very well at Campbell's He's just the same; and they have given me such a jolly little bedroom.
I rang up [W.L.] George to-day and went to lunch with him. He's just the same too Everybody's just the same. Lesley who again is opposite me at Fleming's for tea is just the same too. London makes me frightfully vague though. I can't focus to anything properly. I want to be back again. All my work, everything I want is now 31 rue de Tournon. But still I'm going to be awfully business like to-morrow, I hope. Please I'm going to buy pepper & salt trousers if I can find any. Are you happy? I've got my feet wet now – and my tooth hasn't quite stopped aching.
Were you frightened after all? You mustn't be. It's alright. I am determined to leave by the night train on Tuesday, unless unforeseen events i.e. jobs prevent me.

All my love
Jack.

31 rue de Tournon (6ème),
[Paris]
Monday morning [9 February 1914]

Dear Jack.
I am glad that Campbell is looking after you well – glad, too, that you went to see W.L.G.[eorge]. That was a good idea. Lesley writes me – the weather is beastly – and here it is so warm and sunny that I have sat with my window open yesterday and today. (Yes, dear, mentioned 'with intent'.) I wish you would buy a pair of shoes as well as the pepper & salt trousers. Try to. You want them so badly and I've no faith in those cheap Boulevard beauties.
Everything, here, too 'is just the same'. The femme de ménage is singing in the kitchen – a most improbable song. It runs along – very blithe and nice – for about five notes and then it *drops* – any distance you like, but a little deeper each time. If the 'aspects' were not good that song would frighten me no end – *provided* that I was

in a little house on the edge of the steppes with a mushroom shaped cloud over it & no smoke coming out of the chimney etc. etc. But things being what they are, my romantic mind imagines it a kind of 15th century French Provincial Ride-a-Cock-Horse – you know the business – dashing off on someone's knee to get a pound of butter and being suddenly 'tumbled into the gutter.' Which, after all, is a very pleasant place to fall. I wonder if Queens played this Disturbing Game with their youngest pages.

My door has been mended. I am told that a workman came at nine, wrenched out the remains of the old panel, tapped the wood with an iron hammer, clapped in a new panel, clattered over the hall – but I did not hear a sound. I slept until a quarter to ten.

You will tell me the exact time of your arrival. Won't you? If it is early morning I'll not meet you but at any other hour I would like to go to the station. You have all my love.

> Tig.

No letters have come. I sent a 'bleu' on Saturday for you –

[London]
[10 February 1914]

MUST SEE BANKRUPTCY FRIDAY BETTER STAY REPLY

9, Selwood Terrace,
South Kensington, S.W.
February 10 1914

Darling,

I'm afraid you didn't understand my wire, it was so brief. On Monday Gordon inquired about my bankruptcy business from a friend of his who is Assistant Receiver; and this friend said the only thing for me to do was to go to see them immediately. If I didn't they wd. put out a warrant after me; if I did they wd be very nice as the bankruptcy wasn't my fault. Accordingly, this Tuesday morning I went. They were nice. They said they wouldn't make any attempt to touch my earnings, and that there wdn't be any difficulty, *if* I filed a statement of my affairs immediately. The man told me to write to all the people to whom I owed money and find out exactly what I owed and bring the results to him on Friday morning when they wd draw up my statement for me. After that, I shd. only have to attend my public examination in March. So today I've written to everybody. It seems that I can do no good by returning to Paris before Friday, as I only lose the fare; and we've got so very little money. That's why I wired. If I get the answers I may manage to do the business on Thursday morning and get off Thursday evening. Only I see plainly that I must get the business off my mind, or I shall get into serious trouble.

Then about the other, even more important business, I don't know whether I made it all plain, as I was so agitated when I wrote. It amounts to this. I can't expect more than £6 a month from the *Times*; and I can expect nothing from the *Westminster*, if I decide not to return. My other attempts to find work haven't turned out well – the *British Review* won't, & the *Nation* Editor is in Egypt so that I can have no reply for 2 months. It doesn't seem to be any use looking to that. The *Westminster*, if I decide for it will take me on, as art-critic & regular reviewer, and give me £5 a week, but I must decide within three weeks.

Darling, you must try to decide for me. I don't feel that I can face working in Paris, with only £6 a month to come in, and that quite uncertain. I couldn't do anything with that idea over my head. Don't you think that somehow we had better try to exchange our flat for a year with somebody and meanwhile work here somewhere till we've got some money to fall back on i.e. produce all we can, at least 1 novel each during the year, and then if we see a fair chance clear off to our flat in Paris for good? But write to me and tell me what you think. I know we have over a week to talk about it when I get back; but I want you now. Even that arrangement depends upon exchanging flats – but somehow that shouldn't be difficult; and then we shd. always have our home in Paris, & cd. look upon it as an enforced holiday. I shd. be happy anywhere with you, so long as you had a proper working-room. (Darling, just an interruption – I love you. I can just see you there, and now we're straining against each other to make us both brave. Oh darling – you are me) But we mustn't decide in a hurry. One thing we can*not* do – that is *move* in the real sense of the word. Even if our pride wd. allow it our purse won't.

Darling, I've kissed you and I feel brave as anything

Jack.

31 rue de Tournon (6ème),
[Paris]
[10 February 1914]

Dear Jack.

If you are staying so long I had better send you this to answer. Do not worry about anything here. We are alright. I'm afraid I am rather childish about people coming & going – and just, now, at this moment when the little boy has handed me your telegram – the disappointment is hard to bear.

Your room is ready for you. It looks lovely – Do whatever is best, dear, but remember that all the people are very little and that really & truly we are awfully strong –

Very well, dear
Tig.

[9 Selwood Terrace,
South Kensington, S.W.]
Feb. 10. 1914
Tuesday 1 a.m.

I saw the bankruptcy man today and I am glad that I did for, as long as you do what you are told, they seem to be very kindly disposed at least to one in my situation. I think that this business at least will turn out well enough.

As for the other, even now I am no wiser than before. I am not sure whether my immediate preference for sticking to the *Westminster* is not merely prudential. I think even that I would throw the whole business over if we had not got that flat in Paris – but that if we are really poor will hang about our necks and weaken us because we can't afford it on less than £250 a year, & perhaps hardly even on that. I wish that I could see my way clear.

All the while I feel that I shd. be better if I had Tig close by me. It's a ghastly business not having enough money to afford even £2 10.0 for an extra fare to Paris & back

I'll go on with this as a letter. I'm no use at keeping a diary. I feel that it's just irony. On Monday morning I was going about so cheerful, spending 5.16.6 on my clothes, and telling the man at the shop to be sure and send them early Tuesday morning, for I was leaving by the night train, and then at 3 to see Spender, & at 4 to see Richmond. It's taken me a long while to understand it. We can't give up Paris it's a symbol of something free for us; nor can I (and that is we) live there yet.

Tig you are perfect. I had to tell the Campbells all the story of how we met and how we lived together – two years ago – to keep myself from feeling miserable. It certainly made me feel happy. I have a little tiny camp bed, like the one we used to sleep in together when we first came to Chancery Lane, and I went to sleep and you ached and never said a word. Now, though we're wiser perhaps we're in something of the same hole again, & again a camp bed, and only me sleeping in it. But that's not symbolical: I need you more than ever: I feel I can't move without you. Dear heart I kiss you good-night, to wake to your morning letter. Good-night

Tig. Tig

		31 rue de Tournon (6ème),
excuse writing	Tired	[Paris]
Wednesday		[11 February 1914]

Well, Jack dear.

I expect I did not understand your wire quite fully. Telegrams are always frightening. Now that I've read your letter I am able to write to you more sensibly. You are right to stay until the matter of the bankruptcy is fixed up. I quite understand that, dear, and I am thankful they are more or less nice. Don't rush and don't consider me. If you find it more convenient to stay longer, just wire me.

Now about the other and 'more important' affair. It is difficult to discuss by letter. I do not think that it is any good you staying anywhere if you are worried about money. A constant strain like that wears you out quicker than anything. If we cannot live over here on £10 a month (and we can't) there's an end of this place for the present. I *think* that you had better do what you think – I mean take the Westminster job for at least a year and feel the security of a regular £5 a week for that time. Your work needs freedom from these grinding fears. About exchanging flats I expect it would not be difficult. But it would take time, I am sure. What is at the back of your darling mind? Is it your idea to stay at Campbell's and me to stay here until the exchange is effected? Tell me quite plainly, won't you? Did you take a return ticket. Would you rather stay on now and save the money and manage things by letter? You know Jack darling, quite seriously speaking, I can be happy in any place where we are together, but without you all places alike are deserted for me. No more now.

Tig.

Don't send any more postcards – like you did today, please dear.

[9 Selwood Terrace,
South Kensington, S.W.]
[11 February 1914]
12 a.m.

Wednesday Morning,

Darling,

I got your letter this morning and I felt awfully sad. I wanted to come over to-day just to see you – but I don't think it wd. be right. We can't afford it, & I should have to come back for Friday morning. In the letter you got yesterday morning I explained all that I could.

Oh, darling don't imagine that I don't know the disappointment & didn't feel it myself. There's something I feel even more. Continually I have before my face the picture of how you would look if I were to arrive tonight, and it makes me cry. Yet I know you understand. Something seems determined to play with us again; but though the worries are not all over after Friday, the bankruptcy is practically cleared off; and then we shall be able to think clearly about the rest. Darling, if you can manage it, write me a word of advice about it, not that I'm helpless – but it wd make me feel as though you were talking to me about it.

Thursday, Friday, Saturday – oh, it seems long: but, darling, the end *must* come then. Don't think about the people who come & go. Shut the door fast and think of us both together.

Your darling
Jack

Lyons. Oxford St,
[11 February 1914]
5 o'clock

Darling,
I'm here with Lesley. You will have a letter from me at the time
you get this if not before. I'm not any forrader yet about the whole
business. The question seems to me whether, supposing we could
find a decent place in London, you feel that you could work there.
That's all important. And I'm not quite sure whether you could.
What do you think; or do you think that what we ought to do is to
risk everything and hang on – now I've got to the old question.
O Tig, I nearly came at mid-day to-day; but how could I with the
money we have. It wouldn't have been right. But darling, I love you
too dearly not to be missing you terribly at every minute of the day.
Try to think that just now I'm cuddled up with you in the morning
& the alarm has just stopped sounding. My head is on your breast,
and I'm very sleepy and warm. You're more awake, because you
always are; but I'm just only awake enough to be trying to kiss you
lazily, and then my head flops down to snuggle between your
breasts.
For that's where I am really, darling.
Jack.

cheque enclosed   31 rue de Tournon (6ème),
                                       [Paris]
Thursday   [12 February 1914]

My dear one.
You are good to me. Two letters this morning and a telegram
yesterday afternoon. I wished that I might have sent you one in
return but I thought you would not expect it so I ... guarded the
money. It would be a great relief to talk over everything, but by the
time you get this letter it will be Friday morning and unless your
plans have changed you will have no time to reply to me except 'in
person'. I talked over 'the business' with you yesterday as much as I
could by letter and without you. Depend upon us – we're quite
strong enough now to find a way out of our difficulties and we *will*
and be happy, too, and do our work. (By being happy I mean happy
together in the 'odd times', you know.) And if I can get a room in
London that hasn't another opening out of it and isn't the logical

end of a passage I can work there as well as anywhere – supposing
we arrange to leave here at once.

I read the letter that you wrote me with Lesley and my breast
ached, my dearest.

Tig.

Can you let me know the *exact time* of your arrival. If you feel
you'd rather keep the money, don't worry to, but I have been very
careful of my money here, & everything is paid up to date – the two
weeks laundry & the femme de ménage and I have 60 francs left.

[9 Selwood Terrace,
South Kensington, S.W.]
[12 February 1914]
7 o'clock
Thursday

Tig darling,

I have just got the bankruptcy business over, and I am coming by
the 10 a.m. train tomorrow morning Friday which gets in about 8
o'clock or a little before, just after half past seven.

Darling, I shall be happy to see you again – then we can get every
thing right.

Love – to catch the post

Jack.

March–May
1915

Following their return from Paris in March 1914, the lives of Katherine and Murry remained unsettled. They moved from one dreary London flat to another before taking Rose Tree Cottage at the Lee, near Great Missenden (and near the Lawrences' Chesham cottage). Katherine's closest friend, Ida Baker, was on a prolonged visit to her family in Rhodesia. Murry, on the other hand, had entered into an intense intellectual friendship with D.H. Lawrence and the Irish barrister, Gordon Campbell.

Feeling increasingly lonely and left out, Katherine began exchanging love-letters with Murry's bohemian friend, Francis Carco, whom she had come to know in Paris. When she decided in February 1915 to join Carco in the French war zone of Gray, Murry offered surprisingly little resistance. But as his letters show, he was confident their relationship would survive. He was right. The affair was a humiliating fiasco and ten days later Katherine came back to him.

Although reconciled with Murry, she went twice more to Paris, where she had the use of Carco's empty flat on the quai aux Fleurs. During these two visits, from 18 to 31 March and 5 to 19 May, she began writing *The Aloe*, the long first version of 'Prelude'. Murry, meanwhile, had taken rooms at 95 Elgin Crescent in London. After Katherine's return in May 1915, they finally found a house that was to her liking at 5 Acacia Road in St John's Wood.

Greatham,
Pulborough
Sussex.
16 February, 1915

Tuesday

Darling,
You see that one night alone was enough. I had to run off to the

Lawrences, feeling that they might be kind to me. They have been – and I will remember it in their favour. You see it's no use plunging into solitude after having been with you – but in a few days I may very possibly be quite sick with the L's (or they with me) and then to be alone in my shed will appear delightful. Anyhow I couldn't work – my cold has got quite bad again, so a change of atmosphere will do me good, I think. Of course this cottage is a palace. One enormous dining-room with great beams, the size of a good barn, three bedrooms, a bath-room and a wonderful kitchen. For comfort it beats Mary's Mill, (though it is after Mary's style) because it's not overcrowded with things. I must confess I envy these people their money. It's the kind of cottage we could live in so much better than they. However, we were born to be poor. It's horrible to think that I'm already getting quite sick of our cottage at the Lee, but there it is. It seems as though we shall never be satisfied without perfection, that we can never afford.

That sounds very gloomy, but I'm not – only worried a bit by the cold. Rather I'm glad that I'm not sleeping alone in that cottage tonight. I walked here 4 most confusing miles from the station, and at length in despair and in total darkness, I knocked at this door to ask the way. I was pleasantly bouleversed to find Lorenzo at the door. Inside was a lady called Cynthia Asquith – not born but married Asquith – who was rather nice of the clever kind; much better than the women the L's generally pick up, though there was a great deal too much 'Lady Cynthia' about it all. L. enjoys it a bit, himself – while Frieda almost wallows.

I am eagerly waiting your letter to me. L says he saw you in London last night.

To be continued tomorrow morning.

Wednesday Morning.

Darling Tig – Someone is going to London, so that I have a chance of sending this little letter off earlier. I will write again by the 7 o'clock post tonight. Jack.

Greatham,
[Pulborough, Sussex]
Feb. 18. 1915

Darling Tig.

I enclose a registered letter from Carco. It appears that the right address in Elgin Crescent was 95, not 91, and the man was there on

Monday. I have just had a card from him & have written to arrange a meeting as I pass through London home. I don't quite know when I shall go – probably as soon as my cold is better. Nothing has happened since yesterday. The Lawrences continue to be very kind to me, except that Frieda has ferreted out my novel which she reads in secret somewhere. That annoys me, though I don't know why it should. I feel exactly as I did once when I got ill at Oxford & Fox took me away to his house to stay until I was better. The feeling is a kind of pleasant irresponsibility. The cottage is light & pleasant; & I have a convincing excuse for doing nothing. I am still waiting for a letter.

(I've just come back from a short walk since writing what goes before – and, inevitably Frieda has read what I've written before. I can't help thinking that it serves her right.) When I say that I am waiting for your letter, I don't mean that I'm worried at not getting one, for I have calculated the time and don't expect anything until tomorrow morning. Let it be a long one

           Jack.

                                    Paris
1st morning   [19 March 1915]

My dearest darling,
    I have just had déjeuner – a large bowl of hot milk and a small rather inferior orange – but still not dressed or washed or at all a nice girl I want to write to you. The sun is very warm today and lazy – the kind of sun that loves to make patterns out of shadows and puts freckles on sleeping babies – a pleasant creature.
    Bogey, I had a vile and loathsome journey. We trailed out of London in a fog that thickened all the way – A hideous little French woman in a mackintosh with a little girl in a dirty face and a sailor suit filled and overflowed my carriage. The child combed its hair with a lump of brown bread, spat apple in our faces – made the Ultimate impossible noises – ugh! how vile. Only one thing rather struck me. It pointed out of the window and peeped its eternal 'qu'est ce?' 'C'est de la *terre*, ma petite', said the mother, indifferent as a cabbage.
    Folkstone looked like a picture painted on a coffin lid and Boulogne looked like one painted on a sardine tin – Between them

rocked an oily sea – I stayed on deck and felt nothing when the destroyer signalled our ship – We were 2 hours late arriving and then the train to Paris did not even trot once – sauntered – meandered – Happily an old Scotchman, one time captain of the California, that big ship that went down in the fog off Tory Island – sat opposite to me and we 'got chatting.' He was a Scotchman, with a pretty soft accent. When he laughed he put his hand over his eyes & his face never changed – only his belly shook – but he was 'extremely nice' – quite as good as 1/- worth of Conrad – At Amiens he found a tea wagon and bought ham and fresh rolls and oranges and wine and would not be paid so I ate hearty – Paris looked exactly like anywhere else – it smelled faintly of lavatories. The trees appeared to have shed their buds. So I took a room (the same room) and piled up coats and shawls on my bed to 'sleep and forget'. It was all merely dull beyond words and stupid and meaningless.

But today the sun is out. I must dress and follow him. Bless you, my dearest dear – I love you *utterly* – *utterly* – beyond words – & I will not be sad. I will not take our staying in our own rooms for a little as anything serious – How are you? What are you doing?

Address my letters to the post until I give you another address –

This is a silly old letter – like eating ashes with a fish fork – but it is not meant to be. I rather wanted to tell you the truth. I read last night in the *Figaro* that the 16ᵉ Section (Carco's) are to be sent to TURKEY. Alas! the day –

Jaggle Bogey, love tell me about you, your book, your rooms – Everything

> Your
> Tig.

> 9, Selwood Terrace,
> South Kensington

Friday   [19 March 1915]

Dear darling,

I don't think there is very much fun to be had out of furnishing rooms alone. It just seems like a great waste, of energy & money & time. There's no-one to enjoy it.

I'm dog-tired. In the middle of the day I sent you a cross p.c. about the man who was to have upholstered the sofa. In case the p.c. does not reach you, I asked where he was to be found. I hunted all over Baker St. for a couple of hours in vain. Please give me some directions that will do.

I was at the job of finding cheap furniture all day to-day. It's cheap & nasty; but it can't be helped. We couldn't afford better. Then I've been putting up shelves in the kitchen. I bought a chest of drawers for 16/- (wh: I shall have to paint to-morrow) but I can't find a cupboard anywhere.

No, I'm not going on with this now. I'm too tired

[Paris]
[19 March 1915]

Darling

I went to Chartier to lunch and had a macquereau grillé et épinards à la creme. It was very strange to be there alone – I felt that I was a tiny little girl and standing on a chair looking into an aquarium. It was not a sad feeling , only strange and a bit 'femme seuleish' – As I came out it began to snow. A wind like a carving knife cut through the streets – and everybody began to run – so did I into a café and there I sat and drank a cup of hot black coffee. Then for the first time I felt in Paris. It was a little café & hideous – with a black marble top to the counter garni with lozenges of white and orange. Chauffeurs and their wives & fat men with immense photographic apparatus sat in it – and a white fox terrier bitch – thin and eager ran among the tables. Against the window beat a dirty French flag, fraying out in the wind and then flapping on the glass. Does black coffee make you drunk – do you think? I felt quite enivrée (Oh Jack I *won't* do this. It's like George Moore. Don't be cross) and could have sat there years, smoking & sipping and thinking and watching the flakes of snow. And then you know the strange silence that falls upon your heart – the same silence that comes just one minute before the curtain rises. I felt that and knew that I should write here. I wish that you would write a poem about that silence sometime, my bogey. It is so *peculiar* – even one's whole physical being seems arrested. It is a kind of dying before the new breath is blown into you. As I write I can almost see the poem you will make – I see the Lord alighting upon the breast of the man and He is very fierce. (Are you laughing at me?) So after this intense emotion I dashed out of the café bought some oranges and a packet of rusks and went back to the hotel. Me voici. The garçon has just polished the handles of the door. They are winking and smelling somethink horrible. The sky is still full of snow – but everything is clear to see – the trees against the tall houses – so rich and so fine and on the grey streets the shiny black hats of the cabmen are like blobs of Lawrence's paint. It's very quiet. A bird chirrups – a man in wooden shoes goes by. Now I shall start working. Goodbye, my dear one.

The same night. Very strange is my love for you tonight – don't have it psychoanalysed – I saw you suddenly lying in a hot bath, blinking up at me – your charming beautiful body half under the water. I sat on the edge of the bath in my vest waiting to come in. Everything in the room was wet with steam and it was night time and you were rather languid. 'Tig chuck over that sponge.' No, I'll not think of you like that – I'll shut my teeth and not listen to my heart. It begins to cry as if it were a child in an empty room & to beat on the door and say Jack – Jack – Jack and Tig – I'll be better when I've had a letter. Ah my God, how can I love him like this. Do I love you so much more than you love me or do you too – feel like this?

Tig

Saturday morning. Just off to see if there are any letters. I'm alright, dearest.

95 Elgin Crescent,
[London]

Monday Night. Half past ten.   [22 March 1915]

Tiggle Darling,

How wonderful were your letters this morning – they are so wonderful that they are almost you. And I haven't written half so many or half so long. But I wrote immediately, the same night that you went, so that I can't understand why you haven't got one.

But, darling, if my letters are funny or cross or dull, like this one, remember (I'm not asking for pity) that they were written while I was dropping with fatigue. I've never felt so tired as I have doing these rooms – it was because I couldn't get decent rest on C's couch. I had four nights of that. This is my first night In the rooms. I've just stopped work on them. Oh dear, how bare they look. Bare, but good. They swallowed up our sticks, and the one or two bits I could buy. Now there remain 8/- and the rent to pay, I suppose, to-morrow. So I shall have to review four novels tomorrow morning early. Honestly I rather enjoy being so hard up. It made the penny bazaar I went to to-day terribly important. But what's the good of a palace without my princess, my wonderful. Oh, Tiggle, we are the lovers of the world.

We are the lovers that were dreamed by God
When first he set his image on the clay
And made it man & woman: on that day
He dreamed a spirit should inspire the clod
He fashioned human

No I'm no poet tonight, I'm a painter and polished by profession and mind. But the poem shall be made to you – my queen. Oh! What shall I call you – are there no new words for that wonderful firm breasted child woman that has lain in my arms, that darling queen who is all things in her one perfect self.

I would not have thee nearer than thou art
E'n thus do all perfections shine in thee
Like to a gem to whose translucent heart
The myriad rays return and severally
Unite in one remote and flawless flame

Another beginning ...
Darling, I haven't anything to say but that I love you. But I think I shall say it properly soon. It's no use to tell you how I have been running all over London, to tell you again how the curtains don't fit, and how I have to use the blinds that were (providentially in the rooms) – it's no use because there's nothing true in it. It's not me at all; I have spent 4 days in a dream. Tomorrow I begin to live again, discreetly, and not tempting providence by a premature turn on the roundabout. But there it is, what was to be done has been done – all save the sofa, you black angel.

More to the point, tomorrow I will begin to write real letters, I hope – not hallucinated effusions like this.

I wrote to Orage a really very nice letter – I got a reply 'No thanks'. I won't pretend I'm not hurt about it. I am very deeply hurt. And it rankles nastily in my brain. I had never dreamt that it was possible that he should give me a slap in the eye like that. It was not right, anyhow. No, Orage may be a brainy fellow, as he is, but he's not one of my kind. My kind don't, can't do things like that.

I'm very sorry about it and sore. Just at the moment when I'd really hardened myself against people, I was foolish enough to let myself go because you believe in him.

For God's sake don't think these last words are against you. Only now I feel sure that what you admire in Orage – or rather your admiration – belongs to you of three years ago.

Perhaps I'm all wrong; but I could never bring it off with him now – never never.

Yes, you can see I'm hurt – I can't let the thing alone. It tapped in my brain all day 'Fool, fool'. I'm made to be a lonely one, now – lonelier, I believe, than you even.

Self-pity damnit, you mean little swine of a J.M.

Tig darling, it's all because I'm tired out – but why should it make lumps in my throat because a man won't see me? *Please* never breathe a word of what I've written, or ever suggest in any way to him to make advances. Kaput!

> Bogey.

No curtains yet.

> [13 quai aux Fleurs,
> Paris]
Monday night.   [22 March 1915]

Dear Bogey,

When I wrote to you this afternoon I was not a nice girl – I know – Now, sitting writing to you by the light of a candil – with the whole house so quiet & closed and all the people in the cellars – I am sorry. The trumpets sounded about an hour ago. All the lights are out – except one on the bridge – very far and one by the police station at the corner. I have been standing at the open window – search lights sweep the sky. They are very lovely, lighting up one by one the white clouds. Now and then someone passes, or a cart all dark gallops by. When the alarm sounded the sirens & fire whistles & motors all answered. I was in the street – and in a moment or two it was almost pitch dark – just here and there a flicker as someone lighted a cigarette. When I arrived at the Quai aux Fleurs & saw all the people grouped in the doorways and when people cried out 'n'allez pas comme ça dans la rue' I was really rather thrilled. The concierge, all the house and an obscure little old man who is always on the scene on every occasion asked me if I would 'descendre' but I hate the idea & I came up – of course all the gas was turned off – and hung out of the window. It was extremely terrifying suddenly – in fact (prosaic!) I was nearly sick! But after that the wonderful things happening & especially a conversation between a man at a fifth floor window and a thin man on the quai got me over my mal d'estomac – Those two men talking – their voices in the dark and the things they said are unforgettable – also – a fool who came along the quai whistling his hands in his pockets and as big drops of rain fell shouted with a laugh – 'Mais ils seraient mouillés – ces oiseaux des canailles.' The rain – the dark, the silence & the voices of the 2 men – the beauty of the river and the houses that seemed to be floating on the water – Ah, Jack!

As I wrote that more bugles sounded. Again I ran into the bedroom with the lamp, again opened the window. A big motor passed – a man in front blowing a trumpet – you heard from far & near the voices raised. 'C'est fini?' 'Fini, alors?' The few people in the street ran blindly after the motor & then stopped – I went on the landing with my big rusty key to put on the gas again, because it's cold and I wanted a fire. The little man came up the stairs & of course I couldn't find the letter or the number and of course he knew all about it. 'Attendez – attendez. Voulez-vous allez voir si le gaz prend'. He was far greater fool than I – but I mercied him bien & managed it myself. These raids after all are *not* funny. They are extremely terrifying and one feels such a horror of the whole idea of the thing. It seems so cruel and senseless – and then, to glide over the sky like that and hurl a bomb – n'importe où – is diabolic – and doesn't bear thinking about. (There go the trumpets again & the sirens & the whistles. Another scare!) All over again. At B's [Beatrice Hastings's] this afternoon there arrived 'du monde' including a very lovely young woman – married & *curious* – blonde – passionate – We danced together. I was still so angry about the horrid state of things.

(Oh God – it's all off again!) I opened the shutters – the motors flew by sounding the alarm – I can't talk about the tea party tonight. At any rate it isn't worth it really. It ended in a great row. I enjoyed it in a way, but Beatrice was very impossible – she must have drunk nearly a bottle of brandy & when at 9 o'clock I left & refused either to stay any longer or to spend the night there she flared up in a *fury* & we parted for life again – It seemed *so* utter rubbish in the face of all this – now. A very decent and pleasant man saw me home happily. Otherwise I think I might have been sitting in a Y.M.C.A. until this moment – it was so very dark. But a lovely evening – very soft with rain falling. B. makes me sad tonight. I never touched anything but soda water & so I really realised how the other people played on her drunkenness & she was so half charming and such an *utter fool*.

It is raining fast now on the shutters – a sound I love to hear – England feels so far away at this moment – oh very far – and I am quite suddenly sad for you. I want you as I write – and my love rises, my darling & fills my breast. Perhaps tomorrow in your letter you may sound happier. Oh, my little lover, my dear dearest I shall write no more now – I must go to bed & drink some hot milk pour me faire dormir tout de suite.

Goodnight, my heart's treasure
Tig.

95 Elgin Crescent,
[London]

Thursday: 11.45.   [25 March 1915]

Tiggle,

This morning I got the letter you wrote on Monday. I think those Zeppelins must be terrifying, really – and just before your letter came I read in the stop-press of my morning paper that another one had been signalled coming towards Paris at 10.30 last night. But there was nothing in the evening paper about it. So perhaps it didn't come. I hope not; for though it's silly, I'm always thinking that if they do kill anybody it must be you. I had a terrible turn when I saw the placard on Monday (it may have been Tuesday)

ZEPPELINS OVER PARIS
ONE WOMAN KILLED

If they had only put THE in front of the second line, I shd. have been done for, for a dead snip. It made me very sad to hear that about Beatrice Hastings, because I know she must have come near being a fine woman; and I know too that what really upsets you in her now, is the completeness of something which was – perhaps only a little bit – in you, that used to terrify me and almost killed me dead – I mean the Cabaret bit. You see Beatrice (tho' I never have seen her) seems to be a smaller specimen of your kind. Well, they don't turn up very often. They're absolutely different from women in general; and all women in general are against them. It's easy to see why. It's not because you criticise them or are clever; but because they see in you the ideal they never can attain. You are as I said six weeks ago – the eternal woman. The others are wives or mothers or Rebecca Wests – all of them are females. All their activity consists in feverish reactions because they haven't a man or a baby in bed with them at night. When they have – well they don't have any activity at all. They're negatives – in you they come up against a positive and they hate it. They put up right & wrong against you, whose greatness is that there is no right and wrong save what you feel to be you or not-you. Well with so much against you, it's a hard row to hoe, to be really *you*. (You is a type – the wonderful type from Aspasia to B.B. Colette Vagabonde, and you above all moderns) Naturally the tendency is to be extravagant and outrageous, retaliating against the hostility that puts up right & wrong against you. You by the sheer fact of your genius – genius is with you only being wonderfully what you are – have got through that without hurting yourself, and are very near to getting absolutely rid of your wickedness (that's only a figure of speech). Because of that, you'll stick to me: not so much because you love me, which you do, but because you know that you are more the real you, the good you, with me. I stick to you because I adore you, and you are the only woman I have ever seen and the only one I ever shall see. No woman could take me away from you. I could prove it logically almost, but that's off the point.

Well B.B. just hadn't enough to pull her through. When she said she left O[rage] because he wasn't passionate enough – that was a lie, I know. She was only excusing herself. It wasn't a failure in O. but in her – and I think I could tell you the reason why she failed, but again that don't matter.

The point is that I'm always thinking about you and I feel that I know more about you than you do yourself. (You think that is swank). I will put it more acceptably when I say that I know how big you are better than you do now. I used to know much less of course.

I mustn't go on gassing like this. To-day I've been trying to take up my novel again. It was awfully hard work, and then I couldn't get going – and that is more tiring than anything I know. And so I am tired now. I am missing you badly – but I couldn't help doing that, could I? Life gets frightfully empty when you aren't here. It might be alright if I could then make up on the roundabout what I lose on the swings. Most likely I will tomorrow. I'll tell you. I wish we had hundreds and hundreds of pounds and that I was there with you. I hope my good letters have begun to arrive.

Tiggle – why aren't you in my arms in my big bed tonight?

Boge.

[13 quai aux Fleurs,
Paris]

Thursday morning   [25 March 1915]

My own Bogey –

Yesterday I had your letters at last. But first I *never* got a cross postcard about the sofa: you never mentioned it until this letter. Here are the directions. Take a bus to Blandford Street which is off Baker Street. Walk down it and turn into South Street. King has got a filthy little shop with a sewing machine in the window and some fly blown cards which say 'Loose Covers'. More than that I can't tell you myself. Have you written to him and enclosed a stamped envelope? If not, I would do that *at once*.

You seem to have done perfect wonders with the rooms – the carpentering job I saw and heard as plain as if I'd been there – to the very sand papering. All the things are floating in my brain on a sea of blue ripolin. I feel those rooms will be lovely. If Frieda is there ask her about the curtains. She can sew even though I don't think she'd have ideas. I saw such jolly low stools yesterday – very firm with rush seats 1.75. I wish I could send you 2 or 3. They are nice.

I had a great day yesterday. The Muses descended in a ring like the angels on the Botticelli Nativity roof – or so it seemed to 'humble' little Tig and I fell into the open arms of my first novel. I have finished a huge chunk but I shall have to copy it on thin paper for you. I expect you will think I am a dotty when you read it – but – tell me what you think – won't you? It's queer stuff. It's the spring makes me write like this. Yesterday I had a fair wallow in it and then I shut up shop & went for a long walk along the quai – very far. It was dusk when I started – but dark when I got home. The lights came out as I walked – & the boats danced by. Leaning over the bridge I suddenly discovered that one of those boats was exactly what I want my novel to be – Not big, almost 'grotesque' in shape I mean perhaps *heavy* – – with people rather dark and seen strangely as they move in the sharp light and shadow and I want bright shivering lights in it and the sound of water. (This, my lad, by way of uplift.) But I *think* the novel will be alright. Of course it is not what you could call serious – but then I can't be just at this time of year & I've always felt a spring novel would be lovely to write.

Today I must go to Cooks with my last goldin sovereign in my hand to be changed – I am getting on alright as regards money & being very careful. Cooked vegetables for supper at 20 the demi livre are a great find and I drink trois sous de lait a day. This place is perfect for working.

I read your letter yesterday in the Luxembourg gardens. An old gentleman seeing my tender smiles offered me half his umbrella & I found that it was raining but as he had on a pair of tangerine coloured eye glasses I declined. I thought he was a Conrad spy. My own dear darling – what are you doing about a bed? Surely not that vile sofa all these nights!

I have adopted Stendhal. Every night I read him now & first thing in the morning. This is a vague letter but it carries love and love and kisses from your

Tig.

	[13 quai aux Fleurs, Paris]
Friday evening.	[26 March 1915]

Dearest darling,

I am in such a state of worry and suspense that I can't write to you tonight or send you anything. When I came back from the fruitless search for letters the concierge began a long story about an Alsatian in the house who had received yesterday a four page letter for the name of Bowden. Another came today, said she: I gave it back to the postman. I literally screamed – I have *written* this name for her & she'd utterly forgotten it thinking of me only as Mansfield – Since then I've simply rushed from post office to office – The Alsatian is out: I'm waiting for her & the postman now. My heart dies in my breast with terror at the thought of a letter of yours being lost – I simply don't exist. I suppose I exaggerate – but I'd plunge into the Seine – or lie on a railway line rather than lose a letter. You know Bogey, my heart is simply crying all the time and I am frightened, desolate, useless for anything.

Oh, my precious – my beloved little Jag, forgive Tig such a silly scrawl – But Life ought not to do such things to you & to me – I could *kill* the concierge – yes, with pleasure – 'Une lettre d'Angleterre dans un couvert bleu' –

Courage! But at this moment I am simply running as fast as I can and crying my loudest into your arms –

I will write you properly tomorrow. This is just to say that I love you and that you are the breath of life to me

Tig.

[13 quai aux Fleurs,
Paris]
Saturday –   [27 March 1915]

My Bogey, my little King,
    I'm doing the unpardonable thing – writing in pencil, but I'm in
bed still and having breakfast, so please forgive. I kept my eye upon
the hole of the door until 12 o'clock last night when the Alsatian
deigned to ascend. As she did *not* know this flat was occupied she
had a pretty fright at sight of me in the inky darkness – but after a
long disappearance when I decided to hit her if she had not got it
she appeared. V'la! At the same time – carrying her little làmp and
all wrapped up in a shawl & wonderfully beautiful I thought – she
put her hand on my arm – 'AttAndez!' she said – & disappeared &
brought me back a pink hyacinth growing in a pot – 'Ca sAnt de la
vraie fleur' said she – Then I came in and read your Monday night
letter – I read it and then I read it again – Then I dropped it into my
heart and it made ever bigger circles of love – flowing over and over
until I was quite healed of that torment of waiting. I love you – you
know. I love you with every inch of me – You are wonderful – you
are my perfect lover. There is nobody but you. Hold me, Bogey,
when I write those words, for I am in your arms, your darling head
in my hands & I am kissing – kissing –
    The rooms sound lovely. I hope by now the sofa is there. I hope
another cheque has come. The moment Kay sends my money I will
send some to you.
    I think Orage wants kicking. Just that – Of course what is so
peculiarly detestable is his habit of lying *so* charmingly – his 'I
should be delighted, Katherina,' rings in my ears. Beatrice I have
not seen since her famous party. It's an ugly memory. I am glad it
happened so soon – I think next morning she must have felt
horribly ashamed of herself for she was drunk and jealous and
everybody knew it. I am thankful that I stood firm – I feel so utterly
superior to her now –
    To tell you the truth, both of them are bitter because they have
nearly known love and broken and we know love and are happy –
Bogey, *really* and *truly* how happy we are. Now I am giving you all
sorts of little hugs and kisses and now big ones and long long
kisses – –
    No – I really *must* get up. What a farce it is to be alone in bed in
the spring when you are alive –

                        Tig.

95 Elgin Crescent,
[London]
Monday,   [29 March 1915]

Tiggle darling,
   The letter you got just before this was written on Friday and not
posted until Monday. In my terrible hurry, going to the Lawrences I
forgot it.
   I came back this morning and found two of your letters – one
when an Alsatian woman had managed to defraud you of one of
mine, and the other when you had got it. I'm terribly glad it did
come.
   I don't know what to write at this moment (1.30). There's
nothing to say about the L's. L. talks an awful lot about you and
me, and I'm sure I don't understand one-tenth of it all. The other
nine-tenths are wrong; but I don't trouble to correct it. You see
there is good feeling (as Kot wd. say) between me & L. & nothing
else really matters. I wouldn't gain anything by trying to put him
right. For instance, he says that it gave him quite a shock to
discover how crude I was physically, apparently as between you
and me. I listened; but it didn't give me a shock at all, for I haven't
the least idea of what he was driving at. I suppose he meant
something; but I'm not quite sure.
   So there's really nothing to say about my week-end. And about
my return, nothing. One thing is over everything – the ghastly cold
weather. It's always just beginning to snow; and if it doesn't bring it
off it's because it's too cold. The stuff just gets frozen into ice before
it gets going at all.
   I don't understand Orage a bit – and there's the end of him.
Perhaps he is too old and in life has gone a bit bad. I don't know.
Now I laugh at myself for being hurt. What does it matter? Only it's
funny the way I go about saying to myself I won't be hurt any more
(just as I said in that auctioneer's shop I won't be swindled) and I
always let myself in. It's nothing to be proud of; I suppose. But I
don't get angry with myself. I only laugh. Perhaps I am simpler than
they are. And to be simple is a good thing, Tiggle, I know. I am so
much better than I was – not good yet, of course, but really better
than I was. Now there's a bad pride still in me, but perhaps that will
go soon – and then I shall begin to be something. It sounds like
Snodgrass in *Pickwick*, who 'took his coat off and loudly
announced to the bystanders several times that he was going to
begin.' Then, sometimes, I think I'm a funny little chap – just like

that – and give myself a small pat on the head or a pinch of the ear and say 'You'll grow up one of these days' – but I never shall, never. I shall only become a funnier little chap. But you'll stick to me. I know that somehow, and don't think about it very much. I stand for the good in you & you for the good in me. We can't leave off now, nor ever, so long as it is good: and I can't imagine that it can ever be otherwise.

How little I do think about now, to be sure. I don't think you would find me talking very much, nowadays. I feel quite extraordinarily calm and peaceful. But I do want you. It's wonderful to think about that – to have somebody near me who understands me as you do, and will tell me the truth, and do true things to me. Even now that I begin to imagine our caresses, my head snuggling against your wonderful breasts, my lips feeling slowly over them till I kiss – it is all so true. Do you understand what I mean. The word is funny. But I mean it's not just desire, or wickedness, or excitement, but the being of two good souls and bodies together & making suddenly a better thing. Now I would have you back. Something in me says why is Tig not here now? and another thing says why should she be – she is there and Tiggle – more truly Tiggle for being there. But those two things do not really drag me different ways. I can wait, quite content and happy, till you come: simply, I suppose, because I have no shadow of a doubt any more either of you or me.

Good-night, darling

Boge.

95 Elgin Crescent,
[London]
Saturday Evening   [8 May 1915]

Wig Darling,

I got your letter this morning. I wish you were here now.

The Lawrences have just been. Yesterday, thinking that I ought to be nice to them, I invited them here to supper tonight at 7 o'clock. All day I've been with my brother because it was his birthday, and did not get back till 5.30. Then for an hour and a half I slaved to get supper ready. They turned up with an extra man at 8.30. Isn't it silly that that should upset me? I should have been alright if Frieda hadn't been there. I was hurt that they were late, seeing that they knew I had to get it all myself, but to find Frieda fatuously laughing on the doorstep, as though it were so very Bohemian to be an hour and a half late – no, that was a little too much. After an hour of it, she decided that I was dull, and to prove to me what a party should be began to sing German sentimental songs in that idiotic voice of hers. Lawrence kept on saying à propos of the cottage in Bucks, you & I and Katherine & Frieda will never have so good a time as we did some of those evenings at your cottage. It makes me think furiously. He must be blind to certain things. I do look back on some moments with a kind of feeling that it won't happen again – but on the evenings in Rose Tree Cottage, never. I think I have fifty times the capacity for delight now that I had then. But I do like Lawrence; though I *feel* that he is deteriorating – really getting feeble. Frieda is the Red Woman, the Whore of Babylon, the Abomination of Desolations that was to Fornicate in the High Places, and the Holy of Holies. I've just remembered that bit of Revelations – isn't it really Frieda, spiritually speaking?

I feel inclined to write a play about the evening – called 'Un Peu de Charcuterie' – I got some from Appenrodt; of which the aforesaid F. wolved over one half before anybody else had even begun to eat – and then she said that spring-onions (also provided) she could not eat because they were vulgar. Then the strange man they brought was continually saying quite unintelligible misfires in French & German and asking Frieda if it was right. You've no idea of the bestial cumulative effect.

I met my brother at S. Ken. I was surprised he was late. He didn't turn up till 12.10. Then, the moment he saw me he began to cry. So I had to walk him down to Thurloe Square to find out what was the matter. He'd got on to a 19 bus – and it had taken him to Sloane Square. He hadn't any money & he made sure I would be gone. So he had run all the way from Sloane Square to S. Kensington (– and he didn't know the road at all –) as fast as he could. It was a melancholy & typical beginning. I used to be just like that. But he had a lemon squash which seemed to revive him, and then we rowed for 2 hours round the Serpentine. It was wonderfully beautiful in Kensington Gardens to-day. Then a good Dairy Express Lunch; then he came home with me to tea and then had to rush home. But as he said while he was having tea in our kitchen. 'I *think* I've enjoyed myself to-day'; which seems to me a masterpiece.

My mother sent me a note asking if you would go to tea with her on Wednesday – 'She hasn't seen you for so long' – but I'll say – unless forbidden – something nice from you when I go.

Goodbye, Wig darling, – I'm quite alright now I've talked to you

Boge

95 [Elgin Crescent,
London]
9 May, 1915.
Sunday

Dear Wig.

I just had a funny thought. I was cooking a bloater for supper, just now, and I wondered how you did without a gas-stove. I felt sorry for you because you hadn't got a gas-stove. Oh – I'm too silly. Fancy putting that down.

I've been in all day – Sunday – working for the *Daily News*. In twenty minutes I am going out to see the Lawrences; but I know I am going to be offensive to Frieda, for plainly I hate her. I shall have to be very careful. Part of the afternoon I spent sewing a button on my trousers, a tape on my pants, & sewing up the waistcoat pocket of my old flannel suit. I did it all beautifully, especially the white-cotton hemstitch that shows on my flannel waistcoat pocket.

To-day's been windy, sunny, & cold. At least I think it has been cold, because I left off my pants first thing in the morning and had to put them on again in the evening. (What an awful lot there is about pants in this letter). Early in the morning I went out to buy some tobacco from the sylph I told you about. She's very cold to me, not cold – I don't mind that – but she despises me profoundly. I wouldn't go there at all, only it's the only shop open on Sunday. I always drop my change; she makes me so nervous.

What else have I done to-day? I can't think of anything. I thought about you several times. First, as I do every morning, that you were very wigged to take away the sponge – but I am getting quite expert in bathing myself with my hands. Then when I did my sewing I thought it was sad that you weren't there to show it to, because I'd done it better than you could, at any rate as well. I'm always thinking about you when I think of anything at all; but except when my thoughts are passionate, it's wonderfully calm and happy to think about you. I just smile a little, and feel that I were talking to someone quietly in a boat (I think in Venice) on a midsummer night. It is wonderful to be so secure and beautifully – tender or sensitive, I don't know the word.

But this has been a quiet day. I've got nothing to tell you except what I know you can read in every word I've written.

Boge.

Tuesday morning.
A letter from you.

[13 quai aux Fleurs,
Paris]
[11 May 1915]

My dearest of all

I have just got your Saturday evening letter and you can imagine what I feel about the supper party & about Frieda. I could *murder* her. Everything you told me made me boil and made my heart fly out for my Bogey – What a great fat *sod* she is – I should like to send a pig to kill her – a real filthy pig ... Lawrence has got queer blind places, hasn't he?

Poor Arthur – the beginning of the day sounded very like a little you. But I envied him being on the Serpentine with you. Lesley and I used to go in the old days but I've never been since. It's a lovely thing to do.

Yesterday was simply hellish for me. My work went very well, but all the same – I suffered abominably. I felt so alien and so far away – & everybody cheated me – everybody was ugly – and beyond words cruel. I finally got to such a state that I could go nowhere to eat because of the people and I could hardly speak. At half past ten I shut up shop & went to bed, but not to sleep. The three apaches of the cinema, L'Fantome, Bêbé, & le faux Curé tried the key of the door all night & tip toed on the landing. Finally through the shutters there came two chinks of day. Do I sound foolish and cowardly? Oh, but yesterday was simply Hell. In the evening (I'd gone out to get a lamp glass. The concierge with relish, had smashed mine) I sat in a little garden by a laburnum tree – I felt the dark dropping over me and the shadows enfolding and I died and came to life again 'time & time again' as Mrs C. used to say. I went to buy bread at a funny shop. The woman hadn't got a nose and her mouth had been sewn up and then opened again at the side of her face. She had a wall eye. When she came into the lamp light with the bread I nearly screamed, but she clapped her poor hand to her head & smiled at me. I cannot forget it. This morning things are better. It is such a fine day, but I could not stand a month of yesterdays. I'd come home in a coffin, Jaggle.

My darling, my dearest – your letter written so beautifully is on the table. It expresses you so. I love you with every bit of me – I am your own woman your

Wig

Shut your eyes a minute. Hold me very hard – Now I am giving you little kisses & now a big big kiss.

PS. I have opened your letter again to say that your Sunday one is just come, so I am rich today with 2 letters. Don't cast your clouts before May is out – in other words, keep your pants on, Boge. (How absurd it sounds.) I should like to have seen the sewing – but I shall, shan't I? Found another BUG in the kitchen today (did I tell you about the first which nearly bit off my hand?) and also a large black louse with white spots on it. I am being so careful – careful of money. You'd be surprised – Every sou is counted out and put down in my book. I detest money – Isn't it a long time since I've heard from Lesley?

I'm sorry the sylph is cold to you, my dear love – and I hope the Lawrences were nicer. The concierge has just refused to get me some milk. It's ½ past 11 & I've had no breakfast. She *is* a swine.

Tig.

[95 Elgin Crescent,
London]
Tuesday.   [11 May 1915]

Wig darling,
I've just got your letter of Sunday evening, saying that you haven't had a letter from me. Darling, I write to you every night by the 12 o'clock post. Perhaps they would get to you quicker if I put the arrondissement on the envelope. I have quite forgotten which it is, so please tell me in your next letter.

I went to see Lawrence last night as I said. He was very sad. Poor devil he is so lonely, with that bitch of a Frieda, always playing traitor, and hurting him in every secret and intimate part of his soul. It's no good until he can get away from her – she's really wearing him out. No, it depressed me terribly to be with him last night. It was all so unreasonable & cruel, – but it's no use to go on with that. But I think I shall ask him to come away with me for a fortnight's holiday during this summer to see if I can urge him to the point of leaving her. Not that I think I can do very much directly; but I have an idea that he might be happy were he away with me for a bit, because he would know that I was loving him. It does make a difference. – Wig, how wonderful *we* are!

Well, I'd been talking to him for about an hour, Kot being the silent corner-man, Frieda happily away at a concert, when who should turn up but Gilbert & Miss Muir – you remember Miss Muir, who walked over with me & Gilbert one day when I was staying with G & M & you with the L's. Gilbert was in a very good mood. I liked him more than I have at any time during the last 2 years. Yes he was very good and I was happy that he was still our friend. I lunched with him to-day, and amiably gave him a piece of my mind about himself & his writing. He took it awfully well. He seems to have a respect for what I say – perhaps that's why I'm liking him now. Tomorrow I'm going to tea with Miss Muir & him. She's nice, I think, – at any rate she got me by admiring you – not in the silly envious coarse way of Frieda, but sincerely. She thinks you're very beautiful and that we're an awfully fine pair. Perhaps I tumble into that kind of trap too easily. – I don't know, but I like tumbling.

Gilbert's going to see Pinker about my book so with D.H.L. too, something ought to happen. Won't it be fine if we both appear together. Tig and Wig

I didn't make the books big enough to write titles on.

Oh, about that supper. It was D.S. MacColl, Aitken, Muirhead Bone & me. They were very nice, particularly nice to me. But I thought them all a bit stupid. I couldn't talk to them at all. I wasn't nervous or bored, but I just couldn't. They're alright, but they aren't my tribes. And, I can't believe Muirhead Bone is as big an artist as I thought he was. He must be a second-rater with a great technical skill.

Jarvis has just been for his 10/6, chatting away – saying the same thing a half-dozen times: but I can't help liking him.
Wig, Wig, Wig
You are a darling
I love you

Boge.

[13 quai aux Fleurs,
Paris]
[?13 May 1915]

Dear Boge,
This is about the 4th letter I have written and torn up (the others I mean. This I will send) The others were nothing. My rheumatism is simply dreadful. I am very tired with it – *dead* tired and sick of it, but my work goes 'alright'.
Fancy GIVING YOURSELF UP to LOVING someone for a fortnight, as you say you will do for Lawrence in the summer. My strike! I think you are quite right, but it does surprise me as an idea.
You *are* seeing a lot of people, Bogey. You always do when I am away – I wish I knew where Harris was in Paris. I've a perfect mania to see him – & to hear his bitter laugh.
Quelle vie.
I send back this letter. I don't know what to say – *Why* do the fowls come in? I am ill and alone voilà tout.

Tig.

[13 quai aux Fleurs,
Paris]
Friday afternoon.   [14 May 1915]

My dearest darling –
I am determined to come home on Wednesday; I'll arrive at Victoria at 9 o'clock – My work is finished my freedom gained. If I stay they will ① cut the gas off ② arrest me as a spy ③ F[rancis] C[arco] is coming to Paris at the end of next week. Voilà des beaux raisons! Besides which I have only to polish my work now; it's all really accompli. I am simply bursting to come. If this throws you

into a fury do not attend me à la gare – or come & don't recognise me or something.

Ah, Bogey be glad – Such a *good* Wig is coming back with money in her pocket, too – for I have lived MOST CAREFULLY –
But what with Bugs and no gas and a heart full of love and fun – I cannot cannot cannot stay alone. So there you are – Do my letters arrive all safely – I write every day – I am very silly ce soir – drunk on a black coffee – dearest – I believe – But Life is fun – and I'll take up my leg and walk. What perhaps is the source of my amusement is that I was marched off to the police station today – as I was here without papiers de séjour I thought it was all up ± the cheek of those police – where was my husband – how many children have you – None – 'Pourquoi pas' said the inspector. I was a frozen Union Jackess – There is a darling baby in this café with me. She is drowning her brioche in a cup of weak coffee – drowning it *deliberately* holding it down with a spoon!

Dearest darling –
I am hanging up the curtain in the little house today – Ah, I do simply love you – you funny boy – Anoint your derrière, love with Zinc ointment. Buy steak for Wednesday – They are selling huge asparagras here – so big that it looks like the first sentence of a Willy novel. I love love love you – will this letter arrive on Monday – then start the week with my arms tight round you a moment – for I adore you Bogey and I am only yours. Wednesday then, dearest Heart. I shall see your old grey hat at Victoria. But come on the platform – this time – & I will lean out of the Kerridge and wave.

> Always your
> Wig

[London]
[15 May 1915]

COME BACK DARLING. MURRY

[95 Elgin Crescent,
London]

Saturday Morning,   [15 May 1915]

Wig darling,
I'm hoping while I write this that it will never get to you, because
you'll have had my wire and been able to come back.
Your letter this morning was terrible. I don't know *when* you
wrote it, but you had torn up 3 already. Oh, darling it was awful to
read. I don't know what to say except that we mustn't be apart
while you're like this. It isn't right. Come to London again and we'll
find a room somewhere, where you can work all day – or I'll go
back to the country so that you can have these rooms until your
book is finished. But I can't bear the thought of you ill over there –
so far away.
And now I wonder whether the wire has got to you, and whether
you will come back if it does. You see I've only got that awful note
– and I know I shan't hear from you again – I can't hear from you
again – till Monday. Oh Tig – I wonder whether you will wire in
answer so that I get it to-night.
Oh my precious – life seems so cruelly hard to you that you can't
bear it alone. The last words of your letter were 'I am ill & alone –
voilà tout'. Tig, you must know what that means to me. You must
be coming home. You wouldn't just write that and stay. Oh darling
I can hear your tears in every word of the letter – and I can't do
anything.
No, I've got nothing even to say. I just wonder whether you are
coming, and how I shall wait until Monday.

                    Boge.

[13 quai aux Fleurs,
Paris]

Saturday afternoon.   [15 May 1915]

I got very sane after I had written to you yesterday – I wish
something in you didn't make me feel a 'silly' when I want to write
at full tilt. It's because you never do; you're such a guarded and
careful little Bogey – and so frightened I shall 'make a scene'. I
won't, dear, I promise you. I'm not *at* all sure this afternoon
whether I'll come on Wednesday or whether I'll wait a week.
Perhaps I'd better wait a week. If I *do* come I *won't* wire if I *don't*

come I *will* wire. It's a fair toss up. Yesterday evening I sat in a little parc and played with the idea with a *sou*. The sou said every time 'Yes, go – ' but that was yesterday. And this morning again your calm letter as though we were 'seule pour la vie' shook up against the apple cart.

You sent me a letter from Lesley – which was simply marvellous. She wrote, as she can, you know of all sorts of things, grass and birds and little animals and herself and our friendship with that kind of careless, very intimate joy – There is something quite absolute in Lesley – She said at the end of a page – 'Katie, dearie – what is *Eternity*?' She's about the nearest thing to 'eternal' that I could ever imagine. I wish she were not so far away. Things are so changed now. You and I still love each other, but you haven't the need of me you had then and somehow I do always have to be '*needed*' to be happy. I've expressed that abominably – and it's not even quite true, for what I call your need of me was more or less an illusion on my part. You're an amazing person in the way you can accept just so much and no more – No, I'm beating about the bush and not really saying what I want to – *and* it really doesn't matter – But I do wish my tall, pale friend were here to walk with and sit with. You're not the slightest use – for it doesn't come natural for you to desire to do such things with me. It's I who plead like 'une petite pensionnaire' to be taken out on a Saturday afternoon or to a music hall –

A lovely woman sits in here with me. She's got a fool of a man with her that she hates beyond words. So would I. She wears a big rose under her chin – her eyes are lovely but very shadowed with a purple ring. She is not *only* bored: she is trying not to cry. Three fat jossers at a table nearby are vastly amused. Two dirty little froggies smoking pipes 'a l'anglaise' & ragging each other are next to me. They occasionally sing at me – or snap their fingers. They are the most hideous little touts – Blast them! Now, I might have known it, my lovely woman is playing a game of cards with her cavalier – Mon dieu! She does look lovely with the fan of cards in her hand, the other hand hovering over and her lips just pouting. I must go. This is a fool of a letter. What makes you disgruntled? Is your book worrying you? No, I can't send any of mine because I'm too dependent on it as a whole under my hand. The BUGS are still flourishing in the kitchen. One violated me last night.

Pretty business this German chasing – and a pity they have to photograph such decent, honest looking wretches as the belles proies. It's a filthy trick; there's no difference between England and

Germany when the mob gets a hand in things – No difference between any nation on earth – They are all equally loathsome.

Goodbye for now, my dear. *Hanged* if I know whether I'll see you on Wednesday or not – If I do wire that I am not coming you might send me that £1; just to reassure me – will you – Oh, Bogey – dearest –

Tig.

December 1915

The social horizons of Katherine and Murry expanded in 1915. D.H. Lawrence and Frieda came to live in Hampstead and with Murry planned the launching of a new magazine, *Signature*. Murry and Katherine also came into contact with some of the writers and artists who belonged to the set entertained by Lady Ottoline Morrell at Garsington Manor. Katherine's only brother, Leslie ('Chummie'), moreover, had arrived in England in February 1915 to train as an officer in a British regiment. During his leaves, the two spent some happy periods together, talking about the people and places they remembered in New Zealand. Leslie's death while training in October 1915 left Katherine numb with grief. Unable to remain in the house where he had so recently visited, she went with Murry to Bandol in the South of France. But he, feeling shut out by the intensity of her mourning, returned to England and spent Christmas at the Garsington Manor house-party. When Katherine summoned, however, Murry lost no time in joining her at the Villa Pauline in Bandol.

[Hôtel Beau Rivage,
Bandol]
[10 December 1915]

Friday.

Jag-Bog,
   I don't know whether you expect me to write to you every day but I shall do so (D.V.) & you will too, won't you? Once a day really isn't too often & it's my only dear signal that you are well. Today came your Paris letter with the swindle from Cooks (which made me furious!) & the lady with the Dates. 'Net gain 4d' re baggage was very *pa* of you. I heard you saying that. Darling, what a frightful adventure with O Hara San. What a Minx to take off her

61

head like that – but you ought to have known, Bogey. You are always accusing me of the same thing. I hope you do see De la Mare – thank you for sending me his note.

Yesterday I went for a long walk round by the sea towards St. Cyr (which is very beautiful & wild & like my NZ.) & then I struck inland & came home by little lanes & crooked ways bordered with olive trees – past the flower farms – I thought I should never get home again. I got quite lost & though I kept hearing voices the walls were always in the way & when I peered through the gates there was never a soul to be seen except jonquils & daffodils & big blue violets & white roses. The sun went down – I passed a little villa called 'Allons-y' and coo-ed but a Fearful White Dog happily attached to a pump answered me so effectually that I decided to strike into a wood & have done with it. But at that moment a far too agile malignant looking goat appeared – vaulted over a wall just ahead of me – I rushed in the opposite direction and got found at last.

My work is shaping for the first time today – I feel nearer it. I can see the people walking on the shore & the flowery clusters hanging on the trees – – if you know what I mean. It has only been a dim coast & a glint of foam before – The days go by quickly.

My precious one, I long for your first London letter. I expect it will arrive on Sunday or Monday – so I *must* be patient. Take care of yourself, my darling boy. Buy something for your hair & use it. Do keep warm. Buy yourself another pair of those pants. Do keep happy. Eat good food. Don't call this 'swank' on my part. It is not – Perhaps it *is* partly that I love to frown at you & give your tie a perfectly unnecessary little tug. Even though you do say 'for God's sake woman, let me alone.'

I kiss you on your eyes & your lips & the top curl of your hair.

Tig.

But don't　c/o Kot,
write there.　[London]
Sunday　　　　[12 December 1915]

Wig darling,

I have been waiting for a letter from you – but nothing has come yet. Probably the posts take longer than we imagined – but I shall get anxious soon.

I am now in that room of which I spoke (41 Devonshire St.); but I don't like it very much. However, before taking it I told them plainly that I would only stay until I had found a studio. The room is a rather pretty little attic right at the top of the house – but it isn't very clean, and it's a terrible trouble doing for one's self. Kot, as I told you is very angry with me for being here at all; and I am sure he will compel me to find a studio within a week. The chief trouble with this room is that, in addition to its not being quite clean anywhere, the bed is only an apology, lumpy and hard – in fact a disreputable example of the old familiar kind of chair bedstead. There are a few draughts as well. However, I'm not at all sad, except at having received no letter from you.

Goodyear has been here on 5 days leave. His boat left Le Havre at the same time as my own; but we didn't see each other until we met at Campbell's on Friday night. On Saturday G. stood me a dinner at Treviglio's, after I had taken him to see Lawrence, and then he came back with me here and stayed the night. Now, as an old campaign [sic].

He can sleep, even on a dirty floor, with the greatest satisfaction. He is now sick of the war and desperately anxious to be a free man again. But he has become awfully nice – really one of us; and he tells some very funny stories of his experiences. He lives with a Welsh brewer in a lovely cottage, belonging to a French peasant on whom he is billeted, and they spend all the time devising how to steal the necessary stores from the quarter-master sergeant. I have given him your address and told him to write you immediately.

I think that Lawrence was really & truly pleased to see me back again. I feel that he is very fond indeed of you and me – and that he feels that we are the only people who really care for him in the way he wants to be cared for. Our going away had depressed him very much: already – I have been to see him twice – I notice that he is much more cheerful. Kot is also happier, I think. Lawrence is writing to you to-day.

There is a mangy old cat on these stairs – very frightening at night-time. But he has chummed up with me, drunk my milk and eaten my sausage (he was so starved that in his ravenous appetite he made a beastly mess on the floor) and now he sits in front of my fire wagging his tail for the first time, I should think, since the war began. I am glad to have him for all his manginess – only I dare not touch him yet.

My first two nights – I was ashamed to say so – I stayed at the Campbells. Gordon is now completely done for, and terribly depressing. I think he is really a lost soul. Biddy is lovely as ever –

she has had her photograph taken with yr. locket round her neck. Shall I get you one of the photographs? They aren't very good because she was frightened – and Paddy who is in the photograph too was more terrified still. O Tig, why haven't I got a photograph of you as a baby? All my mind will insist on picturing you as one. You are always rising up before my eyes as you must have been when you were three years old, with those wonderful darling fingers, that bend as no woman's ever could. That little tiny crook in them is almost making me cry now – with love and pride and delight. When you get to these words, just hold up your finger and bend it as you do for me – and think that there is only one who carries that beauty locked in his heart for ever – that he is wicked at times and cowardly and cruel through cowardice, and yet loves you with some power that you have given him, so much is it beyond his own compass. Darling.

I am very anxious about your money. Please when you write explain to me exactly how it is going and how much you would like. I'm sure I can get it from anybody – *Times, Westminster* etc.

Kot has just been in to see me for a minute or two; and in the interval I have been looking up the Jiggisons in the little red-book. I haven't been able to get the Weekly *Times* – but the *Literary Supplement* was sent on Friday. The *Times* will follow tomorrow, Monday.

To-night, I am going to the Dreys for dinner. I don't want to at all; but I have to keep my promise. Besides I have to soften the resumption of my job I will tell you in my tomorrow letter of what happens.

To-day it is very cold here in London. Before midday it even snowed a little.

My darling – for my sake, next time you go out wear your goblin hat. I want to think of you in it, then you are most mine.

Jag.

[Hôtel Beau Rivage,
Bandol]

A windy Sunday.   [12 December 1915]

Dearest and only one,
I really do think I may expect your first London letter tomorrow & I ought to hear from Kay, too. I've not had a sign so far.

For some unaccountable reason, chéri, I've got our Marseilles fever again with all its symptoms – loss of appetite, shivering fits, dysentery. What on earth can it be? I really think it is a noisome fever from some black man in a café near to The Vieux Port. At any rate it's horrid & I am a ragged creature today. If I hadn't got William Shakespeare I should be in the ultimate cart, but he reads well to a touch of fever. However, I expect I shall be a better girl by the time you get this, so don't go and worry, darling of my heart. I bought a most superior exercise book yesterday for 4 sous *but* at about five o'clock the eternal silence was broken by a rap at my door & a pretty creature with gold rings in her ears, Spanish boots like Bogey's & flashing eyes & teeth brought in a basket – My laundry. I only send a *morsel* – the veriest fragmint & Lord! there was a bill for 3.15. *How* the rings the teeth eyes & boots vanished – counting the precious money into her hand I paid for them, every one. I shall have to cut myself a little pair of football shorts out of the *Radical.* I can see that – How are you? Where are you? What are you doing now? ...

The salon my dear has become impossible ground while the wife of that Englishman remains in this hotel. Did you remark her – she is a Belgian – I never met her like – she out Belgians anything imaginable. However I'll be even with her and put her to paper and have done with her. I shall creep to the post and back but that's my limit today. Otherwise I'll keep my room & try & write & read. Send me a book, precious when you can. Take care of yourself – I kiss you, Bogey – I am

Tig.

23 Worsley Road,
Hampstead. N.W.
Thursday – late afternoon.   [16 December 1915]

Wig darling,
This morning I had two letters. When you wrote them, you had not yet got one of mine – the other arrived as you were writing. Both your letters made me sad; for in both you were ill. Oh, my dear darling, can you understand – of course you can, better than I – how small and infinitely precious, infinitely fragile you appear to me? I am afraid for you, and our letters take so long. You say that perhaps when I get your letters, you are no longer ill. I feel that you

may be worse. I feel, too, all the love that your letters bring, and I wonder are mine strong enough to carry something back to you. Because of my love for you & yours for me – Tig, precious, it is for *Toujours* – it has *Toujours* written upon it – because of our love, I feel a stranger in my own land. This England is my own land, I know, but yet the persons in it, even those who are in some way dear to me, seem to be blunt of understanding. They seem to laugh when they should not, and to talk when they should be silent, and not to know how precious is the thing of ours I carry in my heart. To me it is something that I must bear in my cupped hands ever so lightly, like a flame – (not that it may be blown out, but that it burns so brightly that they could not see it at all,) or rather like that little bird you carried in the room at Cholesbury, or even like O'Hara San herself who is to me so delicate that I dare hardly breathe when I smoothe her hair. I wonder now, sitting here, whether you and I in our common love are not too fine for those, even those, whom we call our friends. Wouldn't they be somehow different, Wig, somehow more sensitive if they really knew. Or do we suffer just because we have been chosen out of all others to keep the one flame alive until we too have given it over to others? I feel myself somehow aloof, terribly apart, though I would be of them. I try to conquer myself to work with them. But I am not I any more, I am you, and our common spirit will not submit. All our friends hurt me; Kot very deeply – Campbell insufferably; Lawrence least of all – but all of them hurt. I wonder are we, am I, as selfish and hard as they are? Perhaps, but I do not believe it; and now I seem to discover that even those silences & gruffnesses wh: you do not like in me – they are going away, dearest, I am sure, so that I may be a new Jag to take you into my arms at meeting – were a God-given protection against the unmeant brutalities of people.

And now I am afraid you will think I am sad on my own account as well as on yours. It is not true, at all. I am sad for your illness, my nut brown goblin (and this morning I called to you in the dark, whistled my empty windy whistle to you, as you swung so sadly on that gate, and I think you must have heard) but in what I have told you before I am not sad. I am just laying my head upon your cool and wonderful breast, and telling you what I have found in the world to which I was sent. For you and I are not of the world, darling; we belong to our own kingdom, which truly is when we stand hand in hand, even when we are cross together like two little boys. Somehow we were born again in each other, tiny children, pure and shining, with large sad eyes and shocked hair, each to be the other's doll. I cannot speak save to you – and to you I have no need of words.

Oh, my dearest – I must not write any more like this; I do not believe it will make you happier, but rather sadder, for something in real love is sad – that knowledge of apartness, of an enemy world in which we dare not stay too long for the peril of our souls. And that is the sadness that has hold of me tonight. It is not sadness at all, but the final triumph of our love. Darling it is *toujours*. If you would not say the word now that I have opened all my heart, I feel that I should die. But I hear you saying it: I even see your lips shaped to the word.

There I go again. I will not. Dearest, I am sending you the money I spoke of, in this letter. Tomorrow I will send you a couple of Colettes rescued from the ruins of 5 Acacia Road. To-day I sent you another *Literary Supplement* & the *Daily News*. How long will you stay?

Jag.

	[Hôtel Beau Rivage,
	[Bandol]
Vendredi.	[17 December 1915]

My dear love,

I am afraid that the courier is past & my letters are drowned for it is as wild a day as ever I have seen – a sky like lead, a boiling sea, the coast hidden by thick mist, a loud noise of wind and such rain dashing on the windows. It is very cold, too, and (3.30) dark already. My maid however lit me a splendid fire this morning & after lunch when the room was warm I got up & am sitting by it now in the armchair. I don't feel *very grand* & though the fire isn't like that wretched affair at Cassis and burns merrily and warm, it seems to light the shadows & to prick an ear to the quiet. How quiet it is – except for the storm outside! Much quieter than Day's Bay!

No, the courier has just come & there *is* a letter after all with no address – 'Somewhere in Hampstead.' I am glad you have moved there if you are more comfortable, darling. I am sure you were wretched doing your own chores in the other place. And I do hope you will soon be able to get your studio and be free of your wretched worries in that respect. It always seems such a waste of time looking for a bed – especially for people like you and me who are so particular – I hope you have a big fire and a GOOD breakfast, darling Bogey and that you will now refresh yourself with one of your Turkish Bath Tickets – (which are in your 'gentleman's companion'.)

I am sorry I made you sad about that little villa. I heard of another last night from my Englishman – four rooms – good stoves – electric light, heating, a verandah, a garden all furnished, and so sheltered that you can dine out every day – 88 francs a month. The man who has just taken it says he buys fish at the market for practically nothing and rosebuds at 1d a dozen – so I should live off fish and rosebuds – But no, I'll not speak of these things – for it's useless & foolish – I'll remember that England & the Printing Press won the day & left me on the field – Don't think I don't understand – I do understand, absolutely, my love. Ah, Bogey, as I write to you my heart is full of love for you – and I long to press your head to my breast. Do not forget me – we have had the loveliest times together – you know. Shut your eyes and so many sweet things press on your eyelids –

> I am
> Tig.

> [Hôtel Beau Rivage,
> Bandol]
> [19 December 1915]
> Sunday before Xmas.

My dearest love,

I have just got the letter that you wrote me on Thursday night – with the money in it. Papers have come, too, which I have not opened yet and other letters are waiting – but I want to speak to you très sérieusement – Your letter made you 'real' to me in the deepest sense of the word, I believe, almost for the first time. You say just those things which I have felt. I am *of* you as you write just as you are *of* me.

Now I will say toujours because now at last I know you. We are in a world apart & we shall always be in a world apart – in our own Kingdom which *is* finer and rarer. Shut the gates of it for a minute – & let us stand there. Let us kiss each other, we three. Yes, Bogey, I shall love you *for always*.

> Tig.

Later. I've just read the *Times Lit Sup*, the *New Statesman*, the *Daily News*, a letter from Beatrice Campbell, Kay and Marie. For the papers many thanks darling; they were a great feast. The *New Statesman* is a dead horse – but still – horse it is & there you are – Beatrice (très entre nous) wrote me a nice letter. She's a queer mixture for she is really loving & affectionate & yet she is malicious. She was about you and Lawrence *re* me, you understand. How you were so happy on your own and a lot of rubbish & how Lawrence had spoken against me at Clive Bell's. It is unpleasant hearing, that kind of thing, and smells faintly of their drawing room which is a most distasteful memory to me. By the way, I wrote to Lawrence the other day – a wild kind of letter, if I think of it and not fair to 'us'. You understand? It was just after I had been in bed and without letters & I had a fit of positive despair when life seemed to me to be absolutely over – & I wrote rather in that strain. I only tell you because when I have read your despairing letters to your friends I have always felt that you betrayed us and our love a little and I feel if you should see mine (don't! for it's nothing & the mention is making it a mountain) you might feel a little the same. I am sorry I wrote it – To tell you the truth I am come to the conclusion that our happiness rests with us and with nobody else at all and that we ought to build for ourselves and by ourselves. We are very rich together for we are real true lovers – and we are young and born in each other. Therefore I think we ought to develop together – keep very close together (spiritually, mon chér!) and make ourselves, on our island, a palace and gardens and arbours and boats for you and flowery bushes for me – and we ought not to court other people at all yet awhile. Later it will be different. Do you know what I mean and do you agree with me? Writing to you I love you simply boundlessly. My love for you is always being new born; the heavenly dews descend upon it & I'll not believe it is the same flower as yesterday. You see – how I believe in you! I have a store of belief in you that couldn't be exhausted! How I admire you! How I love you – we are two little boys walking with our arms (which won't quite reach) round each other's shoulders & telling each other secrets & stopping to look at things. We must not fail our love.

At the end of your letter you ask me how long I am going to stay – I do not know at all, my precious. You'd better tell me what you think. Now I'll add a word tomorrow.

                                                    Lundi le matin.
A lovely 'gold dust' day – From early morning the fishermen have

been passing & little boats with red sails put out at dawn. I am dressed to go to the post with my 2 mandats –

When I woke this morning & opened the shutters & saw the dimpling sea I knew I was beginning to love this place – this South of France – Yesterday I went for a walk. The palm trees after the rain were magnificent – so firm and so green and standing up like stiff bouquets before the Lord. The shop people, too, are very kind. You are a regular customer – after a day or two – & my Englishman says they are very honest.

Last night in the salon I had a long talk with a woman who is here for her health. A woman about 50. She has been nursing since the beginning of the war somewhere near Arles. She is of the Midi and has a very pronounced accent – which is *extremely* fascinating – and she knows and adores 'mon pays' – She told me all about the coast, about all sorts of little places 'de toute beauté' – and as she talked I began to see this place – not romantically but truly. I like it and more than like it. This woman was reading the *Letters of Taine* ... She told me such good stories of the black soldiers – I must not forget them. I hope I shall speak a great deal with her because she is very good for my French too. She has a good vocabulary and a way of *spacing* her words giving them a very nice, just quantity. Oh, Bogey, it is the most heavenly day. Every little tree feels it and waves faintly from delight. The femme de chambre called to the gardener, just now as she beat the next door mattress out of the window – 'Fait bon?' & he said 'Ah, délicieux!' Which seemed to me very funny for a gardener, especially this little chap – Now I must button my boots with a tiger's tail and go out –
Goodbye dearest love

      Tig.

                     23 Worsley Road
                     Hampstead, N.W.
Monday evening 10 p.m.   [20 December 1915]

Wig – I know it's silly to sit down and write again to-day but what am I to do? I have had no answer to my wire. Perhaps you couldn't send one, as you wrote that you could not on Wednesday. But that is worst of all – that you should be so terribly ill. Oh, Wig, I pray that there will be some answer tomorrow morning. Perhaps this address had not reached you yet and you telegraphed to Kottilianski.

I could not just go out and eat and come straight back here. Je m'énerve, to-day when I am alone. I went to the Lawrences for an hour. They had got your letter to-day. They did not show it me. I didn't ask to see it; I couldn't look at what you wrote to anybody else – and perhaps you told them not to show it. But Lawrence went for me, about you, terribly. Had I been alive I should have been hurt; but I'm not alive to-day. I'm just numbed. He said that it was all my fault, that I was a coward, that I never offered you a new life, that I would not break with my past, that your illness was all due to your misery and that I had made you miserable, by always whining & never making a decision; that I should never have left you there. I do not know how much of it is true – perhaps all, perhaps nothing. I can't really think about it, tho' I try. To me we seemed to be so happy together, and that happiness made me feel happy even when we parted. It breathed out of your first letters.

Wig, do you just treat me as a child? Do you make your letters seem happy to deceive me? Do you just pretend to be happy in order to make me happy? And what has happened – is it that you were unhappy all the while & now do not care to conceal it any more?

Perhaps I am just blind. Lawrence says to me that your superficial happiness never deceived him. I don't know what to answer, except that he never knew you. Was all our secret life together just a game you played to amuse me as a child, so that I should not know how sad at heart you were?

Lawrence confuses me utterly now. Another day, I should not have cared, for I should have felt in my heart that you and I understood each other, and that we couldn't tell our secret to anybody. I should just have listened with a smile, with my love curled up warm in my heart so that I could touch it and feel safe, while he said monstrous things. But to-night I have lost my treasure. He says these things and I feel that perhaps some of them may be true. There is nothing curled round my heart to make me feel miles away from the world he talks about. He let drop by accident that you had written that 'there was nothing for you in life'. And now instead of my warm love, that creeps about me like a poison, and I feel that so soon as you have said that there is nothing for me. He says to me 'that unless I promise you happiness, I will lose you', and even though happiness for him means Florida, I feel that there was something in your letter made him say that.

Oh, darling, is there nothing left of that which was *ours*. I know that Chummie's death was terrible, and that the pain tugs at your heart for ever; but I trusted that even then we should be yet greater lovers than we were. And now I think that all that was just my own brutality – my insensibility.

[Hôtel Beau Rivage,
Bandol]
[22 December 1915]

Mercredi –

Bogey, my dearest love,

I wish you could see the winds playing on the dark blue sea today, and two big sailing vessels have come in & are rocking like our white boat rocked when you were here – The sea is what *I* call very high this morning and the clouds are like swans – It's a lovely morning; the air tastes like fruit. Yesterday I went for a long scrambling walk in the woods – on the other side of the railway. There are no roads there – just little tracks & old mule paths. Parts are quite wild and overgrown, then in all sorts of unexpected faery places you find a little clearing – the ground cultivated in tiny red terraces & sheltered by olive trees (full of tiny black fruit). There grow the jonquils, daffodils, new green peas and big abundant rose bushes – A tiny (this word is yours really: it's haunting me today –) villa is close by with a painted front and a well or a petite source at the bottom of the garden. They are dream places – Every now and then I would hear a rustle in the bushes and an old old woman her head tied up in a black kerchief would come creeping through the thick tangle with a bunch of that pink heath across her shoulders. 'B'jour ma petite dame' She would munch and nod – and with a skinny finger point me my way – Once I found myself right at the very top of a hill and below there lay an immense valley – surrounded by mountains – very high ones & it was so clear you could see every pointed pine, every little zig zag track – the black stems of the olives showing sooty and soft among the silvery green – One could see for miles and miles – There was, far in the distance a tiny town planted on a little knoll – just like a far away city in a Dürer etching – and now and again you would see two cypresses & then if you looked carefully you found a little house – for two cypresses planted side by side portent bonheur – On the other side of me there was the sea & Bandol & the next bay Sanary – Oh, Bogey, how I longed for my playfellow. Why weren't you with me – Why didn't you lean over the fence and ask the old old man what that plant was & hear him say it was the immortelle & it flowers for eight years and then dies and its yellow flowers come out in June – The sun went down as I found the Saint Cyr road back to Bandol. The people were coming home – & the children were running from school – As I came into Bandol I heard a loud chanting & down the Avenue des Palmiers there came four little boys in white carrying a cross & incense braziers – an old priest with white hair chanting – four men following each carrying a corner of a black & silver cloth – then a coffin carried on a table by six men & the whole village following – the last man of all being an old chap with a wooden leg – It was extremely fantastic and beautiful in the bright strange light. No post came yesterday. I expect it was delayed. I am longing for a letter today, my precious – Do you feel in this letter my love for you today – It is as warm as a bird's nest – Bogey – but don't mind when I say that in all these walks & in all my growing love for this country and people I cannot but wish infinitely that you were here to share it and complete my happiness –

My own – my darling love. Take me in your arms and kiss me – and I will kiss you too and hold you Bogey & tell you all I can't write. I am your woman

  Tig.

As I write a *third* ship is coming in & you are walking on the deck in your corduroy trousers & Spanish boots – an Awful Knife in your sash. Can you see me if I wave?

23 Worsley Road
Hampstead. N.W.

Wednesday. 7.30.   22 December, 1915.

Dear darling,

 I feel so miserable without you to-night. It has been round about me all day. Yet I was happy enough with your telegrams last night – a second one, all in French, came very late at night, quite unexpected – but it didn't last with me, somehow. I think that your illness and your awful loneliness has shaken me. I have lost the old confidence. I want terribly to be near you, to have the warm comfort of your actual presence. Without you, I am lost.

 And your letters – just one word or one sentence of them – stab me. When you wrote in your Friday–Saturday letter about the villa at 88 francs, when I read 'But no, I won't speak of these things – for it's useless and foolish – I'll remember that England and the Printing Press won the day and left me on the field' – oh, Wig, that has haunted me all day long. Why did I leave you? I keep on asking myself the question, and I find no answer. I can remember nothing of what urged me back. It must have been strong and overwhelming – but it is all gone. There is no printing press – that vanished like smoke. There is no England. There is only you, whom I left. Why, how, did it seem all so simple & natural then, and now it's like a nightmare that never ends?

Wig, is it all too late. Could you not even now get a villa? and I could come. I should not go away again. England is simply a foolish word without you. You are everything – everything. Will you not get a villa – surely you could find one; I could find the money to come, and even if I could earn nothing, I might live on only a tiny bit of your money. Surely it isn't too late. Or [do] you mistrust me now, for a coward? Darling, for an hour I've stopped, just thinking – shall I borrow the money and come to you now? Shall I wait in the hope that you will come back? Shall I wait a little while until you have found a villa and then come? – for I should have nothing at all & could not afford to stop in the hôtel.

These three chase one another through my brain incessantly till I am dizzy with them. I don't exist any longer – but I am only a torment of longing to be with you. And then, if I come – I am terrified that I should be a burden.

Your Sunday letter has just come, while I was writing. Another stab. 'I have a présentiment that I shall never see Albion's shores again.' Oh, Tig, if it's only a jest, it nearly tears my heart out.

Darling, will you promise me this – that you will try to get a tiny villa for us both immediately – that if you can you will telegraph to me 'Come immediately. Ill.' (Then they will visa my passport immediately. I have arranged with the nice man who took me last time) I will borrow £10 – Lorenzo has £100 – and come, just as I am. I will be there within 3 days of when you wire. I can't live away from you. I don't desire even to be alive. It is one incessant hunger. Oh, my Tig, *I implore you to do this* if you can. We could live in a villa for £3 a week, easy, couldn't we darling?

Wig, I want to sit by you, to hold your hand, to talk all my heart to you. I have only just learnt – oh Tig, the things I have to tell you or my heart will burst. And don't think I will fail again – never, never. We will live like little goblins in our nest and go hand in hand for ever. I have lost the world in finding you. I have not cared to do anything since I left you. Journalism is past. I am only a lover after all. Tig, Tig, do this for me. Even though you have found me wanting, give me this one chance more. We will go from sunshine to sunshine.

If you cannot do this, then come back to me. I will make a nest – where we can talk. It's to talk to you, to hear your voice, to pour out all the things that have been crushed to death in my heart – all the things that I was too hard to give.

I must, must be with you   Jag.

[Bandol]
[27 December 1915]

ILL COME IMMEDIATELY URGENT WIRE ARRIVAL

          KATHERINE

                              [Hôtel Beau Rivage,
                              Bandol]
Monday morning.   [27 December 1915]

Even if you never came I cannot but love you more for the evening and the night and the early morning I have spent thinking that you *are* coming. It was Sunday so I could not send you a telegram until today. I somehow – Oh, how did I? got through last evening but sitting in the salon among unreal fantastic people & sewing and talking. For I knew I would not sleep. What drowsy bliss slept in my breast. Oh Jack, I hardly dared to breathe. A woman here told me how to buy our stores & what to pay & how to make soup with 2 sous worth of bones – and what day the woman with the good apples was at the market and how to manage une femme de ménage. I heard – I dared not look at her – I felt my smiles chasing in my eyes – I saw the villa, perhaps a cactus near the gate, you writing at a little table, me arranging some flowers & then sitting down to write, too. Both of us gathering pine cones and drift wood and bruyère for our fire – I thought of what I would have ready for you, soup & perhaps fish, coffee, toast because charbon de bois which is *much cheaper* than coal makes lovely toast, I hear, a pot of confitures, a vase of roses. And then I thought de notre bon lit et de nous deux tout seule, seule cachée dans la nuit – the fire perhaps just tinkling – the sea sounding outside et vous et moi, mon chéri ... with happiness fast asleep on the roof with its head under its wing, like a dove. And then I saw us waking in the morning & putting on the big kettle & letting in the femme de ménage. She hangs her shawl behind the kitchen door. 'Vous savez il fait beau –'

Finally I could bear it no longer. I came up to my room & took a hot bath & then curled up in bed & smoked & tried to read a new Dickens. No use. The sea was very loud. I looked at the watch and saw it said 25 to 12 & then I went to sleep. When I looked again it was nearly four. So I turned on the light & read & waited waited for day. How the light changed I never shall forget. I put on my big purple hat & opened the shutters & sat on the window sill. It was all primrosey with black mountains – A sailing ship put out to sea. I saw all the little men on board – and how the sail was put up & how when it caught the breath of wind the ship went fast. Two more of our big ships, with a rattle of chains, hoisted anchor & put out to sea. I saw the bending straining bodies of the men. And then came the fishers bringing in their pots. Then the first bird – At seven I heard my little maid lighting the stove so I ran out and asked for my déjeuner, washed in cold water, kissed my roses – put on my goblin hat and flew into the garden. The market was there – with 2 funny Spaniards beating drums. Such flowers! Such violets! But I kept my pennies for you & me. I thought I should have to have a small fête so when I went to the post office I put *new relief nibs* in all the awful old crusty pens – The sea, and sky this morning are LITERALLY a DARK NAVY (See Aunt Li). I sent your telegrams ran home to find the maid beating the carpets and the white dog overslept & pretending he had been awake for hours on the terrace. Now I am going with a gent in corduroys to look at a furnished villa of his.

This letter may never reach you for I shall not send it until your answer comes. Oh, my love, I cannot walk fast enough. My heart is eaten by love like the Spartan boy's inside. Love eats & eats at my heart and I feel everybody must know. I keep thinking 'we shall go to Sanary – to that little village in the mountains – I will show him all the walks', and then I think and think of the long journey & perhaps you will not come – If you do then it is the miracle.

There are faeries, faeries everywhere. I would not be surprised if I were to find them putting fir boughs in the hall, and wreaths upon the door handles and swags and garlands over the windows.

Love presses on my forehead like a crown – my head is heavy – heavy – I must not think of you ... But I keep talking to myself in my Tig voice as though you could hear ... The other coming to France I can hardly remember. It was all so curious, so uncertain, and so joyless. Was it? Or is it my fancy – I feel we are coming together for the first time. In your letter you say 'we shall go from sunshine to sunshine.' Yes, that is just what I feel. Today too, my brother smiles. Two more ships have put out to sea. One had 11 sails and one had 12 twelve. And now a little destroyer has come rushing in. My only thought is – are you on the destroyer? A little low gray boat snipping through the water like a pair of scissors.

	23 Worsley Road
	Hampstead, N.W.
Tuesday night 10.45	28 December, 1915

Wig, my darling love.

I am full of hope that I shall be with you before this letter and that we shall read it together and laugh tears. Therefore it must be short. A long letter would make me feel that we should be kept from each other.

I came back from Garsington to-day. There this morning I had both your telegrams saying that I should come. When I arrived here another came – imploring me not to. That one finished me. It seemed suddenly so childish – not childish, but criminal – to stay away from you a day longer. Whatever happens I must be with you: we will live together in our villa, until the summer comes. Oh, how we'll be happy & careless.

I have to go to the Consulate tomorrow morning (Wednesday) – I shall start on Thursday. I have just a tremor of terror that they may make difficulties – they have passed so many new laws in the last few days. I hope & pray they won't & with your telegram I think I can persuade them. Oh my darling – may it all come true & on Saturday – I shall be holding your darling face in my hands   Jag.

	[Hôtel Beau Rivage,
	Bandol]
Wednesday night.	[29 December 1915]

I am like that disciple who said: 'Lord I believe. Help thou my unbelief.' As I was dressing & your letter was already sealed the heavy steps really came along the corridor – the knock at the door –

the old man with the blue folded paper that I scarcely dared to take and having taken – could not open – Oh, I sat by the side of my bed – & opened it, little by little. I read all those directions for the sending of urgent telegrams & telegrams in the night – At last I said: He is not coming & opened it and read your message. Since then I have never ceased for one moment to tremble – I shall never never be calm until I am on your heart. I felt 'now he is coming that villa is taken' and I ran, ran along the quai. One day I shall tell you all this at length, but it was not taken until I saw the woman & took it. I went through it again. It is quite perfect in its way – It is always what I felt there was somewhere in the world for us – in Spain or Italy – And the people to whom it belongs who live next door are such good decent, honest people, eager to have us, eager to make us comfortable & happy. 'Je suis toujours là. Vous avez seulement de frapper si vous aurez besoin de quelque chose.' The sun shone in every room & on the little stone verandah danced the shadow of a tree. Is this true? Is it coming true?

I have to sign the agreement & pay a month in advance tomorrow. Then to order the coal & wood & see my femme de ménage who has already been found 'pour 3 heures le matin et pour faire mes petites courses, n'est ce pas?'

All the rest of the day I do not know how I have spent it. Such a lovely wild day brimming over with colour & light. I have found the shortest way to our home by a road you do not know, through fields of jonquils & past the olive trees that blow so silver & black today. There are high walls on the road & nobody goes – I thought – we shall stand here & kiss each other. Then I thought, but if we do I think I shall faint for joy – Yes, I have found a lovely way – And I have made out a list of our modest provisions – that I shall buy on Friday. In fact I have made out more than one list – For I can't even write nor read. This evening in the salon someone said that already there was conscription in England – Oh, God is it too late – Are you coming?

I have loved you before for 3 years with my heart and my mind but it seems to me that I have never loved you *avec mon âme* as I do now. I love you with all our future life – our life together which seems only now to have taken root and to be alive and growing up in the sun – *I* do not love you – but Love possesses me utterly love for you and for our life and for all our richness and joy. I have never felt anything like it before. In fact I did not comprehend the possibility of such a thing. I seem to have only played on the fringe of love and lived a kind of reflected life that was not really my own but that came from my past – Now all that is cast away – Oh, my soul – if you come now we shall realise something that it seems to me never has been – such warmth and such richness and such virtue there is in you and in me – Is it too late? You are *really* coming?

This morning I went to the little church and prayed. It is very nice there – I prayed for us three – for you and me and Chummie. It was so gay and yet solemn there –

Bogey, come quickly quickly. My heart will break.

July 1916–December 1917

Katherine and Murry enjoyed three happy and productive months together at the Villa Pauline in Bandol. Then, with some misgivings, they allowed themselves to be persuaded by D.H. Lawrence to take a cottage near him and Frieda in Cornwall. Lawrence, already embittered by the war, and quarrelsome, proved a difficult friend. In June, Katherine and Murry moved away from him to Sunnyside Cottage in Mylor, another part of Cornwall. Alleviating Katherine's dissatisfactions with life that summer was her friendship with Lady Ottoline, whom she visited at Garsington Manor. By September Katherine and Murry had moved back to London, where he had obtained employment as a translator with Military Intelligence.

In February 1917, after living together for a time in Bloomsbury, Katherine and Murry took separate rooms: she at 141A Church Street, Chelsea, and he at 47 Redcliffe Road, Fulham. While Murry was preoccupied with his demanding work at the War Office, Katherine was reworking *The Aloe* as the long short story 'Prelude'.

<table>
<tr><td></td><td>[24 Norfolk Road,
St John's Wood]</td></tr>
<tr><td>Wednesday –</td><td>[12 July 1916]</td></tr>
</table>

My dear Bogey –

This morning I received a book and a note & a shilling on page 50. But the letter to which you refer has never come. Perhaps it is just delayed, but I don't see why – So your note was a little difficult to understand. I suppose the letter explained the book. I'll read it (the book) on my journey to Garsington.

You could not have given me much less news of you – Not a personal word – nor half a phrase –

So I suppose you don't want any from me & I'll not give it –
You are a funny boy – and you *do* rather offend me –

Tig –

Ever so many thanks for the 1/-. You should not have sent it –

[Sunnyside Cottage,
Mylor, Cornwall]
Thursday Morning   [13 July 1916]

Wig darling,
I've just got the note you wrote on Wednesday. It is too awful. I
posted the book on Tuesday, *after* I posted you a long letter
explaining everything about the boat. I cannot understand why you
didn't have it on Wednesday morning.
We seem to be fated to suffer because of letters when we are
away from each other. Now I don't even know whether the letter I
sent on Wednesday has reached you. If the other didn't why should
this. Anyhow I'm going out to send you a telegram.
It is too awful. Only last night when I was sitting in your room, I
was so happy about us. It suddenly came over me that the war must
end, and that we were really free. We could always spend half the
year in France, in every kind of out of the way place. We have really
achieved what we used to dream of as an ideal. But now the fact of
my letter having gone astray seems to have upset it all.
It hasn't really, I suppose, but I feel so miserable & depressed –
particularly because you wouldn't send me a word about yourself,
on purpose. I know it must have hurt you not to get a letter. 'Really
you *do* rather offend me'. But why wouldn't you give me credit for
having written & posted it? Did you really think I would *pretend* to
have done so? That worries me.
However, in spite of myself, I'm hoping that everything is alright
and that the letter really did arrive at last. I can't believe it was lost.
These things don't happen. I shall simply go on as though it had
turned up.
I did my *Times* article yesterday. In the afternoon I went out in
the boat. I'm rather chary of venturing too far into the open,
knowing what it costs to get back. It was just as well, for yesterday
when I had sailed as far as Restronguet creek, that is the next one to
ours going towards Truro, I suddenly discovered that I had left the
rowlocks behind. Luckily I wasn't more than a half mile from the

shore. So I stood up in the boat, just like a shipwrecked mariner and paddled with an oar first one side & then the other until I got to land, then, feeling very much like Robinson Crusoe, I hunted about for some pieces of stick & made myself rowlocks – and so home. At all events I learn. I shall never forget rowlocks again.

The syringa is wonderfully out. I smell it religiously every evening – yesterday it was faint & lemony; faint I think because we have had too much rain. But it reminds me of our magnolia at Runcton, and for some reason I always feel sad when I think of Runcton. To get over that I went to the back, to the bed that I was digging before you went away, and began to plant late cabbages. I don't believe that any self-respecting late cabbage ever comes up if planted in July, but I had to plant something. I feel miserable, besides, if I have a bed with nothing in it. Then I tied up all the beans to their sticks: some of them are terribly lazy at climbing. I look hard at them every morning & sometimes they don't seem to move at all: perhaps they were longing to be tied up.

I bought 3 flower pots yesterday to put my dahlia seedlings in – and I think I shall get some more & put the stocks in. Then they'll grow quickly and we shall be able to plant them out in the garden.

I come down from your room into the kitchen every night at about half past ten. Last night my milk boiled over while I was reading and of course the primus flared up & smoked. To clear out the room I opened the door. In about ten minutes in came a big thing between a great moth & a dragon fly, and began to buzzzz about the room. I didn't like it at all & tried to kill it, with your felt hat. The more I swiped at it the more it buzzed at me, until suddenly I made a great hit at it and the wind I made put the lamp out. I was frightened – it was pitch dark & buzzzz – all the while. I knew if I lit a match the thing would come straight for the light, and I nearly dropped the lampglass. However I got it alight, and made another great swipe at the thing. I don't think I killed it, but it didn't buzz any more – so I didn't mind. But I felt rather like Pyotr Stepanovich & Kirillov.

I am working as hard as I can at these translations, so that we can have a really free time when you come back. You say I didn't write a personal word. What can I write? That I love and adore you – but darling, you know it. You are the only soul in the world: without you I am quite alone. That I miss you terribly. I don't want to say that. For though I do miss you awfully, I should be quite happy, really quite happy, if I knew that the change was doing you good. But I don't see how it will, if you have to worry so much. Oh, curse the post. When I think of that letter I am mad with rage & despair.

Good-bye, my darling – but please believe that though I may be a funny boy, every morning I write you a long letter: and do you write me one in return.

Jag.

<table>
<tr><td></td><td>[Sunnyside Cottage,
Mylor, Cornwall]</td></tr>
<tr><td>Very late Friday night.</td><td>[18 August 1916]</td></tr>
</table>

My own,
    I shall not be able to post this letter until I have heard from you where you are going to sleep after tonight. Never-the-less I must write and tell you ...
    That it only dawned upon me this evening that perhaps you will not be here again for a long time. That you won't see these dahlias of this year again reflected in your mirror & and that the lemon verbena in a jar on my table will be all withered and dry.
    As I thought that, sitting, smoking in the dusky room Peter Wilkins came in with a fallen-all-too-fallen leaf in his mouth, and I remembered that the michaelmas daisies were out and lo! it was autumn.
    Is it just my fancy – the beauty of this house tonight? This round lamp on the round table, the rich flowers, the tick of the clock dropping into the quiet – and the dark outside and the apples swelling and a swimming sense of deep water. May brought me this evening some of this year's apples. 'Good to eat'. They are small & coloured like pale strawberries. I wish that you were with me, my love. It is not because you are absent that I feel so free of distraction, so poised and so still – I feel that I am 'free' even of sun and wind – like a tree whose every leaf has 'turned'.
    I love you tonight beyond measure. Have I ever told you how I love your shoulders? When I hold you by your shoulders – put my arm round you & feel your fine delicious skin – warm & yet cool, like milk – and your slender bones – the bones of your shoulders ...
Goodnight, my heart.
I am your own girl.

[Sunnyside Cottage,
Mylor, Cornwall]

Sunday Night.   [20 August 1916]

Dearest,

This evening I watered the flowers & went into the orchard and
into that 'walled garden' where you cut down the nettles – on your
birthday – wasn't it? I am simply prostrate with misery; I can do
nothing – Are we *never* to be happy – never never? We haven't had
any 'life' together at all yet – in fact it's only on the rarest occasion
that we have any confidential intercourse –

The day is dying – very grandly – I can hear the water lapping &
I can hear some sheep on the hill. It's ages since I really talked to
you – for when Goodyear was here – no – you *wouldn't* respond.
But it's all of little account. What misery I have known! If it goes on
like this I'll make an end to it in October – I can bear no more.

Tig.

[Sunnyside Cottage,
Mylor, Cornwall]

Tuesday.   [22 August 1916]

Dearest Jack

I am going up to Mylor to post this; I'll send you a wire from
there too – to cancel if I can, my horrid letter of yesterday – But I
could not help it. Now I shall write fully in answer to yours of this
morning. If they do accept you provisionally, would that be sure
enough for you to decide finally to leave Cornwall for the present?
If they don't accept you are you coming back here? Heavens! I am
really very much in the dark! And won't you have to find some
place to live in in London as soon as possible? The whole affair
seems to me so dreadfully in the vague.

But I'll get down to earth. If they accept you provisionally I shall
wind up here – pack your clothes & my clothes – & travel up to
London on Friday morning. As to what books and papers you want
– as you have said nothing – you must leave it to me – I'll do my
best – I shall stay the night in London and come down to
Garsington by a train which (I think) leaves Paddington at 2.30. If
this is all O.K. wire me to Charing X where I'll go for a telegram *or*
letter post restante – in the name of Bowden – in case I have to

produce my identification disc. I'll call for letter or wire on Friday evening and Saturday not later than twelve o'clock – Then *if* all this happens we may have a moment to talk things out & arrange our plans. I can't stay much after Monday at Garsington. Salute Lady Ottoline for me –

> Always, dearest –
> Tig.

Cheque for £1.15. enclosed.

[47 Redcliffe Road,
Fulham]

Saturday Night   May 18th 1917

My darling
　Do not imagine, because you find these lines in your private book that I have been trespassing. You know I have not – and where else shall I leave a love letter? For I long to write you a love letter tonight. You are all about me – I seem to breathe you – hear you – feel you in me and of me – What am I doing here? You are away – I have seen you in the train, at the station, driving up, sitting in the lamplight, talking, greeting people – washing your hands – – And I am here – in your tent – sitting at your table – There are some wallflower petals on the table & a dead match, a blue pencil and a Magdeburgische Zeitung. I am just as much at home as they.
　When dusk came – flowing up the silent garden – lapping against the blind windows – my first & last terror started up – I was making some coffee in the kitchen. It was so violent so dreadful I put down the coffee-pot – and simply ran away – *ran ran* out of the studio and up the street with my bag under one arm and a block of writing paper and a pen under the other. I felt that if I could get here & find the Fraulein I should be 'safe' – I found her and I lighted your gas, wound up your clock – drew your curtains – & embraced your black overcoat before I sat down – frightened no longer. Do not be angry with me, Bogey – ça a été plus fort que moi … That is why I am here.
　When you came to tea this afternoon you took a brioche broke it in half & padded the inside doughy bit with two fingers. You always do that with a bun or a roll or a piece of bread – It is your way – your head a little on one side the while …
　– When you opened your suitcase I saw your old feltie & a

French book and a comb all higgledy piggledy – 'Tig. I've only got 3 handkerchiefs' – Why should that memory be so sweet to me? ...

Last night, there was a moment before you got into bed. You stood, quite naked, bending forward a little – talking. It was only for an instant. I saw you – I loved you so – loved your body with such tenderness – Ah my dear – And I am not thinking now of 'passion'. No, of that other thing that makes me feel that every inch of you is so precious to me. Your soft shoulders – your creamy warm skin, your ears, cold like shells are cold – your long legs & your feet that I love to clasp with my feet – the feeling of your belly – & your thin young back – Just below that bone that sticks out at the back of your neck you have a little mole. It is partly because we are young that I feel this tenderness – I love your youth – I could not bear that it should be touched even by a cold wind if I were the Lord.

We two, you know have everything before us, and we shall do very great things – I have perfect faith in us – and so perfect is my love for you that I am, as it were, still, silent to my very soul. I want nobody but you for my lover and my friend and to nobody but you shall I be *faithful*.

> I am yours for ever
> Tig.

> [141A Church Street,
> Chelsea]
> [late July 1917]

My dear Jack,

I got up at that moment to re-read your article on Leon Bloy. The memory of it suddenly *rose* in my mind, like a scent. I don't like it. I don't see its use at all, even artistically. It's a 'Signature' style of writing and its *appeal* is in some obscure way – to me – mind me – I suppose only to me – indecent. I feel that you are going to uncover yourself and quiver. Sometimes when you write you seem to abase yourself like Dostoievsky did. It's *perfectly* natural to you I know, but oh my God, don't do it. It's just the same when you say – talking to Fergusson and me – if I am not killed – if *they don't kill* me. I always laugh at you then because I am ashamed that you should speak so.

What is it? Is it your desire to torture yourself or to pity yourself or something far subtler? I only know that it's tremendously important because it's your way of damnation.

I feel (forgive fanciful me) that when certain winds blow across your soul they bring the smell from that dark pit & the uneasy sound from those hollow caverns – & you long to lean over the dark driving danger & just not fall in – But letting us all see meanwhile how low you lean –

Even your style of writing changes then – little short sentences – a hand lifted above the waves – the toss of a curly head above the swirling tumble – It's a terrible thing to be alone – yes it is – it is – but don't lower your mask until you have another mask prepared beneath – As terrible as you like – but a *mask*.

K.M.

Forgive me for not telling you frankly when you read it to me – what I felt. I was wrong.

[141A Church Street,
Chelsea]
10.VIII. [1917]

My dear Jack
 I am re-reading your poems & taking a note or two. Here they are:
 Torment is damned good. Better than I'd even thought. The way the passionate pace of it quickens in verses 4 5 and 6 is amazing & then the way it 'ebbs' into quiet. Musically speaking it's a little meisterwerk. Anyway it's real love poetry and an achievement.
 The effect of *The Tryst* is alright. The clichés are there once or twice but they are *fresh* rather than *current* (I mean rare by that).
 The Quest comes off. It's what you might call legitimately romantic. And it's got a kind of dark boyish plume in its hat that's very captivating. I like it immensely.
 I *cannot* see anything in *Backward*. I've read it as fairly as I can. It's simply streaky with not even the best streaky Masefield, and so I tells you. Think well before you publish this. I'll blush for you if you do. Dear Jack, you may have a red carpet hassock with yellow flowers on it which makes you weep for tender remembrance but you won't put it in your lovely room. It *isn't* you. Enough! It's an awful thought [that] 'the coming man' may open your book at this!
 The Critic in Judgment is so good even as it stands that it's hard

to keep one's head about it. It's like a lifting of the mist, a glimpse of the Blue Mountains and you – blast you – a young poet walking airy in their bright shadow.

The *Tig* poem will blow away if I lay even a feather on it. The last line is too easy.

You are 'in your stride' in *The Return*. There's a kind of dark mysterious sobbing in your love poetry – which shakes the heart. I feel that your lady, leaning from her tower, her hair all blowing out – says 'is that he – or a dark shadow – or a young tree bending in the night wind'. And really you are all these things.

To Jules Laforgue is frightfully good & brilliantly clear. Bitterness, fatigue, and a queer ageless quality – and all controlled. It's your control of that poem – the shaft of light you bring to bear upon Laforgue is so good. You might be the wan moon at the window of the morgue where he lies.

Villa Pauline is charming but the last line is flat.

So is the last line of *I Know The Sea* – and the sentiment of the second half is fatigué.

Sanary is delightful.

The City of the Hills. Here you are again, singing your own song. It's a very lovely little poem – very 'rich' somehow in weight like dark grapes are rich in weight ... if you know what I mean.

Nunc Dimittis for some reason which I can't quite explain leaves me cold.

Now, my dear friend for your poems of Remembrance. I'll not take them separately. To say that they are the only poems that have come out of this war isn't enough. They are *wonderful – wonderful – wonderful.* There they are – 'you've done it' as we say. If you knew how strangely each dead boy lies – lies in your poems as in a very perfect tomb – And at last, when they are all buried and hidden, you pause a little, and pluck a few forlorn notes and suddenly break into your song

'O unreturning travellers, O friends ...' as the night falls.

Well, you see. I'm quite overcome and weeping as I write. Je t'embrasse, mon ami

K.M.

December 1917–April 1918

In November 1917 Murry became ill with overwork and was threatened with tuberculosis. Katherine arranged for him to spend two months' sick-leave at Garsington. Ironically, it was she who, visiting him there, caught a bad chill, which in December was diagnosed as a spot on her lung. Not believing that she was seriously ill, she accepted medical advice to escape from the rest of the English winter to the South of France. On 7 January 1918 she set out for Bandol, where she and Murry had previously been so happy. But the conditions of life there had changed terribly. Her letters to Murry between January and April 1918 document the protracted nightmare that followed as her health deteriorated and she found herself helplessly trapped in war-torn France.

[141A Church Street,
Chelsea]
Friday.   [14 December 1917]

My darling Boy,
 My temper is serene again. I am so sorry that I let fly yesterday but it did and *does* seem to me a bit steep de la parte de Miss Wright – I have a lot of 'things' to say ... Miss Palmer came here last evening. I have taken that flat for a year for 11/- a week. She is having it colour washed cleaned swept, painted where necessary. Not badsome ... She was very nice and decent. Je suis très contente. I don't know just when I shall move my bits of things for I want to have the floors & curtings done & the kitchen dresser painted etc before I do. However, it is amicably arranged. I like the place. I feel so free there. I have *adored* this cubby hole & that is a fact. I'm not unfaithful to it even now but it's plain to see that it is over.
 About the South of France,– please don't mention it, Betsy. I just *couldn't*. I am really not in the least seriously ill. It would be a pure joke to pretend that I was, and I am a little lion as you know most times. The South of France must joliment attendre. But this is exceedingly important. Don't you DARE come back here until you have to. You'd undo all the good you've done, and worry me to

death. I should have to spend all my time collecting food for the Xmas season & so on – and where you are all is so simple. Oh, my love, PLEASE BE REASONABLE FOR JUST THIS ONE XMAS. Praps I'll come down *or* I shall stay here but the idea that you should post up simply horrifies me. I implore you, most seriously to be wise about this. When I think of your coal, housekeeper during the holidays, shops shut, etc. etc. I feel quite hysterical. I should be tortured. I, of course, here have got coal. L.M. & Chaddie & Belle have stuffed this place with food for me. I eat like a warrior, and drink pints of milk a day. But if I have to feel that you are neglecting yourself in your rooms I shan't bite another crust and I'll throw the milk down the drain, my temper will be vile. Bogey stop torturing me *at once*, or I'll tell.

I feel much better today except for this worrying idea. In fact I feel, simply dandy. I ate nearly ½ lb. steak last night & I've got 9 newlaid eggs, 1 lb butter, dates, filletted haddock, cream – etc etc in the larder. I shall be as fat as butter and as brown as a Maori if only you will behave. But of course you will – darling.

$$X \quad X \quad X \quad X$$
$$X \quad X \quad X \quad X$$

I have an idea that your hair will never grow until you take it to New Zealand – Then it will sprout up and wave in the breeze like a little fern tree – all one lovely crinkle. I feel that if Mother were only to pat it with her tiny white hands and frown at it there would be no holding it. I hope that is true.

What a nice letter from Milne. He is a rare nice boy. He must come and make a long stay with us when Sullivan is there too. There is something *shy* and *loving* in this letter which endears him to me – and he is 'serious' – Thank you for letting me see it. I send you a kind of cabbage from Anne [Drey] – bless her – 'Pantalons solides' might be the title of all her pictures.

I did not do any work yesterday – That was another reason why I felt jumpy. But today I am going it & shall have to make an effort to be nice to Brettushka. H[er] L[adyship] hasn't been here again. I wonder what has happened to her? She seems to have quite disappeared – It's a nice day here. Very quiet – and warm. Even the milkman crying milk sounds to me like a bird trying its note – a funny sort of big bird you know – a bird penguinian.

The clock ticks on tip toe and the yellow curtains wave gently – I love such a day – It is such a rest – not having been outside for these days. I love to be out of the streets and buses – out of the nudging crowds – Oh, I must work. The very shadows are my friends. Don't forget to weigh yourself again when the week is up – & if you are not heavier you must melt a horseshoe in your next glass of milk so as not to disappoint me. Dearest of all. I am

> Your loving, cautious playfellow
> Wig.

[141A Church Street,
Chelsea]

Sunday   [23 December 1917]

My dearest –
Here is the certificate which the doctor has just given me. Is it alright? He says that left lung of mine that had the *loud deafening* creak in it is 'no end better' but there is a SPOT in my right lung which 'confirms him in his opinion that it is absolutely imperative that I go out of this country & Keep out of it all through the future winters'. It is evidement rather a bad 'un of its kind – at any rate it would become so if I did not fly. About Oxfordshire. He says it is far wiser that I stay here until I am well enough to travel & don't attempt the country; that was even when I explained about the hot pipes and glasses of hot milk on trays. The programme seems to be (if I don't want to do this mysterious crocking up) to sit tight, pack and make for the sun. See? What do you think? Although I am still snapping up fishes like a sea lion, steaks like a land lion, milk like a snake (or is that only a 'tale'?) and eggs honey, creamb, butter and nourishing trimmings galore, they seem to go to a sort of Dead Letter Office. However he has given me a tonic today which will put that right. Of course I feel now that I've only to get into the sun and I'll simply burst into leaf and flower again. It is this old place that does it to me and I keep sweeping out *our* house with a branch of acacia tree, picking a rose to tuck into my bodice and then hurrying off just in time to catch the train which tumbles you, my treasure, in my arms. And I keep going into that room and putting my arm round you and saying: 'Look there's that diamond of light in the shutter' –
I know quite well, I appreciate absolutely that you must be faithful to England. Hell it would be to know you were away & felt its call, but all the same you will have to have two homes & we shall have to have all our babies in pairs, so that we possess a complete 'set' in either place.

Je t'aime! Je t'aime!!

This man is coming again on Thursday to unstrap me and overhaul me. In the meantime I think that the passport affair should be got under way & the Hotel Beau Rivage written to – to make sure – don't you? I thought – tell them Madame will be there for 2 months at least so she will require une belle chambre avec vue sur la mer & beaucoup de soleil – & to reply ˙immediately. You, who write so much better than I had better send that letter & don't forget your *name problem*. But don't mention LUNGS or they will take fright. You know the French. They'd imagine I had come there to gallop away.

Should I forward you my old passport. Tell me. I shall send *this* and if you need it *that* registré of course. I was so glad of your wire this morning; it put a flower on my Sunday.

These my present letters are really such *self engrossed dull* matron affairs that I groan to think about them after they are gone. But you see I feel that life has changed so and it has all happened so quickly – all my plans are altered – my future is touched by this, all *our* future rather. It's like suddenly mounting a very fresh, very unfamiliar horse – a *queer queer* feeling.

As to 'working' I can't just now. However I have heaps to read and to think over against the time when I shall get down to it again – What is so difficult to realise is that this has happened to *me* and not to *you*. That seems just nonsense. And oh dear, what a serious talk I shall have to have with you before I do go, about taking care of *yourself*. It's almost funny in a way – isn't it? One thing – which must be your idée mère – is don't you worry about me. Keep happy! We can afford to be happier than anybody – you and I. And just think how I shall write. I wish we could have been married before I go – but it don't really signify. (*Burn my letters*) You are so grown into my heart that we are like the two wings of one bird.

Goodbye for now, my own. Have you weighed yourself again? I am sorry to plague you but you know how one feels. And don't dare not to tell the ABSOLUTE TRUTH. I am ever your own

Wig.

P.S. If the certificate is not right I think you had better write to Ainger direct. Tell me if you do. I notice for one thing he has left the date out. Ribni says 'Happy Xmas' & he's going to take off his kimono & hang up one of the sleeves tomorrow. And he says we've got two oranges & 2 tangerines & nuts and flowers in this place – see? *And* you are not to forget him or he may creep into your pocket next time you're here & give you an awful fright. *And* 'tell that Old Mousey that I like him.'

Monday.

Dearest
    This letter could not be registered yesterday so I am adding a word. Also, as you see I am sending you the passport. I do hope all this will not take too long. As I am going I have a great longing to be ready – and I feel today absolutely strong enough to travel – The spiritual fact qu'on voyage vers le soleil is such a staff!
    Sullivan came last night. He was particularly nice. And he told me a story about you which is so *frightfully good*. Do you know it – Allen's remark about you? I'll not repeat it in case you do.

Paris
[9 January 1918]
5.30 P.M.
Wednesday.

My precious darling.
    I shall not be able to write you a 'proper' letter until I arrive in Bandol. It is so difficult to get calm and I have spent an immense day rushing after my luggage and to Cooks (who wouldn't 'arrange' my affairs for me) and to the P.L.M. However it is all done now and I am in a café near the station, with my grand malle registrée, my little uns at le consigne, writing to you before I go to Duval where we went to get some dinner before the train goes.
    Everything on the whole has gone wonderfully. It's not a nice journey now a days & it was immensely complicated this time by the blizzards. We left South Hampton at about 9 o'clock & did not arrive at Havre until after 10 next morning. We anchored for hours outside Havre in a snow storm & lay tossing & pitching & rolling – – You won't believe me when I say that I enjoyed it. I did. For one

thing I had a splendid supper when I got on board – a *whack* of cold lean beef & pigheels, bread, butter ad lib, tea, and plenty of good bread – Then I took a nip of brandy & went right to bed – in a little cabin – very clean and warm – with an excellent stewardess in attendance. The upper berth was a general's widow (more of her later) except for her imitation of a cat with a fish bone in its throat I was divinely comfortable & slept & woke slept & woke but did not move until we reached Havre. Then I tumbled up on deck to find everything white with snow – I shall tell you nothing in detail now for I mean to write it all. It was too wonderful to miss. We had to spend the day in Havre so I took a bedroom at a hotel had breakfast & washed & went to sleep, until late lunch. The food in France is simply wonderful. *Bread* that makes one hungry to look at, butter, sugar, meat, 7 kinds of cheese for lunch & 7 hors d'oeuvres. Then we started for Paris at 5 to arrive at 9.20. The carriage was packed, *un*heated with a broken window & the snow drifting in. This was very vile. But a red cross old party took me in charge & rubbed me and cossetted me & finally made me eat a dinner which cost 6 francs but saved me as we did not arrive until 2 A.M. Then a plunge into the pitch dark and snow as all the entrances to the Terminus were shut except the one in the street. God! how thankful I was that I had reserved a room. Crowds were turned away, but I staggered up a palatial staircase, through ballrooms, reception rooms, *hollows* glittering with chandeliers to a yellow & blue brocade bedroom which seemed to be worth £50 to me. I slept like a top and got up early and (L'Heure! Liberté! *La* Presse!) saw about all my affairs. It is snowing hard. The streets are all ice and water – and so slippery qu'on marche comme un poulet malade. All the same I am unreasonably deeply happy. I thought I would be disenchanted with France this time, but for the first time I seem to recognise my love for it and to understand *why*. It is because, whatever happens, I never feel *indifferent*. I feel that indifference is really foreign to my nature and that to live in a state of it is to live in the only Hell I really appreciate. There is too, dispassionately speaking, a wonderful spirit here – so much humour, life, gaiety, sorrow, one cannot see it all & not think with amazement of the strange cement like state of England. Yes, they do feel the war, but with a difference.

But this, too, I must write about seriously.

My treasure this is not a letter. It is a kind of intake of breath before I really begin to tell you all. Ah, how I love you here! The

spring of my joy is that we belong to each other and that you and I
are lovers and wedded to each other –
You are mine and I am yours for ever. I can't 'get over' that. It
simply fills my being with a kind of rich joy which I know I shall
express marvellously marvellously for you & through you.
Ribni – our little John the Baptist. Kiss him for me –
As for you – you are my own – and I am forever yours

Tig

Hôtel Beau Rivage,
Bandol
Friday.   [11 January 1918]

My dearest Bogey,
My enthusiastic letter from Paris has been in my mind ever since.
And mocked me. I took it to post; it was dark by then, piercing cold
and so wet underfoot that one's feet felt like 2 walking toads. After
a great deal of bother I got established in the train (no pillows to be
had now-a-days) and then the fun began. I liked my fellow
passengers – but God! how stiff one got and my feet hurt and the
flat iron became hot enough to burn the buttoned back against
which I leaned. There was no restaurant car on the train – no
chance of getting anything hot – a blinding snowstorm until we
reached Valence. I must confess the country was exquisite at
sunrise – exquisite but we did not arrive at Marseilles until *one*
o'clock. Good! As I got out a pimp getting *in* to hold a seat for some
super pimp gave me such a blow on the chest that it is blue today. I
thought 'this is Marseilles sans doute'. Feeling very tired and
hungry I carried my luggage 3 miles to the consigne & finding that
the train left for Bandol at 3.30. decided to have a snack at the
Buffet just outside – that place under a glass verandah. It was rather
full so I sat down opposite an elderly lady who eyed me so strangely
that I asked if 'cette place est prise.' 'Non Madame' said she,
insolent beyond everything, 'mais il y a des autres tables ne'est ce
pas. Je préfère beaucoup que vous ne venez pas ici. D'abord – j'ai
déjà fini mon déjeuner, et c'est très dégoutant de vous voir
commencer car j'ai l'estomac delicat, et puis – –' and then she
raised her eyebrows & left it at that. You can judge what I ate after
that – and what I thought. At 1.30 I went to get my baggage

registered – waited for one hour in a queue for my ticket & then was told I could not have one until my passport was viséd. I had that done, waited again, carried my luggage to the platform finally at 3 o'clock juste, and waited there in a crowd until four. Then a train came in at another platform & the people swarmed in just like apes climbing into bushes – & I had just thrown my rugs into it when it was stated that it was only for permissionaires & did not stop before Toulon. Good again! I staggered out, & got into *another* train on *another* platform, asked 3 people if it was the right one who did not know – & sat down in the corner – completely dished. There were 5 Serbian officers in the compartment with me & their 2 dogs. Never shall I say another word against Serbians. They looked like Maidens' Dreams – excessively handsome & well cared for – graceful, young, dashing with fine teeth & eyes. But that did not matter. What *did* was that after shunting for 2 hours – five yards forward five back – there was a free fight at the station between a mob of soldiers & the civilians. The soldiers demanded the train – & that les civils should evacuate it. Not with good temper, but furious – very ugly, & VILE. They banged on the windows, wrenched open the doors & threw out the people & their luggage after them. They came to our carriage swarmed in – told the officers they too must go and one caught hold of me as though I were a sort of packet of rugs – I never said a word for I was far too tired and vague to care about anything except I was determined not to *cry* – but one of the officers then let out – threw out the soldiers – said I was his wife & had been travelling with him five days – & when the chef militaire de la gare came, said the same – threw HIM OUT – banged the door, took off their dogs' leads & held the door shut. The others then pressed against the connecting door between the carriages & there we remained in a state of siege until seven o'clock when the train started. You should have heard the squalling and banging. They pinned the curtains together and I hid behind them until we were under way. By this time it was pitch dark & I knew I should never find the station as a terrific mistral was blowing & you could not hear the stations cried – but as we came to each stop they pulled the window down and shouted in their curious clipped French to know which it was. Ah, but they were very nice chaps – splendid chaps – I'll not forget them. We reached Bandol at 9. I felt that my grande malle was gone for ever but I seized the other 2 & dashed across the line. I could not have walked here but happily the boy from the Hotel des Bains was at the station & though he said 'qu'il n'etait pas bon avec le patron' he brought me.

When I arrived the hall was rather cold and smoky – a strange woman came out wiping her mouth with a serviette ... I realised in a flash that the hotel had changed hands. She said she had received *no* letter but there were plenty of rooms – and proceeded to lead me to them – My own was taken – I chose finally the one next door which had 2 beds on the condition that she removed one – Also it was the cheapest 12 francs a day – The others have had l'eau courant put into them and cost 13. The big stoves were not lighted in the passages ... I asked for hot water and a hot water bottle. Had some soup, wrapped up to the eyes & simply fell into bed after finishing the brandy in my flask. For I felt that the whole affair wanted thoroughly sleeping over and not thinking about ...

In the morning when I opened the persiennes it was so lovely outside, I stayed in bed until lunch. Ma grande malle really did turn up. Then I got up, and after lunch went into the town. The Meynets are gone for the present. The tabac woman did not know me & had no tobacco. Nobody remembered me at all – I bought writing things and a few bull eyes – about a penny for two, they were, and suddenly I met Maam Gamel. She, too did not recognise me until I had explained who I was – Then she was very kind – 'Ah! Ah! Ah! vous êtes beaucoup changée vous avez été *ben* malade, n'est ce pas. Vous n'avez plus votre air de p'tite gosse vous *saavez*!' I went with her to the shop, which is just the same & saw the old mother who was most tender about you. I bought a tiny pot of cherry jam, and came home – to find my room not yet done –

You can see, love I am depressed. I feel faible still after cet voyage, but I shall get better and I shall arrange things here as soon as I have la force nécessaire. The place is even to my blind eyes as lovely as ever, glittering with light, with the deep hyacinth blue sea, the wonderful flashing palms and the mountains, violet in the shadow, and jade green in the sun. The mimosa outside my window is in bud – Don't worry about me. Having got over that journey and that Paris thaw I shall never fall by the way – & when my room is ready I shall *work*. That I do feel, and that is what matters Bogey. I am not even very sad. It has been a bit of a bang though, hasn't it? and I'll tell you exactly what I feel like. I feel like a fly who has been dropped into the milk jug & fished out again but is still too milky & drowned to start cleaning up yet. Letters will take a long time, perhaps 6 or 8 days – so do not worry if you do not hear. And take care of yourself & LOVE ME. As I LOVE YOU. Ah, this is not the day to start writing about that, for my bosom begins to ache & my arms fly out to embrace you. I want you. I am lonely & very fainting by the way but only for now – you know. Always your own woman

       Tig

This is one of the truthful letters we promised each other my precious one ...

[Hôtel Beau Rivage,
Bandol]

Saturday.   12 January 1918

Bogey,
    You are to write as often as you can at first – see? Because letters take so long, so long, et jé suis malade. I have just got up and am sitting wrapped up in all my clothes & my wooly cover & your geranium jacket over & the Kashmir shawl over that & Ottoline's pink one round my legs & the rug folded on the floor – The fire is alight but it will not burn unless I keep the iron shade right down!! The old old story. It is bitterly cold – and a deep strange grey light over the sea & sky. I have got up because I <u>must</u> work & I can't in bed. If I am going to languish in Foreign Parts all alone I must have a great deal of work done – or it will be no use.
    Please Bogey write me warm letters – tellement il fait froid. Ah, do let everything be lovely 'chez vous'; that would be the greatest joy I could have. That *you* are well and comfortable and that you think of me and work in the evenings.
    You can't get any cigarettes here; nothing but cigars. There is a 'crise' in tobacco, too. This hotel is so quiet. There are only four uglies in it. I wonder they keep it open. I shall write to Madame Geffroi tomorrow.
    If L.M. was here she could blow up that fire.
    My little precious. My love, my child playfellow. Didn't we wave to each other a long time that day?
    Say you want me back in April. Tell me I *must* come back then.

        Your
        Wig.

[47 Redcliffe Road,
Fulham]
[14 January 1918]
Monday night. 11.45.

Wig my precious,
 I got your Bandol letter this evening. I won't talk about it now because this is only a fragment written, while the kettle boils, to go with a letter to-morrow. I have just been writing a political article for the *Nation*. As I got up from my chair, I saw your letter lying on the little round table in front of me. I had to kiss it: then I stood by the fire and looked at the clock, and loved you so much that I thought my heart would burst. I wondered whether something would tell you that I was full of love of you, wanting you to know I loved you so deeply, at a quarter to twelve on Monday night. Then I got down your photograph. It's stuck in a corner of the looking glass. And I was knocked all of a heap by your beauty again. It's the photo where you have the black jacket on, and the marguerite in your button hole. And there is all that wonderful, secret child-ness, trembling about that impossibly delicate mouth. You darling, darling, darling. That's only the first words of what I said to you. You exquisite, incredible woman.
 At that point his kettle boiled and he, being tired, had to go to bed. One thing before he goes, however. *Don't worry about money*: just ask for as much as you want.
 To-morrow I shall let myself go on the matter of that journey. Tuesday morning on way to office.
 I have decided to post this now – all alone. I shall send my long letter on Wednesday, darling.

       Boge.

[47 Redcliffe Road,
Fulham]
[15 January, 1918]
Tuesday evening. 8 o'clock.

My Wig, my precious Wig
 I have just had your second letter, written on Saturday. How I curse myself that I haven't written every day since you went. But I

will: I made up my mind to it this morning. Even if it's only a tiny word – something will come every day. Thank God, your letters seem to come quickly. Let me hope it is the same with mine.

Darling, I won't say I'm terrified by your journey, because you'll do something desperate to reassure me. But I am – I can't help being – worried about you. Oh, you are so tiny, such a fairy child, and so far away! My heart aches. If only there were some means of whispering all my love to you now so that you could hear just as I write ... If only I knew that you were well; instead I know you are ill ... If only I could send Ribni even to you just to make your heart warm ... If only I could come myself to you. All these thoughts buzz in my brain.

That journey! My precious, it is a nightmare to me. It seems to me now that it must have killed you. Oh, I wish that you had never, never gone. Everything seems so terribly to have changed; and what we thought would be a triumph ride into the sun, has been something utterly different.

I am frightened for you. But because I say this, I beseech you, Wig, don't tell me anything but the truth about yourself. I know you are telling me the truth now, and though it frightens me, it makes me warm, because I think that love can go no farther.

Write to Madame Geoffroi 1 Avenue Victor Hugo, Carpentras, (Vaucluse). I shall feel better if I know that she would look after you. But how shall I feel really better until I hold you tight in my arms again? And yet I daren't say I want you back, because you will come back. I want you back terribly: not because I miss you terribly, not because days without the sound of your voice are lonely days – all these things would fade away, if I knew you were well and happy, if I knew there was sunshine and that you were breathing it in. I want you back because you are small, and ill & so far away; because you are the only thing in the world, because you are the whole world to me; because you are so fragile, and the thought that I cannot look after you at all, even in my clumsy way, torments me.

Perhaps the weather will change. It must. It's not so cold in London now; though there is a deluge of half-melted snow pouring from the sky. What's the good of the South if the sea is grey?

Darling, look here. I don't want you back, so long as you are really well. If you are strong and can work and are happy, I would not say a word to bring you back even in April. I love you too much. But if you would say you were coming back then, such a thrill would go through my heart that it might burst.

Wig, don't worry about me. I swear to you, straight dinkum, that I am absolutely comfortable. I never see anyone in the evening: and I like that. I am full of your presence; and if the office weighs me down all day, I bound up again in the evening. I can talk to you then. And what is the use of anybody if it's not you? I'm very comfortable, and just now, ever since you've gone, I've been working hard at articles for the *Times* & the *Nation* so that we shall soon be swimming in funds again. Take it for granted that I could not be more comfortable. You saw the rooms. I could not ask for more. My one, my only anxiety is for you.

Oh, if you could only feel how warm my heart is for you, warmer than any nest!

                    Boge.

                                        [Hôtel Beau Rivage,
                                        Bandol]
Sunday.   [20 January 1918]

My Own Precious
    I LOVE YOU.
    I AM EVER SO MUCH BETTER
    I AM COMING BACK IN APRIL.
    BE HAPPY MY DEAR LOVE
    ONLY WRITE TWICE A WEEK
    OR YOU WILL BE 2 TIRED.
    MY MONEY IS QUITE SATISFACTORY
There is the bulletin. Oh Bogey I WISH that I had not told you the truth, for your two sad letters today, the one when my awful remark about malade jumped up & down the typewriter & the other wrung my heart this morning. It is quite true. I have been *bloody ill* but these last 2 days I feel ever such a great deal better & quite a different child. Chiefly because I know that I am not going to get worse & that we shall be together again. I really *did*, at one or two times, think I would 'peg out' here, never having had a heron or a heronette and that simply horrified me. But now though the local pain is still there everything else in me is against it & not for it – I feel *hungry* and I keep making plans. i.e. I shall bring him, in my old biscuit tin, ½ a pound of mountain butter, a little pot of cherry jam, a tiny handful of sweet dried figs. & in my box I'll pack 4 of the biggest pine cones I can find.

It's the 20th of January today. By the 20th of April we shall be married & sitting among our children I expect in some flowery field making daisy & buttercup chains. *If* I don't break off into a thousand pieces for love of you before then. My mother sent us great and little blessings today – to 'you & Jack'. She has a feeling that 'a happy future is unfolding for you both', though of course our letters haven't arrived yet. She told me a way to make bread which sounds very easy for our farm. She says after the war she is going to do the cooking in their house & Father is going to do all the washing. Father bought the entire library with that house which sounds a pearl. He has just finished reading *Robinson Crusoe*.

My Grandma Beauchamp is dead. She had a stroke & died.

Aunt Li has never recovered from her stroke.

Bee's husband has hanged himself in an outhouse.

As Mother says we seem to be all on strike or on string out here.

I had a nice letter from Ainger today, asking me to tell him how I got on & I had a letter from Belle & Chaddie. In fact I had 11 letters. But they might all have gone down that wind. Yours were the only ones I really coveted – devoured –

Oh my cherished one – I wish I could somehow tell you *here* and *now* that I feel inclined to lie on my back & play with Ribni. If we were together we'd make some coffee & a bright fire & sit and talk curled up in one round. Next month I shall go to Marseilles for 2 days to see Cooks & to get some books. To see Cooks about all that one has to do to get back so as I can be ready.

It is dark and very windy today. The sea is all teeth and fury. It rained all night. But I would not be surprised if the sun came out next week. I feel I have lifted up my head again and all my petals have spread out ready to catch a ray. But I wish I had a pigeon to send this letter more quickly.

It's Sunday and some strangers came here for lunch – we had bouille baisse. I wondered what you had.

Yes, I am not one but *two* – I am *you* as well as myself. You are another part of me just as I am a part of you.

Goodbye for now, my bogey.

Yours ever
Wig.

[47 Redcliffe Road,
Fulham]
[20 January 1918]
Sunday Night. 9.40.

My precious darling,
    Will you tell me if this letter gets to you at the same time as the one I wrote last night, which I posted early this afternoon, because, if it does, I might as well write a long one on Sunday instead of two short ones. What I want to arrange is that you should get a letter (if I'm terribly hard worked it may be only a postcard) every day. So if you'd just tell me whenever two come at once, I may be able to get it right by rearranging the times when I post them. The P.O. here can't tell me anything. They just say that no-one knows when the mails go to France, and that you have to take your chance. It may be true; but I suspect it isn't.
    Arthur has been here to-day. He wanted your address so that he might write to you; but I turned the subject of conversation, because I didn't want him, or my mother, to see that you were still Madame B. So that you must take the will for the deed on his part. He told me a story about Wordsworth – where he can have got it from, I don't know. It's stupid, but characteristic, and it makes me love the old fellow rather. One day Wordsworth was dining with a friend. Some rather aged, yellowish peas were served. The friend in order to turn it off said to W. 'Forgive me, but I forgot to send these peas to Kensington'. 'To Kensington', says W. 'Why pray?' 'Because that is the way to Turnham Green'. W. thought this an extremely good joke, resolved to remember it, and to let it fly on the first opportunity. It came very soon. He was dining with a friend whose peas were also rather passé. He turned to the lady of the house. 'Madame, I'm afraid you forgot to send these peas to Kensington'. 'To Kensington, Mr. W., why pray?' 'Because that is the way to make them green'. And he roared with laughter.
    Lesley also has been here. She is evidently very upset with anxiety about you; but for some odd reason (not so very odd) I am impelled with her to take up a very impassive attitude about you. I dislike the kind of her anxiety so much that there are moments when I assume almost a callous air about you, my darling. I say: 'I'm sure she's better'. Then she says: 'Do you believe what she says' (i.e. in your wire of yesterday). I reply, very short: 'Absolutely'. If I'm not careful I shall fall into my old habit and regard her as a kind of ghoul, fattening on your illness, although I know it's wrong & that

she's really a brick. But something makes it quite impossible to unburden my heart and my anxieties to her. I am all but silent when she is here. And when she asks: 'But don't you think it's likely Madame Geoffroy has been a disappointment?', I say 'I know she's devoted to Tig & Tig's devoted to her', although I'm asking myself exactly the same question. I can't make up my mind whether I am unfair to her, whether it is in fact that I resent anyone else than myself being so concerned about you. There's something of that, I'm sure, because when I said 'Don't you think, instead of hesitating, the best thing to do would be to send her a straightforward wire: "Would you like Lesley to come?" ' and she replied: 'Whatever she said, I know she wants me' – I had a kind of jealous resentment.

Oh, that old marché of which you sent me the picture and the neat little station with the stupid train! To think that the place where we were so happy, where we entered on the phase of our perfect love, should have become morne and desolate. Those wounded mangy sheep!

My precious, I hope & pray that your weather has changed. It is really almost warm here in London now, warmer, at any rate, than it has been for two months. Oh child, you small and tiny jewel, why can't we speak to each other? Why do we have to wait so long for the answers. Darling, je t'adore

        Boge.

> [Hôtel Beau Rivage,
> Bandol]
> February 1st 1918

IMPORTANT

Dearest

I have made a resolution tonight. I mean to come back next month, *March*, as soon as Kay has sent me my money. I can see, from all signs, that if I don't get back then I may not get back at all – the difficulties of transport will be so great. Tell nobody. Of course a wangle will be necessary for the authorities. But the King of the Nuts at Havre told me that if I had any 'urgent family affairs' I could of course get back before 'my time'. ∴ do you send me after the 1st of the March a telegram saying *Mother worse come back soon as possible Bowden* and I shall have that to show.

I can stick this anxiety until then but no longer – *Don't send me any money*, of course. I have plenty. And tell me just, frankly, what you think of this. I have headed the page important so when you refer to it say you have got the important letter & then I'll know which one you mean. By that time I shall be as well as I ever shall be during the war & – & – Oh I must come. I can't stick it out for longer. But tell me very frankly 'vos idées'.

Your woman
Wig.

If you can afford a wire before you answer this letter – just the word *agree* if you do agree – it would be Heaven.

Wiggie.

[47 Redcliffe Road,
Fulham]
[3 February 1918]
Sunday 9.15

My precious darling.

I have a whole evening to myself to-night. Article sent off to the *Times* & nothing to write for the *Nation* till to-morrow. If it were not that the night is already far spent, I could find it in me to court the Muses. Perhaps I will, even yet. I would certainly if my cold had wholly gone; there is something radically impossible in writing poetry with a cold in the head. Mine really is going, but it takes such a cursedly long while tidying up beforehand.

Lesley was here this morning to lunch. She brought me some flowers yesterday for wh: I was very grateful. I love to have them in my room, but I always forget to buy them. Also, which is even more important, she brought me four fresh herrings. 1 I had for breakfast; 2 we had for lunch, & 1 for to-morrow morning. I cooked them with genius – there's no other word for it.

I suppose things do happen to me; but it must be that I don't take any notice of them, for when I look into my mind to take something out for you, it's empty of anything else but your own letters. It's no use our complaining about this state of affairs. We know that it might be very, very much worse; and we know what we're up to & whither we are bound. Still, *cependant*, it must be confessed that I am rather a second-rate affair.

However, I stole enough time from my articles on Friday & Saturday to read a most delightful book by R[obert] L[ouis] S[tevenson] *Prince Otto*. Have you ever read it? There's some most uncommon beautiful writing in it in parts; and in others it's damnably witty. Shall I send it across? The only drawback is that it isn't very long & you'll read it at a sitting.

That's been my only literary recreation since you went. To think that a month has gone since you went away! Really, to put me in that office is like putting a tortoise into a dung-heap for the winter. I believe I shall have to [be] poked out with a stick. No I won't, when Spring comes, that's you, I'll be found trundling along out of some quite unexpected corner, nibbling something. Do tortoises nibble? I don't know.

I had a long talk with Arthur about the printing press to-day. We were very matter of fact, I almost seemed to hold the sheets of bright clean paper in my hand. Phew, I shall be bitterly disappointed if it doesn't come off. But it will. Besides, I quite seriously believe it will be the only way to keep going practically.

Tell me all about flowers, and smells, & the sea. Are there many pine-cones. Have you been to Cape Sixpence. No, of course not: it's too far. What has happened to our house. Tell me some more golden things. My head is a bit cobwebby. It needs to have a rainbow put inside.

My darling, my own – hooray for the registry office in April!

Boge

[Hôtel Beau Rivage,
Bandol]
February 3rd 1918.
Sunday morning.

Dearest,
It is early for me to be up, but I had such a longing for a cigarette, and as I sit here in my pyjamas smoking a very good one I'll begin your letter. There was nothing from you yesterday & the facteur hasn't been yet today – however – –

I really feel I *ought* to send you some boughs and songs, for never was there a place more suited, but to tell you the truth I am pretty well absorbed in what I am writing & walk the bloody countryside with a 2d note book shutting out les amandiers. But I don't want to discuss it in case it don't come off .....

I've two 'kick offs' in the writing game. *One* is joy – real joy – the thing that made me write when we lived at Pauline, and that sort of writing I could only do in just that state of being in some perfectly blissful way *at peace.* Then something delicate and lovely seems to open before my eyes, like a flower without thought of a frost or a cold breath – knowing that all about it is warm and tender and 'steady'. And *that* I try, ever so humbly to express.

The other 'kick off' is my old original one, and (had I not known love) it would have been my all. Not hate or destruction (both are beneath contempt as real motives) but an *extremely* deep sense of hopelessness – of everything doomed to disaster – almost wilfully, stupidly – like the almond tree and 'pas de nougat pour le noël, – There! as I took out a cigarette paper I got it exactly – *a cry against corruption* that is *absolutely* the nail on the head. Not a protest – a *cry*, and I mean corruption in the widest sense of the word, of course –

I am at present fully launched, right out in the deep sea with this second state. I may not be able to 'make my passage' – I may have to put back & have another try, that's why I don't want to talk about it – & have breath for so little more than a hail. But I must say the boat feels to be driving along the deep water as though it smelt port – (no darling, better say 'harbour' or you'll think I am rushing into a public house)

After lunch.

My Boge,

I have just read your Tuesday note, written after *another* raid. You sound awfully tired, darling and awfully disenchanted. You are overworking ... it's too plain. (Curse my old shoes. Keep them for me. don't worry about them any more.)

Yes I agree with you – blow the old war. It is a toss up whether it don't get every one of us before it's done. Except for the first warm days here when I really did seem to almost forget it it's never out of my mind & everything is poisoned by it. It's *here in* me the whole time, eating me away – and I am simply terrified by it – It's at the root of my homesickness & anxiety & panic – I think. It took being alone here and unable to work to make me fully fully *accept* it. But now I don't think that even you would beat me. I have got the pull of you in a way because I am working but I solemnly assure [you] that every moment away from my work is MISERY. And the human contact – just the pass the time away chat distracts you – & that of course I don't have at all. I miss it very much. Birds & flowers and dreaming seas don't do it. Being a biped – I must have a two legged person to *talk* to – You can't imagine how I feel that I walk alone in a sort of black glittering case like a beetle – – – –

Queer business ...

By the way I dreamed the other night that Frieda came to you & asked you for money. She 'knew you had some', she bullied you into giving her £5. I woke terrified lest this might happen. Never let it. Your money is really earned with your blood. Never give it away. You need it; you must have it. PLEASE please!

I wonder what you will say to my 'important' letter & if you agree will they let me through? Can they keep me out of my own country? These are a couple of refrains which are pretty persistent. They say here that after March this railway will probably be closed till June ...

My own precious I love you *eternally*

        Your
        Wig.

                [Hôtel Beau Rivage,
                Bandol]
                [3 February 1918]
                Sunday Night

My precious

I don't dare to work any more tonight. I suffer so frightfully from insomnia here and from night terrors. That is why I asked for another Dickens; if I read him in bed he diverts my mind. My work excites me so tremendously that I almost feel *insane* at night and I have been at it with hardly a break all day. A great deal is copied and carefully addressed to you, in case any misfortune should happen to me. Cheerful! But there is a great black bird flying over me and I am so frightened he'll settle – so terrified. I don't know exactly what *kind* he is.

If I were not working here, with war and anxiety I should go mad, I think. My night terrors here are rather complicated by packs & packs of growling, roaring, ravening, prowl and prowl around dogs.

God! How tired I am! And I'd love to curl up against you and sleep.

Goodnight, my blessed one. Don't forget me in your busy life.

Monday. February 4th.

Dearest

No letter from you today. I had one from Ida written on *Friday* –
so the posts have got a real grudge against you and me ... I am
posting you the first chapter of my new work today. I have been hard
put to it to get it copied in time to send it off but I am so EXCEEDINGLY
anxious for your opinion.

It needs perhaps some explanation. The subject I mean lui qui
parle is of course taken from – Carco & Gertler & God knows who.
It has been more or less in my mind ever since I first felt strongly
about the French. But I hope you'll see (of course you will) that I am
not writing with a sting. I'm not, indeed!

I read the fair copy just now and couldn't think where the devil I
had got the bloody thing from – I can't even now. It's a mystery.
There's so much much less taken from life than anybody would
credit. The African laundress I had a bone of – but only a bone – Dick
Harmon of course is partly is ..

Oh God – is it good? I am frightened. For I stand or fall by it. It's as
far as I can get at present and I have gone for it, bitten deeper &
deeper & deeper than ever I have before. You'll laugh a bit about the
song. I could see Goodyear grin as he read that.... But what is it like!
Tell me – don't spare me. Is it the long breathe as I feel to my soul it is
– or is it a false alarm? You'll give me your *dead honest opinion* –
won't you Bogey?

If this gets lost I break my pen –

I am only at the moment a person who works comes up to read
newspapers, AND to wait for postmen goes down again, drinks tea.
Outside the window is the scenic railway – all complete & behind
that pretty piece is the war –

Forgive an empty head. It rattled all night. I can't manage this
sleeping business.

Goodbye for now my heart's treasure.

> *Yours* yours only for ever
> Wig.

[47 Redcliffe Road,
Fulham]
[7 February 1918]
Thursday 8 o'clock

My precious,

Your Sunday (Feb 3) letter came this morning. Somehow it told me more nearly what you felt, and how you were, than any letter you have written me. Perhaps that was because I feel exactly the things you feel. I too have two motives for writing – happiness (Villa Pauline): and a despairing 'cry against corruption'. The absolute exactness of identity between this last and my own motives struck me profoundly, rather as though I had been on the point of crying out, and you had cried instead – the miraculous, unearthly feeling of complete communion.

And – I don't need to tell you – that I fear the war: it is like a plague, or some great monster waiting. Alone, I feel helpless, (at best) fatalistic; when we are together I feel that we have such virtue in us that we shall, somehow, be able to withstand it. But being apart – it's no good, no good at all.

I wish I knew something definite, whether you will be able to manage to persuade the Consulate. I feel that you will; but until I really know, I shall be anxious still.

I don't know what to say, my Wig: I'm not depressed, I'm not happy. I seem to be in a sort of limbo where everything is half-and-half; quite obviously, there is only half of me here. I was quite calm & deliberate & sober when I said, the other day, that my soul had left me to nestle with you. It seems to be such a simple matter of fact.

I think it is a very good thing that I am working hard. I mistrust myself when I am left alone and writing articles eases the strain. Without it I should be rushing from deep depression to a sort of hysterical nonchalance, and that would perhaps break something.

But how glad, unutterably glad, I am that you are coming back. The sweetest part of my life now is when I think of us sitting together in the kitchen eating: of us lying together in each other's arms, with your head on my shoulder. I dare not think.

Boge.

12.15

Lesley Moore has since been here. She has sprung a complete surprise on me, & now that an hour has gone since she left I am beginning to be very doubtful.

She said she had determined to go to France. She has managed, by getting a certificate from Ainger, to get a passport visa'd, and she was leaving on Saturday. It was no use; she said, my saying anything about it because she had determined to go.

I was completely bowled out. I told her that you had decided to come back at the beginning of March. That made no difference, she said, she would help you come back. I didn't, however, insist, while she was here on dissuading her.

But now I feel that she has absolutely no right to go without asking you first. I feel also that it may make it more difficult for you to return; you may well manage the officials alone on our plan, but she would complicate it. That may be foolish – I don't know. But I now feel overwhelmingly that she mustn't go without asking you. Am I right? Oh, I wish I knew. I could kill any person out of hand who made it impossible for you to return, or delayed your return by a day. I'll do all I can to prevent her.

O my precious love, I want you back. My mind is all dithering, just now. It's so hard for me to decide this thing.

> Boge.

Friday Morning.

I got your M.S.S. this morning. I am going to wire you. I'll write to-night

I've changed my mind about Lesley Moore. It would take the worst of the strain off if I knew she was with you.

Do all that you humanly can to come back. I know you will.

Oh, Lord I wish I could make up my mind about this. I was certain it was wrong last night; certain it was right this morning & now again I don't know

If by any devilish chance you can't get back, then I would have her with you, but if you can, I feel that she may make it more difficult.

Wig, Wig – I'm a poor rabbit of a thing – frightened of my love for you.

Later.

Lesley has just telephoned me to say that there is a chance that she may be able to get some official document from the Air Board, saying that she must get back as soon as possible. If she can do this it completely alters the situation; for that may help you to get back. If she gets it – she is going to the Air Board tomorrow morning – I am all for her going

Good-bye, my precious love.

[London]
[8 February 1918]

STORY RECEIVED MAGNIFICENT

MURLY

[47 Redcliffe Road,
Fulham]
[8 February 1918]
Friday 10 o'clock

My precious,
    Your MS (1st part of Je ne parle pas) came this morning. It's not only first rate; it's overwhelming. The description, no, not description, creation, of that café is extraordinary. (I've just read it again, since I began). The whole thing is extraordinary. I don't know what you're going to do at all. But I'm absolutely fascinated.
    I'll try to tell you what I feel. In the first place my sensation is like that which I had when I read Dostoevsky's *Letters from the Underworld*. That is, it's utterly unlike any sensation I have ever yet had from any writing of yours, or any writing at all except D's.
    Secondly, although it's unlike D. in that unearthly way he has of putting you in a place & stopping the world – everything stands still, becomes timeless, – and though you have – the Lord knows how – kept this up all through, so that the first page & the last seem to be simultaneous, happening in the same icy moment – and this is the final, large impression the whole chapter leaves,————————
    Yet, it's different. Like this. Raoul Duquette isn't what he would be if it were either Dostoevsky (or me) writing, for then he would be Dostoevsky thinking aloud. But instead of this, you have got this strange person, who's strange, not, as D's man would be, because he has thought everything to a standstill, but because he is conscious of a piece out of him. I don't quite know what words to put it in. Yes, he's conscious of having no roots. He sees a person like Dick who has roots and he realises the difference. But what it is he hasn't got, he doesn't know. Nor do I.
    What you are going to do with them I haven't the faintest idea. But I am ravenous to know. It's all of such a different kind to any of your other work. Different, I mean, in scope & skeleton & structure, the exquisite exactness – the this & nothing else – of your

vision in the detail is there just as before. How can I put it? This is the only writing of yours I know that seems to be *dangerous*. Do you understand what I mean – by the adjective? It's *dangerous* to stop the world for a timeless moment.

To put it another way. Here you seem to have begun to drag the depths of your *consciousness*. Before you did something quite different, and I am certain that you will again. But somehow it has happened that on this one occasion you were driven to make an utterly new approach, to express something different. I mean it like this. Ordinarily what you express & satisfy is your desire to write, because you are a born writer, and a writer born with a true vision of the world. Now you express & satisfy some other desire, perhaps because for a moment you doubt or have not got the other vision. The world is shut out. You are looking into yourself.

Does all that seem nonsense? I feel certain that it is true, and also I see how apposite it was I that began by likening this story of yours, though you are essentially a Tolstoy writer, to Dostoevsky.

The thing is tremendous – but my impatience to have more of it is awful.

I'm rather worn out just for the moment by the continual underneath anxiety about your return. The L.M. affair hasn't moved since I wrote this morning. If she gets that letter from the Air Board, I am all for her going. She could bring you back safely. But I shan't be any good at anything till you are back here.

Wig – if we could only hold each other tight in our arms now

When I say I'm rather worn out, of course I don't mean anything serious. What I mean is that the anxiety & the hope always moving inside me are like a little chain tethering me. Whatever I do, or write, or think there comes the jerk.

> I love you.
> Boge.

[Hôtel Beau Rivage,
Bandol]
Saturday 9th   [February 1918]

My own
    The postman brought today a roll of papers from you but no letter. It will come tomorrow p'raps. I was just brushing my fringe when I heard a clumpety clump in the passage that my heart seemed

to recognise long before I did. It began to dance and beat – Yes, it was the Aged with your ADORABLE telegram Sthry receivid mafnificent Murly. I read and of course this bowled me over so much that the pins won't keep in my hair and my buttons pop like fuschia buds and my strings all squeak when they're pulled. Well the only response I *can* make is to send you the next chapter which I'll post as before on Monday. But oh dear oh dear! You have lighted such a candle! Great *beams* will come out of my eyes at lunch and play like search lights over the pomme de terres and terrify these insect children.

Now of course my only faint fear is:– 'will he like the next chapter as much?' Well I must 'wait and see' – I must say when I wrote about the *tea* last night – that's a funny little typical bit – I came all over & nearly cried those sort of sweet tears that I've only known since I loved you. I say Boge – haven't I got a *bit of you*. Funny thing is I think you'll always come walking into my stories (and now of course I see future generations finding you in all my books 'The man she was in love with').

No, dear love. I must wait until I've had lunch before I go on with this letter. I am too much of a 'gash baloon' altogether. *1.15.* Well, I wish you had eaten my tournedos; it was such a good 'un. The great thing here is the meat which is superb. Oh, but now I am turned towards *home* everything is good. I eat you. I see you. And my heart (apart from my work) does nothing but store up things to give you – plans for our life – wherever it is. Shall we really, really next month curl up together on the divan & talk with Rib sitting in the fender playing on a minute comb and paper? I'd die without you. 'Hang there, like fruit, my soul, till the tree die!' The tree *would* die –

I have just looked at the *T.L.S.*, read your Sturge Moore review which touched me. The last sentence is perfect & 'noted' that Mr. M.M. had an article of really high quality in the *Quarterly*.

How *damned* depressing and hideously inadequate that Versailles conference has been – But what I do feel is that handful can't stop the dyke from breaking now – (Is that true?) I mean there *is* – isn't there perfectly immense pressure upon it & L[loyd] G[eorge] & Co may put their hands in the hole (like the little boy in *Great Deeds Done by Little People* that Grandma used to read me on Sundays) but it's no use. Oh, I *don't* know. When I think I am not coming home and that 'all is over' – when that mood gets me of course I don't believe it ever will end until we are all killed as surely as if we were in the trenches. Not that *love* and *you* falsify my feeling about it – make it less terrible but they do fortify gainst it. Yes that is too true! Now I am waiting for a letter from you tomorrow – Sunday. The post will be late & hundreds and hundreds of imaginary Juliettes will come along the passage to my door before the real one comes. But I can bear *that* as long as the real one *does* come.

I am yours eternally
Wig

[47 Redcliffe Road,
Fulham]
February 9 [1918]
Saturday 11.30 p.m.

My precious,
I saw L.M. off by the 4. o'clock train to-day: by the time this gets to you she will be with you. What decided me that it was right that she should go – though of course I had absolutely nothing at all to do with it, because she had firmly decided – was reading your story on Friday morning. You'll understand. I wobbled again towards noon – the record of what I went through is in the letter sent on Friday. The reason why I wobbled was the same original one: I felt that somehow her being there might make it more difficult for you to come back. When she told me that she would be able to get back through the Air Board, my fear disappeared.

My darling one. I want to make my mind, now that the thing has been done and I am, tant soit peu, calm again, quite clear to you, to be absolutely candid.

First, I want you back. I can't bear this separation.

Second, my fear about you is much lessened by my knowledge that L.M. is with you. But it is still there.

Third. In spite of (1) & (2) you must not think that you must come because of me. If you are not fit, if it would make you stronger to stay there longer now that L.M. is there to look after you, if in any way you hesitate to face the journey, if you think you would be able to work by taking a villa, then I *want* you to stay. For us to be parted is not a good thing; but if I know you are being cared for and getting stronger, then I can put up with it, (I won't say indefinitely because it's not true) for some months. I shall be perfectly *all right*, if you now decide to stay on. I shan't even be disappointed. I know that you love me & I know that I love you, and, though there are moments when I could cry because I haven't got you to clasp in my arms, I have to remember that I am after all almost a complete machine until the war is over, and lately, because the money has been going rather fast, I have become worse than ever.

Fourth, you *simply must not worry* about me. Everything goes well. I feed myself, I look after myself, I can truly say (*to you*) I am absolutely fit. I keep very much to myself. I have to in order to do the extra work, & I have no inclination to do otherwise – quite the other way. The moment anything upsetting occurs, I will let you know. I have been nervous, very nervous, about you; but – I don't know why – it hasn't pulled me down in the least. There is not the faintest reason why I should not go on.

I think that's all. I wanted to make it perfectly plain so that you should have something to go on when you make a decision. It comes to this – that I, your faithful, passionate lover, declare that you must not come back for my sake. It's only the selfish part of my love that says: I want you back. I say that it is your duty, as my lover – my darling lover, *to think only of what will be best for you.* In that way, you will love me best of all.

What a little solemn Boge I have been to be sure! But you will read my heart in between the lines, if it's not in them. Good-night, my love.

B.

Hullo Jag.   [Hôtel Beau Rivage,
                                         Bandol]
Sunday still & Monday after.   [10 February 1918]

My own
    I am just going to ignore this wire from L.M. until I hear further. If I really did give way to it it would do neither of us any good, and it CAN'T be bad news. So there, and you must understand. £10 is *more* than enough. I'll get no money for March from Kay. *When I feel the hour has come I will wire how is MOTHER? and then you will reply mother worse operation necessary come soon possible. See?* (But it won't be before March.) That's not mad. Is it? I have ample ample money. I shall take care of myself *because* of you *for* you, I'll wire from Marseilles & from Paris ...
    I have just put up in an envelope the rest of our story. Again this

fusion of our minds. You talk of love poetry – all I write or ever ever will write will be the fruit of our love – love prose – This time for instance as I went on and *on* I fed on our love. Nightingales if you like brought me heavenly manna. Could I have done it without you? No, a million times. You can see us can't you sprouting on every page. Even Rib had a part. I don't want to exaggerate the importance of this story or to harp on it; but it's a tribute to Love you understand and the very best I can do just now. Take it. It's yours. But what [I] felt so curiously as I wrote it was – ah! I am in a way *grown up* as a writer – a sort of authority – just as [I] felt about your poetry. Pray God you like it now you've got it all.

I *dreamed* a short story last night even down to its name which was 'Sun & Moon'. It was very light. I dreamed it all – about children. I got up at 6.30 & made a note or two because I knew it would fade. I'll send it sometime this week. It's so nice. I didn't dream that I read it. No I was in it part of it & it played round invisible me. But the hero is not more than 5. In my dream I saw a supper table with the eyes of 5. It was awfully queer – especially a plate of half melted icecream ... but I'll send it to you. Nothing is any good to me – no thought – no beauty – no idea – unless I have given it to you and it has become the property of these wealthiest little proprietors in the whole world Wig & Bogey & Bogey & Wig. Assistant *Rib*. En cas d'absence *Rib*.

I have asked you to wire when you get this second packet my own because of the sousmarins. Bogey I have MOUNDS of money. I shall arrive (without my March allowance) with a great deal. So don't worry, please, and dearest darling precious love guard yourself for me – oh *keep safe for me*.

See I ignore this black foreboding telegram. I feel that is what you would have me to do until I know why she is so awfully coming. I will keep this letter open till tomorrow's post has been.

Monday. But the bloody thing kept me awake all night. I didn't sleep an hour I suppose. Now with this morning comes your Wednesday letter and the 2 books, my heart. Did you read in my other letter I would not come till March? It seems to me my case is stronger with the authorities if I have been longer here – & the days will go by. Oh please please don't worry my own – and don't worry about my wire *till* you hear from me *as* arranged on page 1. I feel so calm about it now it is decided. All this of course is subject to 'all being well' & the mystery explained. What horrifies me further is I received from L.M. this morning 2 hysterical mad screams – 'Oh my darling make the doctor let me come' 'Oh my darling *eat*'. If she comes with news of you that you're ill – you want me – something has happened then I shall understand. If she comes for any other reason I've done with her – But what could her other reason be? I have asked her *not* to come on my account. Oh it's a circle: I *must* keep calm. I wrote & finished the dream story yesterday – and dedicated it to Rib. I knew I would not write it at all if I didn't on the spot & it kept me 'quiet'. Otherwise apart from this black ghoulish thought all seems Ah so fair – I am coming. I've done some work. I am turned towards home – We are going to live in a biscuit box – and be the two most charming biscuit crumbs together. No, Beaufort Mansions is tempting, but London is not our home – we only have a sort of biscuit tin there. Our home is a cottage with a gold roof & silver windows.

I can expect HER tomorrow night. Not before. Well I must work & bide her coming.

YOURS YOURS every day & hour & breath I'd say I am more your own

Wig.

	[Hôtel Beau Rivage, Bandol]
Monday 11th 8 P.M.	[February 1918]

No L.M. tonight. I thought she might arrive by this evening's train. Every sound from outside is *her – she*. What the HELL *does* it mean. What *can* it mean!

I am mad to begin another *big* story, now that 'Sun and Moon' is ready to send you but between me and the difficult and desirable country looms this misty peak. Perhaps your letter tomorrow will lift the veil ... Bogey if all is well with you, and yet it's so strange. Like our Rib I cannot believe that all is *not* well with you – even though my mind can find no other earthly excuse for her ... I simply can't listen to my mind. No, my heart won't hear it. My heart is an enemy to it. But the suspense! I walked & walked it this afternoon after I had posted your letter & the MS recommandé. I was like a blind shepherd driving a flock of – I knew not what ...

This note (so neat, isn't it – such little stitches!) is to say that I love you eight hours more than I did when I said it before.

Wig.

Tuesday. With All the Flags of Love Flying.

My precious,
   Your Thursday letter & the page explaining L.M. has come &
your Friday letter about my story.
   My heart was right. Rib was right again. This relief is boundless &
yet I *knew* it. There was just this 'panic' like there always is. And my
own lover, be calm. Don't feel the strain. See? I am very calm about
coming back. I will manage it – beautifully. Don't be frightened. I
feel so strong. (I want to write about your Friday letter bang off first
but I'll just finish with L.M. first.) Bogey I have done with her. I asked
her not to come; said, I didn't want her & then she wired me 'leaving'
– That ends it. She's a revolting hysterical ghoul. She's never content
except when she can eat me. My God!! But I shall keep great control.
As she has come I of course must see her & she must be here, but I
can't stop working for her. Till I get back I shall not alter my
programme in the smallest particular for her. She's done it; very well.
She must suffer for her infernal hysteria. I don't think it will make it
more difficult for me to get back, because it is not until March that I
am coming & I may travel with her but I shall ignore *her* object in
returning. She'd *like* me to be paralysed of course – or blind –
preferably blind. However I shall keep cool & explain that I only can
see her at meals & a walk in the afternoon. All the mornings I always
keep my room. After lunch I write or read till 2. When I come in at
five it's my *great* time to write till dinner & after dinner I read. She
must find some occupation. I *loathe* her so much for this and for the
drivel and moaning of her letters to me here that I shall never soften.
If I did bang would go my work again. *Finis.*
   Now about your letter about the first chapter. I read it & I wept for
joy. How can you so marvellously understand – and so receive my
love offering. Ah, it will take all of the longest life I can live to repay
you. I *did* feel (I do) that this story is the real thing & that I did not
once (as far as I know) shirk it. Please God I'll do much better for us –
but I felt there I can lay down my pen now I've made that and give it
to Bogey. Yes I did feel that. But Christ! a devil about the size of a flea
nips in my ear 'suppose he's disappointed with the 2nd half?' I'll
send you 'Sun & Moon' today, registré, *but of course* don't *wire*
about *it*. And, unless the mountain arrives here & milks me of money
I must tell you I have a surprise for you on that score, which will
make you happy: *To tell you your fortune I do not pretend* it sounds
like. You know that machine we stuck a penny in. Yes I'm sure I shall
be able to manage it. You know the programme? *Wait* for my wire

how is mother That is the signal. Then wire *mother worse operation necessary return soon as possible.*

I don't think there can be a big big battle before March because the ground's not hard enough. (That sounds like Rib speaking.) Now I know about this woman I am myself again. She will have to look after herself – but she's nicely finished my (really on the whole) odious friendship. My new story is signalled. And I love you I adore you. To eat in a kitchen with you is my ultimate wishing ring.

                    Your own woman
                    Wig.

                                        47 Redcliffe Road,
                                        Fulham,
Friday 8.30   [15 February 1918]

My precious darling,
    Your stories came safely this morning. I hadn't time to read them before I went to the office; so I took them with me and read them at lunch. After which I sent you the shilling wire.
    They are quite first-chop. I wasn't prepared for the tragic turn of 'Je ne parle pas', and it upset me – I'm an awful child. But it's lovely, lovely. I must read it right through again to taste fully the growth of the quality of that ending out of that beginning. The lift is amazing. And how the devil you got that sharp outline for Mouse I don't know. And then there's 'Sun & Moon' – with the little grey whiskered man. It's quite perfect, and the symbolical value it has stretches out illimitably. It's so damned true of us now, isn't it? These people think we can be fed on broken meats, and that we can feel delight in ice-houses when the roof has been pushed in by their hateful spoons. Save that we walk away hand in hand to our secret darksome cave – it's all true. Go on, my darling, stick to it if you can with L.M. there: what a writer you are!
    Well, well, it's no use talking of L.M. She played me in or up completely. When you tell me that you asked her *not* to come on yr. account, well then I feel vicious against her. But this will be all in the past when you get this.
    After three weeks warm weather it has begun to get cold here, but of course, nothing like so cold as it was the day you went away. I haven't been such a good little machine this week as last. I've really done nothing except a *Nation* article on Monday. On

Wednesday I really was done up, dead to the world, codfish eyes, and a face like an artichoke. Purely mental, understand, physical turn out spanking. On Thursday I was inclined to be feeble and laugh helplessly (of course, I didn't) and I felt on the whole happy & careless, rather as though my mind had gone off on a spree and How the deuce do I know when it's coming back, & why should I care, anyway? To-day, returning sanity, but still rather weak in the head. Before I go to bed to-night I shall have pulled myself together. It's an odd experience, and though it's not really fair I put it down to the tax on my nervous energies that the L.M. affair put on me, so that when it came to Wednesday, I just flopped like a cuttlefish on to the typewriter. But this work of yours is a tonic. I've told you the exact truth of the last 3 days, because it's our bargain. But you must understand that physically I'm in perfect health, and I stood it like Sun himself would stand that disaster.

And I want you to promise me that if you think you will be able to work better by staying down there & turning L.M. into an abject slave – It's the very best you can do with her and better than she deserves – you will do so. Don't come and be caught by an ugly March wind, my darling, unless you really must. If you can't work down there, then you're better here. And you know how I should hug you. But if you can, and if you are looking after yourself and getting strong, then it's your duty to me as your Boge to stay

> Goodnight
> Boge

Rib says: 'That was a good story she gave me, especially the bit about the nut-door-handle.'

[Hôtel Beau Rivage,
Bandol]
[1918]

February 19th   (Your Thursday & Friday letters received)

Dearest

I want to tell you some things which are a bit awful – so hold me *hard*. I have not been so well these last few days. Today I saw a doctor. There happens by an extraordinary chance to be an English doctor here just now, & L. M. got him to come. Look here! I can't leave this place till April – it's no earthly go. I can't & mustn't – see.

Can't risk a draught or a chill & mustn't walk. I've got a bit of a temperature & I am not so fat as I was when I came – & Bogey, this is NOT serious does NOT keep me in bed is absolutely easily curable, but I have been spitting a bit of blood. See? Of course I'll tell you? But if you worry – unless you laugh like Rib does I can't tell you: you mustn't type it on the typewriter or anything like that my precious – my own – and after all Lawrence often used to – so did I think [Aunt] Belle Trinder. But while it goes on I've got to be most enormously careful. See? I've got this doctor & I've got the Slave – so I am provided for, & determined to stick it out till April & not come back till the first week of *then*. It's agony to be parted from you but it would be imbecile to get the March winds as I am so parky – and everybody would be madly cross – & I couldn't stick in bed in 47. I'd only be a worry. So here I stay & work – and try to bear it. I've *ample* money for everything & my journey money fastened up with a pin and locked away.

I can do all this and everything as long as I know you are taking care of yourself and that you don't worry about me and do *feed* and don't overwork too dreadfully. I am afraid it must be done. Before [the] doctor came (you can imagine) I was so frightened. Now I'm confiding ... it's not serious. But when I saw the bright arterial blood I nearly had a fit. But he says it's absolutely curable – and if I sit in the sun till April I'll then come back & see a specialist and Papa will pay for that – He can look at my wings with his spyglass & decide. Of course this man says this coast is my eye because it's not bracing. Still now I am here – here I must stay & he is looking after me & I am to have injections of strichnine & other stuff – I don't know what, and more food still. So it's a good thing L. M. came (even though I feel in some mysterious way *she has done it*. That's because I *loathe* her so – I do.) Still I'll use her as a slave. As I shall be here a whole month longer I can get a lot of work done & that may bring pennies. Oh, I can bear it – or anything as long as you are well. And tell me when [you] feel a boiled haddock – don't disguise anything because I won't disguise things from you. See how I tell you *bang out* because our love will stand it. My money is splendid – and I shall *work work work*. In April there can't be the same chance of a snowstorm or a wind that might make 'pas de nougat pour le noël' for us both. I think it must be – And then, please God we'll be married, & see how lucky I am I can work! I had your letter about the 2nd part of 'Je ne parle pas' & I feel you are disappointed ... Is that true & if it is true please tell me why – This is a silly old letter all about my wings. Forgive it, my love, and answer it as soon as you can. Oh my own precious don't work too hard – & love me love me till April. Your own little

Wig.

[War Office,
Watergate House,
Adelphi W.C.2]
Saturday Morning [23 February 1918]

This morning I got your letter of February 19, the one about the doctor and the wings. It was a bit of a shock, because, you see, I had made up my mind that the reason why you had to stay was quite different. But I'll keep up, never fear. And though I don't think I shall ever forgive myself for letting you make that journey, we *know* and we'll fight the old devil and win. We can't make decisions until you've returned and seen a specialist; but we'll make the right one and win. Let me look at the best side of it. You might very well have tried to make the return journey alone; you might have been alone. No, from this day forth I'll forgive L.M. everything.

I swear to you that I'll not worry, that I'll feed myself, that nothing will happen to me about which you need worry in the least. And, Wig, if you in return aren't absolutely frank about money, you'll hurt our love. All that I've said about money was by way of objection to spending it on a L. M. caprice. Absolutely everything is in the service of our love, and if you don't treat it in this way, it's a crime.

I am writing in the office, and, as usual, people are continually disturbing me. I find it very hard to think straight. But all I really want to say is: Don't worry about me: I am as fit as a fiddle, and the worst that I can truly say is that I am lonely without you.

Then as for your story. Honestly & truthfully I was *not* disappointed. I was bowled out, utterly bowled out by it. Child, don't you know that I am a child? I was so passionately fond of the Mouse that it nearly broke my heart. I hadn't time to see it objectively. I haven't since then had time to read the story straight through from beginning to end and give you a critical, 'objective', judgement on it. Look here, you must see that what you call my disappointment – the word's true enough – was just my confession that you had done it – done it absolutely. My disappointment as a child was my satisfaction as an artist. Perhaps I didn't put this clearly: I can't have done. I was too much under the influence of my immediate emotions. But there it is. 'Sun & Moon' were really tinies. His tragedy would be put right. But Mouse & Dick, they were too much like us. If they had been exactly like it wouldn't have upset me because I know we're alright. But they were different, our brothers & sisters spiritually. D'you understand?

My eye is better. It's a kind of eyestrain, I think and I'll have to get some more glasses.

My precious darling – eat, eat. I love you beyond all that I can tell

Boge

[Hôtel Beau Rivage,
Bandol]

Thursday   [28 February 1918]

(I'll pay back these wires because it's not fair but they do make such a galumptious moment!)

My darling Heart

It's three o'clock; I've just finished this new story 'Bliss' and am sending it to you. But though my God! I *have* enjoyed writing it I am an absolute rag for the rest of the day and you must forgive no letter at all. I will write at length tomorrow. Oh, tell me what you think of *our* new story (that's quite sincere.) Please try and like it and I am now free to start another. One extraordinary thing has happened to me since I came over here! Once I start them they haunt me, pursue me and plague me until they are finished and as good as I can do.

You will again 'recognise' some of the people. *Eddie* of course is a fish out of the Garsington pond (which gives me joy) and Harry is touched with W.L.G[eorge]. Miss Fulton is 'my own invention' – oh you'll see for yourself.

No letter today. That's because of England's Sunday post. I'll get one tomorrow.

I walked to a little valley yesterday that I longed to show you. I sat on a warm stone there: all the almond flowers are gone but the trees are in new leaf and they were full of loving mating birds – quarrelling, you know about whether to turn the stair carpet under or to cut it off straight. And the trees were playing ball with a little breeze, tossing it to each other –

I sat a long time on my stone, then scratched your initials with a pin and came away – *loving* you. I am really spankingly well again and have absolutely NO NEED of any money. So don't you talk about it, but keep it tied up tight but use it for your darling eye. You can feel how I am wheeling this old letter along in a creaking barrow. My head is *gone*. I'll send a long one (letter not head). I love you beyond all measure and for ever and ever I am your own girl.

Wig.

[47 Redcliffe Road,
Fulham]
Tuesday. Mar 5. 11.20 [1918]

My own precious darling,
To-day came in the morning your Thursday letter; in the evening your Wednesday one & the story. Your letter I read while I was cooking my evening egg. It was wonderful. Surely, if one could look at them in a quite detached sort of way – I can't for the life of me – they must be absolute masterpieces of letters. When I read them I go hot and cold with a kind of intoxication of love and delight.

Now – I feel sure you won't forgive me, and yet I know you will – I'm not going to say much about your story; because what I should say now wouldn't be worth while. One can't write about your work jumping out of a railway train; and until Saturday when I shall have got Rousseau – curse him – off my chest, my mind is just like a clattering engine on the District Railway. Unless the skies fall, I shall have all Sunday to myself, and I intend to devote what part of it I am awake to saying slowly and carefully what I want to say not merely about 'Bliss' but about 'Je ne parle pas francais'. You mustn't be cross with me. I know you want to know what I think almost as much as I want to know what you think of my stuff. I don't know (really, don't know) whether what I've done is good until you tell me; and we're both the same. But I'd rather cut my hand off than say clumsy things in a desperate hurry. You see, I can criticise your work; I know all about it; it's as natural to me as breathing: but it's as hard to write what I think as to write a poem. I'm not satisfied if I do it with less singleness of heart, less leisure, & less *purity* than I must have to write a poem. If I say things hurriedly, they aren't true; you feel they aren't true and are disquieted, just as I should be, and just as you were over what I said of the second part of 'Je ne parle pas'. Therefore, though you may be disappointed, I shan't attempt to say anything till Sunday, more than what I shall say in my wire to-morrow: First Chop. But how they're first chop and the little bits where your pen seems to have trembled, all the things that will tell you what your criticisms tell me – all that I *must* leave till Sunday. When I say what I have to say, you have to feel that it is your very self judging your own work. I am your conscience in writing, just as you are mine. I can't bear to give you a superficial word. If I do I'm against us.

Don't think that while I've written all this, I might have written something about 'Bliss'. I couldn't have done it, just as I couldn't have written a poem; I have to be in a state of grace. And I can't be in a state of grace while every moment is till Saturday night when I go to bed parcelled out to the second.

I agree absolutely with what you say about 'Le P'tit' – the physical part, the cheat of the French words. But it seemed to be very interesting precisely because it showed what falsity a Frenchman who seems to have in himself something of the Tchehov spirit is condemned to by being French. Look for instance at the end of 'Nausicaa'. Something about 'the last time she ever wore the chemise of virginity'. It is so *utterly wrong* that there's nothing to be said. But in Ajalbert I felt the conflict between natural truth & Frenchness. They are not quite one. I feel as it were that I can get a knife in between the false and dirty & the true & pure; and I also felt that he must somehow be conscious of it, be ashamed of himself for his own concessions (whether to the Old Adam in himself or to his public I don't know – probably both). But there was *beauty*, snatches of real beauty, in the description & the vision of both those stories They reminded me of your work, very much. The sense of spring in 'Le P'tit' particularly. I felt these were stories you would have written as I would have them written. And I felt that I was judging them by the side of the real story by K.M.

So I have written criticism after all. But not the real stuff; you will have that, I warrant you, on Sunday.

My darling send me another letter like the one I had this evening to-morrow. My soul took wings. I lived in the Heron for a blissful moment. I am sure, absolutely sure, it will come. My God, we've waited long enough haven't we?

Je te baise
Boge.

[London]

[6 March 1918]

YOUR BLISS MINE

BOGE MURRY

[47 Redcliffe Road,
Fulham]
March 10 [1918]
Sunday Morning

My darling,
Everything went as I mapped it out. I finished Rousseau last night and, I think, it's pretty good. This morning I got up late, read 'Bliss' again after breakfast, shaved, and here I am. It's one o'clock already. I feel inclined to smile because of my good conscience. 'I said I'd do it and I did'.
Now about 'Bliss'. It's very, very good. Idea, proportion, lay-out, all are good. But there are one or two things about it – nothing to do with its essence – which don't seem to me quite right. They are only details, but they seem to me ever so slightly discordant. They are two. The first is that Eddie *Wangle* is not the right name. You are caricaturing by calling him that. And your story won't admit any caricature. They are preposterous people, the Norman Knights & Eddie, but they are real. You mustn't do more than show you are *aware* of their preposterousness. You mustn't be laughing at, or angry about, it. Do you see what I mean when I say that Norman Knight is exquisitely right as a name, & Eddie *Wangle* wrong? It is a Dickens touch & you're not Dickens – you're Tchehov – more than Tchehov.
Secondly. You put a number of phrases in inverted commas. For instance. 'These last she had bought to "*tone in*" '. 'She only wanted to get "in touch" with him'. Now, I think I know perfectly what you are after. Bertha is a soul with exquisite perceptions & exquisite demands on life, which she doesn't know how to express. She is a kind of artist manqué – artist in our big sense of the word. Now that's damned hard to express in the particular, I can see. I can also see that you can't just drop the inverted commas. I also see that her clumsy phrases are at the heart of her. But I think that, being what she is, she would avoid the phrases and, however impatiently, prefer her own dumbness. 'These last she had bought

... for the sake of the new drawing room carpet. Yes, that did sound rather far-fetched ...' 'What had she to say? She'd nothing to say. She only wanted ... She couldn't absurdly cry: "Hasn't it been a divine afternoon?" ' Do you see what I am driving at? It's always for the same kind of thing that you use the inverted commas, when Bertha is trying to express more perfect satisfaction or communion. For instance again about Pearl Fulton. 'The provoking thing was that though they had been about together and met a number of times and really *"talked"*.' 'Harry & she were as much in love as ever and they got on together splendidly and were really good *"pals"*.'

You see, Bertha is not actually talking. If she were she would probably have to use the words. But she is thinking – and in *her thought* she would refuse them.

I don't know whether I'm right. The thing seems to be so tenuous that it slips away under my pen. I would like to know, very much, *very much indeed*, what you think. For at moments I fear that I am becoming super-subtle.

Now, once more, the story is beautiful. I mean absolutely no more than to say that to my ear its perfection is marred by two discords, ever so slight. In worrying about them to find what the reason of them was, I may have made a mistake. My explanation may be wrong, tho' I don't think so. But that's unimportant. The question is whether your ear tells you the same thing as mine. I feel sure it must. I feel that when I am working and in the excitement of the work my ear becomes for the moment dulled, yours remains perfectly sensitive: I feel that I am the same with your work. But write to me immediately & tell me. These correspondences of ours have given me such unlimited confidence: I want to know definitely whether I am in any way presuming upon them.

I got your Wednesday letter last night. It's no use talking about these identities of ours. I have now not the slightest doubt (seriously) that we are manifestations of the same being. One might be a coincidence, two might be; but ever since the Heron began, we have gone on and on. Don't think me mystical if I explain it like this. The night when we *discussed the Heron together*, We became one being. The quality of that evening I shall always remember; and with these correspondences it recurs to me again & again. I feel certain that what I say is true. We became one being and this one being expressed itself that night in the Heron. Therefore the Heron is more than the symbol of our love; it is the artistic creation of our one being. From that night on we have been fused in soul, so that our correspondences now seem to me the most natural & inevitable thing in the world. Now, I am perfectly aware that if I were to say this to anyone else but you they would think me raving. But to me it is simple truth, simple truth in exactly the same way as 2 + 2 = 4. Everything now conspires to tell me that I am right. You will see from this Rousseau article when it appears – that Rousseau was of the same kind as us. What I have written about him seems to be luminously simple; but it is *all new*. No-one has had the faintest idea of what I have discovered about him before. And I feel certain that we shall find, in just the same way, the secret of all the great men we love. No-one else can understand them except us – no-one else at all. And when we go away from the world to the Heron we shall discover the secret of them all, have them dwelling with us like friends. Sometimes now I begin to think tremulously *high* thoughts, thoughts that make me dizzy. Suddenly, I seem to know the secret of the universe. And this at least I know, beyond all doubt, that I know the way to the secret and that my life will be spent in trying to make the pathway clear. I know this, too, that you and I are *geniuses*. I didn't know it before the real meaning of the Heron began to dawn upon me as it has lately done. You saw that into your work and mine a new strong wind of *power* had come. I didn't know *why* it had come: – Why we two, at the moment when we seemed more frail than all other creatures of the earth, should become suddenly *strong winged in the spirit*. Now, I begin to see. What I said about the Heron just now is part of the explanation. But behind that I feel there is a bigger explanation still. You and I are manifestations of the same being, yes, but that same being is also a manifestation. I feel I am on the way to discovering of what.

I have bought Lamb. I opened it *at random*. I opened it at a letter he wrote about Coleridge & Wordsworth's *Lyrical Ballads* when they first came out. I've marked the place with a piece of paper and I'm going to send you the volume to-morrow, so that you can see exactly how deep my sense is that our life has passed out of our hands. You will understand.

I'm sorry about your being tormented by Geoffroi. People are no use, no use at all. Try to save yourself. I was glad of those postcards of les Charmettes, though. Was that too just an accident? You can't buy them in Bandol, can you? I would like to know because I want to keep a record of these 'coincidences'. You see it makes me feel rather queer when just as I am on the last page of my Rousseau article which has as many *seeds* of discovery as Dostoevsky, I get your letter saying that mine about Ben Jonson, the Elizabethans & Keats reached you the day after you had written to me, and *in the same letter* a collection of pictures of the place that really made Rousseau what he was!

Another thing, if any of my letters are alive still, will you keep them? I have all yours – and I think they may be important to us one day.

At the end of this week I'm going to send you £5. It may come in useful. One can't have too much money on a journey – and if you don't use it, it don't matter.

I didn't write to you yesterday. I thought that one long one was better than two shorts. I shall post this one this afternoon, so that I shan't have one to post to-morrow morning. There's been a fog this morning, but now the sun is up (2.30) and the sky clear, so I shall, when I have prepared my casseroles, trundle out.

My Wig – you're coming back!

Boge

[Hôtel Beau Rivage,
Bandol]

Thursday. [14 March 1918]

My Precious

I have just received your *Sunday* letter. It was very noble of you to do as you did and so beautifully keep your promise about my story. You're, of course, absolutely right about 'Wangle'. He shall be resprinkled mit leichtern Fingern, and I'm with you about the commas. What I *meant* (I hope it don't sound highfalutin) was, Bertha, not being an artist, was yet artist manqué enough to realise that those words and expressions were not & couldn't be hers – They were, as it were *quoted* by her, borrowed with ... an eyebrow ... Yet she'd none of her own ... But this I agree is not permissible – I can't grant all that in my dear reader. It's very exquisite of you to understand so *nearly* –

You know (seriously) I don't feel as though I have really written anything until you have passed your judgment – just as I should never feel that I had had a child, even though it were there & screwing up its fists at me until you had held it and said 'yes it's a good kid.' Without *that* I am just in a state of 'attente' – you understand.

I have, of course, kept all of your letters ever since my arrival here, knowing that they will be of use to us one day –

All that you write of the *Heron* and of our 'departure' is so true and clear to me that I can only look at you & smile & say 'yes Bogey'. You see – the Heron is the Miracle ... I can't write about it today. Very soon we shall talk – for ever – and as we talk we shall become more and more at peace and wisdom from on High shall descend upon us –

I hope Lamb arrives in time to go home with me as fellow traveller. (I will make a corner for him so that he shall come to no harm.) And I *don't want* the £5 dearest love. However, if you send it I shall just keep it. I heard from Cooks this morning. There is evidently great difficulty in getting places on the Marseilles–Paris rapide. But otherwise all seems more or less plain – I think I shall leave the middle of *next week*. Though I write that I don't feel it – Somehow a curious *numbness* is beginning in me about this journey – or a sort of feeling that it is all going to take place in the pitch dark – with no thought of place or time – Rib must be a little crusader & sit with his feet crossed 'for luck' all the while I cross the Channel. I am still terrified of that part of the journey – I keep thinking myself into a little boat with a bundle or not a bundle on my lap and the cold sea water round us – & you & the Heron you & the Heron – all my solid earth and all my Heaven far away. But it's silly of Wig. It's a gay sunny day and the tamarisk trees are *blowing* into leaf. Tomorrow I half expect an answer to my telegram – Did it surprise you awfully ...

> Goodbye shipmate
> Wig.

[Hôtel Beau Rivage,
Bandol]

Saturday. (No letter today)   [16 March 1918]

Dear Love

I must tell you just how matters stand and you must help me please, if you can. L.M. saw the Consul at Marseilles yesterday. *She* can return without any trouble but my telegram re Mother will not do at all. It appears that everyone who came to the Riviera 'for fun' this year has been recalled by the same sort of thing and the French authorities will not allow it. It is absolutely insufficient. What I have to do is to *write* to the authorities at Bedford Square asking their permission to return before my time is up i.e. before the END of April. They, having looked into my reasons, communicate with the Consul at Marseilles and either grant me a permit or do not grant me one. The Consul at Marseilles says he has *no power over the matter at all.* So this you see will take a most confounded time and I have had to cancel my wire of yesterday by sending you another today – I am, as well, *extremely* anxious not to travel without L.M. as she'd be such a help to me on the journey.

My plans then are as follows: I shall endeavour to obtain from the English doctor here a chit to the effect that it is no longer advisable for me to remain on this coast and then, if I have to go to England it *is* necessary for me to have a companion. As L. M. is practically forced to return *now* that means I'd have to be let through with her. This 'chit' he may or may not give me. I can't see him until tomorrow afternoon (such is the press of illness at Bandol) and then it depends very much in what mood the man is – He is so exceedingly shady and suspicious that he may have a lively fear of signing his name to anything; on the other hand he may do it just for that reason. If he *won't* I'll write to Bedford Square & state this same case and I thought I might also plead that I wish to remarry on the 7th of April & wish to return to make preparations. I can't *tell* whether that is wise or not. I'd give anything for your advice on that point. Indeed I really think I will not mention this marriage until t'other has failed. If I can reinforce my plea with the chit I think there will be no difficulty, otherwise there will be ... L. M. of course, will stay for the present and as long as anything is unsettled she will stay – Yes, I am now brought so low as to be thankful.

It is all very vile and unlooked for. This new 'strictness' has only been established during the last fortnight on account of all the false reasons people have given. I do not think I *could* wait here for another whole month – I mean – until May. The idea almost frightens me. I feel there is a plot to keep us apart – & then *our marriage* – – –

I suppose you can do nothing from your side – *influence* nobody – ask nobody? In case you can I give you the number of my passport 177256. You see dearest Bogey, I write in this *numb dumb* way, because at present I know nothing & the idea that the war can do *this* in addition to all it has done to us *strikes* me and lays me low for the moment. I'll get up again. I'm only speaking 'spiritually' but at present, after I had packed & taken my tickets (*transferable*)

I should cry if I wrote any more. I feel I can't *bear* this absence a great deal longer – & yet – – – they *will* torture me. If any change occurs I will wire you and do you wire me if you can think of anything I ought to do or anything that *can* be done. What about that friend of Pierre MacOrlan? Any use? I sit thinking & thinking. Curse this doctor – he's either the victim of a big bottle or a little 'un & not fit to be seen today – & he's the only person who can help – a little sot with poached eyes who bites his fingers.

No, we must comfort and sustain each other a *great deal.* Comfort me! Put your arms round me! It's raining here, too & the rain is all over my floor & it's blowing & cold & I feel so *far* so *far* and oh how my homesick heart *faints* for you & you only – Love me

Wig.

But harder to bear than anything is *your* disappointment. That's what hurts – oh! like sin!

Marseilles Monday.
Café de Noailles
[18 March 1918]

Dearest,

Everything seems changed – My whole life is *uprooted* and this calm of living in Bandol & even with the G[eoffroi]s and L. M. feels like *calm* compared to this violent battle. I arrived here, very late this evening, too late for the Consul or for Cooks: the train was 2 hours en retard. And so I got a room at the Hotel de Russie, had some food and here I am. I must bring you up to date with this Battle of the Wig. Last night after I wrote you I felt desperate & sent L. M. after Doctor Poached Eyes. Even though it really was rather late. He was at dinner – fatal time! but promised to turn up. Whereupon I set to – turned L. M. out of my room – dressed in my red frock & a black swanny round my neck, *made* up – drew chairs to the fire – & waited for this little toad. If you could have come in you would have been horribly shocked I think. I have not felt so cynical for years – I knew my man & I determined to get him by the only weapon I could – & that *he* could understand. He came, far more than 3 parts on – and I sat down & played the old game with him – listened – looked – smoked his cigarettes – and asked finally for a chit that would satisfy the consul. He gave me the chit but whether it will I'll not know till tomorrow. It could not be more urgent in its way – I dictated it & had to spell it <u>&</u> lean over him as he wrote <u>&</u> hear him say – what dirty hogs do say – I am sure he is here because he has killed some poor girl with a dirty buttonhook – He is a maniac on *venereal* diseases & *passion* – Ah, the filthy little brute! There I sat and smiled & let him talk. I was determined to get him for our purpose, any way that didn't involve letting him touch me. He could say what he liked: I laughed and spelled – and was so sweet and soft & so *obliged*. Even if this chit fails I think he can get me through in other ways – He has, for all this shadiness, a good deal of very useful influence in high quarters in Marseilles & Toulon – & it's all at my disposal. So I'll use it.

Oh dear oh dear! I feel so strange. An old dead sad wretched self blows about – whirls about in my feverish brain – & I sit here in this café – drinking & looking at the mirrors & smoking and thinking how utterly corrupt life is – how hideous human beings are – how loathsome it was to catch this toad as I did – with *such* a weapon – I keep hearing him say, very thick 'any trouble is a pleasure for a lovely woman' & seeing my *soft smile* ... I am very sick, Bogey.

Marseilles is so hot and loud – They scream the newspapers and all the shops seem full of caged birds – parrots & canaries – shrieking too – And old hags sell nuts & oranges – & I run up & down *on fire* – Anything – anything to get home! – It all spins like a feverish dream. I am not *un*happy or happy. I am just as it were in the thick of a bombardment – writing you, here, from a *front* line trench. I do remember that the fruit trees on the way were all in flower & there were such big daisies in the grass & a little baby smiled at me in the train – But nothing matters until I have seen the Consul. I am staying tonight at the Hotel de Russie. It is clean and good. I have *Elle & Lui* to read – But this is all a dream you see. I want to come home – to come home – Tomorrow I'll wire you after I've seen the man. Under it – above it – through it I am yours – fighting & tired but yours for ever

Wig.

[47 Redcliffe Road,
Fulham]
Tuesday Night. 8.20.   [19 March 1918]

My own darling precious child,
     The letter that I somehow *dreaded* came to-day – to-night – the
one you sent on Saturday when L.M. had returned. I'm like you
now: it only takes a straw to knock me down, and this is a sledge
hammer. I will see Sydney Waterlow to-morrow in case he knows
some-one at the Foreign Office who can help; and I'll wire the
result.
     Didn't you say that doctor said that not only you ought not stay
down there, but that you ought to come home and see a big man in
London as soon as you were fit to travel? Won't the devil write that
on a bit of paper. Surely that would get you through! But, since I
haven't had any telegram, it looks as though he wouldn't give you
the 'chit'. I calculate that since you couldn't see him the day you
wrote, you would have seen him on Saturday. If he had given it you
would have wired. Or would you have sent L.M. back to the
Consulate first to see if it was all right. In that case she couldn't go
until Monday and I might very well not get a wire till to-morrow,
Wednesday. That's how my mind is running.
     Who else could I see except Sydney? That friend of Pierre
MacAlan's – curse it – I have completely forgotten his name. Like a
fool, I never made a note of it. I shall write to Chaddie to-night. She
may possibly know some military fellow who has something to do
with the French Military Permit Office. If anything at all comes into
my mind – which is a whirling, aching blank – I'll do it and wire.
     I am trying hard to pull myself together. My disappointment
hurts you and your disappointment tortures me. We mustn't. It's no
use thinking about each other's disappointment; I feel if I went on
thinking about yours very long my mind would certainly snap. It's
very rickety. O my own wig, my arms are tight round you – if only
they were strong arms, and if only they could pull you nearer
somehow.
     And I am absolutely tongue-tied – like you numb and dumb.
When you need it most, I can't express my love. It all ties up into a
hard choking ball inside me: and my letter grows cold. If I could
only make it warm.
     Whatever happens, don't let L. M. leave without you *under any
circumstances*. If you try the marriage reason, try it last of all. The
medical is the one. Surely that doctor will repeat what he said – that

you ought to see a specialist in London?

Wig, I'll turn every stone I know how: but I feel very helpless just at this moment. I'll have to wait till to-morrow for a ray of hope from this side. Till then I'll just pray that something good has happened.

And to all this is added the fact that I am haunted by the thought that I didn't write to you from Wednesday until Sunday. Just when you will have needed letters most. Forgive me, Wig, a week ago I was dancing with delight at the thought of your return.

Your most loving, wretched Boge.

Café de France,
rue Cannebière,
Marseilles
Bulletin du Front: 19 ième [March] 1918

I advanced to the consul and gained a local success, taking the trench as far as Paris. I expect to advance again under cover of *gas* on Saturday. The enemy is in great strength but the morale of the Wig is excellent. Please explain this to Ribni & make him salute.

Dearest of all

Well as far as I know the 'wangle' has succeeded. At any rate I have leave to go as far as Paris & try my luck there – and I don't think – having got so far & pleading as I shall – they can withhold their consent to my going further – Especially as L. M. (lunatic attendant) has permission. The Consul here was *not* agreeable about the affair – but whether that was just a formality or not I don't know – I rather think it was. After having been there I went to the police – & had my passeport viséd again & then to Cooks to take the ticket. It is still a divine day, a sort of *anguishing* beauty of spring – wonder if you know what I mean. I mean something so definite – I have bought myself a bottil of genet fleuri (which I can't afford) so that I shall be a little perfumed bride (*if* I get back). I think I shall today. Oh, how much I could tell you. I have lived through lives & lives since I last wrote to you in calm – That night at the hotel – par exemple – but *that* I have written at four oclock this morning. It's pretty good I think – this city seems to me to be stranger & stranger. Does one always have fever here? And are these things here to be seen or are they all 'dreams' – Birds on the trees – so big – so fat – flowers to sell, lovelier and more

poisonous-looking than flowers could be, & the beggars – who are
like the beggars of the 14 Century (Wig that is swank) and then the
blacks & the women with white faces and pale pale gold hair & red
dresses & little tiny feet – Women – who seem themselves to be a
sort of *VICE.* L. M. has of course just been like an immense baby
without a perambulator. I have carried her everywhere, paid for
her, ordered for her, arranged for her bath – showed her the cabinet
– & answered all the questions that my grandmother used to ask
my father when *she* came from Picton to gay, wild, evil Wellington.
I go back this evening, pack tomorrow & leave by the early
Thursday train. In Paris on Friday – start for Havre Saturday (all
being well) & I suppose at that rate England on Tuesday – or
perhaps Monday. But that is still dark. At any rate the lighthouse
throws a beam as far as Paris. Oh, my *lean* purse. Its *bones* – its
stringiness. But all is well – I am so full of black coffee that if you
see at the station a dark copper-coloured little Wig don't despise
her – Now I must go back to the trenches & go over the top to the
station – Goodbye – breathlessly with all my loving heart.

Wig.

[Paris]
[22 March 1918]

KEPT PARIS TEN DAYS ADDRESS COOKS DONT NEED
MONEY FONDEST LOVE BOWDEN

[47 Redcliffe Road,
Fulham]
[23 March 1918]
Saturday Morning

My darling,
    I got your wire saying you were held up in Paris for ten days just
before I started to the office this morning, where I have just arrived.
It seems as though the stars in their courses are fighting against us;
but they won't win. But when, after all you have gone through, the
German offensive begins on the very day you start for Paris – it's
hard to be reconciled. Still, I feel that you are ever so much nearer in
Paris: and though the ten days are hard, I feel that you are almost

within reach. When I have finished this short note, I'm going out to telegraph to you. You say you don't want any money: I am just putting three pound notes in this letter which may do as a tiny reserve. But I've got money; so please do wire me if you'd like any, and don't let things get so low as they did before I sent the fiver.

The Colonel's given me a week's leave from next Friday onwards. If you could only get back at the next week end, we should have nearly a week together without the old office!

O lord, lord, my own wonderful darling, I can't write at all any more. Mind you, I don't worry any thing like so much now you are in Paris. But I am now so impatient for the happiness of seeing you, that I can't write anything coherent at all. I try to kill the hours in the evening by writing poetry; but it's very hard. I send you something I wrote the night before last.

Why do you have to wait the ten days? I mean is it because of the trains or because you have to apply to the Military Permit Office in London. Sydney Waterlow has written about you to the head of the military section of the M.P.O., Colonel Danielson; so that, if the second is the reason, it should go through quickly. But I have an idea that it's the offensive & the trains, particularly as your telegram says nothing about passport difficulties.

Wig, I love you.

Boge.

[Select Hôtel,
Paris]
Thursday.   [28 March 1918]

Darling Heart

Three letters came from you today. 2 Saturdays & 1 Sunday; one of the letters had £3 in it. I have received no wire at all. This is the first news. Upon getting it I wired you, rather at length: because my letters have been depressed and I wanted to get near you if I could a bit quickly. But they say at the 'poste' there are at least 48 hours delay for telegrams in England – so God knows when this will arrive. *I do not want any money at all.* Please keep this secret. Mother sent me some money to make myself a lovely girl the day I was married, but she said I was not even to tell Chaddie, as it was her 'secret funds'. This money I am spending and it will see me and the mountain through. That is provided we are allowed to leave

France – One can't say anything for certain with this battle raging and the whole infernal upset – here and everywhere. I have lost confidence for some ghastly reason. I go on, do all there is to do, make all possible efforts, but my heart don't pay any heed. *It's gone quite dead.* I feel I suffered and hoped & tried to pull through unendurably before the moment. Now the snail simply can't put out its horns again for the moment. It will of course – mais – – – And topping it all this long *inevitable* wait for letters – – – And this great half-idiot woman at my heels always with 'Katie what shall we do now?' ... God what Hell one does live through!

The Military Permit people although they will not let me through without having heard from Bedford Square are not the Great Brick. It's the police.

Any person who stays longer than 48 hours in Paris must obtain a permit to leave France – This sauf conduit takes from 8 to 10 days to obtain – & is, even then, uncertain – as to one day or another. Have you had any dealings with the French police? They are like the Russian police rather in D[ostoevsky]'s books. I don't want to discuss them here – I went again to the office yesterday, but they laughed in my face at the idea of my getting a permit sooner. In fact my anxiety seemed to amuse & delight them so much – and the fact that I was *une anglaise* in a predicament that I did my case no good, I fear.

I hope Sydney's man helps; it sounded a good idea. I was infinitely relieved to have letters from you after so very long, dearest – and the lovely little poem – But I can't help it. To be sincere, j'ai très fatiguée aujourd'hui. Nothing serious – only I am *tired out* and everything seems so far away – As though you were in London & I were passing Cape Horn.

You won't send me any money – will you? I have 300 francs. That is enough to pay both our bills, HER food etc. – all the extra booking expenses. I've worked it all out.

Here is an Easter card for Rib. *He* mustn't be a sad one: he's my brave little boy who looks through his telescope every morning & comes down & blows in it & shakes it out as though it were a trumpet & says: 'I think I can see something ...'

> Goodbye darling –
> Wig.

If you were not there, I'd really die, you know. I only live, I think, *with you*. Without you I'd give up.

[Paris]
[29 March 1918]

CIVILIAN TRAFFIC SUSPENDED ASK KAY SEND APRIL
ALLOWANCE COOKS

ALL WELL LOVE BOWDEN

[47 Redcliffe Road,
Fulham]
[1 April 1918]
Monday Night

My darling, my precious,
I have just had your *Tuesday* & Thursday letters.
I must pull myself together. For our sake, my mouse, try to
believe I am holding you in my arms. My heart, too, seems to be
numb; and something goes on weeping, weeping inside me. If I
thought of what has happened to us – how you have been caught
and our love *tortured*, deliberately, foully tortured – I think I
should go clean mad.
I don't know how to comfort you, just as I can't comfort myself. I
tried on the strength of your wire to believe there was some chance
that you might be allowed to start on Tuesday, to-morrow. But
your Thursday letter has killed that hope dead. What, in God's
name, is there to hold on to? Every time that our hope, our love
stretches out to something, even only a tiny happiness, the black
thing descends & withers it.
Yesterday was a slow Hell. To-day I have been to the office;
Somehow it's better there. But even yesterday, something was alive
in me still. I had managed to deceive myself with your telegram.
And Rib spent all the day fanning my spark of hope into a flame.
Yes, I must tell you about Rib. At any rate it's better than going
on about my own despair. He was wonderful yesterday. His hair
was all towsled somehow and he was perched on top of the
cushions in some queer way, that made him look *as though he had
just been born.* Yes, that's it, – as though he had just popped up
from somewhere where he had been asleep, in a sunflower perhaps.
And I felt – I tried to call myself a fool & to suppress it – that
something had whispered to him that you were coming. *For the first
time* he looked as though you really were on your way. And,
somehow, in spite of myself I believed it.

Yes, and even now – I just went over & had a long look at him – I do somewhere in me believe it. I can't help having faith in Rib. He's waiting and watching , for sure. I can't be mistaken.

No, it's useless to try to go on convincing one's self: besides the disappointment's so bitter.

Oh, my child, I daren't try to express my heart; it would frighten you, it's so sad. The hopelessness of your Thursday letter has frozen it up. Still, though to-morrow will be another hell, I'm glad I'm not going to the office. I couldn't bear to be with all those people: much rather be with my dull, aching, worn out old heart alone. The office is only a drug. And I don't want drugs.

Perhaps there may be a letter from you to-morrow giving me a tiny thread of hope to build on again. If only I didn't feel so bitter with myself for deceiving me, for letting me deceive myself. I can't even express my love. It's as though it were choking

Oh, Wig, my mouse, my secret soul: you are there suffering and I am dead without you. Surely, life can't be so awful as not to bring us together again quickly now. It's getting desperate. I feel that I had come to the top of the water for the last time. Of course, it won't be the last. Just as I never come to the end of my despair, I shan't come to the end of my hope either. Boge (smaller than that)

[Café Mahieu,
Paris]

Tuesday.   [2 April 1918]

My darling Heart

No letter again today but I hardly expected one – I mean by that I knew that the English post would be disorganised for Easter – Tomorrow, perhaps I shall have 2 at least – That's what I look for today.

Since yesterday the 'lutte' as they say has continued – Gunfire last evening – and at 3.15 this morning one woke to hear the air *screaming*. That's the effect of these sirens; they have a most diabolical sound. I dressed and went down to the Caves – Everybody else was there – the place was packed with hideous humanity. *So* hideous indeed that one felt a bomb on them wouldn't perhaps be as cruel after all. I don't think I can go to the caves again – The cold and agony of those stone dusty steps & these filthy people *smoking* in that air – I crept back to bed & to sleep & woke to a perfect deafening roar of gunfire. It was followed by the sound of people running in the streets. I got up again & went to look. Very ugly, very horrible. The whole top of a house as it were bitten out – all the windows broken – and the road of course, covered with ruin. There were trees on both sides of the street & these had just come into their new green. A great many branches were broken but on the others strange bits of clothes and paper hung. A nightdress – a chemise – a tie – they looked extraordinarily pitiful dangling in the sunny light. One thing which confirms me again in my dreadful feeling that I live wherever I am in another Sodom & Gomorrah – – This. Two workmen arrived to clear away the debris. One found, under the dust, a woman's silk petticoat. He put it on & danced a step or two for the laughing crowd – – – That filled me with such horror that I'll never never get out of my mind the fling of his feet & his grin and the broken trees and the broken house.

I have just posted you a book – because of the pages about Dostoievsky. The woman, Sonia Kovalevsky, is awfully nice; her friend Anna is a b—ch, I think. But perhaps that is because I can't stand women, Bogey – who 'pretend' to friendship.

I am writing to you in the Café Mahieu. It is a divine, warm day. I keep thinking & thinking only of you – my darling – & wishing & wishing – you know what. I went to Cooks this morning. The man seemed to think the boats would start again at the end of this week – but no, I don't dare to hope until I have been to the M.P.O. tomorrow.

On my way here I fell in with an accident. A man on the pavement said he had broken his ankle. A large crowd collected, but nobody believed him. Two policemen nearly *swore* him away – but as he groaned & sweated a great deal they decided to take off his boot & sock & see. After *pulling off* the boot I said – 'cut the sock, don't drag it' – & really it is just a fluke I wasn't arrested. You should have heard the 'taisez-vous' that was flung at me & the rest. So they pulled it off, and the ankle was all broken. His whole foot was at right angles, pale green in colour with black nails. 'When did you do it' they asked him & the fool said 'pas aujourd'hui'. At that the whole crowd began to laugh, looked at the foot & laughed – He had evidently been going about for days with this foot & I should think it will have to be amputated – But God what a joke it was for these Parisians!

Bogey, the dreadful beauty of this spring terrifies me – and Bogey darling Heart I keep wondering if your holiday is begun. Where are you? Have you seen any flowers or bees? What can I say? Nothing

except that I am far from my own & all else doesn't matter –
Perhaps tomorrow – that is my only cry – Tomorrow – tomorrow –
Oh please don't give me up – & don't shut your heart to me.
Keep it very warm & ready won't you – *My heart* is such a frail one
now. It beats so fast if I look at the letter rack & hardly beats at all
when I look away –

God help us.

> Your own
> Wig.
> who loves you *terribly*.

> 47 [Redcliffe Road
> Fulham]
> [3 April 1918]
> Wednesday afternoon

Kay said he had instructed Cooks about yr. money.

My precious darling,

Today I went to see Chaddie, and after that I went on to Kay to
see if he could do anything. He was decent and he promised to send
a private letter to the High Commissioner immediately. Of
course, I know that nothing can be done so long as all civilian
traffic is suspended; but I can't help thinking that it won't at any
rate do any harm, if we can get someone to put in a word – You see,
I'm frightened lest, when the civilian traffic does begin again, only
people with influence will be allowed to get on the train.

Kay having promised to do that has made me feel a bit more
hopeful, put forth a very very tender bud. If a raw wind nips it
again, I don't know what I shall do. Then, there's that ominous
remark they made to you at the Consulate, that 8 days suspension
of traffic seemed optimistic. But I have to believe in the 8 days as I
believed in the 10 days before, simply because I can no other. My
faith is pinned on the 17th now. It must be that you will be here a
fortnight to-day.

I spent the second day of my *holiday* wandering about London
trying to kill the time between seeing Chaddie at 12.30 and seeing
Kay at 3.15. I wandered up and down Tottenham Court Road and
felt that all that I saw was a dream in a fever. The sun was shining,
though when I went out in the morning there was a fog. I looked in
shop after shop, and prayed for the Heron. I can't remember a

single thing. The whole of London seems to be made up of dirty cardboard. Some-one has merely to touch it in the right place and it will all fall flat to the ground. I feel terribly hungry for real things – trees, and a solid oak-floor, copper pans thick as shell-cases. All the strong, solid things are being devoured by the war, and only the shams are left. And among all these shams, one pines away, and my blood seems to get thin. Together, we were strong enough to battle through. Without you, I have absolutely nothing to fall back upon. I can almost believe that my imagination is only a queer unreal fever; it is so far divorced from the earth where its roots should be, like one of those freak flowers that grow when they plant the seed in the darkness and it makes its painful way ever so far to a little speck of light where it breaks into a too fragile blossom. I want to be a stout rose or an apple; I don't want to be anything orchidageous. In other words, being parted from you, I use literature as a drug, and now, at the crisis, I feel that I have taken too many tabloids. A sense of emptiness hangs over me.

Of course, the real reason is that the disappointment of your not coming has been just like a sudden fall, stepping on nothing. It will all disappear like the mist the moment you come. No, Rib was quite right: I did wrong to let you go. But whereas for one or two days lately I felt that we were being washed apart again after our finger-tips had touched, to-day I feel that we are creeping nearer. It's too slow – oh God, how slow. But we are coming nearer. And to feel that is something after these last despairs.

My mouse, be sure all day long that Rib & Boge are watching and waiting.

[Select Hôtel,
Paris]

Saturday Night –   [6 April 1918]

Precious, dearest, darling Heart

I am so hopeful tonight. Two letters have come from you today – one written on Tuesday evening & one on Wednesday afternoon – & they bring you so ... tremblingly near. I had a phone message from Sydney's man at the Embassy today, too, went to see him & he said that I would *definitely* get across on Wednesday – He gave me a card to the M.P.O. telling them that it was *urgent* I should go (he was a great ponce). And the M.P.O. still say that a boat will go on Wednesday – though Cooks say it is most uncertain. I think it is absurd *not* to regard it as uncertain – for it is a race between Wednesday & this second battle – and those vile Germans are still marching on. But everybody & every tree & every person & every breath seems now to *incline* towards Wednesday – If that again is just a big black hole & again there comes the uncertainty – and the waiting I don't know what I *shall do*. I am glad Kay was decent. Kiss your darling little Mummy for me – I am so glad that I am going to be her real daughter-in-law. & oh how I want to see the little brother again – the dear lad. But all these things come after.

First of all there is just YOU. L. M. has just lifted 150 off me: she can't help it & it's alright of course – I've plenty & she'll pay me back but I wish she was not dead drunk as a result of one dubonnet. She is – & can only (as she says) 'giggle' … If you knew – – –

The bombardment has gone on again today & it's 8.30. I've had news. I'd better get back as soon as possible – But there is still a good quarter of an hour. I haven't had any *bread* since this new rule came in. I do want a crust – As to butter it don't exist.

Do you know IF I ever do get back it will be just a week before our wedding – & your mother must ask us to tea (we'll say it's the anniversary for she must *never* know) & we'll take her flowers – lovely ones – & be very gay children – Shall we? – Shall we? Is it all before us? Not all swept away?

I spend my nights now playing Demon patience. I sit up-in bed & play & play. This morning at 3 oclock a mouse jumped into my waste paper basket & began to squeak –

But I can hardly tell you these things. Wednesday begins to more than loom – Again I think – I must take him back a peppermill – & another of those red & green cups & saucers. God! If ever I do get back then I feel our trial will be over for ever.

But the German army & the big gun & the raids and all this vast horror still rolls between.

Bogey – hope *for* me – I've been so tortured that I must have someone to *help* me *hope*. Your letters are my salvation – but that – you know.

　　Your own Wig.

[47 Redcliffe Road,
Fulham]
[8 April 1918]
Monday Night

My darling,
To-night I had your Saturday letter saying you had got *one* of mine.

But, even more wonderful, I had a reply from Sydney enclosing the actual letter sent him by his man, Joseph Addison, of the Paris Embassy.

He said that you would be allowed to travel by the Wednesday boat. From the way he put it, that can only mean that you will be allowed to go on Wednesday *in any case*, whether the boat is nominally for civilians or not.

Well, I'm not going to write any more, first because I'm too overcome by the news; second, because you'll never get it, that's certain; third, because I expect a wire from you to-morrow.

But, darling, if you should by any chance get this – it's to say Rib and I are at the window again, thank God.

Boge.

Bar Monaco.
[Paris]
[9 April 1918]
Tuesday.

Dearest Love
I am simply *desperate*. I had your two wires today – one at the hotel & one at Cooks – but you can never have got a wire I sent immediately after my Friday letter saying *let's hope on it's all the best*. No you can't have got it. And there is a letter from you today referring to things I know nothing of – that you have already written about. This letter was written on Friday: it's the one about the letter press. Oh Bogey, will it never end? I have spent the day *rushing* from the police to the police – Now it all seems nearly finished & I've only to pack & try & get back tomorrow. I keep on writing – you know why – & now of course it's in case the boat is submarined. I think I should keep on writing even under the sea ... Yes, of course I should. I have bought 2 quarts of butter – and am going to try to bring them – but that's all I can afford cette fois ...

We leave at 7 tomorrow. You know that, though. I am speechless with anxiety & hope. I will write to you in Havre tomorrow, darling, more leisurely.

Oh God this Friday letter has something of you in it which carries me straight into your heart – It's a letter so like you – Oh my darling heart I do love you so – & I too am terribly timidly just beginning to think of a bud of hope. Ever so tiny a one.

I have simply everything to tell you – everything & I can't help today – telephoning – endlessly – 'Put me through to Mr Middleton Murry. Is that you Boge?' And then I can't say any more – Can you think what I feel like – my treasure? My courage is just about mouse high – & I am nobody but your tiny timid loving

Mouse –

Give the worm a kiss & show him my new passport photograph.

[Southampton]
[11 April 1918]

ARRIVE WATERLOO ABOUT 11.30 THIS MORNING.

TIG

May–June
1918

Katherine Mansfield arrived back in London on 11 April 1918, a shadow of her former self. Nevertheless, on 3 May, her divorce from George Bowden now absolute, she and Murry were finally married. But they had little to celebrate. Murry's dark rooms at 47 Redcliffe Road were no place for a sick woman, and he, already overburdened by his work at the War Office, was in no position to look after her. Reluctantly, Katherine agreed to go to the Headland Hotel in Looe, Cornwall, where her friend Anne Estelle Drey (née Rice) was now living. In the meantime, Murry negotiated the lease and redecoration of a house in Hampstead that they called 'The Elephant'.

Katherine's letters from Looe reflect her attempt to accept the fact that she was now in the grip of an incurable illness. Murry, in his turn, struggled to cope with his wife's black moods as well as the pressures of work that brought him to the edge of a nervous breakdown. After five weeks apart, he was finally able to join her in Looe for ten days' holiday. They returned to London together, having agreed that Katherine should not enter a sanatorium but instead try a 'cure' at home.

[Looe]
[17 May 1918]

SUPERB ARRIVAL EVERYTHING SIMPLY SPLENDID HEAD-LAND HOTEL

FONDEST LOVE WIG

148

47 [Redcliffe Road,
Fulham.]
[17 May 1918]

My darling wife, my precious Wig.

When I got home this evening, I felt very depressed. Somehow I couldn't reconcile myself to being alone again. It seemed so devilish that we should have written to each other: when I hold you in my arms again I'll never let you go.

But the depression didn't last long. I just thought how miserable I should have been if you had still been here in these rooms without a breath of air: but I longed to have some word from you. Then I got my supper. One egg or two egg omelette? I said to myself, and decided that you would like me to eat a two-egger. So I did. My child, do the same for me. Whenever you think of me, eat something extra. I know it's hard – devilish hard – but if you don't, I shall pine away.

It is very strange; but to-night I can't express myself at all. It's as though I were a bird whose throat had been strained by trying to sing some incredibly passionate song. It's not that I'm worried. I know that you will do what you have to do; and I know that you will turn the corner – just because I have implicit faith in your loyalty to our love. But the passionate anguish of the love I feel has been like a revelation to me, and I am silent.

Oh, my darling, my wig, my wife

Boge.

Headland Hotel
Looe
Cornwall
17.v.18

For dinner there was:

soup
fish cutlets
mutton chops
greens
pancakes with cherry jam
cheese & biscuits
coffee
butter
½ pint milk

My dear husband

I have been sitting in a big armchair by the *three* open windows of my room wondering how I shall group or arrange events so that I may present them to you more or less coherently. But I can't. They *won't* group or arrange themselves. I am like a photographer in front of ever such a funny crowd whom I've orders to photograph but who won't be still to be photographed – but get up, change their position – slink away at the back – pop up in front – take their hats off and on – Who *is* the most Important One – Who *is* Front Middle Seated? The morning with you was quite unreal – another dream nightmare. When I kissed you did we wake? No. When you kissed my hand I did feel a kind of thrill of anguish. (Will you understand that?) But it was all a part of this racing vile dream. Let us try & shut our eyes to it and go on as though it had not been – at least for the present, at least until the – the plaster is off your finger and the place healed again – – –

I had a very comfortable journey – The country, in the bright swooning light was simply bowed down with beauty, heavy, weighed down with treasure – Shelley's moonlight may glittered everywhere, the wild flowers are in such a profusion that it's almost an agony to see them and know that they are there – I have never seen anything more solemn and splendid than England in May – and I have never seen a spring with less of the *jeune fille* in it. – God! Why are you caged up there – why is our youth passing while the world renews itself in its glory!

I must confess, of course that, standing in the middle of the goldy fields, hanging from every tree, floating in every little river and perched on top of every hill there was a Thermos flask filled with boiling coffee – I have so often seen people in trains, armed with these affairs, *appearing* to uncork them and pretending that real steam and real heat flows out – but I've never believed them – until today – At Plymouth I got out and bought two wheatmeal bigglechicks from the scrupulously clean refreshment room (fresh hot meat & potato pasties still for sale) and made an excellent tea. But indeed I had such constant recourse to the bottil that some soldiers in the carriage could not quite believe my exquisite signs of satisfaction were tout à fait sober! But 'twas nectar darling – & of course we shall never never be without one again – Only think for a moment. One need never want again for a cup of tea at one of those 'odd' moments which always come on journeys to us.

Anne & Drey were at Liskeard – Anne – just as I had imagined –

bronze coloured with light periwinkle eyes – carrying a huge white bag bulging with *her* thermos flask & a vest of Drey's (I didn't find where *it* came from or how) & a box of paints and a handful of hedge flowers – and the 'most beautiful lemon'. Drey was awfully kind. He did everything – We featherstitched off to Looe – It was very hot – all glowing & quiet with loud birds singing & the bluebells smelled like honey. The approach to Looe is amazing. It's not 'English', certainly not French or German – I must wait to describe it. The hotel buggy met us driven by a white haired very independent boy who drove the horse as though it were a terribly fierce ramping white dragon – just to impress us – you know – We drove through lanes like great flowery loops with the sea below and huge gulls sailing over – or preening themselves upon the roof tiles until we came to this hotel which stands in its garden facing the open sea. It could not be a more enchanting position. The hotel is large, 'utterly first class' – *dreadfully expensive* – It has a glassed in winter garden for bad weather with long chairs – a verandah – the garden hung between the sun and sea. Anne had taken for me a really vast room with three windows all south – the sun comes in first thing in the morning until 3 in the afternoon. It is clean as a pin – gay – with a deep armchair – a bed with two mattresses – Just across the corridor is a 1st class bathroom with constant hot water & a lavatory so superb that it & the salle de bains might be part of a sanatorium. For everything (except the cream), for four meals a day served in my room – breakfast in bed – the extra meat & so on it is 4½ guineas. There! I know it's dreadful – I can't possibly live here under £5 a week alors – & I've only just four. But I think I ought to stay here at least until I am strong enough to look for another room because for a 'cure' it could not be better. The old servant unpacked for me, gave me hot water – took away my water bottil just now on her own & filled it – In fact, Bogey it *is* a sanatorium without being one – as it were. The manageress gets the butter – so I am sending mine back to you. You see it's included here – And, will you please send my *sugar card*? She'll get me that, too. I think it's easiest. She says she'll give me butter at each meal & ½ pint milk at each meal – ¼ of butter every two days!! Don't you think I ought to stay here – just at first & get a stronger girl? I know it's hugely dear but I feel it is right – that I will get well quicker here than elsewhere. All is so clean and attended to. Anne had arranged everything, of course, & filled the room with flowers – She has just walked across to say 'goodnight'. She really *is* wonderful down here

– like part of the spring – radiant with life. It's ten o'clock – I am going to bed. My room has all the sea spread before it – Now with the blinds down there floats in the old old sound – which really makes me very very sad – It makes me feel what a blind, dreadful – losing & finding affair our life has been – just lately – with how few golden moments – how little little rest. But I am not across the water & you are coming down for your holiday – *next month*. It is agony to be away from you but what must be – must be – Forgive me if I have been – what was it? I've forgotten. I find it *so* hard to be ill – But ah! if you knew how I loved you and am for ever your loving wife

<table>
<tr><td></td><td>47 [Redcliffe Road,
Fulham]</td></tr>
<tr><td>Monday. Evening.</td><td>[20 May 1918]</td></tr>
</table>

Darling Wig-wife.

How can I tell you of the joy with which your letters have filled me? I feel gay, light-hearted, full of sun and air, utterly confident – everything that you would have me. When I think that you should have found *the* place, that if you are only a moderately good Wig, an eating-resting Wig you will certainly have knocked the backbone out of your old illness by the end of the summer, when I think that at long last the aspegs are *all* good, I feel just as though the only thing to do is to stand on my head and sing: I dreamt that I dwell-helt in marbill halls.

When I had read your letters, I went off to my looking glass. Truly, honestly, I didn't recognise myself. I don't believe you would have known your smiling Boge; with a spotted bow-tie that looked for all the world like a little dog who was smiling too. Straight dinkum, I *could* not be happier than I am. And yet, strangely enough, when your train went out and I left the old station and plunged into the sunlight, I knew the good thing was going to happen, the only good thing that could happen. I knew it, and I suddenly passed into a state of grace. Everything I did was a good thing. I made my Aunt better; I lifted my father out of his depression; I made the flower-woman laugh; and even Sheppard smiled again.

I've only one hole to pick in your letter. Why do you say it's dreadfully expensive? It's dreadfully cheap. You know it is. I'll send you £8 at the beginning of every month. Do you think that will be enough. Just think, quietly. I have just got a rise of £8 a month. I have only got to go on writing a few articles and I shall be saving just as much as ever. You can't deny the stars are fighting for us at long last. But if you say another word about its being too expensive, or about looking for another place I'll come down expressly and beat you.

And, then, how dare you worry about me? You must know that news like that makes me so happy that I can hardly hold myself. The old office becomes delightful, really delightful – I mean that seriously. If I were not in it, I should try to get in. When you are ill, the only thing that satisfies me is to be earning enough money to make you well. Just think that for the first time we really need money and we really have it. I feel that I could hug the old office. Write to me and tell me that you are gaining a pound a week at least, and I'll keep so well that you'll think I came fresh out of the Heron when you see me next month. You understand, don't you. We are lovers for ever. You pine away & I pine; you flourish & I flourish.

Now, before I forget (1) would you like the £8 before the first of June? You've only to say the word (2) About the sugarcard, you'll have to go on with the present arrangement till July 13th. If the Manageress would like a different kind of sugar next time just tell me. (3) Shall I send you your Charles Lamb or any other books (4) I don't in the least see why you should review any books unless you want to *very much*. But I send you a book the *Times* sent me. They want ½ col – the same as you did last time. But if you don't feel disposed, don't worry a bit. I don't matter a tinker's curse. (5) Write to me as often as you can & tell me the things I want to know. Most days, I shall probably send you only a post-card and a long letter on Sunday. But you will have a p.c. every day. I would write every day if it were not that I feel certain of the Heron again and I *want*, really want, to write articles for it. (6) Don't get too uppish and start climbing hills. That's the only thing I'm afraid of – that because you know you're getting better, you'll begin to behave as though you're quite well. You just mustn't. Think of me. (7) Wash Rib's face & kiss him from me. (8) Remember always that you are my very soul, & behave according

Boge.

I've sent off nearly all the prospectuses – and your story to Harrison. Now, I'm going to read your letter again.

[Headland Hotel,
Looe, Cornwall]

Monday –   [20 May 1918]

Darling little husband

Drey has brought me your Friday letter – & it is a sad one – Yes, you feel – oh – like I do – and what – of all other things – seems so hard is how we swore *not* to let each other go again – & then how soon – – – we were gone – Yesterday, thinking of all this in the afternoon I wept so – I could not bear it. I thought I must come back & *die* there rather than always this living apart. But now that I am stronger today I feel that all may *yet* be well – & the Heron – now I am away from London is so clear & perfect. Try & look after yourself for my sake: try & *eat* and try & *be happy* – I opened this letter to say Anne & Drey have both been here – & the doctor, too. He says I am getting on all right. I must stay in bed for the present – & I must take cod liver oil & iron mixed!! He is just like a student in a Tchekhov book – But he promises me that as soon as my left lung calms down I can go out & drive – and sit on the beach. Oh – such glorious prospecks! Anne is being perfect – I am *eating* all I see & milk 4 times a day & butter & cream. Bacon for breakfast, newlaid egg-wegs – The food is excellent.

Your own wife.

But you know, Bogey, *I shall always be homesick.*

Wig.

[Headland Hotel,
Looe, Cornwall]

Thursday – In bed. 11 A.M.   [23 May 1918]

The old un has just brought your Monday night letter 'right up' – Your letters all arrive perfectly now. My wire was sent really – in a panic, because of that *cursed* raid – which you evidently in the 13th Corinth. manner 'winked at' – the raid, I mean –

I don't worry. But for God's sake *don't* keep anything from me so that I shan't worry – That is so appaling to think of.

Today I am going for a walk – down to the Surgery to be weighed. The weather has changed. It rained in the night & this morning the light is so uncertain – so exquisite – running silver over the sea.

An idea – – – –

Are you really only happy when I am not there? Can you conceive of yourself buying crimson roses and smiling at the flower woman if I were within 50 miles? Isn't it true that, now, even though you are a prisoner, your time is your own. Even if you are 'lonely' you are not being 'driven distracted' – Do you remember when you put your handkerchief to your lips and turned away from me? And when you asked me if I still believed in the Heron? Is it true that if I were flourishing you would flourish ever so much more easily & abundantly without the strain & wear of my actual presence – We could write each other letters & send each other work & you would quite forget that I was 29 & brown – People would ask is she fair or dark & you'd answer in a kind of daze – 'oh I think her hair's yellow.'

Well – well – it's not quite a perfect scheme. For I should have to hack off my parent stem *such* a branch – oh, such a branch that spreads over you and delights to shade you & to see you in dappled light & to refresh you & to carry you a (quite unremarked) sweet perfume – But it is NOT the same for you. You are always pale, exhausted, in a kind of anguish of set fatigue when I am by. Now I feel in your letters, this is lifting and you are breathing again – 'She's away and she is famously "alright" – Now I can get on.'

Of course L.M. would keep us one remove from each other – She'd be a help that way – Did you reckon on that when you were so anxious to keep her. For, of course, as you realised, I'd have given her the chuck for ever after the Gwynne affair if it hadn't been for your eagerness –

You are simply, incredibly perfect to me – You are always 'in advance' of one's most cherished hopes – dreams – of what a lover might be –

But whether I am not really *a curse* … I wonder –

Mrs Maufe's letter was most lovely –

Goodbye for now, dearest Bogey.

Wig.

[47 Redcliffe Road,
Fulham]
[24 May 1918]
Friday Morning 9.30

My darling,

I'll be late for the office, but I can't leave yr. Thursday letter unanswered till to-night. I mean the one 'Are you really only happy when I am not there?'

Well, what's the use of answering it anyhow. Besides I can't. It's comic how with one letter I am left shivering & naked. This time I do feel lonely. You say it all so beautifully that you must have meant it as it was written. It's a blow, a blow.

Oh, damn, what's the good of writing this? I'll not send it: it'll only make you sad, as I am.

Shut up shop, Boge Murry, take your love away. Good God, what a child. Crying, crying, crying. Are you really only happy when she's not there?

My darling, don't believe all this – it can't be true – I've read yr. letter upside down or something. You really mean something quite different. It'll all be right and when you get this I shan't be sad any longer.

Friday Evening

My precious Wig-wife,

I've been rather depressed to-day. I started it by weeping over your letter. I send you what I wrote then: but it's not as bad as that now. It's really quite all right. But it gave me a fearful shock.

You see, worm, it's true that I *was* happy when you went away. I was so confident that the sun & food and Anne and the 'absolutely ideal' place would make you well. I wanted you to go, because I could see that London was knocking you up absolutely. Just because I care for nothing else in the world but you, because the only thing I have to look forward to in life is living at your side – I wanted you to go away. I feel so sure that if I was ill you would be the same; I felt so certain that you understood, that your letter this morning just bowled me out.

But as I say, I'm better now. I know you can't have meant it *like that*, and that I have just been silly. I can't bear the thought that you think my love so imperfect. It's the only thing I am jealous about, because I've fought a hard fight to make it perfect until it has become all there is of me. When I see you sick & ailing, I die; when I think that you are getting well, I straighten my stalk & begin to blossom like a flower.

And then you ask: Can you conceive of yourself buying crimson roses and smiling at the flower woman if I were within 50 miles? I feel I can't answer, more than that I feel I *ought* not answer. But love casteth away pride – besides it's my love that's pierced & not my pride – so I reply.

If you were well and at my side and we were to buy roses together, I might not smile at the woman, I might be solemn even. But she would smile at us. We should leave such warmth in her heart that she would never, never forget.

Do you think that when I'm away from you I *am* happy. Do you think I live at all? I go right apart from the world. I exist. But to think that you are getting well, that brings me happiness – compared to the utter grinding despair of watching you *not* eat, watching you *not* rest, it is heavenly. I'm not happy though. I can never be happy apart from you. And just because I want to be with you, to live *our* life, I want you to get strong. I would wait years – yes years – apart if I knew that that was the only way we could make sure of having *our* life one day.

When I asked you if you still believed in the Heron – I meant only this one thing, that if you believed in it, then you would eat then you would rest no matter what it cost you. I said it at a moment when I was mad watching you. I'm not a cow or a werewolf, after all. I'm your lover. Everything rests on your wonderful body & lovely soul. I grow desperate seeing you pine: hearing you growing well I lift up my head. 'You are always pale, exhausted, in a kind of anguish of set fatigue when I am by. Now I feel in your letters this is lifting & you are breathing again.' It's absolutely true. But that you should have misunderstood!

Well, worm, it's silly to go on like this. Your to-morrow letter will be quite different.

I ought not have written this I know. But I have to tell the truth about what I feel, don't I. And you'll know where I'm all wrong & you'll set it all right again. But please don't doubt my love – it hurts too much.

I got your wire about signing about Hampstead. You will have had my letter this morning. I have written to them to say that on thinking it over I must insist on their taking the responsibility for complete decoration to my satisfaction and for putting a supply of hot-water in the bath-room. I know they won't accept this; but I don't think they'll break off immediately, so that if you were finally to decide for it we could get it. And if you decide against I have only to stand firm.

Goodbye – Wig-wife. Don't have any more of those 'ideas', though

     Boge

A new complication. This very minute Miss Palmer has been here to say she has *let* this flat.

However, the people haven't signed the agreement yet. So I can wait till I get your letter to-morrow & then tell her to postpone matters.

> [Headland Hotel,
> Looe, Cornwall]
> [24 May 1918]

Dearest Bogey

This is a final fling from me before we land the monster – –

Would it perhaps be better to cry off? To tell the agents I have been sent to a sanatorium – 'suddenly worse' – &, until we have the Heron – to live like this – I to take 'provisionally' furnished rooms in Hampstead where you could come for the week-ends. Such things are not too difficult to find – I should take them with attendance, of course – Then, when I wish to go to the country or the sea – je suis *absolument* libre. Moving, all we must buy, will completely exhaust our Heron money – of that there is NO doubt, and we cannot be in the least certain of getting it back. It will & it must be an infernal strain – L.M. will certainly cost £2 a week, but apart from that I really am frightened to take her for better and for worse – My love for her is so divided by my extreme *hate* for her that I really think the latter has it. I feel she'll stand between us – that you & she will be against me – That will be at its worst my feeling – I don't mean 'simply' against me. I mean, of course, absurdly nonsensically abnormally subtly –

The other arrangement leaves you at 47 for the week but then you only sleep there – & it is quiet in the evenings for your work – The weekends we could always share. Then we are really saving for the Heron – not touching Heron money – I feel the elephant will be '47 in the kitchen' over again – in some degree – *with* L.M. J'ai peur – Don't you think perhaps it is the Heron or nothing? You see, your QUITE INDEPENDENT idea that we should be separate until the late autumn 'frees' me in thought. I think it is the right idea. I'll wander away this summer – & when I do go back I'll establish myself in rooms in Hampstead –

Please reply to this fully darling & *don't* hate me for it.

> Wig.

But of course I am ready to be persuaded – I write this because I

must be honest – I *feel* it at the time – very strongly – Do you be
dead honest too – then we'll understand.

[47 Redcliffe Road,
Fulham]
[25 May 1918]
Saturday Night. 11.15

My precious Wig-wife,
    I hate the thought that I can't get a letter from you till Monday
morning. I feel the need to talk to you, to be near you, so much. I
have to take decisions which are our decisions – and that can't be
done unless we are us (forgive that awful phrase, but I can't express
what I mean otherwise).
    You see, my darling, the letters that you have written me the last
two days don't help me to see clearly. They seem to have been
written in the idea that I could be, and am, happy separated from
you. I may have given you that idea: but it's a terribly wrong one,
and if I take decisions, or rather you take decisions, on that basis –
the whole thing will be wrong. I want a letter from you that will put
me in the state of grace, which I have lost now for two days, again. I
am afraid of any decisions we take while this mood is on us.
Nothing good can come of things we do when we are separated in
spirit.
    I am still appalled by that notion of yours that you would live in
rooms in Hampstead while I would stay at 47 and come to see you
for week ends. It not only frightens me in itself, just as an idea:
more frightening still is the thought that you could have such an
idea, and that you should think that I would not be frightened by it.
You stay away in the country – well, I bear that, and I am even glad
of it, because I believe that will help you to get well, and that is the
only thing – really, the only thing – I care about in the world. But
the idea of the Hampstead House was that it enabled us to be
together – and to be together is all that life holds for us. For you to
be in London & me to be apart – well, it just seems a mockery. I
can't believe you really mean it.
    If you are afraid of the Elephant because of L.M. – I understand
that *absolutely*. L.M. shall not be there: we'll find either the real
Dearly or another. If you are afraid of the Elephant just as the
Elephant – a big house with a basement – then I understand that
perfectly and, though I don't think it more frightening than Acacia

Road, if your feeling persists, we'll do our best to drive the Elephant away, while we ourselves clamber down his tail on to the ground. (I know from your letter that you don't want to stay in the country for the sake of staying in the country. You said you had never dreamed of staying till the late autumn. I explained what the intention of my words was.)

Oh, how hard things are to make clear! It's like this, darling. If you had said 'Boge, don't take the Elephant: it frightens me: let's find one that fits us more: *I'll* stay in the country till you do: and when it's quite ready I'll come back' – I should be quite calm & happy. But you said something quite different: and my head is still spinning with disappointment.

But when I put all these things out like this, as clearly as I can, I feel that I am pressing you, driving you, like a little horse, through a gate. But that I will not do. If there is any pressure here, ignore it, my worm, it's not *really* there. I am only trying to make it quite clear to you that you were absolutely & utterly mistaken in thinking that I could ever be happy apart from you. I have told you why my letters were happy, and why I *was* happy when you had gone. My happiness began when your telegram came a week ago to-day

Superb arrival everything simply splendid fondest love Wig.

My god, wouldn't you have been happy if I had sent you that, after you had been watching me cooped up in 47 eating nothing, hurrying about, never resting, though these were the things that were absolutely necessary. I was *happy*, I felt good, I began to *be* again. But when you wrote that you had the idea that I was happy *because* you had gone away, my happiness ended. Oh, I have not been happy since.

Forgive me, my darling, for returning again & again to this. I won't any more. But it circles round & round in my head & gives me no peace.

Please tell me how much you weighed – you were going out to weigh yourself on Thursday, you said – but you never said how much. And the whole world hangs on these things for me: on these things & your Monday letter. Child, if only I could put my arms round you – everything would be plain once more, I know.

I sent you *The Possessed* & a French book to review to-day. I'll send you the *Pageant* on Monday.

Be honest with me, Wig – don't spare me. If you think my love is cold – if you think I have changed in any way – tell me truly.

A whole day till Monday.

I got your telegram about the Elephant to-day. I haven't signed anything. But your telegram was sent before any of my letters can have arrived. All depends on Monday

Your unhappy Boge.

Sunday Afternoon.

I have just been to the Post Office to see whether I can manage that this letter gets to you to-morrow morning. They tell me that there's a good chance if I post it in the late fee box before half past five. I hope it comes off. I feel completely détraqué. How I hang on your letter to-morrow.

Whatever you decide about the Elephant, I shall clear out of here. I've lived too many nightmare hours in it. I hate it, and it hates me. I shall let the other people have it anyhow and go somewhere else.

L.M. brought me some cigarettes for you. I am sending them with this by letter post.

[Headland Hotel,
Looe, Cornwall]
[27 May 1918]

While you read this feel that my arms are round you & your head is hidden – & I'm telling you it all – with every part of me.

Monday.

My dearest own

I think, reading your three letters this morning I suffered every atom that you suffered. Nay, more, because it was I who inflicted it on you – you who came crying to me & saying 'this is what you have done to me! This!' Even now I can't get calm & I am all torn to pieces by love and hideous remorse & regret. I must try & explain all this away & it is so difficult – so difficult – with these great clumsy words. I could do it were I to see you – in a moment – in a breath. Only *one thing*. Never never have I ever said to myself – 'shut up shop take your love away'. If you ever feel that don't tell me until you do take it away. It really nearly killed me. The sky – the whole world fell. Before I begin to speak – you must know that you're all life to me. God – haven't all my letters said just that. Hasn't all my suffering & misery been just because of that, because of my terrible – exhausting – utterly INTENSE love. But you must have understood that? That was the whole why & wherefore –

You see, I was in the S. of F. from December till April. What was it like on the whole – just HELL. As you know it nearly killed me. Then I came back to rest with you. All my longings, all my desires, all my dreams & hopes had been just to be with you and – to come back to my home. Bien! I came. Heard how ill I was, scarcely seem to have seen you – except through a mist of anxious – felt that ALL your idea was for me to get away into the country again – Well I understood that – although please try & realise the appaling blow it was to me to uproot again – & so soon – with hardly a word spoken – Please do try & realise that. Plus the knowledge that I was more ill than I'd thought & that all my precious 'privacy', my love of 'self contained' life – doing all for myself in my own way – doing all – enfin for you was to be taken away from me – was 'bad' for me – enfin.

However it was only for a month or six weeks that I was to be alone. Then you came down for your holiday & we went back together – I arrived – & found I was to be here (without a word explaining why this change had been) at LEAST 4 months – until the *late* autumn – No word of your coming – no word of anything else. It was the sort of ultimate comble. It knocked me back onto my own lonely self. I was in despair as you know, and I saw Life quite differently. I felt that if all I had oh so passionately pleaded & protested without shame or fear about my love – my longing for married life – as soon as possible – was to be just delayed – not understood – I could endure no more – & I fell into the dark hollow which waits for me always – the old one – & I wrote from there – I felt he has not this same great devouring need of me that I have of him – He *can* exist apart from me. I have been in the S. of F. nearly four months & here is another four – He will never realise that I am only WELL when we are 'together' – All else is a mockery of health. I depend on him as a woman depends on a man & a child on its little playfellow, but he, as long as he knows I am alright, he can play 'apart' –

Now do you see a little bit? Is it a little bit clearer? But there is more to say.

Our marriage – You cannot imagine what that was to have meant to me. It's fantastic – I suppose. It was to have shone – apart from all else in my life – And it really was only part of the nightmare, after all. You never once held me in your arms & called me your wife. In fact the whole affair was like my silly birthday. I had to keep on making you remember it – – – –

And then – all the L.M. complex is – taking the reins out of my hands. I am to sit quiet & look at the country – I can't – I can't. Don't you know that LIFE – married Life with you – co-equal – *partners* – jealously alone – jealous of every other creature near – is what I want – I am jealous – jealous of our privacy – just like an eagle. If I felt that you & she discussed me even for my own good – I'd have to fly out of the nest & dash myself on the rocks below.

My little Boge-husband, you don't know me even yet. I adore you & you only – I shall not take my love away ever – not even long after I am dead. Silly little button flowers will grow on my very grave with Bogey written on the petals ... Do you understand now? (Maintenant, c'est moi qui pleure.)

There is my answer for ever to you.

Now about the Elephant. Get it if you can & we will make it a Singing Elephant with all our hearts –

As I wired you this morning I am not going to leave this hotel after all. I cannot explain to another landlady that my lungs is weak – Also the fag of wondering what I shall order to eat would mean I'd order nothing. Here it comes – one eats it – & it's over. And they know me here, now, & are more than kind to me. The old 'un, Mrs Honey is 'pure Heron' – Bless her – I can always hear her & my Gran'ma talking as they put the linen away. So here I shall remain & I will take your money, please. Unless it leaves you short. I will take it from you – You must try & come here, as we did once arrange – even for a week & we'll have a sail boat and go 'whiffing for pollocks'. I am working hard & Pagello says I have made remarkable great strides.

So now, please God let us be calm again. *I will not be sad.* Let us be calm. Let our love keep us quiet & safe – like two children in a great big quiet field – sitting there hidden in the flowers & grasses.

Oh, thou who hast all of my heart. Accept me –

I am simply for ever & ever your own little

    Wig.

I have told the manageress I am staying for the whole of June – *at least.*

The books came & the cigarettes – thank you, love. Tell me all the practical things. Don't spare me – Tell me all the worries. They are my RIGHT. I must have them & discuss them. You are NOT to have any worry *un*shared.

M.I. 7D,
War Office,
Watergate House
Adelphi, W.C.2.

Tuesday 1.30   28 May, 1918.

My precious, wonderful wife.

I was so overcome by your letter this morning that I forgot to take out with me the letter I wrote last night.

I have read your letter three–four times. I shall wear it near my heart. That only means in my pocket, I suppose, really: but I have to carry it about with me, shall have to always. Such an influence of love flows out of it that I can never let it go far from me.

I think you are right when you say I don't know you, even yet. There is something, some final perfection of perfection, in you that [I] did not understand. I did feel it, I did know it was there; but I had never seen it face to face, never felt its fragrance steal so close about my heart.

I don't need to defend myself to you. The only thing I want to say is that perhaps you didn't quite know how *afraid* I was. How my soul was struck dumb with terror at your illness. I seemed neither to be able to speak nor to breathe. I could never say what I wanted to say to you, things that I cannot *say*. When we were married, my longing to fold you in my arms was terrible; but more terrible still was the thought which held me back. No, I mustn't: I shall hurt her. At that moment the knowledge of your illness blinded me like a flash of lightning – tore right through my heart. And from this there came another thing. I felt that I couldn't tell you all my love because if I did, if I once let out the flower that was bursting in my heart, I could not have let you go and you couldn't have gone. I felt that we were being killed by the devouring passion of our love: I chose to hold it back – it cost me more pain than I have ever known or ever will know again. I was held up only by the one thought that never left my mind for an instant: She must rest or she will die. One night I lay awake by your side for years and listened to your breathing.

My darling, our marriage meant, was to mean & has meant, as much to me as it did to you. Of that I am sure, utterly sure, even though you may smile a little & slowly nod your head. But my happiness withered in my heart – I shall never forget how it withered when I looked at you as you came into the restaurant. Perhaps I should have fought the devil of despair – but I am only Boge – a child.

I never meant, and never wrote, worm, that *you* said 'Boge

Murry take your love away'. That was me speaking to myself.

To be together and to be at rest – that is my only desire, my one longing. It does not eat out my heart so much now that I know we are one again; but all the same it's there and never leaves me alone.

About Lesley I feel just as you do. I have always felt that she drove a wedge between us – not that she did, not that she wanted to even. But no living person can share our life, nor even pretend to. Neither Johnny nor Anne nor she, no-one understands. She was at 47 last night wanting to know how you were. I couldn't say a word. I felt that it was too secret, and too sacred, and that if I tore it out of my heart, I should die.

Now, I know that we can trust each other absolutely. You will do for our love's sake all that you must do to get well. Any housekeeper would do for us, so long as she was clean & good: but, if it's Lesley M., then she is only a housekeeper – a friend as well perhaps – but in essence a housekeeper. But I think it would be far better for me to find someone else.

How hard it is to write things – one look, one kiss, once my arms round you, and all that I am groping at would be said.

My one, my only idea, when you went away was to get the Elephant ready as soon as I could & bring you back. But I was fearful – fearful as I always am – of seeming to bring pressure on you. When your letters came saying you were so happy & getting so well, I felt I must not *call* you back. The thought of months without [you] was a nightmare. When I wrote it I was praying that you should say: I'd rather come back. But I dared not ask you.

Wig – wig – when I read your letter I *am* in your arms. I am calm & happy.

[Headland Hotel
Looe, Cornwall]
[29 May 1918]

Wednesday.

Dearest of All

Your Tuesday letter written at the office is here – I have just exchanged my breakfast tray with a poor little sole's bone on it with the old un for it. (Here's pretty writing!) I don't know what to say about it.

'If you read it once you must read it twice
It will make *your* heart smell sweet & ni-ice.'

as the lavender gypsies just don't sing. *Re* health (as Papa would say) I am really bonzer. I went for a walk yesterday – really a walk & today I feel better than ever & am going out in a boat. Are you coming down here at all? For a week? The manageress would board us bed us light us & clean our little shoes for £6½ the two of us. That is a monster room with a balcony. Well – just say. And you have not told me how to write to my bank so as I am extremely short I shall have to ask you for the June £8 by wire. You see I've had a chemist's bill as well as all these old extras.

I *want* that Elephant now. If it falls through we must try for a flat but there are no flats are there – And yes, if we could get another person clean & honest they'd be better than L.M. I feel – Because you see we can't treat her just as a housekeeper – & I *have* I must say this horror still even though I know it's 'wrong' – I have to tear a delicate veil from my heart before I can speak to her – & I feel I oughtn't to tear it. Is that nonsense?

Darling love this is absolute Heronian weather – and I think our Heron must be somewhere near here – because it is so amazingly open – and healthy – And now that the black monkeys have folded up their little tents (I see *and* hear them) I am beginning to feel like Anne does about this place – Also now that I *can* walk & look over the walls –

Forty-nine sailing boats sailed 'into the roads' yesterday. I counted them for you – There they all were, skimming about – – – This place is 4 miles from Polperro – 10 from Fowey. You can go across country to Fowey in a Jingle. Anne & I mean to do it one day. But now – before I finish this letter I talk to you seriously and at length about 'our plans'. (See next page)
Grand Sérieux!

If we do not have L.M. one bother will be the moving. We shall absolutely need HER for that. She's the only person to be trusted to pack all that is at 47 & to understand *where* that all shall go at the other place – Also, tied as you are, there must be a second person who can see to ALL sorts of various things, like measuring for curtains – buying the 'odd' things, ringing up the builders and so on. The *so on* is really very important. It is absolutely impossible for you to attend to this & your work. No strange woman could. She's the only one. But if we took her at all like that it would have to be for ever. We could not say – leave your factory. Do all this. Then find us a housekeeper & decamp. So what I think is this: now you & I know just *how* we want to live – just *how* we think about all of L.M. and you know what a jealous woman I am. I think that if we can overlook 'all the other things' we ought to regard her as God-given & take her & if she don't like her position as a 'housekeeper & friend' – well – she can chuck it. But we shall find no-one like her for the first months. Phone her. See her. Tell her my letter to her is cancelled – & explain. Will you? *She* will understand. The devilish thing is that now I have told you *all* I feel about her – I feel that nothing would be simpler than for the three of us to live together in Harmony.

Tck! Now how long will you be at 47? What do you intend to do? And try, precious, in your *rushing* life (I know how few minutes you have) not to be done by the agents. They generally leave us roasted oh such a brown!

I have heard from Virginia who dislikes the drawings very much. So does Leonard. Well, they would – wouldn't they? It's their press. I suppose they'd better not use them. Just a plain blue cover with Prelude on it. To Hell with other people's presses! I'll send you her letter, however – & I'll write to her & ask her to send you a proof of the cover – I don't want Roger Fly on it, at any rate (That 'Fly' seems to me awfully funny. It must be the sun on my brain.) Don't bother to type 'Carnation'. Let it be. You've enough to do. I am of course in heaven that you like it 'cos I did, too. And you 'understood' – I meant it to be 'delicate' – just that. Has a parcel from Lewis with two little pantalons of mine turned up. Oh will you please send them to me?

Oh, my Boge, my precious own darling – Anne is painting me & old Rib – Rib of course – is violently flattered & keeps flattening down his fringe at the thought. He is getting very brown. He is going to bring a tame shrimp HOME, please, he says. All my letter is just one thing – I love you – in every way – always – for ever –

> I am yours eternally.
> Tig.
> Give Johnny [Fergusson] a big hug from me.

> [47 Redcliffe Road,
> Fulham]
> [6 June 1918]
> Thursday Morning

My darling Wig-wife,

I didn't get a letter this morning – It was rather a blow. But I think that perhaps you forgot to put 1½d. instead of 1d. on it; and it's being delayed. So I won't worry you with a wire until I have seen whether the night post brings me anything. The two books you sent back arrived safely, also a review of *Pour Toi, Patrie*, which I forgot to mention before.

The agents telephoned me yesterday morning to say that the Elephant was now practically settled and that they hoped to have the agreement signed within a week – so, failing the utterly unexpected accident, we should be able to go ahead. I have to see about the decoration next. I am to be given a month rent free to get the things done. I hope we can manage it in the time. The agent suggested on the telephone that we should have possession before June 24. If we got possession say ten days from now & we could get the decorators to go ahead, it's possible that the Elephant might be ready, washed & curry-combed, with a rope ladder hanging down his tail by the third week in July. But not possibly before. So there still remains the question what you will do for those three weeks. It might be a good thing to go down to Garsington, after all – because then I could consult you during the week-ends. I wish I'd had a letter this morning. Your letters do make such a difference. It's on them I live all the day & not on my bacon & eggs.

Will you try to visualise the Elephant for a moment and give instructions about the colours for the walls & paint? I know we talked it out before but I want to hear again.

For instance shall we have a plain-white distemper for the staircase, or shall we have a pale yellow? I know you don't want a plain white for your own rooms – but what about the paint for the woodwork in both cases. The Kitchen of course as white as white can be; also the garden – basement room – or should that have a tinge of colour, and if so, what colour? What about the front door & the gate? Take things one by one and tell me the colour.

Oh, blow, I want that letter. The day seems so empty without it.

Thursday Afternoon.

I am sending you a *Mercure de France*. I want you to read the things by Duhamel in it: 'La Recherche de la Grace'. It seems to me very remarkable indeed that there should be another man not merely feeling what we feel, but using our words to express what he feels. Our 'state of Grace' is exactly what he means – you see. Coming after *Civilization* – which again expressed a great many of the things I feel – it gave me a very queer feeling. The only thing that make[s] me sad is that he should be happy because he has had a son. I'm glad he has; but I am terribly envious – terribly. However, we will have one, won't we? I don't know why I should be so longing for a child – but there it is, I am. I want someone who'll know how perfect you are, someone to whom I wink & nod about you, have laughs with, someone who'll be the dead spit of you – a Rib who'll talk just a little bit more.

It's a queer thing to write about these things in the office – queerer still when it happens as it did just now that this should be seized by someone taking a bundle of papers off my desk and only rescued by me dashing down the stairs. It's a queer world. I don't like it very much.

Please let there be a letter for me when I get home, my darling heart.

Boge.

	[Headland Hotel,
	Looe, Cornwall]
Friday.	[7 June 1918]

Darling Heart.

All the morning a thin fine mist-rain came spinning down – and the only people on the plage were the seagulls. I saw them (when I got out of bed for my cigarettes) standing on the wet lovely sand in rows waiting for the waves that came in heavy and reluctant and soft like *cream* waves – I never had such a bird's eye view of voluptuousness ... Then Anne came, with some berries for me & sat on the bed & smoked and talked about hospitals in New York & the helpless feeling of the patient & the triumphant sensation of the nurses being a question of ANGLES. The patient being horizontal etc. etc. *Then* I had a hot bath and dressed and went across to East Looe & bought a shady chapeau (feltie is too hot.) The little hand glass had an emerald bow on it; it looked exactly like a cat. When I heard myself explaining to the girl – 'the hat must appear to be painted on the head – *one* with the head an ensemble – not a projection, as it were' and saw her Cornish eyes gazing at me – *horrified*, I walked out – feeling very humbled. Everything smells so good – oh so good – & two men are lying on their backs painting the belly of 'The Good Fairy' – They are wearing green overalls & they are painting her bright red – The ferryman says we're in for another three months spell of fine weather – You will like him. His boat is called the *Annie*. He is particularly handsome & fine –

though he has only one eye – and only one 'good' arm & that one ends in a thumbless hand – (He was blown up in that explosion – oh *yess*!) All the same he don't look in the least mutilated –

It is very warm now – 'soft' you know – Cornish weather, and the sea is half green half violet. I had a very large, commodious, tough old mutton chop for lunch while everybody else had a teeny little veau cutlet. This caused horrible bad blood –

Ladies: I wish I had thought to apply for *extra* rations. I could have – quaite easily with may health.

I pretended of course that it was divinely tender – melted in the mouth, & I tried to waft the choppishness of it in their direction.

No post today – not a sign – Mrs Honey promises there shall be one this afternoon. She has confided in the manageress: 'it's in my heart and I must out with it. I *dearly love* my little fine leddy' – – Oh, if only she could be at the Heron with her 'little maidy' to help her – She's only got one tooth and she's small with these rose cheeks & big soft blue eyes & white hair but how fond I am of her –

Now the tide is nearly high. I've just been on the balcony. I heard a boat *hooting*. It's a queer little lugger with one orange sail and a tiny funnel. A man has put off from it in a boat – not rowing – standing up and – sort of deep sea punting along. The lugger is called the Eliza Mary & she comes from FY.

People have such funny names here – there's a man called Mutton and another called Crab. You must please take me into the Jolly Sailorman when you come down – It's so lovely I *must* see inside.

The post has come. There's only this. 'Tis a book. Oh dear – it had a letter in it. This was simply *heavenly* – But why hasn't my letter come? I have been infinitely careful about the 1½d. It's just delayed, my darling love. But I know what it means to start the day without one. I am a sort of hollow cave until the letter comes – All day I've waited for this – I shall talk over the elephant on a separate page & you must say yea yea and nay nay as you will – It's just suggestions – Talk them over with me won't you – You know – oh well I'll talk of that on the separate page.

One of my suggestions.

Shall I come up today (Friday) week for a week & discuss Elephant in all its bearings with you going as I know now how to go – *dead slow* & then shall we go to the Bailiff's Cottage for your holiday? & I stay on there? We save a lot of money & a lot of mental energy this way. But on the other hand you don't see Looe.

And I don't know which would be more of a holiday for you. But this is well considered before it's written so don't FAIL to answer it.

Goodbye for today my Bogey
Wig.

If you agree to my 'suggestion' wire, will you love?

Suggestions for the Trappings of the Elephant.

I think front door, windy frames & gate a bright green. A house must be handsome to support blue – & green seems more in its period. But not a cooked spinach green – an 'emerald' green –

Kitchen and garden room & basement generally WHITE with all the woodwork & dresser a bright light BLUE – what they call *hyacinth* blue, I think. China and glass & food & fruit look so lovely with these 2 colours – 'Praps it's Wedgewood blue. Do you know what I mean?

All the rest of the woodwork in the house is best WHITE – don't you feel? One can always paint a fireplace with flat ripolin if one wants to, later, but I think, coloured woodwork, unless one is going in for an immensely intensive colour scheme looks patchy. We'd better, I think then, put, as it were, a *white frame to the house* inside. This applies to the staircase, too.

For the hall & staircase – walls I suggest a good *grey*. Yellow ties one in the matter of a carpet & altogether grey with a purple carpet and *brass stair rods* which give the grey the 'gilt' it wants and drawings with a gilt frame or two – *or* one could have a blue staircarpet (lovely with grey). Grey is so kind to you as you come in – don't you think?

With all our furniture in my eye I really am inclined to say *grey* again for the huge big two in one studio. I don't know exactly why – but I am a bit 'off' yellow walls. I feel yellow wants introducing in curtains etc – but one can use purples, blues, reds, & greens with grey – & especially as you're so fond of *chintz*. It's the best background for it. However if you incline to yellow for the studio – c'est entendu. Again books are good against grey & inclined to go a bit muddy against yellow. Does that seem nonsense?

I'd like my two rooms to be WHITE – quite white. Both of them.

I suggest for L.M. who of course must choose for herself GREEN – the green of my spongebag. All her bits of Rhodesian fur and everything would be lovely with green – all *tawny* colours, and the washstand set, par exemple. She ought not to have white I am *sure*. No – stop it – the room faces North – a really *deep* yellow? It's not a big room – But that's for her to say. I'd STILL say green.

Why not have a little delicate flowery paper for your bedroom? If not I'd have *pink* with white paint like we had at Acacia road. Oh that would be lovely wouldn't it? With coloured much patterned 'fruity' curtains – & your workroom I'd have a deep cream – (with engravings of the poets against it.)

I hope this don't sound dull. But I have and so have you a horror of *patchiness*. People are so *patchy*, and I think one must most carefully avoid smacks in the eye. A cushion, or a bowl or a curtain are pleasant little flips but a door skirting board & mantelpiece are positive *blows*. I feel that the body of the house enfin ought to be *spring* – real spring & we'll put all the other seasons in it, in their time. But this [is] absolutely nothing but 'suggestions'. You tell me, dearest, what you feel – and say if you think me a very dull little puppy –

Don't forget the kitchen range is broken.

[Headland Hotel,
Looe, Cornwall]
Sunday.   [9 June 1918]

Precious darling

I have just been writing about *Gus Bofa*. Now I want to write to you. It all feels so different today; it's been raining and 'tis loövely air as Mrs Honey says. No sun – rather cold – the curtains blowing – very desolate & far away from everybody – 11500 miles away at least … Oh dear! I wish I were in London (but you'd be angry). I wish I could have some tea (but you wouldn't let me go into the kitchen). In the middle of *last* night I decided I couldn't stand – not another day – not another hour – but I have decided that so often. In France *and* in Looe. And have stood it. 'So *that* proves', as they would say 'it was a false alarm.' It doesn't. Each time I have decided that I've died again – Talk about a pussy's nine lives: I must have 900. Nearly every night at 11 o'clock I begin wishing it were 11 a.m. I walk up & down – look at the bed – look at the writing table – look in the glass & am frightened of that girl with burning eyes – think 'will my candle last until it's light?' & then sit for a long time *staring* at the carpet – *so* long that it's only a fluke that one ever looks up again. And oh God! this terrifying idea that one must *die* & maybe *going* to die … The Clovelly Mansions, S. of F. writing 'a few last words' business … This will sound like exaggeration but it isn't. If you knew with what feelings I watch the last gleam of light fade! ... If I could just stroll into your room – even if you were asleep & BE with you a moment – 'all would be well.' But I really have suffered such AGONIES from loneliness and illness combined that I'll never be quite whole again. I don't think I'll ever believe that they won't recur – that some grinning Fate won't suggest that I go away by myself to get well of something!! Of course externally & during the day one smiles and chats & says one has had a pretty rotten time, perhaps – but God! God! Tchekhov would understand: Dostoevsky wouldn't. Because he's never been in the same situation. He's been poor and ill & worried but enfin – the wife *has* been there to sell her petticoat – or there has been a neighbour. He wouldn't be alone. But Tchekhov has known just EXACTLY this that I know. I discover it in his work – often.

I have discovered the ONLY TREATMENT for consumption It is NOT to cut the malade off from life: neither in a sanatorium nor in a land with milk rivers, butter mountains & cream valleys. One is just as bad as the other. Johnny Keats' anchovy has more nourishment than both together. DON'T YOU AGREE???

However I'll cling to the rope & bob up & down until Friday week but not a day later. Look here! dear. Do please give me every bit of your attention just to hear this. I MUST NOT BE LEFT ALONE. It's not a case of L.M. or a trained nurse you know. It's different. But that really IS a cry for help. So do remember.

Your Wigwife.

This letter is not to make you sad. I expect my tomorrow's will appear to absolutely deny it. But it will not really. This *does* stand for all time & I *must* let you know.

[not posted]

[Headland Hotel,
Looe, Cornwall]
Monday.   [10 June 1918]

Dearest Bogey

Here's my *third* letter. I've torn up one attempt, kept another as 'interesting evidence' & this one I'll send. It's a process of clarifying ... you know.

Truth is – it is one of my très mauvais jours – as bad as can be –

I'm filthy black – But what's the use of saying so? No use at all – It only 'confirms' me though in my determination not to spend another day here after you are gone – I could NOT stand it. That's as much as I'll stay. I'll try & stick it until Friday week & no doubt I shall – but not a day more!! Tak por tak!

I think a letter of yours is lost. Here is your Friday letter (postmark Sat. 5.30 pm. W.C.) and a 'note' from Sunday. But you 'pass over' my wire and my notebooks and the p.cs. or are all these things delayed at your end – or hadn't you time – you were too tired? Oh there are a thousand reasons. And enfin – the notebook wasn't grand' chose – postcards are a waste of money & the telegram was quite unnecessary – and out of the air – Still I would just 'like to know' – Also would you try & remember to tell me if my review was alright?

That's very superb about the £13. Especially the recovery of last year's –

No, darling I shan't buy anything on my own. No energy – I shall buy a bottle of Beaune however – because I feel I must take some stimulant regular – plus – the milk – cod liver oil iron etc – Wine that maketh glad the heart of man – What heavenly words – Are they true – do you think? Then I shall be a drunkard – But they are not true.

Addio. I'm in despair you see. Laissez moi. Let me wave my jade white hand & go. I love you *un*speakably – with a strong stress on the first syllable today.

Tig.

[47 Redcliffe Road,
Fulham]
[11 June 1918]
Tuesday Evening 7.45

My darling,
I got your wire: 'Fully understand about holidays Friday week alas' at lunchtime today. How hateful this business of wires is – it's always like hearing your voice far away at the end of a long tunnel.

This morning your Saturday & Monday letters came. The Monday one was very black; and of course I got frightened & depressed. It's awful – the thought of your just hanging on there torturing yourself until I come down. And yet I feel so deeply that it's wrong for you to come back here to London. You simply can't live properly in these rooms: they're a death trap – hateful & malign. I want to burn them up. Darling, we'll come back together and then you must go to Garsington. I'll come down every week-end until the Elephant is ready. Oh, I don't know whether you won't hate the suggestion and think that I'm pushing you away again. You know I'm not, don't you? We settled that once and for all.

No, you didn't lose one of my letters last week-end. There was the Friday night letter and nothing but the note on Sunday until Monday. For once I was really too tired. I was done up absolutely. I couldn't remember anything at all. I'm ever so much better to-day, but I'm not as they say 'what I was'. It's terribly hard for me to attend to anything – hard to form words into sentences. So I forgot to answer all the things you spoke to me. I didn't forget them; I just couldn't grasp them quite when I wanted to.

If it weren't for the despair, I should have said that I was suffering the same thing as you when you wrote your Monday letter. I had no energy; but I wasn't in despair, particularly. I would have given anything to be drunk. (Before I forget, the review was excellent and I was very glad to have the postcards. I like to know the kind of place you're in, because if I try to gather anything out of the impressions your letters give me I am left with something that is a hell one day and a divine fairy land another.) Getting your Saturday & Monday letters together this morning was a queer shock.

Well, I suppose there's nothing to be done with your depression worm. I wish I could comfort you, but there's not much comfort to be got out of a thing like me, because I only have to glance at your letter, I don't really have to read the words – the shape and fashion of the letters tells me – to be utterly cast down until one morning one of your letters comes with sunlight & happiness dancing all over it. Then I blink and smile & jump up again. We are like that, aren't we worm?

I don't think much of this life. I can't say I hate it exactly. I can't get it into focus to direct my hate upon it. It just surrounds me like a mist of dust. I twiddle my legs off in the morning & twiddle them back again at night, but what comes between or follows after I don't really know. I have a vague recollection of having tried hard to concentrate and squeeze something out of my brain: but what or why, I don't know. I suppose someone will find me out soon; but before that I shall be down with you, I hope. Then, I feel, everything will be better. I shall look at you & you will look at me, &

something will happen. Lord if you knew how that Cornwall train seems to my imagination to race straight into heaven. I'm almost frightened of finding myself in it. I feel that I might do something stupid like leaning out to get hold of a sunbeam, and that would be the end of me.

Well, my Wig wife, I love and adore you – but I feel more like your rag-doll than your live Boge husband just now

C U R S E   T H E   O F F I C E !

	[Headland Hotel,
Thursday.	Looe, Cornwall]
	[13 June 1918]

My own Darling Heart

I shall not write much today, I am too worried about you. You *can't* go on. I am going out to wire you to see Croft Hill – This you really must do. He will I hope order you immediate leave and you must come here *as soon as possible* & rest absolutely.

I had no letters at all yesterday though I waited ever so. Now this morning your Tuesday & Wednesday letters are here and I feel that the case is immensely urgent. You can obviously stand no more. If you don't do this you may break down very seriously. I implore you to take all the care you can of yourself. (Of course the main cause is my INFERNAL coldness, heartlessness & lack of imagination in having written as I have lately. No more of that, though or the pain will be too great & I'll cry out.)

Try & forgive me – that's all.

Re Elephant. Are you 'legally' free to sign the agreement in view of the fact that you're an undischarged bankrupt? I saw some man was fined yesterday for some offence or other & it made me think. Hadn't I better sign? As your wife with independent means? Don't risk anything. But above all – for God's sake take care of yourself.

Your own Wigwife.

Friday A Week Today   [14 June 1918]

My Precious Bogey
    Wednesday evening when L.M. came & brushed you &
Thursday morning note are come.
    ALSO just as I had tied two lovely purple bows on the shoulders
of my chemise came Mrs Honey with such a sort of sweet piece
from the comb that I am still tasting it – your telegram despatched
this very morning as ever was – saying you are 'chirpy' (When you
use that particular word my heart always overflows. It's such an
exquisitely *brave* word from you – and my 'hurray' in return has a
little catch in its voice.)
    You shall have strawberries, love in this happy land three times a
day – & I don't see why we shouldn't take back a great basketful
for jam, too – & do the government in its cruel blind eye – Oh – the
Picnics! We shall have almost perpetual picnics – whole or half day
ones – There is a river here, you know which I've never yet been up.
Waiting to explore it with you. Then we shall even if we don't buy a
pin or a curtain ring to it – adorn the Elephant here & plan it &
plot it and mark it with E & put it in the oven for Bogey and me.
    Rib: 'She's in one of her worse moods. Look out, parentchik!'
But it's all your fault as Wilkie's girl says – you ought *not* to be so
enchanting.
    Oh, darling Boge, wings or no wings, even if I become a sort of
baby pelican with a bright eye *I* must be the one who looks after
you – until the Heavens open and we behold the Lord with the
Heron upon his right hand. It's not fair – hopelessly not fair that
you should have to drag me in a little cart after you to the office and
then drag me home again & that I should fall over every time I'm
'propped'. No – I refuse – for ever & ever – amen. (We are to have
a couponless poulet to take back.)
    Now I am going to talk to you about what you ought to bring
here – If it means the large suitcase – and it's not too great a
nuisance – bring it for an odd corner would be most welcome on
my return journey. This hotel is a ... 1st class English Pension –
Awful if you had to fraternise but as I have established a squirrel
reputation (only descending to seize my nut or two when the gong
goes & then simply flying back into the branches again) it's quite
alright. But what I mean is – one *changes* in the evening – & though
I don't expect you to join the boiled ones you'd be happier if you

had your – say blue serge – I think to get into after you have been out all day – You'll need of course your slippers, too, and some cricket shirts if you have same. Socks, ties, hanks and spunk bag. Also a belt for wearing when we row away & you throw your coat at me – for not even oriental embroidered braces will do – – Corduroys of course would have you in the lock-up in ½ an hour & a jersey would have the fishing boats after you – 'Spose you'd better wear a straw hat – hadn't you? And don't forget pigglejams. You will of course be met with a jingle – Rib driving.

I thought you'd wear your white silk shirt in the evening with a bow tie. Is that a possible combination – or do I rave? These are just hints. If you want to throw them away & arrive with your rucksack – well – you will, of course!

Pagello – galant uomo – was here last night & made a tour of the battlefield. There is no sign of an *advance* by the enemy – they are still more or less there in force on our left wing – but the moral of the Commander in Chief is excellentissimo today –

This long letter is because Sunday comes in between – a dull old day – no post.

But you must understand it has Love Love Love enough to fill all the letterboxes in the world – It will, my own, if only you'll hold it to your warm heart a minute keep alight until Monday –

Oh God. How she does *love* him – Is it possible? What can she do to express it. Go to the town & buy the ferryman some tobacco – yes, that's what I'll do. Give the old boy a hug from his sister –

As to what I give YOU – & Rib throws up his arms – Yours for ever.

Wig.

Do *please* send me *Colour*. Cigarettes are excellent, thank you.

[47 Redcliffe Road,
Fulham]

Sunday Afternoon.   [16 June 1918]

My precious Wig.

I felt very, very chirpy indeed yesterday morning when I got your Friday letter. It was wonderful; and I never felt such a sham as I did when I marched off to Crofty at 12 o'clock. But the die was cast, and I had to. He was extraordinarily nice, banged me about, said I wasn't ill, but wasn't strong enough really for office work, told me to be very careful, was very glad I was going to live near Hampstead Heath, and finally said I must have one half-day off at least every week (and that he would give me a certificate to that effect) and finally that the very best thing for me was a course of arsenic and iron injections. So I, with the weekly half-holiday singing in my head, said 'Yes, please' without thinking that it wd. probably cost at least five guineas; and I had the first on the spot. I'm to have two more before I come down to you: and nine when I come back.

So that's the end of that story. Weighing it all up, I think the half holiday will be cheap at five guineas. Think of it, Wig, in the Elephant! One day in the week I shall come home at lunch-time and not have to go back any more. It's to be in the middle of the week. Thursday I think. It'll make things pretty different, won't it?

I haven't seen anything of that strawberry glut yet. But my paper to-day says that there may be plenty to-morrow: if I can get any at 1/- a lb, I'll make the jam. I asked my mother yesterday. She said she didn't leave them overnight, but put them straight in the pan. Her strawberry jam last year was jolly good. So I think I'll risk that. No water, she says, and agrees with you.

I'll bring the large suit case and all the implements for making myself look a little gentleman. I'll not go so far as a boiled shirt though. Your idea about the blue serge is good enough; but I must get the missing button sewn on. I won't forget the belt, and I'll buy myself a couple of cricket shirts. One of my two pairs of white flannel trousers has been fairly gobbled up by the moths: and the laundry woman, very rightly, refused to wash it. So I shall have 1 clean pair and the old pair of grey flannels – they've got some green paint on them; but they've also got a pronounced crease – so I'll think they'll do. I'm very weak on coats to wear with my cricket shirt. My black velvet one is down in Garsington. Will slippers do? Or do I need to buy myself some pumps? Say but the word.

Oh, Lord, it's really *very* near now – very, very near. I'm getting everything tidied up now. Last night I finished the front page article for the *Times*. Next week I have to write a leader, the political notes & a review for the *Nation*. 'Twill all be finished on Thursday. Yesterday afternoon I finished the monthly report in fine style – the arsenic having already begun to course thro' my veins – and it only remains to correct the proofs. So it seems to me that things are going very well indeed.

Of course, now I shan't be able to write anything coherent until I see you. That's how I'm always taken. I feel the imbecile smile spreading over my face and I have to give way.

I'm going to lunch with Chaddie on Tuesday at some place in Jermyn street of which I couldn't catch the name. However, it has two little trees in front so that ought to be good enough.

Your *Boge*

[Headland Hotel,
Looe, Cornwall]
Tuesday.   [18 June 1918]

My own Bogey
It is cold as Winter, gray with white horses, solemn boats – a pale light on everything – a feeling of great 'uneasiness' in the air. I think I may have a letter from you by this afternoon's post – none came this morning. *Colour* came – I shook it – held it up [by] its hair & its heels but it hadn't a message – The reproductions are very beautiful – I have had a good look at them – You know 'Poise' is extraordinarily fine, but having gone so tremendously far as Fergusson *has* gone I don't think the *mouth* is quite in the picture – It is – it is more 'in the picture' than most of his other mouths are – but I think it might be more *sensitive* ... more 'finely felt.' Of course I can hear his 'to Hell with rosebuds' but I won't be put off by it: it's too easy & begs the question anyway. To exaggerate awfully (as I always do) he really seems sometimes to fit women with mouths as a dentist might fit them with teeth – & the same thing happens in both cases: the beautiful *individual* movement (mobility) of the face is gone – Looking at 'Poise' again this mouth seems more nearly right than any other – Perhaps that's what sets up the irritation in me. I must say as a picture it properly fascinates me – – –
The magazine as a whole is VILE. Nothing less will do. The article on J.D.F. is such pigwash that I cannot imagine how he allowed it – There is not a hint of even low ability in one word of all the writing from cover to cover – It makes me want to start a paper of course, frightfully, but not a soul would buy our paper. We'd have to make our cow subscribe and all our little newborn chickens & ducks would be presented with life subscriptions – The birds that sang about the Heron I am sure would gladly pay a feather a copy, too, but then in the case of swallows for instance it would [be] such a *job* posting theirs on to funny strange addresses in Africa & Italy – No, no paper. Books.
Bogey, the north wind doth blow – It has found out my bones

again & is playing a fine old tune in them. I should like to come into your room, light a big fire, put a kettle on – & then both of us – curl up in two big chairs – the doors & windows are shut – tight – there are books & I'll make coffee & we'll talk or be quiet. This ain't a day for hotel bedrooms – If I hadn't FRIDAY nailed to the mast – but I have – I have – thank God!

I think you'd better bring down your wooly weskit, darling – to be ready for weather like this. But the Lord may turn his face to Looe again by then. He just must.

I am a silly, dull girl today – I had a nuit *blanche* & my brain is still, as it were, empty with it. But Friday is in this week & thank God! you have not to cross the water – Let us make a solemn vow – never – never to let the seas divide us – Be careful not to lean out of the train window. Have tea at Plymouth – but don't miss the train while you are blowing on it. Cut yourself a large huge sangwich for your lunch. It's better to have too much food when you are travelling. I didn't have half enough on my way down here & had to keep on buying snippets. Above all – keep *warm* & remember you're looking after yourself for me as I do for you.

> Your own
> Wig.

P.S. Look here! I have just taken a room for you. Does that sound awful? It's next to mine. It won't cost any more than if you were in this room with me – but it will give you *platz*. You needn't sleep in it if you don't want to – we are 'side by side' – & as I have bregglechik in bed I thought you would perhaps prefer to dress & so on in your own room – It will cost just the same as this room – I feel we'll both *rest* better like that – It's a nice room – tiny, though.

> Wiggie.

> [2 Portland Villas,
> Hampstead]
> [about 20 November 1918]

My dear Jack
   I confess that these last days my fight with the enemy has been so hard that I just laid down my weapons and ran away, and consented to do what has always seemed to me the final intolerable thing i.e. to go into a Sanatorium.

Today, finally thinking it over, and in view of the fact that it is not, after all, so much a question of *climate* as of *régime* (there are very successful sanatoria in Hampstead and Highgate) I am determined, by my own will, to live the sanatorium life *here*.

(1) Father shall have built for me a really good shelter in the garden where I can lie all day.

(2) He shall also give us two good anthracite stoves.

(3) I shall buy a complete Jaeger outfit for the weather.

(4) I shall have a food chart and live by it.

(5) This new servant releases Ida who has consented to give her whole time to me – as a nurse.

(6) Sorapure shall still be my doctor. I shall have a separate bedroom *always and live by rule*. You must have a bed in your dressing room when the servant comes.

(7) I shall NOT WORRY.

You see, Jack, for the first time today I am determined to get well as Mother would be determined for me. If we are depressed we must keep apart. But I am going through with this and I want you to help me. It CAN be done. Other people have done this in Hampstead. Why not I?

Anything else, any institutional existence would kill me – or being alone, cut off, ill with the other ill. I have really taken my courage up & I'm not going to drop it. I *know* it's possible.

Your own Wig.

September–December
1919

On 14 October 1918 (her thirtieth birthday), Katherine Mansfield was examined by specialists and advised that unless she entered a sanatorium she had only four years to live. Rejecting the advice that would have curtailed, if not put a stop to her writing, she instead made a gallant attempt to go on leading a normal life. From August 1918 until September 1919, with L.M. acting as housekeeper, the Murrys lived at 2 Portland Villas in Hampstead. Early in 1919, Murry was appointed editor of the newly reconstituted *Athenaeum*. Katherine began contributing weekly fiction reviews to the paper, enthusiastically supporting this venture as she had *Rhythm* and the *Blue Review*.

By the middle of 1919, however, it became obvious that her health could not endure another English winter. In September, therefore, Murry escorted her and L.M. to the Italian Riviera for a separation that they had agreed would last until May 1920. But almost from the start, the Casetta Deerholm at Ospedaletti proved unsatisfactory. Katherine's letters reveal her becoming increasingly lonely and despondent without the support of her husband. Finally, on 4 December, she posted Murry the bitter 'New Husband' verses that brought him hastening to her side for Christmas.

[2 Portland Villas,
Hampstead]
September 9th 1919.

My darling Boy

I am leaving this letter with Mr Kay just in case I should pop off suddenly and not have the opportunity or the chance of talking over these things.

If I were you I'd sell off all the furniture and go off on a long sea

183

voyage on a cargo boat, say. Don't stay in London. Cut right away to some lovely place.

Any money I have is yours, of course. I expect there will be enough to bury me. I don't want to be cremated and I don't want a tombstone or anything like that. If it's possible to choose a quiet place – please do. You know how I hate noise.

Should any of my friends care for one of my books to remember me by – use your discretion.

All my MSS I simply leave to you.

I think you had better leave the disposal of all my clothes to L. M.

Give the woolly lamb to Brett, please, and also my black fox fur.

I should like Anne to have my flowery shawl; she loved it so. But that is as you think.

Jeanne must have the greenstone.

Lawrence the little golden bowl back again.

Give Pa all that remains of Chummie.

Perhaps I shall have something Chaddie would like by then; I have nothing now – except perhaps my Chinese skirt.

See that Rib has an honourable old age and don't let my brass pig be lost. I should like Vera to have it.

That's all. But don't let anybody *mourn* me. It can't be helped. I think you ought to marry again and have children. If you do give your little girl the pearl ring.

> Yours for ever
> Wig.
>
> K. Mansfield Murry (for safety's sake).

> [Paris]
> [2 October 1919]
> 11.30 Thursday

My darling Mouse,

I got here (Paris) at 9 this morning, and am catching the boat-train at 12. They say we may have to stay the night at Folkestone. Therefore, although it has been a rush, I thought it better to give Paris a miss altogether and catch the boat to-day. The train is crowded, but I've managed to get a place. I only hope it won't be gone when I return.

My love & my dear – how sweet that sounds really – you have all my heart. Again I feel that it's just been taken out of me and left behind: and there it will remain with you – hiding under my old grey hat I expect – until I come and fetch it & you back for ever. Good-bye my darling. Everything is going well with me

Boge.

[Casetta Deerholm,
Ospedaletti]

3.30 p.m.   [3 October 1919]

Darling,

Your card has just come. Figurez-vous my happy surprise. I am disgusted that you had the extra bother but *much* relieved to think you will be comfortable in the first class express (or moderately so). Of course you couldn't have waited and then travelled in such a caterpillar. There is Felti in the hall. Signs of you are everywhere. I jealously gathered your clothes & sent them to the donna bella this afternoon, making the list *myself*, so that no other hand should touch them. By this same post goes Swinnerton to the office, written in spite of the flies. I hope it is alright. After you had gone I coo-eed when I saw you on a part of the road which was visible – then, when I saw you at the station, I ran up to the bonne's bedroom & remembering your old eyes, waved a *chemise!!* I felt sure you'd see.

No sign of Vince. I sent L.M. to phone. The agent says the people are *here* working but deep in the mountain like gnomes & we may expect them to appear above ground tomorrow [and] the water the day *after*. No Mr. Vince or Miss; they are frauds & I've received their bill. They charged us 2.50 for those custards with our own eggs & milk. Oh, a plague on human beings, only you & I are really the right kind. Here is a letter from Rendall. Kot's parcel came today – with a cheque for £1. The parcel contains sheets & sheets of translation to be 'ultimately published in book form in America'. What a bother! L.M. refused lunch today but only tore a piece of bread, she said she was not hungry – I did not get angry and later discovered her *having her lunch* – Proved at last! She *is* a silly. I'll not mind her, though. The sea is white, with silver fishes of light in it. The waves say Boge – Boge – as they come in – Yes, find the house. Yes, the 28 weeks will pass – Then comes our month of May, and after that our home. Eggs are to be had in Ospedaletti, good ones & figs & mutton cutlets.

The good things that happen to you you may leave untold if you like but you are to tell me *all* the bad things that happen. Then I feel secure of your confidence and I don't worry. See?

I am going to start bang in on Mackenzie & Gilly – so that I shall be a bit ahead. So send along some more books soon, please.

You will be in London when this reaches you and at home. Give it to Wing to sit on for a moment. Oh, darling Heart – *how* I love you – All must go well. I want to know about the house & Violet and if she really does all you require in the way you require. It's so hot – the flies are eating me up. Oh, Bogey, you come up the steps, carrying the pail – a geranium in your waistcoat pocket. You are more loved than anybody in the world by your

> Wig

No 7.   2 Portland Villas,
                                     [Hampstead]
                                     [9 October 1919]
                                     Thursday 10.30 p.m.

My precious wife,

Your Monday letter came this evening to say you had my Paris card. Thank Heaven. I can't imagine why it took so long, seeing that it was posted at a post office before 12 on the Thursday. Surely my English letters – the first was sent on Friday night – will have begun to arrive on the Tuesday. They would if they did things as well in France & Italy as they do in England. Your letters are getting here in 3 days regularly.

You don't tell me how you are. If it was anybody else – someone not quite such a darling as Wig – I should be able to conclude that you were feeling well because your letter was happy. But with you, that doesn't really work. You might have two legs & an arm off, but you'd forget to tell me because of your joy at a letter from me saying my constipation was better. So I must ask you just to forget all about me for half a page of every letter and say exactly how you are – even your temperature.

To-day I've sent you my little present. Please don't think it absurd. It's just a spoon for you to eat your porridge & soup with. The worst of it is you'll always have to use it. I'm very sorry. But I thought it would look nice on your tray. Will it? By the way, darling, don't worry if it doesn't arrive at the same time as this letter, though it was posted today & the letter won't be posted until to-morrow. Your registered letters arrived quite a day & a half after the letter saying they were posted at the same time. And I had a letter today from a man in Spain saying that a registered letter took two days longer than an ordinary one. That's worth remembering if ever you are pressed for time with your review. If you are posting on or after Saturday copy to go in the following week, don't register it. Only register if you post before Saturday.

Another thing that worries me a little. How about your money? Has anything arrived at the Banca d'Italia? Or are you getting it direct from Kay? And how are you off anyhow? I can easily send you some.

I'm jolly glad you've got that revolver. What a cursed shame about that water. If I don't hear good news about it to-morrow, I shall write Mr. Vince a type-written stinker on office paper.

Sydney Waterlow arrived last night, puffing and blowing. I don't think he's going to be a nuisance at all; and he doesn't seem to eat a frightful lot. At any rate Violet seems to give me such a great deal that he comes in very useful for eating it up. He never gets back from his office till 7.30; so I'm going to arrange to be home as often as I can for tea at 4.30 – and have a quiet 3 hours all to myself.

I lunched with Tom Moult to-day. He's nice, but extraordinarily childish. His conceit of his own work is quite staggering. I couldn't get out of asking him & Bessie to dinner on Wednesday; it'll be so funny to see what happens to Sydney. In the restaurant I met Clive with Mary H. Clive very anxious to know whether you would like to meet anybody at San Remo. He apparently knows someone, an Italian, who knows all the local intelligentsia. I didn't commit myself.

I had to buy a new double saucepan to-day: hope it doesn't get broken. Violet also wants a medium-sized saucepan. I'll get an aluminium one. I'm dead nuts on getting the furnishings together for our house.

I wonder will this be your birthday letter. It's meant to be. Just for a moment you must imagine I'm under my old hat. You're in your little room. Now I'm coming ever so softly – just tripped over the gold & red plush bookcase – into your room with your spoon in my hands. Now I've put the spoon in your lap. Now I've got you folded tight. Many happy returns of the day – my little Wig, mouse, darling. This is the last birthday we'll ever be apart – the last, the last, the very last

Boge.

[Casetta Deerholm,
Ospedaletti]
Monday,   [13 October 1919]

My Precious,
  The weather has completely changed it's chilly with a thick thick fog & heavy downpour of rain. The sky is grey, it's like living inside a pearl today – very lovely for a change.
  The October 10 number of the paper I have just gone through. Good Heavens! how good it is – What different eyes – different hair – – to the little measles that came out all spotty while you were away. *This one simply thrills me.* I'll have to get a flagstaff in this garden & when I've read my copies through, fly them – just out of pride – The leading article was excellent – it went so well – I think one ought to begin by – not knocking the reader down exactly but by showing him who is 'master of the house', as Wilkie's girl would say. Scott-James too is admirably to the point and it's a very good article to have. Sheppard is one of your most valuable men, I think. An excellent mellow quality in what he writes & altogether – – – just what the A. can publish so well.
  I wish the 1st letter from America had not been so particular. It's first chop to have secured it but we don't really care so passionately about Mr. Kreymborg – do you think? I do so love a general *survey* or at any rate an ordnance map – before I visit the various paths & farms. Now & again this chap gives me an idea he could write very well.
  Most excellent letter from Italy, I thought – & awfully good dramatic criticism of Tolstoy – so *fresh*. In fact the whole appearance, contents everything has form & substance again. You are evidently a genius as an editor – nothing short of that – a perfect genius. I adore working for you but I do *wish* you'd send me some novels. I am sending an article tomorrow on some novels here, in the bookcase but it is a bit steep to be left without a single one –
  Yes the paper is a noble paper, my son: it most certainly is. I don't know what to do – I am so damned proud of you – you little marvel. I feel if only I had some books here I *would* write a review & that's what all your team feel, I believe. What about Ripmann. Have you ever thought of him again as a possible contributor – an article on languages or the *production of books*, he is a very great nut on printing and so on.
  L.M. has surpassed herself today – At 1.30 I staggered in to ask where the lunch was & it was *not*. She had no kindling & the olive

root won't burn with just paper – After all these days when every afternoon she is up in the hills, roaming the pastures wild. *Then* there were no eggs – then she boiled the coffee in the water she had prepared for spaghetti, reeking with *gros sel* – I got a bit fierce but I apologised at once and really I don't get upset by her at all now – I think she is *very queer* though. You know that lovely room of hers with that view.... I asked her yesterday why she didn't make it nice – and she said she hadn't unpacked 'as you are sending me away in April and at any rate my room is just a passage isn't it – to the lavatory – – –'

Visitor last night. A *very* nice one. While I was waiting for the beans. I saw two honey-ball eyes looking at me from the hall (the front door was open.) When they saw me they *flashed* away but I immediately said as much Wing language as I knew & went quietly to the door with my soup plate. A perfectly lovely tiny cat came in – *gold, white & black* with a body rather like a rabbit. It simply bolted the stray pasta then I gave it some milk & it simply more than bolted that. Then it purred more loudly than any cat I've ever heard. Its purring machine must have been wound up until that moment – It sat under a chair singing like this for a little & then fled into the night again. In my mind I called it 'Genêt'.

I have just looked up – the fog has rolled away – the rain has stopped – The air smells of the geraniums. Tomorrow the gardener comes for the day – the ground will be just right for sowing. There are carts going by. *Yip-y-y-y-ip-yip* say the drivers & the bells go *tring-tring-tring* – The sea sounds as though it were somehow exquisitely refreshed by that mist – all the grass blades are bowed down by a diamond. Oh dear, *I'm awfully happy.* It has been so lovely lying here in the rain – I feel renewed too and bowed down with a diamond too. I love you. I love you. Shall I have a letter by the late post. O Bogey, look at the new leaves on the rose bushes – bright red. Were they there yesterday? There is one hidden frog here; he croaks every evening – He shall be invited to the festa in May. Isn't this rotten paper – it's oiled in places, and you can't write on both sides really. After all a birthday present came from C[haddie] and J[eanne] Came together. An ordinary small 1d. match box, enamelled yellow and painted (very badly) with an ugly little Chinaman–Oriental Department 1/11¾. 'To our darling Katie with our united love & best wishes.' They couldn't have said more if it was a carpet. I shall keep this match box for ever and measure the size of their hearts by it.

Goodbye most precious. Bites are still going strong – Does

Tommy know a fly – just like an ordinary house fly in the face that
stings? *It is here.*
And now I hug you tight & hold you a minute.

      Wig

    No letter. Weekly *Times.* A for October 3 & the 10th, *Nation*
fetched up.

                          2 Portland Villas,
                            [Hampstead]
196 days   [17 October 1919]

My precious Worm,
    Your mottled Monday letter came this morning. How wonderful
your descriptions are – 'like living inside a pearl'. No-one but you
has the genius for these things nowadays. Why the devil the whole
literary world is not at your feet, I'll never understand. You are the
only *genius* in the whole bunch of good ones among us.
    It thrilled me to think you thought so Much of the *Athenaeum* –
too much? I don't know. I agree with you about the American letter
as too particular. But doesn't the man write well for an American;
he really writes. By the way, old girl, I would like to give D. H.
Lawrence a leg-up. What do you say to writing on *Sons & Lovers*
one week – either extra to or instead of your ordinary novels;
saying how it stands out etc. You know what the average is like
nowadays & you can speak your mind. It might help him a bit, you
know. Anyhow, I'll send it across. (In passing, I put your cheque in
your last letter with a stamp on the back.)
    Ripman's an idea. I'll get into touch with him & see whether he
wouldn't look after modern languages from the educational point
of view. L. M. – just a passage to the lavatory – is unspeakable.
That really puts the lid on her. Your notepaper is exactly like
mottled soap – but I can read what's on it. You can't tell how
happy your happy letters make me. Nothing matters. I can do
mountains of work. I've really done ¾ of that announcement list
to-day. To-night I have to go to the play. I'm taking Arthur with
me. Thank heaven James Strachey is back again though.
    I have two determinations – one to make the paper a success
against all competition this winter – the other to write a novel with
among other things some real you and me love in it. There are many
things to be got into it. I don't know how I shall tackle it; I can't get

a scheme, and don't see what good it would do if I had one. I'm sure I wasn't built to work with schemes. One door suddenly opening out of a dark chamber, then another, and another – that's the only way my mind ever works. So, as soon as I can get a breathing space, I shall start in – anywhere, anyhow all I have is a house (very important) & a woman & a man (both very vague). I'm terribly afraid it will be what the critics call a romance. But I can't really say anything until I've dug the first hole. What it must be at all costs is a you & me novel – no rotten old *Still Life*: to show these devils what subtlety & delicateness (in joy & pain) life is capable of. I hope it won't get too big – or no-one will ever publish it.

But first – *Cinnamon* must be finished. I was reading a play by Robert Greene – an Elizabethan – not much good – the other day & I found he had a girl called Angelica, & that he used her name rhythmically & repeatedly just as I have done. That's rather disturbing because they'll say – if they ever say anything, which they won't: no-one ever said a word about my book of *Poems* – I copied.

This is all very egotistic seeing you are the genius & I ain't. But who can I tell it to but you?

> Your devoted loving
> Boge.

198 received (*no* 199)
Books received Benson & Weyman

[Casetta Deerholm,
Ospedaletti]
[20 October 1919]

[[Oh, Bogey why are people swindlers? My heart *bleeds* when they swindle me – doesn't yours? This gardener – he promised to come & put the garden in order for 10 francs & bring some little plants too. It was to be 10 francs a day *with* the plants & now his wife has come & explained the plants are *10 francs more*. And he only came for half a day yesterday but she says he spent the other half looking for the plants – so they between them charged me 30 francs. It isn't the money that matters – though I felt ashamed as I gave in to them & could not look at their eyes – it is that *they are dishonest*. That hurts so! Yes, put the wall round the house. Why will people do such things. I'd rather they turned & beat me. The sun streams through the folded clouds on to the sea in long beams of light – such beams as you see in picture books when the Lord appears – it is a silent day except for the sound of this *false* pick as he digs up the little beds. L.M. is in San Remo. I have to hide from this old man now. I wish he'd go. His wife was all in grey, with big black hollow places where her teeth had been & she said *firmly* 'c'est moi qui vient tous les soirs arroser votre jardin pour vous.' When I said no – her 'C'est bien' was like *steel spittle*. Well, I've cried my cry to you. But my dear love – this vileness – this snail on the underside of the leaf – always there!]]

199 is lost – is roaming in the wilderness. Perhaps I shall still get it. It's awful to miss letters. This today – Mrs. W[aterlow] seems established in the house. Oh I hope not. It's what I had feared. Can't you send her away. She mustn't be there long. No, that's childish, You know what is best from where you are and you will do it but *another woman* – it *hurts*. Still, be sensible, Katherine don't mind. What does it matter – She goes & comes on the stairs – she waits in the hall & I expect she has a key – I *knew* it would happen I *knew* it – She pulls the chairs forward. It makes me feel exactly as if I were dead. I see it all. She talks to Violet & would Violet mind doing this instead of that. Oh, curse my heart – curse it!! [[Why am I not a calm indifferent grown up woman ... and this great cold indifferent world like a silent malignant river & these creatures rolling over one like great logs – crashing into one – I try to keep to one side, to slip down unnoticed among the trembling rainbow coloured bubbles of foam & the faint reeds. I try to turn & turn in a tiny quiet pool – but it's no good – sooner or later one is pushed out into the middle of it all. Oh, my enchanted boy I am really sadder than you. I believe at any rate if they weighed us in the scales we'd both dip as deep –]]

[[Two books have come Stanley Weyman & Stella Benson. Good. I'll do them. Stella Benson seems to me just to miss it; she reminds me of Colette in a way. But I've only *dipped* into her book. A very attractive creature.]]

Father wrote to me: he is only coming as far as Nice or Cannes. Guaranteed no infection, I suppose. I shall go on writing away to him so as to be sure of my position. L. M. is at San Remo buying butter – This week I hope to work more – my hands are still poisoned by the bites & my eyes are not Dorothy Wordsworth eyes – It's a bore. [[Shall I send this letter? Or write another one – a gay one? No, you'll understand. There is a little boat – far out – moving along, *inevitable* it looks & *dead silent* – a little black spot like the spot on a lung – Don't mind me. I am very foolish and ought to be punished. Even as I wrote that the little boat is far away, there have come out of the sea great gold streamers of light such as I never before saw.]] Your own

Wig

2 Portland Villas,
[Hampstead]
190 days   October 24 [1919]

My precious darling,
 I had a very sad letter from you this morning, dated Monday last. You were sad about Mrs Waterlow being here, and also about the gardener, or the gardener's wife, turning out a fraud. Ironically, as usual, your Sunday letter, full of happiness about what the gardener was doing, arrived after the Monday one.
 Oh, child, I wish I was there to comfort you. The sight of the worm in the pear is unbearable to me, I know; but I feel, I know I can bear it better than you. You don't think so & you always want to bear it for me, I know. But I am the stronger for this particular burden. I am far less sensitive, less frail than you. The vision shakes your whole being; it doesn't do that to me any more. Besides being cruder & clumsier, I have a leaden foot which other people would call a philosophy. Of course, it's nothing of the kind. It's merely a sentimental kettleholder. I am able to take hold of things that would have burned me years ago. You haven't got a kettleholder; you're too delicate & fine.
 It doesn't need to be proved. I know. But there is a proof to hand – a strange & interesting one. When you wrote to me, a fortnight ago, to say that you feared Sydney W. would bring strange women into the house, I immediately supposed that you meant a woman of the town, or something corresponding. It never faintly dawned upon me that you meant Mrs. W. That mere fact is enough to show how much cruder & less sensitive I am than you. I hang my head in shame for not having known that you meant an alien feminine influence. I ought, as your lover, to have known it. I *ought*. There's no excuse. But there it is: the damage is done. All I can say is that she never entered your room. What is most yours, is yours intact.
 To-day has been dull, raining and almost close. Mrs Lynd came in to ask news of you this morning. I told her all that I could tell. Would you write to her, if you could – about the house, I mean. I know she wd do for you what she wd. never do for me.

There's not much office news. As I told you I called in Arthur to help with designing of our advertisements. I was very disappointed when Bonwick this morning suddenly said to me why didn't you introduce yr. brother to me when you took over the editorship? He could have had Sears's job – S. is our kindly but utterly incompetent publicity manager. However, it's no use repining over lost opportunities. I must be satisfied that A. made a tremendous impression on Bonwick. It'll probably stand him in good stead some time.

Tell me more, darling, about the blood-shot eye. What a curse it is that we had no time to get your eyes examined & fitted with gig-lamps! Are you sure it comes from too much reading?

Wd. it be possible – returning to the A. – for you to get a week ahead with the novels? You see now that the advertising campaign has begun, I need to have my whole contents on the Friday previous – that is a whole week before publication. As it is, I never know what the novel article will be about until the Tuesday – so that I have to leave it out of the advertisement.

I am sending you Waley's new book of Chinese Poems. You're the only person who can do them – not more than 2 columns, when you feel inclined.

I weighed myself the day before yesterday – 10 stone i.e. a half-stone heavier than I was two years ago. It's not my health you have to worry about.

Unless the weather clears & the rain stops, I shall stay at home working to-morrow.

Good-bye my darling
Boge
xxxxxxxx
xxxxxxx
xxxxxx
xxxxx
xxxx
xxx
xx
x

[Casetta Deerholm,
Ospedaletti]

Thursday,   [30 October 1919]

My darling,
I am sending a review today and I shall send another tomorrow. Things have not gone as fast as I wished (as usual) but from now onward they will improve. I expect you wonder why with such unlimited opportunity I do not just waltz through with things. Alas! up till now it [has] been – not so much my health at all – but my domestic arrangements. Now I have discovered how I can live with L.M. It is by not speaking more than is necessary for the service of the house. Two nights ago we had a 'crise' which made me realise it must be the very last, that if it occurred again I'd have to ask her to go & to make other arrangements. This, of course I don't at all want to do, so the other plan is adopted. I don't know what she thinks – I imagine she is furious but I don't care. It's *such a rest* – you can't imagine. No shouting, no quarrelling, no violence, just quiet: I am basking in it. I can keep it up, too, by an effort of Will; I am *sure* I can. Otherwise there would have been no work done – nothing done – nothing written – for our hate had got to such a pitch that I couldn't take a plate from her hand without shuddering. This *awful relationship* living on in its secret corrupt way beside my relationship with you is very extraordinary; no one would believe it. I am two selves – one my true self – the other that she creates in me to destroy my true self. Still I'll write no more about it & try & think about it less and less so that the fire gets more & more covered. But that's what makes my work so hard & what *paralyses my mind*. It's just like a terrible fog; I'm lost in it and I go mad – just like L[awrence] used to. Here I have thrown things at her – yes, even that – called her a murderer, cursed her – Her three standing remarks 'give me time', 'I'll learn by degrees, Katie' and 'you must first teach me, that's all' are to me too sinister.... I haven't the time to give – However, it's over. And I shall live in silence with her now and put it away. Better a thousand times be lonely than speak to her. But that is *the real reason* why I cannot work as I could, L.M., L.M. and L.M. So after this I'll do better – see?
No letters came today – none yesterday – I am longing for the post. There'll be two tomorrow I expect. It's fine today though still bitter cold: I've been lying still in the sun all the morning – haven't moved. The sea is wonderfully beautiful – so deep and dark – yet with the light on it, moving and glittering.

I heard from Chaddie & Jeanne yesterday, both full of [illegible]. 'How I wish I could send you a great hamper from the orchard of nuts and apples ...' it's a safe wish at this distance. One page was devoted – this is *dead true* to the match box: she knew it would appeal to me – so delighted it had fetched up safe, J. & she both said '*K.*' when they saw it etc. It made me violently jealous that they should have a house and nuts & apples. I *yearn* to beat them – I feel I shall buy all the china I can get here to beat their china & oh if we had more money you could be looking out for oddments too. We must have our house Bogey, next year. Is there any star on the horizon? Chaddie sent me a photograph of myself at three months [i.e. years] old. It was a *dreadful shock*. I had always imagined it – a sweet little laughing thing, rather French, with wistful eyes under a fringe, firmly gripping a spade, showing even then a longing to dig for treasure with her own hands – But this little solemn monster with a wisp of hair looked as though she were just about to fall backwards head over heels. On her feet she wears as far as I can make out a pair of ordinary workman's boots which the photographer, from astonishment or malice has photographed so close up that each tootsie is the size of her head. The only feature about her is her ears which are neatly buttonholed on to the sides of her head & not just safety-pinned on as most babies' are – Even the spade she clasps with the greatest reluctance ... Now I must work. The hot water runs at last – for the first time yesterday – Vince is not going to London until the end of *November*: I thought I'd let you know. Oh, I do hope there is a letter tomorrow darling with news of *you* in it. I am anxious about this ghastly press of work. Otherwise all goes well here, and under my new regime it can only go better. Goodbye my own precious Bogey. When you get this it will be November – 2 months to the New Year.

Your own Wig

2 Portland Villas,
[Hampstead]
[1 November 1919]
Saturday Night.

181 days

My own precious darling,
I got your last letter (Monday) this afternoon. It's a good job they came in the wrong order, because the last was much more like

you (or rather made me think you weren't miserable). The Albatross had been too much for you before. Oh, darling, I do so sympathise: if only I could just appear, to hug you & talk to you, only for a moment. But there – it can't be. But just think my arms are round you, that you really are better at last as you will be, that we are together in our bye in our house, early summer morning, bright light coming through the casement curtains. You and I together – lovers. Oh, my heart something in me faints at the thought of feeling your wonderful body beneath mine again, of kissing your breasts as I used, going from your breasts to your lips & to your breasts again, till the whole of me melted away into you and I became a pulse of your heart. My God, to be lovers again.

I suppose all this is wicked & that I ought not write it; I feel somehow that it is cruel. And yet for once forgive me Worm. The nights come when my physical love for you is unbearable.

Well, the time will come again & soon, if we stick to our bargain to keep going at all costs

I shouldn't have written this letter. I've upset myself and I can't go on.

But my love for you, Worm, is consuming, consuming.

Boge

I'll do something better to-morrow

[Casetta Deerholm,
Ospedaletti]
Sunday in bed   [2 November 1919]

Darling of darlings

I have heard from you twice this week – du reste silence. If I do not get a letter today it will be TOO dreadful. My mind is paralysed with dismay and apprehension, and I am in bed with this horrible storm raging day & night outside – No one to speak to – Like Robinson Crusoe – HE lived alone – Worse – ah, much, much worse –

I have just seen the Hochwohlgeborene Doktor Bobone. I did not want to wait any longer for Ansaldi. Yesterday was so terrible, Boge, in my darkish room – like a cave – unable to write or think – no news – no letters – I sent her to San Remo: because I felt I must at least have someone in touch with me – He stayed about an hour and most thoroughly examined me. I think he is a very good doctor indeed – scientific – dry – *German* and as frank with me as if I'd been a student examining the case – with him. He says the fact I have so little fever is good – all on my side. 'So long as you have not the fevers you do not die. It is de fevers which kills.' I don't think he had at all a *great* opinion of me. On the other hand he said he thought I might go in to see him once a fortnight – go into San Remo! He says the apex of the right lung only is affected; the left is infiltrated to the third rib. He is giving me a medicine *for* tuberculosis. This I don't like. Sorapure said they were so often dangerous. This man said himself it is not one of the dangerous ones. 'It do nothing or it do well' – I suppose I must trust him, then. This villa he approves of for fine weather but when the weather is not fine he says I must stay in bed to be out of draughts & to be warm – Air, to live out in the sun, food, and no vorry, no fever – 'and you will not die. It is the fever kills the patient'. This was his one cry. But when I tried to tell him of my appalling *mental* state of depression he didn't even listen.... No one *listens* to a patient except Sorapure –

Now listen. TRY to send me letters often or cards or papers from the office – anything. If I were there, you'd spend 10 minutes with me – give me those 10 minutes here ... HELP ME HELP ME!! If I veep I getta de fever and I am veeping strong!! I have no negative tonic. I am tired – I can't always write or work or read – Then I have nothing but darkness – I live on this desolate hillside with L.M. munching by me. *But I can fight through all this* if I am in touch with you – If you are ill Arthur *must let me know immediately* – Reality Bogey is ALWAYS less than my dreams and apprehensions. If you will bear that in mind you will make Life easier. SILENCE is the ULTIMATE BLACKNESS – I must stop crying & send this to post – Oh God – what an end of all my fine hopes – to be writing my S. of France letters because of these cursed posts. The weather is perfect hell: the sea roars: it's never never quiet – it eats away the air. The room is half dark and I'm alone all day all day all day every day every day – Mrs. Jones can do up a paper can't she? But you are so pitiful have pity on me & WRITE.

Wig

Nothing is hopeless. Nothing is lost. No new terror has been added no new fear really. But this loneliness is what opens the gates of my soul & lets the wild beasts stream howling through. I shall get over it. Let us keep firm – But write me AT LENGTH.

[2 Portland Villas,
Hampstead]
[3 November 1919]
[179 days]   Monday Night.

Violet took my letter off to the post at the same time that she brought three from you – Thursday & Friday – each more upsetting than the one before. First, you seem to be really ill again. There's no getting over your cough, & your creaking lung & your depression. I feel so utterly helpless; & I am utterly helpless. The horror of the relations between you & L.M. is awful. I feel that I don't even know what to suggest. What's the use of writing that?

I'll go to Sorapure first thing to-morrow morning about the prescription. But how can he prescribe for your depression? I try to explain it all to myself in vain. Have you not been really resting, or is it impossible to rest with L.M.?

It's a fearful blow to me. It would have been that anyhow; but the consciousness that I can *do* nothing is too much. You say that the depression keeps your cough going & keeps you weak. And this depression is just an invisible enemy to me. I can't even approach it; all that there is is to get depressed myself.

What *is* it, Mouse? I know you've tried to conquer it; I almost wish you hadn't, so that I should not have been living in a fool's paradise. Is it something that just comes out of nowhere & seizes you. Has it any form?

Look here, Mouse. If you think it over & decide you'd rather I came out I'll throw up my job. Only you must ask your father to give us £200 – nothing more. But that we must have if I give up the *A*. If he will I'll come out immediately & you can pack L.M. off. I'll look after you myself. I'll understand, if you decide that, that there's no other way of pulling through. And *we must pull through.* But if I do that, we must face the fact that I can't – I haven't the energy or strength – count on making more than £200 during the first year, and that's not enough for us. There's devilish little margin as it is; but we can't live even in the quietest way with none at all. *We must not be worried for money in addition to the other worries.* Think it over, darling, & decide: whatever you decide I'll do like a shot.

Well, well, my darling heart, I thought I was used to these smacks in the face from destiny – but I'm not. Whenever there's a tiny little space I manage to get a great tree of hope going. But they all get blown down – they can't have any roots. If only one would stay.

What is most hateful is that this letter will only be depressing. If by the grace of God it should happen you are feeling better when this reaches you, remember this. That I shall *not* be feeling depressed. I shall be feeling happy just in proportion as you are well.

Oh, Mouse, if only I believed in God: I don't know what to ask to take care of you except our love. That's real enough, but how much power has it.

Boge.

One thing, Worm, the awful weather is *sure* to get better. The Riviera can't be all a fake. Oct–Nov. is a bad time before the fine weather comes. It's terrible here. But that's no consolation. The Italian grammar shall be posted to-morrow

[2 Portland Villas,
Hampstead]
[5 November 1919]
Wednesday Night
11.15.

177 days

My own precious darling,

Your Saturday (Nov. 2) letter came to-night. I'm afraid it's not very comforting. I know you are still wretched. My darling mouse, take heart. Believe somehow that I am really near you and the six months will disappear; but if we are down & despondent, then I feel we shall never climb over them. The mountains will be too high & terrible. Oh my heart, how I love you, adore you, worship you. Try to remember that you *couldn't* have stayed here this winter; it's like a viper, bitter & biting; think that your being there is something positively helping us to come together, as it really is. But if you think that Mentone would be better, why not get Conny & Jinny to find a place & go. We'll manage the money.

I couldn't get the parcel by post off to-day. They made such difficulties about declaration forms and the precise manner of sealing that, since the parcels didn't arrive at the office till 3, by the time I'd got them really ready, the Post Office was shut. But the parcel which Sydney sent in the diplomatic bag went off safely.

Thursday Morning

Your Sunday letter came. Even more shattering still. You have had no letters. I write every day, you know I do. I mustn't give way. I'll just say that I am in body perfectly well; but I don't know how long things will last if this strain goes on. Those silly lines I wrote when I was very young keep singing in my head: 'There's nothing to say: my heart is dead'. It isn't really; but there are moments when I feel it's on the point of giving out.

What can I do to help? I write & write; I try to keep in control of my work & behave like a sane being to the world. But when I feel that you feel that I have not written because you are not receiving my letters – I certainly become very nearly insane. Look here, you must keep things straight, & remember that a letter from me to you goes off every single day. If ever I feel in the slightest degree physically ill, I will wire you immediately: I promise you faithfully across my heart.

But until I feel some spark of hope from your side, it's useless my writing much about myself. It would merely be monotonous & depressing – my nervous agitation is continual, & the effort to keep pace with my work which is heavy is pretty severe. When I feel that you are moderately happy & making headway everything seems easy, easy. Now everything seems hard & requires a particular effort of will.

You know these things. What's the good of writing them? I'll work with all my soul I promise you to keep you supplied with news from the office, & things to read. If I've failed in this, as I have, it's because the work has been really heavy – now Sullivan's away & Aldous ill – and the necessity of keeping up the standard of the paper has been always an anxiety which I could share with no-one. The back *Literary Supplements* have been sent you. But I can't write about the details of the paper now, because I'm so agitated I can't remember anything.

Darling heart, my wonderful Mouse, I think of you years ago as my Squirrel in your little brown hat, the goblin hat, I think of all the happiness we desired & that seemed to be again in our grasp only a month ago, and now. It's not to be borne. One can't go on fighting losing battles. We *can't*. No doctor, even from Heaven, can do anything for your depression, any more than he could for mine. This is our battle. We must win, must win, must win. I'm not hysterical. But you must cling to me; hold on to the certainty that I write every day, that nothing can be wrong with me unless you have a wire, that I am fighting all day long against the misery of the news that comes from you, that somehow I intend to win. Don't say one day 'I can ignore L.M.' & the next 'She is killing me'. It begins to be that I can't believe a word. You must ignore her. I begin to feel from your letters that I'm only a kind of ghost to you: something far finer than I am, but bodiless & unreal.

Worm, my darling Worm, my arms *are* round you. You must believe it, somehow you must, you must.

                    Boge

                                        [Casetta Deerholm,
                                           Ospedaletti]
                                        [7 November 1919]
Friday,   180, 181

My darling

She came back with your Saturday night & Sunday letters (enclosing Butler). They heap coals of fire on my head. But I must tell you – your Saturday letter when you spoke of us being lovers – was like a credo I believe to me. It seemed to bring the future, near and warm and *human* for a minute. At sight of it – of so much life – the birds drew back – flew up and away – And then you seemed to tell me so much of what you were doing and it was home like. Our tiny Wing, clean in patches!

Early summer morning – think of it – a day before us – in the garden and in the house – Peace – Holding each other, kissing each other until we are one world.

It is all memories now – radiant, marvellous faraway memories of happiness. Ah, how terrible life can be – I sometimes see an immense wall of black rock, shining, in a place – just after death perhaps – and *smiling* – the *adamant* of desire. Let us live on memories, then and when the time comes – let us live so fully that the memories are no nearer than far away mountains – –

Arthur sent me another of his letters: you & he eating sausages & mash. *Hug* the old boy for me – tell him he's my brother – My 'Eternity' seemed perfect rubbish: I'll send it if you like. It seemed to go out as I wrote & I raked ashes. I'll send Butler back to-morrow. I'll send Dosty tomorrow. This isn't a letter – it's just a word again with you, my precious lover.

I've paid Porter – It's alright. I wish you'd go, though –

Think of me as your own

                    Mouse

The *Athenaeum* for Ever!!!
Saturday afternoon

[Casetta Deerholm,
Ospedaletti]
[8 November 1919]

My own Bogey
I will give this letter to L.M. to post in San Remo. I went out today and weighed myself & found in a fortnight I had gained over 2 lbs. I weigh 46 *kilo* 70 and last time it was just on 45. This is as you can see extraordinary. Now you will believe that I rest. I went then to the P.O. and found your Monday letter written after three awful ones of mine. What could I do? I could only send that p.c. *Now* I want to say – I would really count it almost as fearful if you gave up the *A.* and came out here as if all were lost. It would in a way mean all was lost; it would mean scrapping our future. Never think of it; never do it. I can imagine nothing more horrible for us both than that. It would mean – looked at from whatever angle that this thing had beaten us and it would mean – Oh – it is not possible to contemplate such a thing. I had rather live here the 2 years than that. That is the solemn truth. You see – I *am* getting better; my body is getting better. I have a theory that perhaps the creaking and pain I had were caused by the moist spot drying up in my bad lung. It's quite possible. Old Bobone of course would not know a thing like that. But then he good as I think he is, does not believe tuberculosis is curable; it's evidently a craze of his. I saw it & he said as much. 'Quick or soon coma de fever' – But never come to me or give up a thing or send me money or bind yourself, whatever I say *now or in the Future.* Please my own precious, NEVER do. We must see this through *successfully*; not otherwise. If you will just accept the fact that I am not gay – see? I will try not to talk of my loneliness & depression nor of L.M. It is a bright sunny day today and I am not in the least tired after my walk – only hungry. [[As usual I thought I was going to have it all my own way – get well – be happy – the horror of my disease over (it *is* a horror) over – peace with L.M. and ease to work in. What a fathead I am! Out of those – I'll get well – and that's all and enough. Let the others wait. *Work* of course – Work is second breath. When you spoke of planting a tree of hope I felt oh – it was *you* to speak so. Plant it – plant it darling – I will not shake it. Let me sit under it & look up at it – spread it over me and meet me there often and let us hold each other close and look up into the boughs for buds and flowers – No, there's no God. That is queer. This morning I wanted to say 'God keep you.' or 'Heaven guard us –' Then I thought of *The Gods* but

they are marble statues with broken noses. There is no God or Heaven or help of any kind but Love. Perhaps Love can do everything. Lo! I have made of love all my religion – Who said that? It's simply marvellous.]]

L.M. is ready to go. I shall have the place to myself. It's nice. Then I turn into a real Mouse and make as tiny a noise as possible – so as not to disturb the life round me –

We shall not get another sou out of Father, darling, not on any account. I wish you wld send him a farewell note to the Hotel Westminster – just for 'the firm' – would you? It *does* please me enormously that he goes back to N.Z. enthusiastic about us. And he is. The worst of it is he keeps writing about us going there. 'Pray God the day be not far off.' It *is* it's very far. I want Sussex and you and Arthur and the cats but only you.

[Casetta Deerholm,
Ospedaletti]
Monday morning,   [10 November 1919]

My own dear Love

Here is another Monday. They do seem to come round so fast – like the horses we saw at the fair – no – the *roosters* that was our one, wasn't it? Do you remember those little Princesses who went round for ever? They wore cotton frocks & tiny leather belts. It's a chill strange day. I breakfasted in Valhalla – cracks of lightning, thunder, tearing rain. Now I'm on the verandy and the clouds are immensely near and distinct like mountains. Will you please say if my Dosty is alright? I sent it rather in fear and trembling, but I meant it. I am doing Virginia for this week's novel. I don't like it, Boge. My private opinion is that it is a lie in the soul. The war never has been: that is what its message is. I don't want G. forbid mobilisation and the violation of Belgium – but the novel can't just leave the war out. There *must* have been a change of heart. It is really fearful to see the 'settling down' of human beings. I feel in the *profoundest* sense that nothing can ever be the same that as artists we are traitors if we feel otherwise – we have to take it into account and find new expressions new moulds for our new thoughts & feelings. Is this exaggeration? What *has* been – stands. But Jane Austen could not write *Northanger Abbey* now – or if she did I'll have none of her. There is a trifling scene in Virginia's book where a charming young creature in a light fantastic attitude plays the flute:

it positively frightens me – to realise this *utter coldness* & indifference. But I will be very careful and do my best to be dignified and sober. Inwardly I despise them all for a set of *cowards*. We have to face our war – they won't. I believe Bogey, our whole strength depends upon our facing things. I mean facing them without any reservation or restraints. I fail because I don't face things. I feel almost I have been ill so long for that reason: we *fear* for that reason: I mean fear can get through our defences for that reason. We've got to stand by our opinions & risk falling by them. Oh, my own Bogey, you are the only one in the world for me. We are really absolutely alone. We're a *queer couple* you know, but we ought to be together – in every sense, really – We just because we are 'like this' ought not to be parted. We shall not be after May. I'll come home then.

Do you want to know how I am? Yesterday upstairs in my room I suddenly wanted to give a small jump – I have not given a small jump for two years – you know the kind – a jump-for-joy – I was frightened. I went over to the window & held on to the sill to be safer – then I went into the middle of the room and *did* jump. And this seemed such a miracle I felt I must tell somebody – There was nobody to tell – so I went over to the mirror – and when I saw my excited face I had to laugh. It was a marvellous experience.

Blessed little Wing! Kiss his nose for me – & whistle in his ear & say your gan'ma loves you – She does – I wish he would have *one* kitten in May – Has he grown very big? And how is Athy? And how does the house look? Does it shine? And do you have nice food? Why can't we meet in dreams & answer all each other's questions – Our nights are wasted. The sea is up to the brim of the world today –

> Your own Wig
> xxx
> xxx

Good News!

[Casetta Deerholm,
Ospedaletti]
[11 November 1919]
175 received
Rutter received

Tuesday

My little mate
(I shall answer your letter après). I have just had the

extraordinary comfort of seeing a really first chop doctor – the man Ansaldi. L.M. was at San Remo. It was getting dusky. There was a ring at the bell & I opened the door & nearly fell into the arms of a beaming, glistening Jewish gentleman mit a vite felt hat. I immediately decided he was a body snatcher & said, most rudely, 'Vous désirez!' At which he replied Ansaldi & abashed me very much. He came in – dark bright skin, gleaming eyes – a slight stoop and said 'Oh vot a nice little house you have here!' The *spit* of the music halls. It made me feel terribly laughy. I don't know: L.M. away, this solitary spot, this queer stranger with his stethoscope in a *purse* – it would be a purse & me in less time than it takes Wing to pounce sitting draped in my flowery shawl with my discarded woollen coats strewing the floor like victims. He examined me before he saw my chart. My bad lung he says is drying there's only a small spot left at the apex – (When I was in London there was a spot the size of a hand.) The other has also a small spot at the apex. I told him my history to date & he says that I have gained weight & can eat are excellent signs. There is no reason (bar accident) why I should not recover. 'Never to be a lion or shoot the chamois or the hare' (*figurez vous* my darling, I'd rather feed them with rose leaves) but to lead a normal life – not the life of an invalid. The chances are he says 99 to 100 that I can do this. He gave me no medicine, saw my prescriptions & said that was just what he would have prescribed. The fact of so little fever, my appetite weight & that I can sleep are all in my favour. He says it will take two years to cure me but I shall be a great deal better by April and able to live at home but *never* to be in London after September. He was urgent about no mental worry *very* urgent but work all you like and be in the air & walk but never to tire yourself. Always stop everything before you are tired. I'll tell you the truth. He said I was not half warmly enough dressed. He was most emphatic on that – though I was wearing my jaeger & a jersey & cardigan – He says this climate is admirable – especially here because the air is *balsamic* & positively healing, but one must take absolutely no risk as regards a chill. Never to go out uncovered & really never to know what it is to feel cold: he says that wastes one's energy, fighting the cold. This I am sure is sensible. But what was so good was his *confidence* in me it made me feel so confident. He told me I had so much *life* even in my skin and eyes and voice that it was abnormal for me to be ill and that was my great 'pull' over other consumptives. He's coming again in a fortnight. But after closely examining my chart & reading *aloud* that writing we couldn't read, he pronounced a definite improvement. Isn't that really superb. (I'll not always be such an egoist.) Of course he told me a chill or influenza might mean disaster or mental worry – but I must try to avoid these things. And also he impressed on me that I'll never be a lion. That of course is bad, one wants to be a lion, but after these years to think I could lead a normal life is lion-like enough.

But here's a brilliant, clever, sympathetic doctor on the spot see? When I go to San Remo I must please to call on him so that he may show me some little politenesses (as though he had a collection of them. I saw them, darling little tinies, sitting on his finger). Then like the bee the lizard & the man in the poem 'he went away' – I went upstairs put on an extra pair of stockings & a scarf & came down & had tea & ate four delicious fresh dried figs with it. Terribly good!

I won't spare money or fires. I'll be as good as gold & May will be *divine*. I shall spend the £2.10.0 on wood Bogey but now *keep* the book money. Keep little Wing & keep him warm.

Rutter is good. I'll do it. But I've sent back Kurt so I must write and ask 'em for a copy. Fancy calling my writing *critical essays*! I saw you wink at Wing & Wing overcome turning a catherine wheel (with a K).

Do you know what time I go to bed here 7.30 or 6.45. There is not a chair or a sofa to sit on: I am driven there. But it's a good idea.

Everything seems to me good tonight except you. You're BEST.

Answer me. It's so curious. I still feel positively shy of you. I can't ask you to kiss me even after I 'broke down' so –

Bogey, when you have the time & if it is *easy* can you send me a woollen scarf – I'll pay you by cheque. (I *must* – you *must* let me pay for things or I shall stamp and rage.) But I mean one of those soft blanketty scarves that goes round once & twice & covers one's mouth. Do you know the kind of thing I mean? Ask Arthur. I feel he might be very practical about clothes. But it must be *woolly* & long & warm. I'll pay up to £2.2.0 for it & you can choose the colour – a grey green I should think or purple – yes, purple – or whatever you like. This is just when you have the time. I expect Jaeger would have them. But I need it here. NOT fearfully urgent – just when you have the leisure.

> Now goodbye to my One.
> Your One
> (a joke.) Too

[Casetta Deerholm,
Ospedaletti]
Wednesday,   [12 November 1919]

My precious own

I got a telegram from you today it was an extra luxury, a *great* joy but it is not to happen again. A nice little boy literally *blew* in with it.

Strange strange day! My party has just gone Connie, Jinnie (admirable person) and Papa. They arrived at about 10.30 (I expected them two hours later). But it didn't matter. The Casetta seemed to turn into a doll's house. Pa couldn't even find room for his glasses. The women's furs & coats & silk wraps & bags were scattered everywhere – Father suggested a run into San Remo, which we took – I was I am just a little corrupted Bogey darling – That big soft purring motor, the rugs & cushions – the warmth, the delicacy – all the uglies so far away. We 'ran' long past San Remo: it was *thrilling* for me. I didn't dare to speak hardly because it was so wonderful & people laughing & silly Pa talking Maori down the whistle to the chauffeur. Very silly – but very nice, somehow. It carried me away. Then we got up & bought a cake & were as they say the cynosure of all eyes & it was nice too. I was glad the chemist saw me (see what a snob you married!) & then while Connie & Jinnie were at Morandi's Pa & I talked and the sun streamed into the car & he said we were like a couple of hot house plants ripening – They have just gone. Jinnie left me a pair of *horn* spegglechiks of her grandfather's (the kind on a long black ribbon which suit me admirably) – She took photos of the Casetta too – & said 'They'll do to send your husband' – I don't know what happened. They seemed to me so many. Father at the last, was wonderfully dear to me – I mean – to be held & kissed & called my precious child was almost too much – to feel someone's arms round me & someone saying 'Get better you little wonder. You're your mother over again'. It's not being called a wonder – it's having *love* present close & warm & to be felt and returned. And then both these women had been desperately homesick for their dogs so they understood Wing – That was nice too.

Pa did not like this place, neither did they. They were horrified by the cold. Pa said at Menton they have had *none* of this bitter wind – that it has never been cold like today – He seemed to think I had made a great mistake to be in such a thin house & so exposed. So, alas! did they – They said Menton was warm, still, with really

exquisite walks sheltered – I said I'd consider going there in the spring. But I won't. When the bad weather is over here will be warm too & I don't want a town – I don't want to uproot. At the same time I was a bit sorry it was so much warmer. I *fed* them & Pa left me five 3 Castles cigarettes!!! He made the running, talking French – telling stories – producing spectacles (he had four pairs of them – Connie had three & Jinnie had three) – At one moment they were all trying each other's on – in this little room – it was like a dream – ༦ᨆᨆ ᨆᨆ ᨆᨆᨆ ᨆᨆ ᨆᨆ
And here on the table are five daisies & an orchid that Pa picked for me & tied with a bit of grass & handed me – If I had much to forgive him I would forgive him much for this little bunch of flowers. What have they to do with it all?

   Wig

         2 Portland Villas,
          [Hampstead]
         [13 November 1919]
169 days.   Thursday 9 p.m.

My own darling wife,
 I haven't had a letter since yesterday morning. The terrible cold that began yesterday has remained; it hasn't stopped freezing and since we have now used up the little anthracite that remained from last year, the house isn't exactly warm. Apparently there's been another strike in the anthracite mines, with the result that the man tells me that he can't give me any hope of anthracite for another month. However, I succeed in making the little cubby hole room pretty warm; and I know a thing or two now about juggling with the 'register' – that black plate that was always so mysterious in the chimney, & that I thought was merely to prevent the soot falling down in the summer-time. I only wish that I knew you made your little room as warm as I do mine.
 In addition to my having asked Bertie R[ussell] to dinner last night, Sydney had asked E.M. Forster to stay the night. He slept on the little camp-bed. Sydney bought a pair of splendid blankets from Heal's, which I am in hopes he'll forget to take away with him, or will sell me at half-price. Violet was very nice about the extra bother, perhaps because Sydney is very nice to her. He's a remarkably considerate old walrus, really – rather like we are, in

that he seems genuinely surprised when a servant tries to make him comfortable. Since the old stove is dead, we had to shift the dining table into the studio; after dinner – potato soup, mutton cutlets & mashed potatoes & brussels sprouts, salad, apple-tart & custard – we migrated to your room, where my heart was warmed – how I wish it had been our country house & you presiding over a select week-end party: it will be, soon, my darling – by the enthusiasm they showed for the *Athenaeum*. The three of them seemed almost as keen on it as we are. I told Bertie your suggestion about the Chinese dialogues & gave him my idea of how you meant it to be worked out. He was very keen, but, he said, he would need to have no distractions in order to do the thing justice. As soon as he had a clear month ahead, he would begin.

Sydney W. has been working hard on an article on George Eliot, which he thinks is going to be good. He's at it now. I was wise to get him to do it, wasn't I? I felt from your letters that I had given you quite enough to do. And I was frightened of the state of anxiety I knew you would get into if you once thought I was reckoning on you for George Eliot also. You see, I reckon on you absolutely for the novels. Your novel page, I know, is one of the features most appreciated in the paper, and any interruption of it would do us great harm. To me, you seem to get better & better every time. You are so *sure*, besides being so delicate. It's quite unlike – in a different class to – anything that's being done in the way of reviewing anywhere to-day. What I feel, and what a great many other people feel, is that as long as your novel page is there, there can't be a really bad number of the *Athenaeum*. The only thing I wish, if it were possible, is that you should manage to get so far ahead that I had your copy on the Friday before the paper comes out so that I had time to put your article in the advertisement which I have to get ready on Friday.

I've done what you may at first sight consider a very rash thing – through Eliot I have asked Wyndham Lewis to write an article for the *A*. But you will see why, I think, when you read my review of his book in this week's number. That's my honest opinion of the book, which I'll send you to-morrow; and holding that opinion I couldn't do less than ask him to contribute. Still, I'm rather nervous and hoping fervently that he'll give us the saner rather than wilder side of himself. But his attack on Roger Fry & the Omegas is really masterly, as you'll see.

Wing has come up to see me to-night, after avoiding me for two days. The reason, I'm bound to confess, is that Violet is having her evening out, & therefore there's no fire in the kitchen. The wicker armchair in the kitchen is really his place. He likes me, but he'll see me blowed before he'll give up a comfortable place without good reason.

I went to Porter this morning. I think he's awfully good; & what a good memory he must have? for he talked to me about what you had told him of the *Athenaeum* with a great deal of intelligence.

This is a very shoppy letter; but that's because I'm waiting for a letter from you. Unless I have one from you to answer [and] respond to I just have to give you details.

Your loving Boge.

Cheque for £12.10 enclosed.

[Casetta Deerholm,
Ospedaletti]

Sunday 8 AM   [16 November 1919]

My own Bogey,

It was a fearful *blow* to get no letters yesterday again I shall never understand it. When L.M. came back after the last chance I *hid* for a moment or two upstairs, just to delay the 'no letters – nothing' – Perhaps my luck will turn today and the sea have a pearl.

Such a night! Immense wind and sea and cold. This is certainly no 'pensive citadel'. This morning the storm still rages, it's a blow. I long to go out and have a walk but I daren't face the wind.

What is this about the novel – Tell me thou little eye among the blind (It's easy to see whom my bedfellow has been.) But seriously Bogey, the more I read the more I feel all these novels will not do. After them I'm a swollen sheep looking up who is not fed. And yet I feel one can lay down no rules. It's not in the least a question of material or style or plot. I can only think in terms like 'a change of heart' – I can't imagine how after the war these men can pick up the old threads as tho' it never had been. Speaking to YOU I'd say we have died and live again. How can that be the same life? It doesn't mean that Life is the less precious or that 'the common things of light and day' are gone. They are not gone, they are intensified, they are illumined. Now we know ourselves for what we are. In a way it's a tragic knowledge – It's as though, even while we live again we face death. But *through Life*: that's the point. We see death in life as we see death in a flower that is fresh unfolded. Our hymn is to the flower's beauty – we would make that beauty immortal because we *know*. Do you feel like this – or otherwise – or how?

But of course you don't imagine I mean by this knowledge 'let us eat and drink ism' – No, I mean 'deserts of vast eternity' – but the difference between you and me is (perhaps I'm wrong) I couldn't tell anybody *bang out* about those deserts – They are my secret. I might write about a boy eating strawberries or a woman combing her hair on a windy morning & that is the only way I can ever mention them. But they *must* be there. Nothing less will do. They can advance & retreat, curtsey caper to the most delicate airs they like but I am bored to Hell by it all. Virginia – *par exemple.*

Here is the sun. I'll get up. My knees are cold, and my feet swim between the sheets like fishes –

Si tu savais com-me je t'ai … me! Oh Bogey darling Heart – I shall never reconcile myself to absence from you never – It's waste of life – But be happy, my precious – Wig

Parsonage House,
Oare,
Pewsey
Sunday 6.30 p.m.   Wilts.
166 days   [16 November 1919]

My darling Wig,

Being here gives me an anguish of desire for our house. You see, it's just the kind of thing we could afford – a solid, thatched house with about nine rooms, perhaps ten, run by a manservant and a maid. Very snug, quite good rooms, some children, yes, it's a rather envious experience. We should have to spend a good deal of money on furniture to get our house as comfortable as this; but then we shall have to do that, anyhow. But what's really worth remembering is that a small country house like this, even though it's not in the Southern counties, is infinitely warmer than 2 Portland Villas. The important thing is to have what they have here, an anthracite kitchen range which burns on night & day and keeps a perpetual supply of hot water to the bathroom, warm linen cupboards, that & one or two other anthracite stoves and a decent fireplace – the problem's solved. I admit that to-day was a particularly beautiful day, a bright blue sky & a hard frost; but it's certain that you could have sat out in front of the house with joy this morning.

The all-important thing is to have enough money to spend on the house. The difficulty that arises is that one can't possibly spend money on a house that doesn't belong to one; & that it's rather hard to think how to provide enough money both to buy a house and to have the necessary alterations done & furniture bought. But Sydney tells me that it is not only possible, but usual when buying a house to leave ⅔ of the purchase money on mortgage; and on the other hand fixtures like an anthracite kitchen range even if one had them in a rented house could always be moved. Still one would drop a lot of money by improving a house that was only rented, unless one had a tremendously long lease.

But the house is really urgent. It's rather difficult to know how to begin. The Waterlows are looking out; and I think you would like the country here, – I believe you've seen it – and even having them for not too close neighbours, for there's no doubt Sydney is very nice indeed, though I don't think I should ever really take to Marge. She's too efficient, and without even that ridiculous charm that Mary Cannan had. The other clue to follow is Sylvia Lynd. Have you by any chance written to her yet? You've probably been too worried & busy. But it's obvious that one can only find things now by having well-disposed people to look for them. I don't know anyone else whom we could enlist. But somehow we must get forward and find something that we can go into next year; and we must somehow scrape together enough money to do the thing properly. It's no use doing it otherwise; of that I'm convinced. But if you make your house really comfortable, the English country can be divine. I'm sure that, given the comfort, you could not only get through the winter in England, but get steadily better & better. I am absolutely convinced of that.

But the comfort – that must really be done regardless of expense. I have no doubt about that either. Anything else is just madness; we have to be prepared to get a builder in & make him do exactly what we want. The full system of central heating is not really necessary; but you must have this anthracite kitchen range & hot water supply, a fine bathroom, good doors & windows, good carpets & a hundred smaller things that make the difference between exquisite comfort & exquisite misery. You see, Wig darling, I can't afford to have any risks taken with you. It simply can't be done.

I haven't been boring about this, I know, because you are as passionately keen on our house as I am. I've put it all in this letter, because being here has filled me with the house question. We can't have a Garsington; but we can have something as solidly comfortable as this, and with our own exquisiteness. After all, Sydney & M. between them, haven't any more money than we have between us. Not, at least, so far as income is concerned. There is an important difference, that Sydney has some capital. But I think we can get over that difficulty, too. Staying here has just put a keen edge upon my determination to have our house as soon as we possibly can. This is a thousand times more comfortable than Portland Villas. I think of your adorable ways, our garden, our work, our long talks in the evening when the work is done, the visits of our friends, the passing of the seasons, – and I want it all to be now, now, now. It won't be long, my darling.

> Your
> Boge.

> [2 Portland Villas,
> Hampstead]

GOOD NEWS RECEIVED. HURRAH!   17 November, 1919
165 days   Monday 5.45

My own darling wife,
    I think it is strictly impossible, as they say in the mathematical books, that I could ever have two letters that give me more joy than the two I had this morning, one giving an account of Ansaldi's visit, the other of yr. father's. Ah, darling, that is the stuff to give your Boge if you want to see him a roaring, rampaging Lion of Happiness. It went through me like a golden wine, and as a matter of fact I became quite light-headed in the office. I simply couldn't work straight, but wandered about with an imbecile sort of smile. One grievous brick about this imbecility is that I forgot to go to Jaeger & buy that wrap – however, I will get it first thing to-morrow morning and have it sent off by noon, so it won't miss a single post.
    Yes, the news is wonderful. All that I wrote yesterday about the house now seems so urgent & near. I am afraid of nothing on earth. But, do you know, I felt it coming? When you told me that you had gained those 2 lbs during that period of misery, I knew in my heart that you had won a decisive battle against the enemy. It was a miracle. O Wig, Wig, Wig. I don't feel a bit like writing a letter; I just want to say and to go on saying: O Wig, Wig. And so strangely news like that seems to bring us so near. I feel that our hands are

almost touching. Somehow glad voices carry farther & quicker; they ring golden & clear; they are not dispersed, but travel like a bubble of glass in the sun, and break only at the lover's ear.

That's very nearly a prose flight – isn't it. And then there's your Father's visit. I love him for it, love him. I can never in the future think of him otherwise than as one of us. To have made you happy, to have been If only for a single day, wholly what you expected him to be – that is a gift that I can never return. I only wish to heaven I had felt more friendly to him a fortnight ago, & could have written him a letter out of my heart. But I was hostile then; – it can't be helped. But I will write him such a letter.

Just a word or two of such news as there is. I came back from Wiltshire this morning. There is a damp mist over London, so damp that the walls of the house are all sodden. That only proves the utter difference between the English country & London. It was wet in the country; but no mist at all. At the office I found an invitation from Virginia to dinner on Friday which I shall probably accept; a letter from Ottoline asking me to go and see her at Bedford Square where she was staying this week to arrange a sale of her furniture in December. I thought I'd go not so much to see her as to see what was in the house. I had the idea that I might try to get perhaps a couple of the smaller things at the sale. What do you think? You see, in my mind, the question of furniture, like everything else to do with the house is getting urgent. And it might be well worth while, considering how good her stuff is, if I tried to lay out £20 wisely at the sale. Of course there's sure to be high bidding; but still one might snap up something. What do you think of the notion? At all events if I go to tea, I will tell you what there is we might try for. I enclose a note from Dent.

But it's no good. I have the conviction that we have turned the corner of our futures; that good things are waiting for us in the hedges & ditches, good things for us, for *Athenaeum*, for Wing. In fact I'm beginning to feel that we only want £2000 left us suddenly to settle the hash of the world. Hurrah for your Father! Hurrah for Ansaldi! Hurrah for Wig! Hurrah for Boge! Hurray for Wing! You darling

    Boge.

But do everything Ansaldi says about wrapping up. Are you sure there's nothing you want except that woolly wrap. *Do tell me* – anything, everything.

P.S. I find I've left Dent's note at the office. Will send to-morrow It said he had written to his aunt.

[Casetta Deerholm,
Ospedaletti]

Thursday   [20 November 1919]

Dearest of All

Your Saturday letter has come: when you are just off for the week-end & you tell me O. has invited you there for Xmas. I strongly advise you to go. It's so comfortable and one always gets ideas for the house – from just being among those Spanish chests.

It's a very dull day here with wild ragged clouds and a cold halting miserable wind. My black fit is on me – not caused by the day altogether. Christ! to *hate* like I do. It's upon me today. You don't know what hatred is because I know you have never hated anyone – not as you have loved – equally. That's what I do. My deadly deadly enemy has got me today and I'm simply a blind force of hatred. Hate is the *other* passion. It has all the opposite effects of Love – It fills you with death and corruption it makes you feel hideous degraded and old – it makes you long to DESTROY – Just as the other is light so this is darkness. I hate like that – a million times multiplied. It's like being under a curse. When L.M. goes I don't know what I shall do. I can only think of breathing – lying *quite still and breathing*. Her great fat arms, her tiny blind breasts, her baby warmth, the underlip always full and a crumb or two or a chocolate stain at the corners – her eyes fixed on me – fixed – waiting for what I shall do that she may copy it. Think what you would feel if you had consumption and lived with a deadly enemy! That's one thing I shall grudge Virginia all her days – that she & Leonard were together. We can't be: we've got to wait our six months but when they are up I WILL not have L.M. near – I shall rather commit suicide – That is dead earnest. In fact, I have made up my mind that I shall commit suicide if I don't tear her up by the roots then. It would be kinder for us both – for you and me of course I mean. We'd have no love otherwise – You'd only slowly grow to think I was first wicked and then mad. You'd be quite right. I'm both with her – mad – really mad like Lawrence was only worse. I leaned over the gate today and dreamed she'd died of heart failure and I heard myself cry out 'Oh what heaven what heaven.'

Should I *not* send this? I must. I want you to know so that when the time comes for her to go you will remember – The worst thing about hate is that it never spends itself – is never exhausted and in this case isn't even shared – So you come up against something which says hit me hit me hate me hate – *feel strongly* about me – one way or the other it doesn't matter which way as long as I make you feel. The man who murders from sheer hate is right to murder; he does it in self defence. Worst of all is that I can't write a book while I live with her – I tried now for two months. It won't go. It's no good.

Does this seem to you just absurd? Can you imagine in the least what it is like? I feel I must let you know even though you wave the knowledge aside or think it just 'Tig's tearing off at a tangent'. It's not. It is a curse, like the curses in old tales.

Well that's enough 'in all conscience' as Mr. Salteena would say – I shall recover darling – as I did before – I'll get over the positive imperative overwhelming suffocating mood of it and pass into the other. But oh! let this cup pass from me in April. It's TOO MUCH –

> Your (in a black cloud hidden away)
> Wigwife

> [Casetta Deerholm,
> Ospedaletti]
> [21 November 1919]
Friday Morning 8.30 after déjeuner   166 received

My own,
    It happened rather luckily yesterday that L.M. and I reached a crise at tea time and after that the frightful urgency of our feelings died down a bit. So I'll not say more about it. It ruined yesterday and made me so tired that I felt I could have slept days and nights away.
    Here is your letter from Oare, about the Waterlows' house. They are lucky – aren't they. Shall we really have such a house? It's not too late? We don't just make up dreams – precious dreams – it's not 'all over'? I get overwhelmed at times that it *is* all over, that we've seen each other for the last time (imagine it!) || no, don't imagine it || and that these letters will one day be published and people will read something in them – in their queer finality – that 'ought to have told us'. This feeling runs exactly parallel with the other – the feeling of hope – They are two roads I can't keep to either – Now I find myself on one, now on the other. Even when you tell me about

the table I think how perfect but at the very same moment I think 'will he sell it – Of course not. He must have a table, after all.' It's all part of what I've said before – haven't I. I say it so many thousand times over in my mind that I forget whether I've written it – once the defences are fallen between you and Death they are not built up again. It needs such a little push – hardly that – just a false step – just not looking – and you are over. Mother, of course, lived in this state for years. Ah, but she lived *surrounded*. She had her husband her children, her home, her friends – physical presences – darling treasures to be cherished – and I've not one of these things. I have only my work. That might be enough for you in like case – for the fine intelligence capable of detachment – but God! God! I'm *rooted* in Life. Even if I hate Life I can't deny it. I spring from it and feed on it. What an egoist the woman is!

And now Love, just supposing by a miracle the blissful thing should happen … I don't remember where it was I stayed with the W.'s. It was near Marlboro' and the country was beautiful. There were forest glades – a beautiful forest. They took me for a walk that was miles too long I remember that. I remember standing in a rank smelling field and seeing them far ahead and waving very gaily when they looked round … But the country does not really matter a great deal does it? As long as it *is* country and one can grow things (Oh MAKE it happen!) But the money question is pretty dreadful – As to furniture there we can always accumulate Eric-or-little-by-little but I should think an anthracite range costs at least £30 or more and alterations – We know what they run one in to. I think we might do it by not paying down. We overdo the paying down, I believe. Other people never have their money in bags – but first we ought to find the house – take it and then consider. That is my idea. The house (like the Jew) first. (I never understood that text.) Oh God! When you say we'll have to get a builder in I suddenly dimly see a hall, a staircase with shavings – a man with a rule and a flat pencil measuring for a cupboard. I hear a saw and the piece of sawn wood creaks and tumbles (such a *final* sound). I hear the squee-quee of a plane – and the back door of the house is open and the smell of the uncared garden – so different to the smell of the cared one – floats through and I put my hand on your sleeve and rest a little against you – and you say 'do you agree' and I nod 'Yes –' But these dreams are so dear that they feel unearthly – they are dreams of Heaven. How could they become reality? *This* is reality – bed, medicine bottle, medicine glass marked with tea and table spoons – guiacol tablets, balimanate of zinc. Come – tell me – tell me *exactly* what I am to do to recover my faith. I was always the one who had a kind of overplus of it you hated it in me – it seemed to deny you so many of your more subtle emotions – You made me feel it was so crude a thing – my belief that couldn't be shaken – Take this all *coolly*: it's all – what? Just add to my diseases a touch of melancholia, let us say. And remember how I adore you for so long as I live.

Wig

[The Athenaeum,
10 Adelphi Terrace, W.C.2]
Saturday Morning
160 days   Nov. 22 [1919]

My precious darling,
Your Monday letter (Nov 18) arrived this morning. First, about the Weekly *Times*. I'm sorry. You see I always intended to send the Weekly *Guardian*, but as it didn't come quick enough when it was ordered, I sent the *Times* instead. When the *G.* began arriving regularly I dropped the *T.* I didn't know you would like them both. I'll send a copy of the *Times* to-day.

I'm getting frightened about the cold at Ospedaletti. It seems to be always prowling about to stab you. I know you are taking every possible care of yourself; but I curse myself for my stupidity in letting you take the risk. Will some more woolly clothes help at all? I think you are terribly wise to go to bed as early as you do. But I don't at all like you saying that your back aches so much with the cold. I feel that I've left you alone not merely to loneliness, but to roaring lions & hissing serpents.

I don't feel depressed about you, darling; but I do feel rather nervous, and angry that we didn't go to Switzerland instead. The only thing I remember is that Sorapure was very much against Switzerland, & very emphatic about some place on the Mediterranean.

Your praise of the Nov. 14 number was very sweet. But the reason why it looked so big & had so many advertisements was that a considerable number were to be distributed as specimen copies. We could guarantee a large circulation to the advertisers, & so they came in. You won't find anything like so many ads. in this one; but I think it's a pretty good number, all the same. Bonwick tells me that under the circularising scheme we are getting about 10 direct orders (i.e. subscriptions) every day, and I suppose one can calculate about as many through the newsagents. About 20 orders every day in all. Which makes 100 a week. The question is whether we can keep this up for six months. If so, we shall be really in a safe position. It's too early to say anything definite yet.

Darling – before I forget – am I to do anything with the ten stories in your cupboard. Shall I send them to Grant Richards? Or give them to Cobden-Sanderson, who, I'm sure, would be glad to have them? Or give them to Virginia? Or do nothing? You see I was dining with Virginia last night, and she asked me point-blank about them. What is your idea? I think the best thing wd. be to get them published as they are & not worry about adding any more to them, You can start fresh on a new book then. If you agree I feel pretty certain that I can fix up their being published in the spring. Do let me know.

Of course, Virginia asked me, as I knew she would, to explain your review. I did my best. But as not only I, but Tomlinson and Sydney and Sullivan all thought it explained itself perfectly, it was rather difficult. I imagine that Virginia was more than a little gêné by it. I explained that what you meant was that she made an abstraction from life, which instead of being potentially complete (forgive the big words) left one important element completely out of account, or rather withered it. I don't suppose that was very comforting. She then said that she thought your novel reviews showed that you were not interested in novels. I thought that was a very illuminating remark, illuminating Virginia of course. What she really meant, as Sydney said, when I reported it to him was that you related novels to life. Virginia can't abide that. You see Virginia & (you and I) are fundamentally at cross purposes. We're right & she's wrong. I'll give you some more of her conversation in this evening's letter. I must work now.

Look after your darling self

> Your
> Boge.

[Ospedaletti]
[22 November 1919]

IGNORI THURSDAY FRIDAY LETTERS FLAG FLIES
FONDEST LOVE – – TIG

[2 Portland Villas,
Hampstead]
[25 November 1919]
157 days   Tuesday 5 p.m.

My own precious Wig-wife.
I feel so ridiculously, tragically impotent, when it's a question of building up yr. defences. You see when you write happily with good news, I always say to myself that's a whole row of bricks in place now, and I'm always surprised when I find they've been knocked down. I shall soon have to believe that I'm a ghastly optimist. I suppose it's because I so long and yearn for the bricks to stay there that I can't believe they can be shifted. Of course, that's stupid – but there it is; and, after all, there is something in it. Remember how even during that period of the most awful depression when I felt absolutely convinced that you were losing ground every day, you were really gaining. I pin my faith on that. It was an amazing miracle; and I believe that from that time forward you have really been building up more than ever has been thrown down. It goes like this, in my imagination.

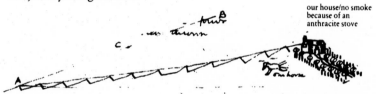

our house/no smoke
because of an
anthracite stove

You see you're always tumbling down. L.M. is always pushing you down for one thing, and you're terribly alone. But you never tumble down as much as you've been going up. You don't go up as fast as you seem to at some moments, because then you'd be at C, the level on which the house is, in the twinkling of an eye; but still you are going up gradually & steadily. You must believe that, darling, because it's been proved. But then you feel that you are walking along the edge of a precipice, that a snake's lurking to sting you, a robber to stab you. That's true. But still every day you gather a little more resistance to the robber. Everyday even though it's only 1 in a 1000, the chances are less of his hitting you. Still that doesn't take away our fear. What we want is someone to take you in a great pair [of] arms and say: Now you are perfectly & absolutely safe. But remember, Mouse, how much definitely nearer that you are than you were a year ago. And you couldn't have faced this winter in

London – it was out of the question. This is the last gasp, darling; – we'll never be parted again.

I always feel when I write about this that I'm pretending it's easy: I don't mean to. I don't know altogether how hard it really is; but I have some imagination & some love. The difficulty is to know how exactly I can turn myself into a stick for you to lean on. I suppose I can only say that I do absolutely believe that you are going to get well, & that next year we shall have our house. Since Ansaldi never a shadow of doubt has crossed my mind and your latest letters don't shake me in the least. I am perfectly convinced. But whether that helps or not, I don't know; I think it would help me.

I sent you *Cinnamon & Angelica* to-day. Please tell me faithfully and mark the MS as much as you like, in pencil though. That will save you the trouble of writing a letter. (Before I forget – did the hydrobromic acid arrive safely. You've never mentioned it since, & I am rather worried. You should also have got the scarf by now.) Your review of Monkhouse & Stern arrived safely to-day: – very excellent as usual.

Oh, the *fake* of this *Georgian Poetry*! It really is a terrible condition of affairs that these people – Eddie M[arsh] & J.C. Squire – should have got such a stranglehold of English poetry. They are spreading a miasma of sickening falsity. Page after page of the Georgian book is not merely bad poetry – that would be a relief – but sham naive, sham everything. Good god. I don't set up to be much of [a] poet myself, but I'm worth 17 out of the 19 put together. That gang has tried to crab us long enough. I begin to feel angry. I want to lash out, & kick their heap of dry bones into the gutter. But I mustn't lose my temper. I get very upset, thinking about it. I feel that they'll manage to arrange that my book falls flat. However, darling, when we're together & in our country castle, we'll pull up the drawbridge and pour boiling water on their heads.

      Your own
      Boge – husband.

              [Casetta Deerholm,
                Ospedaletti]
Wednesday night   [26 November 1919]

My Precious little Paper Boy,

I don't want the *Times* as well as the *Guardian*. I didn't know the *Guardian* was going to be a regular: it's of course 100 times more interesting than t'other. (You see, I am answering your Saturday morning letter). About the 10 stories. They won't all bear reprinting, Boge. I can't afford to publish my early Works yet. If you don't mind I'd rather let them lie & deliver you the new goods in May. In any case I don't want the Woolfs to have any of my new work. We really *are* opposed. I know just how angry Virginia *et C* are with me. They ought not to be for indeed I tried my best to be friendly & erred on the side of kindness. If you read that book you would realise what I feel ... its aristocratic (?) ignoring of all that is outside its own little circle & its wonder, surprise, incredulity that *other people* have heard of William Shakespeare. Though what in God's name THEY find in Shakespeare I don't know! Virginia's cry that she is the flower, the fair flower of the age – that Shakespeare and his peers died that she might be saved that she is the result of God knows *how* many hours in a library – is becoming a mania with her. Intellectual snobbery. She reminds me of Beatrice Hastings who had the same *mania*, B. saying that her work is the talk of *all Paris* my 'dear' & Virginia imagining that England rings with *Night & Day* – It's boundless vanity and conceit – dreadful in woman or man.

The wind has been joined by the robber cold. Both are in highest spirits. There is a perfect uproar going on outside. It makes my room feel like a lighthouse. I seem to see you in another lighthouse. I see my beloved seated at a table, reading or writing or playing with his little cat. All the rest of the world is in chaos – but there is he. It makes every gesture, every movement of yours – *beautiful* – charged with a sort of solemn quiet. Goodnight my love.

Thursday.

Hail, rain, wind, dark. The terracotta in full blast, smelling dreadful as the plaster bakes dry. No, the point about this climate is its extreme variability of temperature. It's never a whole day the same. That's what puts such a terrific strain on one, I think, and that's what makes it truly preposterous for people who are not as well covered & as solid as L.M. They may win through – but why have to fight so hard? Why have to use up one's energies in keeping warm? It's so wasteful. The sea sounds like a big old rake – I was awake more than half the night. At one o'clock I called L.M. & she went down & made some tea. Bogey in my *home* I shall always have the things for tea in my room, so that in the middle of the night I can brew a cup. Mr. Salteena's thrill for tea in bed I feel for tea in the middle of the night. Ten years ago I used to have tea and brown bread & butter every morning at half past two. I don't know why it should be such a gay little feast then. I long for somebody to *laugh* with. I think of such funny little jokes – minute little jokes. Wing would perhaps be the perfect companion of such revels: he *shall* be. I see him stuffing his paw into his mouth or the end of his tail so as not to laugh out loud & wake you.

Oh Boge, I hope I get a letter today or something. It is the *vilest* old day. However, I've *got* to stick it. There's nothing else to do. God! how lonely I am! You know, I sometimes feel a violent hate of Sullivan Elliot [sic] Tomlinson – all of them because they have never suffered what I have had to suffer & especially not THIS. It's just one of the many poisons, I suppose. But to have been *alone* here – that – even you will never know.

Here's L.M. for the letters. Goodbye Bogey

Wig.

Sunday Morning 8 AM.

[Casetta Deerholm,
Ospedaletti]
[30 November 1919]

My Precious Bogey,

It's a real Sunday, calm, quiet, with the sea practising over a voluntary while the verger tiptoes laying out the hymn & prayer books in the strangers' pews. There's a lovely piece of bright sun in my room but bother – it is moving towards great banks of unruffled cloud. Your letter with the house and the horse has come, darling. Yes, I am a ~~~~ but I do my best all the same. I'm *prisoned*. I'll never be right until L M and I part company. About the parcels. The acid sent to Rome has arrived: the other has not, neither has the scarf. But I believe the parcel post takes a month occasionally or even five weeks so they may turn up.... I hope you have a whack at the Georgians. Is Nicholls one? There was a most disgraceful article by him in the *Observer*.

I went to San Remo yesterday afternoon. It was *very* exciting. The shops are all prepared for the Great Fleece. A great many antique shops are open. I suppose they are all frauds. At any rate the prices would be appalling but by Jove! they have got some lovely things! There was a chair yesterday that can't be a fraud covered in the most exquisite needlework on old ivory brocade. Figs and their leaves, pomegranates, apricots, pears, a spotted snake or two all in most gay delicate colours and then there was another great piece of embroidery, all flowers with a little running border of wild strawberry fruits leaves & blossoms. The shops are rather darkish. One looks in and one sees a flash of silver, a mass of copper, dark polished furniture lace, a glass case or two of miniatures & jewels & the old spider with a silk handkerchief over her head sitting quiet, on the watch. I'd be the first fly to go in if my purse were full.

I had to order some cards yesterday but they can't cut me a *plaque* here: the wretched things have to be printed. Boge *would* you send me out some decent ones? I must have them as soon as I can. No address – so I'd better not have many. I went to the market. It was gay there. You remember where they used to sell fried cakes? Yesterday there was a stall covered with them & to one side on a charcoal stove women were cooking pancakes. A queer feeling – markets give me. I feel that – once every hundred years or so I walk about among the stalls, price the fruit, note that the new raisins have come, smell the fried cakes, and see the woman's gesture as she rattles for change in the money bag at her side.... Waiting for the tram Vince came up. Well! He'll commit murder one of these days. If ever man looked like a murderer. He's a fascinating character – a *real* villain. Not a fool – not merely vague (*far* from it). He'll end by having a small hotel at a place like Boulogne or Calais or Dieppe and he'll meet the trains wearing a straw hat and sand shoes. It's autumn here now: the vines are red and yellow: the dark women carry pale chrysanthemums & oranges and lemons are ripe. I came home lit my fire, began to take my shoes off & fell asleep. When I woke up it was dark – the fire just burning – not a sound. I didn't know how long I'd been asleep. Everything was still. I sat there for about ½ an hour then I heard steps outside, and L.M. came in back from the village. It was nearly seven o'clock! I ate dinner came up got into bed & fell asleep again & woke at 11 bitten to death by three *huge* mosquitoes in the net. Murdered them. Went to sleep again & slept till seven! What a pa woman! Oh, Boge, find the house! I am *longing* for it. Christmas is near. *Shall* we next year really keep Christmas? *Shall* we have a tree & put it in a room with the door locked – only you and I allowed to go in & decorate it & then have a small party on Christmas Eve?? We shall go out all wrapped up to the noses, with a pruning hook to cut holly & we'll burn a Christmas log. PERHAPS! You know it's madness to love & live apart. That's what we do. Last time I came back to France do you remember how we *swore* never again, then I went to Looe – and after that we *swore*: never again. Then I came here – Shall we go on doing this? It isn't a married life at all – not what I mean by a married life. How I envy Virginia; no wonder she can write. There is always in her writing a calm freedom of expression as though she were at peace – her roof over her, her own possessions round her – and her man somewhere within call. Boge what have I done that I should have *all* the handicaps – plus a disease and an enemy. And *why* should we believe this won't happen again? We've said as sincerely as we can ever possibly say: 'it will not this is to be the *last* time. We'll *never* let each other go again – We *could* not.' But the time comes, and there's nothing else to be done and – before you say Jack Knife we're apart again, going through it all again. Shall I be in Malaga next winter or Algiers? Odious, odious thought. But really I'd better get used to it. We are the sport of circumstance. It's obviously impossible for us to do anything – but how tired the dice get of being rattled & thrown!

Your
Wig wife.

I long to see *Cinnamon and Angelica*. I expect it will come today.

[2 Portland Villas,
Hampstead]
Monday. Dec. 1.[1919]

151 days

My own Wig-wife,

I got home rather late to-day to find your Monday & Wednesday letters – one had recipes & a darling photograph of the Casetta – and both were brimful of your fragrance. You know the feeling? You begin to open the envelope, and with the first little tear something pops out and settles on your lips, at the corners; and you feel that you are smiling a wonderfully delicate smile, and that anyone with a real knowledge of the things worth knowing would say on the strength of that smile alone: That boy's in love. You know the smile.

The reason why I got home late is because I spent the afternoon at the Sale. The prices were terrific. The exquisite small lacquer cabinets went for about 30 guineas and other things in proportion. However, I made up my mind to buy something – and I'm not displeased. I spent £11 and bought one exquisite writing table for your boudoir room (£7). I think it is a real beauty in very dark mahogany with taper legs and two drawers. It's very firm & steady unlike most tables of the kind; – I know that because it was the table which the auctioneer used all the while. He was a very superior auctioneer, with a manner like a cabinet minister (very expensive). I only tell you that because his taps on the table were so delicate and inaudible that his having used the table doesn't mean there are dents in it.

The other thing I bought was – a clock. You'll laugh. I know you will. You'll think I have a clock mania – and to the extent that I believe every living room ought to have a good clock, I am. I hardly saw it before buying. But Philip [Morrell] who was standing near me whispered that it was given to Ottoline at her wedding by her uncle. I just saw it was rather a fine blue colour in a glass case, and that it was real Dresden. I concluded – very quickly – that it would be very expensive in its internal arrangements, and therefore dirt cheap at £3.15. I just got in with my £4 in time. Still, the clock's rather a dark horse. I'll describe them both to you when they arrive home. There was one lot I regretted not having risked a shot for – but I won't tell you about that. Anyhow it went for 16 guineas, which would have been a lot of money.

I know I haven't very much to show; but I think I steered neatly between rashness & cowardice, & I'm sure you'll love the table. It was a tantalising experience, anyhow. Duncan Grant was with me a good deal of the time, and for some reason we got on well together.

I got to de la Mare's last night: it took 1¾ hours each way. Tommy was there. If I hadn't had a cold, and the journey hadn't been so bad I should have enjoyed it. I let off a great deal about poetry, & prevailed on de la Mare to admit that Drinkwater & Squire at least were no good at all as poets; which was one up at least. But I feel the awful difficulty of taking poetry really seriously as I do. Even de la Mare – delightful, kind & friendly as he is – I believe suspects me of animus. I have an animus, it's true, but I honestly don't believe there's anything impure in it. I do try to test it so hard. I can't find anything but the natural animus a person of my rather heavily serious temperament feels against bad work that masquerades as good. I believe that I am fundamentally straight as a critic. I suppose I ought not mind; but I do hate even my enemies suspecting me of crookedness. Incidentally, this is why I want from you the severest possible criticism of *Cinnamon*. If you possibly can make yourself really hostile: drop on every even faintly weak point. For I know that if I publish my review of *Georgian Poetry* they will wait for *Cinnamon* and break it into pieces if they can. If it is *solidly* good, they will only break themselves.

My difficulty about Sydney's G[eorge] E[liot] was that I've never read a line of her. As compared with Gosse in the *London Mercury* it was a defence of her – and I was glad of that. But I was in no position to judge whether it was really less than fair to her or not. Yes, it's true that he wrote very much under the influence of my review of Hardy. By the way, you spoil me utterly by your praise of my criticism. Your opinion is the only one I care to know, except my own, but you are too generous. Don't you think quite honestly that I'm a little *too* serious; a little heavy. I know the reason is that I take writing intensely seriously; but wouldn't it be possible for me to be just as serious without being so intense? I don't know.

My cold is entering on the heavy stage but I have a feeling that it's not going to be a very bad one. (I just heard Wing squeaking outside & ran down to let him in. He's now squatting in front of the fire.)

Good-bye my precious Wig-wife
I adore you,
Boge.

[Casetta Deerholm,
Ospedaletti]
[1 December 1919]

Darling

I'm rather dashed today. I've got fever and that makes me frightfully depressed. Ansaldi came yesterday. Don't *count* on him. He's a charlatan. He owned yesterday that the reports he gave me were because 'I saw dis lady vants vot you call sheering up. Like de Irishman I told you you could trot and I hope you may be able to walk'. You observe the polite smile with which I listened. The whole interview seems to have been more or less of a fake. He said yesterday for instance *em*phatically that I could not winter in England next year or the year after: that I must have sun and warmth. In fact he behaved precisely like all other doctors in the world but Sorapure do behave. Sorapure is the only man one can trust at all. This one wasn't like Drey in the face for nothing. He *did* give me a good beating. And when I told him of my melancholia he said it was part toxin poisoning and part because you are alone wiz nobody near you to love and sherish you. I tell my patients dat is better dan medicine – *Mrs.* Murry & so on & so on & so on & so on. And then he went away & I sat in my dressing gown & watched

it grow dusk & then dark here – and REALISED how I had been taken in again.
Doesn't matter. What must be, must be. I am writing to Jinnie F. today to ask her if I may come to Menton for a few days. But what's the good? I couldn't go today. My temperature's 102. So one goes round & round & round like the squirrel in the cage. It's a cold grey day. L.M. is at San Remo getting money for me. When I 'get better' again though I'll go to Menton for a few days. I think I *must*. I am *too* lonely. You my own precious don't grieve for me. It's just my melancholia – Tig's black birds. Kiss Wing & know I love you.

Wig

[Casetta Deerholm,
Ospedaletti]
Thursday,   [4 December 1919]

My darling Bogey
I am sending my review of Couperus and Kuprin today. Don't the names go well together! I feel a little better today. My temperature rose again pretty high last night tho' I went to bed at five. I expect it's that which knocks me out so absolutely *morally*. It's pretty frightful – the loneliness the noise of one's heart pounding away – and the feeling that this is ALL there is. I can't master it. I must just go on with it & take what comes. There is nothing else for it, I reviewed the whole situation last night. The old gardener came again yesterday to sow sweet peas. We parleyed through the window – he roaring and I nodding. He wants to dig up the lower terrace & plant zucca, concombres, haricots, tomates, pommes de terre, kakis. And then he performed a pantomime of the servant maid emptying jugs of water on to these delicacies and they growing round and fat – all by next spring.

I've never seen or heard from les dames de San Remo since I did not attend Miss Shuttleworth's lunch. That was the end of that. But it was an appalling day – impossible. Everybody seems to agree that the appalling cold this year has been quite exceptional and that the worst is over. It has not been so cold these last few days. I begin to think that even *with* it this climate is vastly better than England. The sun does shine; the air is pure. If one were not alone here and conscious of every tiny smallest change in the elements and in one's sick body even the cold would not matter so much. And there *is* sun.

Ospedaletti itself is quite the most beautiful little place I've ever seen – far lovelier than Bandol – and behind it that valley must be really exquisite. The cemetery bulks in my vision but then I'm an abnormal creature. If it didn't and if people had to come abroad I should say come here. It's so small, there's no fashion, no parasitic life – the people are self contained and pleasant – you and I in the old days could have been ideally happy here.

You know I am going to Menton I hope for a few days when I am better – to *break the iron ring*. I want to have a talk to Jinnie F. too. If I can be sure of getting better – absolutely sure – would you mind very much if I adopted a child? It's evidently on the cards I may have to spend a good deal of my life – alone – and I can't stick it. I think, I'm sure in fact I could manage as regards money and I want to adopt a baby boy of about *one* if I can get him. I cannot do it if you dislike the idea because of course he would be always with us when we were together just like our own child – and you might hate that.

On the other hand, when I am alone he'd keep me from utter loneliness and from writing these agonising letters!! I thought I'd ask Brett to be his guardian supposing anything were to happen to me. I think she would like it and that would free you from any possible responsibility should you not want to have him & of course you couldn't if I wasn't there. If I must spend next winter abroad I can't spend it alone – and a nurse for him kills two birds with one stone!

But at any rate, my dear darling I can't face life alone not even for six months at a time. The prospect is unbearable. It can't be done. Neither can you and I be together. There's the paper. You CAN'T give it up. We must have the money. You can't earn money away from England and even if you could you mustn't leave England. That is obvious. Your place is *there*. It would spell failure for you to live abroad with me – I absolutely fully realise that. I can imagine what hours we should spend when I realised and you realised the sacrifice – And then there's the house in England which I could come to in the summer & perhaps after a year or two live in always.... But I'll never be sure that a moment of uprooting will not recur and this is what I cannot contemplate. I think quite seriously I shall go out of my mind if I have to suffer a great deal more. There's where the child comes in. I'd love him and he'd love me. We'd look after each other. But when you reply to this consider that he'd be always with me. I'd have to bring a nurse back to England. (She wouldn't cost any more than L.M. however.) But I want you to think of it and write to me as soon as you can for if I go to Menton I'll talk it over with Jinnie.

L.M.'s off to the village. I must give her this letter – goodbye for now darling Bogey ... I hope O's sale was a success (for us I mean). Ever your own

Wig Wife

[Casetta Deerholm,
Ospedaletti]
[4 December 1919]

Darling please keep all these verses for me in the file – will you? I'll polish them up one day have them published – But I've no copies – So don't leave them about – will you. Just thrust them into the old file or into my cupboard.

Wig

5 P.M. Thursday,

My darling
Your Saturday letter telling me of your cold and your Sunday letter are come. I do hope the journey to Penge didn't make the cold worse: it seemed a bit like madness to go and risk waiting at the railway stations – but – what could you do? Wing ought to be trained to balance the paper weight on his nose, like Dora's Gyp did the pencil – you remember? I have been wondering whether you marked the new linen and how: it *is* so important to have it plainly marked & to see it comes back from the wash. I expect Violet is careful, though. Would you put an *ad* of my story in the *T.L.S.* I'll pay – I feel we must sell it now it's been such a labour & that's the the only way it will sell. But it ought to be in before Xmas.

Don't overwork, Boge. I wish I could see your Georgian Poetry review: I tremble a little for you when you go 'eyes out' for or against a thing – I always feel you don't quite get the measure of your opponent – you expose yourself in your enthusiasm and he takes a mean underhand advantage. But perhaps that is nonsense – It's sunset, with a wide, wide pale yellow sky and a blue sea gilded over. I feel horribly weak after this fever attack but calmer – just now – thank the Lord. My heart is so hateful – If you had such a heart. It *bangs˙throbs beats* out 'Tramp tramp tramp the boys are marching' double quick time with very fine double rolls for the kettle drum. How it keeps up I don't know – I always feel it's going to give out. I think every day I shall die of heart failure. I expect it's an inherited feeling from Mother. Oh – *envied* Mother – lucky lucky Mother – so surrounded – so held – so secure! Can't I hear her 'Child, you mustn't be left here ONE INSTANT – and then she'd make miracles happen and by tomorrow she'd have me wrapped up and defied everybody –

But we are firmly held in the web of circumstance – We've got to risk it – to see it through. If you were to leave there our future is wrecked if I came there I'd die – No, once I am better I go to Menton and I'll return here later in the Spring when I'm stronger with a maid so as to be ready for you in May –

L.M. is out to tea with some people in Ospedaletti – gone off with a big bunch of roses for them. The wind sighs in the house and the fire goes *chik-chik* – very small – My fever makes everything 100 times more vivid – like a nightmare is vivid. But it will be over in a day or two, I expect – A bad business! Brett sent me some photographs – Will you thank her for me – I can't lash myself into any kind of a friendly cackle – I thought the photographs very weak – that's all but she sent me a nice letter.

Can you get Lawrence's address for me? I should like to have it –

> Goodbye darling
> I am ever your own
> Wigwife

I am sure Menton will do wonders for my old depression – I've great hopes of it – Bogey forgive me – all you tell me about the house I can't help feeling it's all part of a hideous vile joke that's being played on us – for les autres to read about in days to come. I *can't* see it except like this – I sometimes even get to the pitch of believing that subconsciously you are aware of this, too, and with colossal artistry are piling on delicate agony after delicate agony – so that *when* the joke is explained all will be quite perfect – even to a silver teapot for her –

THE NEW HUSBAND

Someone came to me and said
Forget, forget that you've been wed.
Who's your man to leave you be
Ill and cold in a far country?

Who's the husband – who's the stone
Could leave a child like you alone?

You're like a leaf caught in the wind,
You're like a lamb that's left behind,
When all the flock has pattered away;
You're like a pitiful little stray
Kitten that I'd put in my vest;
You're like a bird that's fallen from nest.

We've none of us too long to live,
Then take me for your man and give
Me all the keys to all your fears
And let me kiss away these tears;
Creep close to me. I mean no harm
My darling. Let me make you warm.

I had received that very day
A letter from the other to say
That in six months – he hoped – no longer
I would be so much better and stronger
That he could close his books and come
With radiant looks to bear me home.

Ha! Ha! Six months, six weeks, six hours
Among these glittering palms and flowers
With Melancholy at my side
For my old nurse and for my guide
Despair – and for my footman Pain
– I'll never see my home again.

Said my new husband: Little dear,
It's time we were away from here.
In the road below there waits my carriage
Ready to drive us to our marriage.
Within my house the feast is spread
And the maids are baking the bridal bread.

I thought with grief upon that other
But then why should he aught discover
Save that I pined away and died?
So I became the stranger's bride
And every moment however fast
It flies – we live as 'twere our last!

147 days

[2 Portland Villas,
Hampstead]
[5 December 1919]
Friday – later

My darling,
Yes, the letter came – saying you had fever – that Ansaldi was a fraud. I don't know what to do; I feel I haven't the energy to react – well, it's no use writing to say that. I must wait until I have the energy.

Saturday Morning 12
I don't even now know any more what to say. I feel, as I suppose you do, very very tired.
You were a darling to write to me about C & A as you did. I know that all you say is right; and I feel in my heart that I ought to rewrite it all from the beginning. But I feel that I can't; I don't want to – C & A doesn't matter. In order to feel that it does a great weight would have to be removed from me. If I am able to work – and I'm not able to just now – it will have to be at something different, something infinitely more bitter. One thinks one's wounds are healing & they aren't.
To get your letter was a blow. It's not that I attach any importance to Ansaldi. The weight you'd gained is far more important than that. But it was a blow to realise that he had such an effect upon you; it filled me not with despair about the final issue, but with despair at my own impotence. I try to make you feel something of my confidence, and the spell won't work, the words won't carry. It's because I don't realise how profoundly lonely you are; your cheerful letters deceive me. But even if I had realised your loneliness, I don't see what I could have done. It's that – not knowing what to do, or what I could have done that has knocked the bottom out of me.
I know it's no use sending you a letter like this; that I'd far better burn the thing. But how can I send you a different kind of letter, where in myself shall I find the mátter of it?
Let's fasten on practical things. *You must go to Mentone.* That's absolutely clear. Surely Jinnie can find you something. You said you

had written to her in your letter. I can rake up some money, somehow. Let me know what you want.

I wish to God I were a man. Somehow I seem to have grown up, gone bald even, without ever becoming a man; and I find it terribly hard to master a situation. I keep on trying: sometimes I think I've got it straightened out a little. But it tangles again immediately. And people seem to think I'm made of whipcord & steel – I'm not, not at all. Je suis tellement triste. My power of running things here, my control, my ability to steer, depends wholly upon my news from you. I could move a mountain when I feel that things are going even moderately well with you; now I could hardly move a mouse. There's one Mouse that I cannot move at all – that's plain.

I don't think we have gained much by being dream-children, do you? We can't help it; we can't change our nature. But things are hard – and so wearisome. Somehow they are always the same – the same bright bloom on the fruit as we reach out to pluck it, the same bitterness when we taste it. I feel at this moment that I shouldn't – Oh it's treachery to write such things.

No, no, no. This is *all wrong*. What truth there is in it is a false truth. We must build, build, build. Scramble to our feet again. But why, why Mouse do you believe Ansaldi? You *know* that you can live in England if you live there properly. You *know* this, & yet you believe Ansaldi. It's that which crushes me.

Forgive me for blaming you. I have no right. It's shriekingly unjust. You are lonely, and ill. These things must be.

I can't send off this letter like this. Perhaps something will come this evening, and I shan't feel so grey. I won't put it in an envelope till then.

I've waited till seven o'clock & nothing has come. Perhaps something will turn up by the last post; but I can't wait until then, or I shall miss the post myself. I've been unable to do a thing all day; I've been terribly nervous & restless.

But this won't do anyhow. At all events I – the absolutely well one – must pull myself together and stand firm as a rock. The awful thing is that a rock can't do anything, but be a rock. And I don't see what good my being a rock will do to you.

At all events let this one thing be clear. For God's sake don't worry about me. I'm safe & well; a word saying that things were better would transform me utterly.

But this love. Is it any good to know that it's absolutely devouring, anguished, devastating: so long as I feel myself as a separate thing at all, I am only love of you.

Boge.

[2 Portland Villas,
Hampstead]
[8 December 1919]
Monday afternoon
144 days 6 p.m.

My own darling,
This morning in bed I got your Thursday letter & the verses called 'The New Husband'. I've wired to you to-day to say I'm coming out for Christmas. I feel there's not much I can say.

I don't think that at any time I've had a bigger blow than that letter & these verses. Even now they hardly seem like a letter & verses – more like a snake with a terrible sting. But it's kind of you to tell me you have those feelings: far better, for me anyhow, than keeping them from me. You have too great a burden to bear; you can't carry it. Whether I can manage mine, I don't know. We'll see when I get out to you.

What is certain is that this can't go on – something must change. What can go on – I don't know yet. My faith at present is that my coming out for a little while will put you right. But I don't see why it should. I feel that everything depends upon me; that I have to do something quite definite, very quickly. But I don't know what it is, and my faculty for doing anything has been suddenly paralysed. At the moment when I have to balance in the middle of the tight-rope I have begun to hesitate.

My plan is to try to get the paper in some sort (!) of order for three weeks ahead during this week, & leave here at the end of the week. The return fare second class is just over £14, so I'm hoping to do it for £20. I mention money, because it's important. But I'll explain these things when I get there.

As you know already, I'm ready to chuck the paper any moment; but I must see my way to money. I've said this many times; but I say it again, because, though I feel you don't agree with me, it's fundamental to any decision I take. At present I'm trying to clear up the remains of last year's debts. Until they are cleared I shall stick to the *A.* That's callous, I suppose. But I can't help it. You know my position as a bankrupt. I dare not leave our debts unpaid – I'm not supposed to have any. Once we're straight – and if things were to go moderately well I shall be straight by April (as I hoped to be by December) – I'll do anything. But I know that to cut off with little money coming in & heavy debts would mean inevitable disaster.

If I felt certain that my being there would really make things right until May, then nothing would matter. But now I can't pretend to a certainty I don't feel. We'll just have to leave it & see. Anyhow, I just couldn't go on with the *A.* if you were to go on feeling like this. I'm absolutely incapable of work, now. That sounds, and is, selfish. But you have told the truth; & I must tell the truth. I'm not made of steel, myself. And it's becoming a great effort to do what I have to do sanely – do you think I can do anything with this ringing in my ears.

> Who's your man to leave you be
> Ill & cold in a far country?
> Who's the husband, who's the stone
> Could leave a child like you alone?

There's nothing to say to that. All that I implore you is to say what you want. That will help.

No, no, no – all this is too *hard.* I don't mean it – something different. But I must keep sane. I'm coming quickly, darling – then we'll see, we'll see.

        Boge.

               [Casetta Deerholm,
                Ospedaletti]
              [9 December 1919]

Dearest

Your wire saying Will come for week Xmas has just arrived – I beg you not to. I beg you to reply by wire that you will not do this. Please please forgive me and remember it was only my pneumonia which made me so miserable. Now I am in bed, and quiet and I'll get over it & be stronger. I know I have *driven* you to this by my letters – I don't want it at all. The idea is perfectly dreadful. We shouldn't be happy <u>and</u> you wouldn't get back. I caution you most seriously on that point. You'd never get your passport from Genoa in time. You'd spend the whole week getting ready to go. Yes, I know it's my fault. I have left you no other loophole, but forgive me & DON'T DO THIS THING. It's not only a question of the money. It's a question of the paper. The paper won't stand it – and more important still the journey is *preposterous* for so few days. You'd not get a week here. The doctor told me only yesterday that people can't GET here without a wait of DAYS in Paris. Xmas will be twice as bad. *Bogey don't do this thing.* You've given me such a proper fright that I set my teeth again and will somehow or other get through. For God's sake wire me that you'll have a peaceful Xmas at Garsington – While I'm ill it's no good. I can't bear it. No, save the money for later in the year. I've driven you to this. I don't want it. It horrifies me. DON'T COME: DON'T COME. Stay there. I'll be calm. I won't be such a vampire again. And consider carefully that quite apart from 'us' there is the fact that one's passport now takes from a fortnight to three weeks to recover from Genoa – that you'd be detained in Paris. It would be a perfect disaster – I *feel* it – Don't do it.

In May I shall be better. All will be different. L.M. will be 'going' – not staying with me and you gone again. I really don't think I *could* stand that. Above all there's no need.

The idea is like you. Thank you from my heart but please don't ever do it.

   Wig.

       [Ospedaletti]
       [9 December 1919]

IMPLORE YOU NOT TO WRITTEN DISMISS IDEA IMMEDI-ATELY GREATEST POSSIBLE MISTAKE BETTER TODAY – – TIG

       [2 Portland Villas,
       Hampstead]
       Dec. 9[1919]
       Tuesday
143 days.   5 p.m.

My own darling,
  Forget all about that horrible letter I wrote you yesterday. I was

overstrung – you only say that of grand pianos, I fear. At any rate I feel it all ought to be wrote again & wrote different.

I don't know whether this letter will get to you before me or not. I got my French visa – for nothing – this afternoon, & I'll get my Italian early to-morrow on the way to the office. But I must get a few things at the office straightened out first; and I should like to have a reply to the wire I sent you to-day, asking what things I should bring. You see I shall travel light so that it will be easy for me to bring anything you need or will like. I hope you will have tumbled to this & wired me a proper list. Anyhow, I shall bring a small Xmas pudding & a decent woolly scarf. There will be no harm in your having two of them if the other turns up; if not, I'll get the insurance money.

As far as I can see we shall certainly have not less than ten days together. I shall have to get back by Sunday, January 4. But I needn't start till January 2. We shall see the New Year in together. With ordinary luck I should be at Ospedaletti not later than December 17–18. Why that will leave a whole fortnight with Christmas in the middle. I shall probably have to do a bit of work while I'm there – but so will you – so that won't matter will it. We'll have a real Christmas dinner, with the pudding I'll bring

But why in God's name, I ask myself now, did we not originally arrange to have Xmas together? I feel it would have spared you half the torment of your loneliness. What a blind fool I am! I scràpe & scrape up money and I throw away the very thing that makes life worth living & money worth having. And even from the purely economical side I lose nothing. For having seen you & having persuaded you, as I know I will that everything will come right; that you *will not* have to spend other winters away, I shall easily be able to do the extra work to make up the cost of the journey.

For, believe me, my own darling Mouse, your fears are all wrong. Well, I won't go into that again. I know you'll believe me when I see you, & talk to you.

I got your cards to-day. I won't send them by post in case they never arrive; I'll bring them.

I have an idea that this journey is going to be one of the easiest & cheapest I ever made. Getting a visa for nothing this afternoon was a werry good omen don't you think? And with no heavy luggage I'll be able to slip across Paris in no time, so that there should be no difficulty about making the connection with the night train to Vintimille, & so avoiding having to stay the night in Paris.

Oh, darling won't it be heaven seeing each other. I shall really hold you in my arms – really you. My heart goes all faint & wobbly at the very thought. Oh, please, don't have any more fever or any more loneliness. It's only a day or two at the most.

I fancy old Bonwick is rather fed up. Serve him damned well right. And he'll be more fed up when I get back for I'm going to demand another £200 a year on my salary. I don't see why I should have to worry about money like this. I'm worth £1000 a year; & they'll have to pay it if they want me. I think I shall have the paper straightened out enough to make it safe to leave. And I'll do some articles myself while I'm with you as I say.

Goodbye, dear heart,

We shall have Christmas & the New Year together after all

Your own
Boge-husband.

I send Arthur's woodcut of the cats that of Wing is a little masterpiece it's the spit of him.

[Ospedaletti]
[10 December 1919]

URGE YOU MOST EARNESTLY NOT TO COME UTTERLY UNNECESSARY ENTREAT YOU TO WAIT TILL MAY LETTER SENT EXPLAINING – – TIG

	2 Portland Villas
	East Heath Road
Thursday 7 p.m.	Hampstead, N.W.3
141 days.	[11 December 1919]

My own precious darling Wig-wife,

I had your second telegram. It's no use you know: I've made up my mind to come. I've been thinking of our meeting, our kisses, our delight, our Christmas dinner, our New Year together. Do you think that I can hold back now having thought of these things? It's just silly of you to talk about 'the greatest possible mistake', when it's – quite obviously – the greatest possible sense.

And listen, Wig. The only real brick all along was the question of money. I wanted to save our money for the house. Well, I decided on Monday that it was a fat lot of use saving money for a house, when it could be used to be happy (if only for a fortnight) with the one person for whom the house was to be made. Last night, I suddenly thought – why shouldn't we have both. Why should we be so hard up, after all we've been through – and it just seemed to me too preposterous. So I sat down & wrote a very friendly, winning, sympathetic letter to old Arnold Rowntree who has a heart, and said I should like my salary raised to £1000. Then, before sending it this morning, I spoke to Bonwick, also in a very friendly way. He absolutely agreed, and said he didn't think there would be any difficulty about it whatever and that I might count on £1000 a year from Jan 1. What do you think of that?

You won't say 'the greatest possible mistake' now, will you? Why, the £20 is a mere flea-bite now. And, mark this, the £200 extra is the direct result of my making up my mind to come. It was only when my mind was made up & I began imagining the delight of our meeting, that I asked myself why should I submit to circumstances which had made that delight impossible for me. I should never have thought of the £1000 without that.

No, darling, you can see plainly, can't you now, that it was the best possible thing to do from *every* point of view. We deserve to be happy, & we will be. But I wish to goodness you would wire me what you want, instead of talking of mistakes. I knew you'd go on like this; but it is an awful waste of telegrams.

What I regret most bitterly is the letter which I wrote you on Monday. Forget it, burn it – it's got nothing to do with me, but only with a me that was harassed and inclined for a moment to throw up the sponge. But once the decision was taken, I've been a changed man. I've thought of nothing but the sheer happiness of being with you. Ask Tommy, ask Sullivan whether they have not seen a new sparkle in my eyes, since Monday.

Well, darling, I've taken the ticket for Monday. I hope to use the week-end making things straight for the *Athenaeum*, writing some articles, & insuring that they don't go off the rails while I'm away.

> Your own loving soon
> arriving Boge husband.

Tuesday night or Wed. morning alors.

[Casetta Deerholm,
Ospedaletti]
[11 December 1919]

My own love
All day long I've lain waiting for the bell that should mean your answer to my telegram saying you are not coming. Sometimes, for days, this bell isn't rung: today there has been an old woman and a child with grapes & a maid to inquire after Madame and a beggar. Each time the bell has rung my heart has felt *suffocated–fainting* and the moment when L.M. went and did not come to me has been an age – an age. I *must* have stopped you! I think of you leaving home – the cold – the dark – your cold – all this vile terrible journey before you – your fatigue. I think of your making arrangements to leave the paper – working, overworking at top top speed. I see you sitting in one of these *loathsome* trains my tired boy and pale, longing to sleep, wrapped in your overcoat – the draughts, the rattle and your uneasiness – your *state of soul*. Oh, can Love keep this horror from you? I'll wire again tomorrow if I do not hear. Be calm, be calm, wait for his answer! It *must* come. I see you with your passport bending over a table, explaining that your wife is ill. I imagine you held up here, unable to get back. If I can only save you from this by those messages. Tonight I would promise to stay here a year I think rather than you should come –
My love goes out to you – running out to you down a dark path saying Keep away, Keep away, Bogey! Can you hear? Will you realise my relief when I know I've been in time? I feel it will make me well again.
God forgive me for what I have done. Those words Chummie spoke as he died. Ever since I've had your telegram they seem *mine*. Can you forgive me? I lie here wondering – Oh my love, oh my love – stay in England! Your own true love

Wig.

[Casetta Deerholm,
Ospedaletti]
In the night   [?12 December 1919]

I am awake and I have re-read your letter. It is stranger than ever. It is half an account of what I have done to you and the other half is all money. And you say I don't appreciate the seriousness of these your views about money. You do me great wrong. But I must not be kept in the dark. Have your creditors come down on you? But if they have – it is since Ottoline's sale? For were the burden of your debts so imperative & terrible you could not have spent any money there – What are these terrible debts? I must be told them. You cannot hint at them and then say I lack sympathy. You are not a pauper. You have £800 a year and you only contribute to my keep – not more than £50 a year at most now. You write as though there were me to be provided for – yourself and all to be done on something like £300. I know you have paid my doctor's bills and that my illness has cost you a great deal. IT WILL COST YOU NO MORE. I cannot take any more money from you ever and as soon as I am well I shall work to make a good deal more so that you have to pay less. But your letter frightens me for you – I think you have allowed this idea of money to take too great a hold on your brain. Either we must do nothing but pay off your debts or you must not care so greatly. It's madness to write like this to your wife & then to buy furniture. It's unworthy of our love surely to taunt me with my lack of understanding. How *could* I understand? I had no idea you still felt these crying claims: I thought all was going fairly smoothly. You must stick to the paper. I have never had another thought. Your being here is impossible from every point of view. I do not want it at all. I thought I had made that plain and about the paper – many many times. You say money is 'fundamental to any decision you make'. Yes of course it is. But I do not need to be told, and truly you should know that. I feel ashamed when I read that.

What I do beg you to do is to stay there, to live quietly and get the paper really going. *Live quietly* – I suppose you laugh. I have made that so impossible in the past. You'll have no cause to blame me in the future for it. I leaned on you – and *broke you*. The truth is that until I was ill you were never called upon 'to play the man' to this extent – and its <u>not</u> your rôle. When you said you ought to be kept you spoke the truth. I feel it. Ever since my illness this crisis I suppose has been impending. When suddenly in an agony I should turn all woman and lean on you. Now it has happened. The crisis is over – You must feel that. It won't return. It's over for good.

And I don't ask you to 'cut off with nothing' or to sacrifice *anything*. All I do ask of both of us is to keep very steady and calm and by May we shall have recovered. But please be calm. You are not asked to do anything quickly – there's *no* decision for you to make.

However ill I am, you are more ill. However weak I am you are

244 Letters Between Katherine Mansfield and John Middleton Murry

weaker – less able to bear things. Have I really put on the last straw? You imply in this letter I have. You make me out so cruel that.... I feel you can't love me in the least – a vampire I am not. That is all.

I am not so hurried now – I want to talk more with you – God knows if I have managed to stop you. I can do no more.

Granted (and I grant absolutely) that I have sent you this 'snake' (though now I'm not talking of the verses but of my depression in general) granted that – are you fair in punishing me so horribly? I know when I write happy letters they make you happy. You ask me to write more and say 'if you want to keep me happy that's the way to do it'. Listen. When I was in Hampstead with you were you always able to put all else aside and make me happy? Did you never come to me, depressed, fearful, uneasy, fatigued and say 'You can't expect me to dance – or act up to what you want?' Did I ask you to make such an effort that your whole nature should change and you should be *really* happy *believing* in happiness. You have even denied you *wanted* happiness – on the heath by a broken tree – I did not think I had to make the effort; I thought you alone – you the secret, secret you would understand. The effort to keep perpetually radiant was too great. But you asked it of me. I did not *only* write to make you and keep you happy. That was important but not of first importance. Of first importance was my desire to be truthful before you, Love I thought, could stand *even that*. Love could penetrate the isolation surrounding another and lovers did not suffer alone. Not that I required of you that you should suffer with me. Never. Never. From the bottom of my heart I can say that. But I took you at your word: it seemed to me almost my duty to tell you all in the greatest possible honesty – anything less would not be *our love*. When you wrote that's the stuff to keep me happy I was full of despair. I knew I could not go on giving it you. It was not as though you were ill and turned to me, strong and well, as a flower would turn to the sun, crying: 'I am in the shadow, shine on me.' Alas, I was no sun. I was in the shadow – and when at times I came into a bright beam and sent it to you it was only *at times* – I keep thinking of Wing as I write this and of our love. Will it all come back or have I the snake laid everything waste. Peace! Peace! It could not be helped. If I have done this, it was a snake in my bosom – yea in my bosom and not I.

I will not receive your dreadful accusations into my soul for they would kill me.

But here is your letter and you tell me I have driven you nearly insane – ruined you – it seems – quenched your hopes even of getting your money affairs straight. You tell me again that you are a bankrupt – It can't be helped. No protestations now.

Remember how we've loved – remember it all all and let us not talk of *money*. It is not necessary to tell me to hint that THEY will come after you & perhaps put you in jail for debt if you run away. I don't ask these things. I never asked them. I believed that the human being did not suffer alone. I showed you my sufferings – I have learned the truth. Do not let us talk of it again. Let us just go on. Let us bury the past – and go on and recover – We shall. Our only chance now is not to lose Hope but to go on and not give each other up.

Your devoted – yours eternally
Your wife

January–April
1920

After Murry's return to London in January 1920, Katherine accepted the suggestion of a wealthy relative, Connie Beauchamp, and her friend, Jinnie Fullerton, that she and L.M. join them in Menton. Meanwhile, Murry helped to negotiate the publication by Constable of Katherine Mansfield's second collected volume, *Bliss and other Stories*. During the weekends he searched for the country house that he yearned for but Katherine privately knew she would never live in. As the correspondence between them reveals, their lives and their personal needs were becoming more and more divergent. Misunderstandings were almost inevitable. At the end of April 1920, having dislodged Sydney Waterlow from 2 Portland Villas, Katherine returned one last time to try to pick up the threads of their shared life in London.

2 Portland Villas,
[Hampstead]
[5 January 1920]
Monday 6.10 pm

My own darling,
I telephoned Rutter to-day, who said he had had a wire from you saying you had sent the article. I didn't know what to suggest save that he should wire you again in case you had sufficient notes of the review to enable you to rewrite it. I'm terribly sorry about the business but I don't see what I can do.
I went down to the office this morning to feel how things were going. I think they are really all right; but I feel very much that when the cat's away the mice begin to play. There's always a general sense of irresponsibility. The paper is filled up just anyhow, and no-one dreams of looking a week ahead. What a joy it will be

when you are back? You and I with our heads together – are the only editors of this paper. It's a mistake to have to let anyone else have control. They are splendid, Sullivan & Huxley, at their jobs – but outside them useless.

The day is cold and has been sunless. It was very hard to get up this morning. The house I found in apple-pie order. But I had rather a shock wh: I didn't care to tell you about in my letter yesterday. When I arrived, Athy was there to meet me, but no Wingley. He hadn't been seen all the morning. He didn't turn up all day. In the evening I went with Arthur who had come to see me over to Brett's for supper. When I came back, feeling intensely worried, in the evening at 10 o'clock, there was Wing on the door mat. He was delighted. When Violet came in, she explained it immediately. 'He had gone to meet me & missed the train'. And somehow, you know, it seemed perfectly simple & true. I'm not quite sure I don't really believe it now. I should be quite broken-hearted if anything happened to him. There never has been a creature who so much belonged to us.

Arthur, I find, made a stupid mistake. (I am rather annoyed with him over it; because I told him so plainly to send by *registered book post*). He sent your two books by parcel post. So Lord knows when you will get them. It is so vexing. In the meantime I'll send you my copy of the ordinary edition of the story. It will show you how beautiful it looks, at any rate.

My book had a fearful slating in the *Daily Telegraph* – conceited, bumptious, platitudinous, everything that is offensive. I haven't a copy of the paper, but I'll buy one to-morrow & send you. But what cheers me more than anything is that Tommy took me aside & said: I think your book's fine, far finer than when I read it in bits. You won't have a great success; but you will have a great influence. Well, that's good enough.

I haven't seen Sydney yet. I'm waiting for him, because I want if possible to go down for [the] weekend. There must be no delay about the house now. (I just want to say once more how glad I am that I came – how happy I was. All the neuralgia dissolves away and only happiness remains, as though someone had slipped a golden fruit into my hand. Good God, Wig, – and to think you said (or was it me?) that it was all over. Why, it's only beginning, darling!)

The first volumes of Thomas Hardy are here. I am glad we have them. They too are ours. We shall be so proud of them in days to come, proud even of the fact that we bought them when we could not afford them.

There was a review of my poems – unexpected – in [the] *Times*

Supplement did you see it? I think it was unsympathetic but fair – the kind of review I like. I had a very nice letter from Edith Sitwell, the editor of *Wheels*, about what I said of Wilfrid Owen – a nice letter, simple & straightforward – and (what is better) enclosing a poem by Owen, not quite as good as 'Strange Meeting', but with beautiful things in it. He's a man I shall feel proud to have published.

> Goodbye, darling
> Boge.

> [Casetta Deerholm,
> Ospedaletti]
> [about 10 January 1920]

My precious Darling

I have just received your Monday letter explaining about Wing. I had been so uneasy about him: now it's alright. I DO love you – this adorable generous letter calling all things OURS. You are a wonderful lover. I shall be terribly proud of you – I feel your book is going to have a great success. Did you see Goldy's letter in *The Nation* – It pleased me *terribly*. Print his poems – ask him to dinner – do anything: he admires my Bogey.

Now my precious please forgive what I am going to say. And do not think you came here all for nothing or anything dreadful like that – It's just my peculiar fate at present which won't leave me – I must tell you, but there is no action for you to take – nothing for you to worry about in the very slightest. I don't ask your help or anything & God forbid I should make you work harder. Just go on as you are and I shall manage what I have to manage.

Bogey I must leave here. The doctor has been today. He says I must go – there are no two opinions. I have been ill this week with my heart – and very nauseated by food & unable to sleep or rest with these fearful fits of crying. I have fought & fought against it but it is all no go. Today he came & I told him. He says I am suffering from acute nervous exhaustion and can't afford to stand any more. My *lung* is very improved but my heart is not and this causes the depression just as the depression he thinks has caused the heart. I've had too much to fight – so he says. I asked if it was within my power to conquer this and he [said] 'no – absolutely impossible.' In fact he was kind & did not seem to think me a coward – so *you* must not. I have known these last few days that I was at the end of my tether – but we won't discuss them. Well, I have written all about it to Jinnie at Menton. The doctor thinks this much the best plan – If she can't find me a place there I shall go to the nursing home at San Remo & send Lesley to Menton to look round. She (L.M.) does understand at last & has been kind. It is not feasible to believe – She was away one day this week – I was alone. It was evening. I had a heart attack in my room & you see there was no one to call. I had to wait till it was over & then get upstairs for the brandy – and I fainted. Well this you see isn't good enough. Yet he says when I do get away I shall get better quickly – just as I did when you were here – When you were here my cough nearly stopped I was always hungry I slept all right. Now don't think that means I regret you are not here now. It does not – All it means is that I must not be alone. I will wire you when I do go. It will be by motor of course. But DON'T worry dearest love. All is well. This has of course thrown my work out utterly – But I've sent the one review this evening and another shall go with this letter tomorrow –

Your letters are meat and drink. I think everybody but you is not to be trusted with the paper. S. & A. would have it ruined in a week. The Shestov! ... *did you ever!* But you are just a little marvel. Oh, our Wing too late for your train! Did you kiss him *enough* to make up? Kiss him again for me. Your true love

     Wig

The carol was lovely. I am so glad about the Hardy. Arthur sent me a really wonderful letter – don't be cross with the dear old boy. Give him a hug from me & tell him I'll write as soon as *I possibly can*. But my pen is very lourde at the moment. My love to Sydney & to Violet. *Did Gertie get my present?* Please ask Violet. Don't forget about chestnuts boiled, put through the sieve & then made the consistency of mashed potatoes.

The Athenaeum,
10 Adelphi Terrace, W.C.2.

Monday. 3 p.m. In the Office.   [12 January 1920]

My own darling,
The Lacket is no good. It's too small, too dark. Emphatically not the thing we want. I walked over to it in a raging storm yesterday afternoon – the wind was terrible. Coming back, it blew me from

one side of the road to the other. I felt rather a worm when I got back, not least because my exhaustion had taken the form of a violent diarrhoea, which has continued until now. Except for that I'm perfectly all right. I arrived at Paddington at 1 o'clock, & gave myself a good, digestible lunch at Gatti's.

One very good suggestion has been made about the house, namely that we should take Roger Fry's for a year or so. It is near Guildford in S. Surrey in a lovely position facing S. with central heating & a properly built open air shelter for sleeping & working in. I don't know whether Roger is willing to let it. I know he doesn't live in it, and that he offered [it] to me for you rent free last summer for as long as we liked. At any rate I'll approach him if only as an additional iron in the fire. It's worth having a superlatively well built modern house on tap in case of an emergency.

Desmond McCarthy was talking to me about Mr. Clough's house last night. He admitted that it was a very fine house but he said it wd. be a great mistake because, to his own knowledge, it was very damp. That, I think, is final.

Altogether we must call Sydney's part of Wiltshire off. I've come to the conclusion that it's no use trusting other people's reports about houses – they've simply no idea of the kind of thing we want and must have. I must simply peg away myself every week-end, marking out a different piece of country, following up every clue I can get hold of.

I feel confident that I shall find it, if I don't allow myself to be distracted from the search. Apart from that week-end with the Wells on the 24–26 Jan, I have no week-end engagements. I must keep them all absolutely free.

Your Tchehov & a parcel of books arrived to-day. I hope I shall find some letters from you when I get home; I have had none since Saturday.

With all my love

> Your own & only
> Boge.

[Casetta Deerholm,
Ospedaletti]
Monday,   [12 January 1920]

My dearest Bogey,

I received your wire yesterday Sunday and am sending by the first post registered this day (Monday) a story called 'The Man without a Temperament'. The MS I send is positively my only copy. I cannot possibly repeat it. May I beg you to see that it is not lost? I have asked Rutter to send either (1) the story to you if he doesn't want to use it or (2) the proofs to you in case he does. But if he does send it to you I would most earnestly intreat you to have it copied for me (at my expense) as it is one of the stories I am giving to Grant Richards and as I have not so much as a shaving or a paring of it wherewith I could reconstruct its like. I hope I do not exaggerate. If I do – forgive me. You know a parent's feelings – they are terrible at this moment. I feel my darling goes among lions. And I think there is not a word I would change or that can be changed so would you examine the proofs with the MS? – –

That my novel review did not arrive on the Tuesday proves that Friday posting is not early enough. You'll have no more of that worry, I promise you.

I have just sealed up my story. I am sorry to say I am nervous about its safety. If you could wire me the word *arrived* when you know it has arrived you would give me very great relief.

Goodbye darling for now

    Wig

Take care of it for me. PLEASE PLEASE.

       [Casetta Deerholm,
        Ospedaletti]
Tuesday Night.   [13 January 1920]

My dearest Bogey,
 Thank you for your letter today and for letting me see the two poems; I think they are exquisite and could not be improved on. I return you them.
 I return also Nevinson's letter. It is an outrage; it made me feel quite sick and faint – the spirit of it seemed to get into the room … and to go on and go on. It is a really revolting letter.
 I am enclosing a letter to Marie Dahlerup which I want you please to read before you send it to her. I am very much afraid that the contents will surprise and anger you. Will you please try to be patient with me while I explain? Bogey I am so sorry – when I have

anything to explain to you now I have a kind of premonitory shiver – I see you turn away so quick and sharp ... But you *really must* please be patient with me now.

I do not want Marie any more. Ever since you left here this time – since this last 'illness' of mine – (what the doctor called acute nervous exhaustion acting on the heart) my feelings towards Lesley are absolutely changed. It is not only that the hatred is gone. Something positive is there which is very like love for her. She has convinced me at last, against all my opposition, that she is trying to do all in her power for me – and that she is devoted to the one idea which is (please forgive my egoism) to see me well again. This time she has fed me, helped me, got up in the middle of the night to make me hot milk and rub my feet, brought me flowers, *served* me as one could not be served if one were not loved. All silently and gently, too, even after all my bitter ravings at her and railings against her. She has simply shown me that she *understands* and I feel that she does. Am I right in feeling you would never have disliked her had it not been for me? How could you have! I look back and think how she tried to run the house for us. She failed – but HOW she tried! I think of her unceasing devotion to us – her patience with me – her trying to help you and to efface herself when we were together. Who else would have done it? Nobody on earth. I know she loves US as no one ever will. She thinks (STILL thinks) it would be the ideal life to be near us and to serve us. In Hampstead she was in a false position. She cannot be a servant – a nurse – a companion – all these things. But to overlook – to help – to keep an eye on OUR possessions (precious to her because she knows what we feel about them) there is no one like her. My hate is quite lifted – quite gone; it is like a curse removed. Lesley has been through the storm with us. I want her to share in the calm – to act Marie's part for us in our country house. Do you agree? I feel I cannot do without her now. Here is some one *tried, trusted*, who understands, who is really bound to me now because of what she has done here for me – I think I would have died without Lesley these last terrible times. You know she has such an affection for you, too, deep and true. 'Jack is JACK.' I know she is not perfect. I know she sometimes will annoy us. God – who won't? And who will leave us so utterly free and yet be *there* in *thought* when we want her. I confess that now I do lean on her. She looks after me; she has become (or I see her now in her true colours) the person who looks after all I cannot attend to. It was only when I refused to acknowledge this – to acknowledge her importance to me – that I hated her. Now that I do, I can be sincere and trust her and of course she, feeling the difference, is a different person. Her self respect has all come back. She thinks *for* me and seems to know my ways as nobody who had not been with me for years, ever could.

This great change will I am sure astonish and I am afraid anger you. I think my hatred must have been connected with my illness in some way. I cannot explain it – only tell you, and though I am afraid I must trust that you will believe me. Will you please tell me what you think? You must realise that now that we are at peace I am never exasperated and she does not annoy me. I only feel 'free' for work and everything.

My dearest, I am still waiting to hear from Menton. It is still early to expect an answer. Foster comes again tomorrow. I got up for an hour or two today but now I am in bed again. Did I tell you we have had an alarm here at night. Some men very late ringing and ringing the bell until finally Lesley shot out of the window – It was so queer – like a siege – very dreadful, really. Lesley did not take off her clothes all night.

Thank you for sending me the Tchehov. I will do my very best – It is awfully good of you to let me do it. Tell me about *yourself* – will you? My darling, remember how I love you – If you knew what your letters mean to me!

Be happy – Fare well. I am your

        devoted Wig

                       [2 Portland Villas,
                       Hampstead]
                       19.1.20
                       Monday 6 p.m.

My own darling

When I got back from Wells's to the office this morning I found your telegram saying that you wd leave Italy on the Wednesday. I wired to the address you gave to say that your story had arrived safely. I am now home. There are no letters from you, which would have worried me exceedingly if your wire had not said 'Postal strike still on'. I have been without any real news of you now for practically a whole week.

Though this is not what I really am thinking about, I'll tell you a little about Wells. The only part of the visit that I really enjoyed was 'the ball game', which I played furiously during the morning & the afternoon with the result that I am as stiff as a poker. I also liked Jane Wells who, besides being kindly in herself, warmed my heart by speaking enthusiastically of your writing in the paper & of Tchehov together. The association of the two, as you know, will always seem to me to show real insight. Anyhow, ball game & Jane – that's the good side of the picture.

H.G. himself struck me as degenerated, shallow, vain and a ludicrous snob. I'm exaggerating things, I know, merely by enumerating them. But he has left a faint bad taste in my mouth; he looks and is a little overripe. He has a double chin, a belly, and a way of talking incessantly & not saying a single thing worth really listening to, much less remembering – nothing that you feel he feels, nothing even particularly clever. Well, since he wasn't an idol of mine, but merely an object of affection, that's all of no great account. Men who aren't big give way to mental and spiritual sloth. But the streak of the snob is a different affair. You've heard of Lady Warwick, the countess who pretends to be a Socialist? Well, H.G. lives under the shadow of her park gates, which is rather suspicious. Anyhow, he is a great friend of the great lady, who came over to dinner on Sunday & travelled up with me in the train.

I have rather a nice taste in aristocrats. Everything else being equal I admire them. I should like to have been one myself. But I do insist on their being aristocrats & holding the creed proper to their kind like Henry Bentinck. But the aristocrat who lives in a park two miles across & pretends to be a Socialist is to me just another form of Bottomley – something that stinks. Of course, Wells hasn't a very delicate nose & he might miss the smell. He might find her friendship tolerable, even amusing; but he must treat her as a joke to preserve his self-respect. Instead of that he's obviously very proud of her; he obviously thought she would impress *me*!; and he was all round & all over her, smirking a little and saying 'Lady Warwick' about as often as a Bond St. counter-jumper.

Well, really, Wig – at our age! It was like the touch of some chemical. He immediately began to exude a strong, unpleasant smell of lower middle class. I couldn't think of him as a writer any more. A writer belongs to no class at all and he carries his impossibility of classification about with him. But Wells – was just lower middle-class. And his two boys (who were there) confirmed the impression, reinforced the smell. You know I can imagine few things more attractive to me than two boys one about 13, the other Arthur's age. Yet I positively disliked these two. They had an effluvium. They were mongrels – a cross between the boardschool boy & the public school boy. You have to be one *or* the other. Each can be perfect if he is intact. But these – no; they were vulgar in soul. I just felt with them how wonderful were the boys you & I have known – Chummie, sans peur & sans reproche, & Arthur, honest as the day

Well, I've given you all that because I think you might like to know. Wells is down & out. He's not important to the likes of us any more.

Will letters addressed to the Casetta be safe? In the one I sent on Friday were cheques for £11.10.0. Also those beautifully bound books are still on the way.

Oh, for a real letter, my own heart. I feel I don't mind what it contains if it's only news of yourself

Your only, loving, adoring
Boge-husband

L'Hermitage,
Menton.
[21 January 1920]
Wednesday.

My precious Husband

... I have escaped. Do you know what that means? There has been a postal strike in Italy. No letters, no wires. *Nothing* comes through. A strike of the railways, and now from today a strike of automobiles. We just got through by taking a roundabout route and escaping the police ...

Boge I have got away from that hell of isolation – from the awful singing at night – from the loneliness and fright. To tell you the truth, I think I have been *mad*, but really, medically mad. A great awful cloud has been on me ... It's nearly killed me. Yes. When Jinnie took me in her arms today she cried as well as I. I felt as though I'd been through some awful deathly strain – and just survived – been rescued from drowning or something like that. You can't understand, it's not possible you should, what that isolation was when you left again and I again was ill ... – if I don't get well here – I'll never get well – Here – after the journey – was this room waiting for me – exquisite – large with four windows – overlooking great gardens & mountains – wonderful flowers – tea with *toast* & honey & butter – a charming maid – and these two dear sweet women to welcome me with papers – books – etc. This is really a superb place in every way – Two doctors live here – they are going to examine me tomorrow – ... The cleanliness is almost supernatural – One feels like a butterfly – One only wants to fan one's wings, on the couch, the chairs. I have a big writing table with a cut-glass inkstand – a waste-paper basket – a great bowl of violets & *your* own anemones and wallflowers in it. The directress is a very nice Frenchwoman only too anxious to look after me and see that there is no change in anything. ... There is also a sort of Swiss nurse in white who has just been in and says she answers the bell at night. She is so good to look at that I shall *have* to ring. Boge Boge Boge –

I've got away from under that ghastly cloud. All is absolutely changed – I'm here with people, with care. I feel a different creature *really* – different eyes, different hair – The garden is gorgeous. There is a big shelter, chauffé – What do you think of that?

Your own Wig.

L'Hermitage,
[Menton]

8.30 a.m.,   [22 January 1920]

My precious own dear

... I have had such a gorgeous night in this huge room, with stars coming through the west and south windows and little airs. At eight arrived the breakfast. I really hope this place is showing off a little and this present behaviour is abnormal. If it isn't, pray see that our new house has folding doors, wide staircases. Nothing else will contain me. Oh, blankets and sheets of such rare quality – blankets that feel like lambs – sheets *glacés*. Electric lamp by the bedside under a small gold shade – great pot of hot water muffled in a real soft thick bath-towel. All these things are acting with such effect upon the infant mind of your girl – and a west view of mountains covered with little pines and a south view of distant sea and olive groves (as seen from 2 marble balconies) that she feels almost intoxicated.

Getting away yesterday was really pretty awful. Ma'am Littardi arrived asking 50 lire for the *hire* of the stove; the youth who has been sleeping arrived asking for 5 lire a night (8 nights) and the laundry arrived with a bill for 57 lire.... The taxi fare was £6, and he demanded 25 *francs* for having seen us through the police at Vintimille. I don't care. I'm still alive and I'm away. But the *comble* was that the day before yesterday when I was gone upstairs to fetch the revolver two beggars came and rang. The door was open – so I came down as quick as I could. But they'd gone & were at the foot of the steps – an old man & an old woman *with a bundle.* I saw them get into a small mule cart and drive away. At 11 p.m. that night I asked L.M. to fetch my overcoat as I wanted to sew on a button – It was gone – with the green scarf – the woolly – Both must have been pinched by the woman – What do you think of that?

Italy – my Italy!

[The Athenaeum,
10 Adelphi Terrace, W.C.2]
[26 January 1920]
Monday
4.30 p.m.

My own darling
Two gorgeous letters from you this morning telling me that you really are at Menton, that you're happy, that the doctor has given good reports – everything that I was longing & praying for – except one thing. What *is* your real address? I've only had it as it came on the telegram. I made it out to be

L'Hermitage
rue P. Morillot
Menton

And some of my letters sent to that address seem to have reached you. But to-day I received from the P.O. an official notification that a telegram I sent to Murry, Hermitage, rue Morillot, Menton on January 19 was not delivered, because you were unknown. That's absolutely bewildering – unless perhaps you weren't actually in Menton on the 19th. & 20th. But then I should have thought that they knew you were coming. However, since you didn't actually get there until Jan 21, I shall presume that the address is correct & the telegram wasn't delivered because you weren't there. But, just to set my mind at rest, will you copy out your address and put it prominently at the top of your next letter.

You will, I hope, have got the notes which I sent you from Sussex. I came back without having found a house, but with the firm conviction that Sussex is a county of *incomparable* beauty. and that I must try might & main to find something there. I walked 30 miles on Saturday and Sunday. The walk on Sunday was divine. Darling, I'm sure you wouldn't believe what the South Downs can do on their day even in January. There was a bright, pale-blue sky, with tufts of cloud. We were walking on the lower slope of the Downs on the north side. Below us, gently sloping away to the right were miles on miles of the Sussex weald rolling away to the north. The strangest & most wonderful thing about it was the colour – it seemed to be all golden, with dark brown splashes where the woods were, and every now & then a glimmer of vivid green. I can't describe it; it needs patience & art. But it's made a profound impression upon me – of wideness & peace, a queer sense that the country instead of being alien wanted to protect & shelter you, almost to lull you into her own richness. I felt – that you and I could grow wise & unfretted there, that the note of hysteria would go out of all that I did.

Well, well, if I didn't find anything, I had a day's sheer happiness, & I came nearer to a knowledge of what I want than I was before. When I got back this morning I found the enclosed note waiting for me. I have made up my mind to go down & see it to-morrow, even though it's the day before press-day. One can't afford to take risks, the demand for houses in the country is so portentous. You see if it's anything like, the rent is so small that we can take it on the spot, even if we change it for something else. Hold thumbs – what if it were the real thing – an old farmhouse!

Your reviews came to-day – Hurrah! The next number of the paper won't be flat anyhow.

I'm working like a horse. My goodness, but what a difference your letters have made.

How's money – let me know, please.

> Boge
> Wig for ever!

Battle is in Sussex.

[L'Hermitage,
Menton]
[26 January 1920]

Monday,

Darling Heart,
    Letters are beginning to roll up from Italy. I am now up to date to the 18th. Only there is not a *word* about the Lacket. Did you see it?

Or did you just give it up? The cheques have arrived; they are *more* than grateful. As you can perhaps imagine I am terribly hard up, & need every single sou. I meant to send Tchehov on Friday night but in the afternoon I was *stricken* with a nervous headache – absolutely dished with it all that Friday – Saturday couldn't *move* – Sunday the same. I think it was the reaction after the *strain*; also I haven't slept since I left that cursed place – The brilliant doctors here prescribed me a forte dose of veronal (qui est si bon!) I refused to take it – They are mad. But today I can lift my head & walk. Feel a bit faible but that is all. I feel certain that the earliest of my reviews must have reached you for this week – the others will roll along & I'll send this week Tchehov. But that finishes my books. Don't novels ever turn up? Susie? Or Mary Hamilton? Or anybody? I can't *make* them up. When you said we must have novels in the paper – was that really quite reasonable? Who in God almighty's name doesn't agree? Could I stop the strike?

Oh you do make me want to *stamp* so hard sometimes. Wing ought to beat you with his tail. The weather here is simply gorgeous today – the room flooded with sun – L.M. is going to try to get a job here – to help with her keep. You see she costs at least 20 francs a day – then they order me wine & frictions & goûter which I *must* have. Oh – that reminds me – The *Lit. Sup.* has come – What a very nice advertisement. But look here, have you time to send a book of mine to *Grant Richards*? DO darling! Can you find time? Look here – you old boy, I must have it sent – a book of short stories. I'll send a list of 'em & if you approve, do for God's sake let him have it at once. I don't know what terms he will make but let me see a copy of your letter to him. I'd sell outright for £20 of course but I want money *now*. Later on I can make it. But can you do this?

I've just written four pages and torn them up. A wave of bitterness came over me. I *must* never let it be known.

C. and J. are coming today with their precious dog. I regret to say I burn to let them know you are an Old Boiled Egg, and have already told Pa same – and intend writing Chaddie and sending V. a card. What a woman – aren't I? I must stop writing. For some horrible reason a Casetta mood is on me. It will pass in two T's. Tell me if you see that story, will you?

> Always your own
> Wig

For Grant Richards.

Je ne Parle pas Français
Bliss
Psychology
A Man of No Temperament
Sun and Moon
'Pictures'
Mr. Reginald Peacock's Day
The Black Cap

I can't remember the others. There were 10 at any rate, and now my new story will be 11. I'd like them called *Short Stories*. Will you discuss this with me?

[2 Portland Villas,
Hampstead]
[29 January 1920]
Thursday Evening 6.20 p.m.

My own darling,
I sent you a wire to-day to say that the only reviews I had received were *Coggins & Limpidus*, and asking how you were. I haven't had any letter from you at Mentone for three days. Letters arrive, and I am always deceived because they look like new ones, but they are letters which you sent from the Casetta.

L'Hermitage sounds a splendid place – and after the horror of the Casetta, a very haven of peace. I feel I can never ask for forgiveness enough for not having understood the torment of the Casetta. Perhaps if I had been calm, I could have done; but I feel that my attitude was always that of putting you up on a shelf in what I thought was a safe place while I went on with the eternal game of hoops of which I told you in my letter yesterday. It was cruel, terribly cruel of me, and there isn't any excuse. I can only hope that you will *think* of me as *someone* who finds it appallingly hard to cope with the world – with the things that happen – and who is always desperately nervous of a disaster. I try to concentrate on the obvious things: and I forget that all the important things aren't obvious at all.

Perhaps you won't think of me too hardly, even though I deserve it.

I shan't be able to get off to the country on Friday this week – I must write a review – and I must go to Ottoline's evening to-night She asked me to dinner, and I accepted, but I couldn't face it & sent a telegram. But I must go this evening. That leaves me only to-morrow night to write a review.

I sent you the *Times Lit. Sup* & the paper myself this morning. The *T.L.S.* has a review of *Prelude* & *Je ne parle pas*. Not so long as it should have been, but as far as it goes, extremely *useful*. Above all, for instance, those lines about the stories being of the length the publishers are afraid of.

Gertie came to see me this afternoon. She's been very ill, & her panel doctor says she must have an operation. She has refused because she says she doesn't trust the doctor. She looks very ill. She wanted the opinion of another doctor. So I sent her with a note to Sorapure, explaining that she was yr. friend and servant and that we wd. pay the fee. I hope that was right. She looks so ill that her doctor is probably right and it's folly to refuse to have the operation. She will probably do what Sorapure says as she knows you have such tremendous confidence in him. But just now a terrible thought overcomes me that it's a breach of medical etiquette. Oh God.

Well, my own darling, let's hope for another real letter from you. Are you writing everyday? Do please, if it's only a word I do.

I love you, love you.
Boge.

PLEASE READ THIS ALL THROUGH

[L'Hermitage,
Menton]
[31 January 1920]
Saturday

My dear Bogey,

I wrote to you on Thursday last when I had heard from you of the arrival of my letters from here, but I did not post the letter. I held it over, hoping with each courier that the need to send it would be over. But now (Saturday) I can wait no longer.

I have received your letters about the house hunting & your Italian letters are coming in, in any order. I fully appreciate the fact that you are working extremely hard & that all your superfluous energy is directed towards finding a house. At the same time, my dear Bogey, you have hurt me *dreadfully* – if you reflect for one moment you will perhaps realise how your 'how's money?' struck me. Did I not tell you the expenses I had coming here – the bills to settle, the hire of the motor, the theft of my overcoat, the more expensive room, the extras such as *goûters frictions* and Lesley to board and keep. Yes, I have told you all these things. Now let me tell you what I 'imagined' you would do on receipt of my first letter from Menton. I imagined you would immediately wire me £10. 'I imagined' you would have written. 'It's gorgeous to know you are there & getting better. Don't worry. Of course, I shall contribute £10 a *month* towards your expenses.' In addition I *counted* on your loving sympathy and understanding, and the fact that you failed me in this is the hardest of all to bear. I don't think you read my letters. I *cannot think* you simply dismissed them like that. This week I have been simply waiting for the letter that has not come & can't come now. It's made it impossible to work. Now I must just re-adjust things & go on and I shall try and send you more for your paper. I have changed my room here for a smaller one but on Wednesday last, for instance, my lungs were radiographed. It cost me *200* francs & the cocher charged me 15 francs pour aller et retour. This morning the doctor lectured me about working (I put it down to 'mon travail') and ordered me an hour's drive by the sea every day pour calmer les nerves. *I* can't afford it.

Therefore I ask you to contribute £10 a month towards my expenses here. If you cannot do so please *wire me at once* for I must make immediate other arrangements. *I cannot wait a day longer.*

It is so bitter to have to ask you this – terribly bitter. Nevertheless I am determined to get well. I will *not* be overcome by anything – not even by the letter you sent me in Italy telling me to remember AS I grew more lonely SO you were loving me more. If you had read that in a book what would you have thought? Well, I thank God I read it here and not at the Casetta.

I've nothing to say to you, Bogey. I am too hurt. I shall not write again.

Your Wife

You will not put me off with just a sentence or two? Consider, Bogey, what you do!

2 Portland Villas,
[Hampstead]
[1 February 1920]

Sunday

I rather counted, Wig darling, on finding a letter from you when I got home to-night. However, I've learned that to count on a letter from you is one of the surest ways of not getting it, so perhaps I didn't really count so much. But when you write to me next, will you please tell me whether you write everyday or not. I don't want to expect what I can't possibly have; – since I wrote to you about a month ago asking you to write everyday, I have expected more letters than I have received by a long chalk.

I got back at 9.15 to-night. This morning I walked from Battle to Winchilsea through Hastings – that is breathtakingly lovely country – and on to Rye & caught the train from there. The house at Winchilsea was a fraud – a semi-detached villa. So I drew blank again this week. However, I copied down all the names of the Rye agents from the various notice-boards, (they were all shut, it being Sunday) in order to write to them to-morrow. I intend to go down to Rye with a bicycle (not *on* it) next week-end & beat the country thoroughly. One can't cover enough ground walking. You won't have to hold thumbs again until Friday next.

Of course I forgot to enclose the letter last night. I always do. But here it is: also cheque for £20. You see it's much better that I should pay you now, in order to be free to make the best terms for your books that I can. Your instruction to sell your book outright is simply horrifying. I'm sure I [can] get you more than £20 merely in advance of royalties. I think it's a good thing that there shd. be a new edition of *In a German Pension*. Though why the devil no-one (publisher, I mean; *we* did) thought of it during the war I don't know. However, let's be happy that two of yr books will be coming out again soon. I am sure the Constable offer was directly the result of the *Times Lit Sup*. Review. So it seems that your success is coming along very quickly.

Wig to sell 10,000 of her new book & come home; Boge to find a lovely house. Ah, life could be beautiful – couldn't it.

> Your own
> Boge-husband.

> [L'Hermitage,
> Menton]
Monday Morning. [2 February 1920]

My dear Bogey

I have just received your Thursday & Friday evening letters – Thank you from my heart for doing that for Gertie. It was a beautiful little act on your part and I am so proud that you should have done it.

About the Grant Richards book (did I tell you he was coming South this month?) I think 'The Black Cap' had better not be included. But I will send you another story 'A Second Helping' – it is called to go in its place. I shall try and get it typed here. My copy of 'Je ne parle pas' or your copy – isn't it? – arrived yesterday. It *looks* lovely but I am not at all satisfied with the story.

About the house, Dear Bogey, why do you TORMENT yourself as you say? Or is that only your way of saying it? I am sure it is the wrong attitude and it will only tire and exhaust you so that you will be 'sick of the whole subject' very soon –

It's no good my writing every day. I can't. I simply feel you don't read the letters – I try and do my own work instead. There's a much better chance that you'll read that one day – though why you should I don't know.

Yes, this is a very suitable place to be in – it is safe and very healthy.

Goodbye dearest

Wig.

Is there really a tearing hurry about the house? I fully appreciate the fact that you do not want to stay at Portland Villas. At the same time it would not matter if we were there until the middle of the summer. And when I come home L.M. can help with the househunting. I mean she could always go for a preliminary inspection in the middle of the week & so save you useless journeys. This is well worth considering. She knows just what we want.

By the way, about that story Rutter has I am awfully sorry to bother you but I must see the proofs myself before it is printed – if it's typed 10 to 1 there will be mistakes and at any rate I can't expect anyone to go through it as I must go through. Every word matters. This is *not* conceit – but it must be so. Will you promise to send the proofs to me if he prints the story? I'll send them back express the same day. If you did not live at such racing speed I would beg you to go through the typed copy with the MS and see that the *spaces* were correct – that where I intend a space there is a space – It's sure to be wrong. But I can't afford mistakes. Another word won't do. I chose every single word.

Will you please answer this when you write?

[The Athenaeum,
10 Adelphi Terrace, W.C.2]
Feb. 2 1920

The enclosed letter explains itself. It gives me the chance of playing off Constable & Grant Richards against each other to get the biggest advance. Your idea of selling outright is preposterous. What I want to know is whether you have pledged yourself in writing in anyway to Richards. If I have a freehand I think I shall be able to get £30 in advance of royalties almost immediately. Any how, though things are tight, I will send You a cheque for £20 to-morrow, if you will repay me when you get the money for your book. But let me know exactly how you stand with Richards. I'll start in on this business on Monday – see both Constable and Richards.

Your own
Boge.

[The Athenaeum,
10 Adelphi Terrace, W.C.2]
[2 February 1920]
Monday in the Office

I was on to Michael Sadler on [the] telephone to-day. I said that the whole question was one of the advance on royalties, and suggested £40. He seemed quite prepared to do that, so much so that I felt I ought to have said £50. Still, I didn't want to frighten him.

Accordingly, I have written to Richards telling him that everything depends upon how much advance he will give, & telling him frankly that some-one else is after it. He may go more than £40, but I doubt it. He's rather a sharper on terms.

Anyhow, I trust I shall be able to send you another cheque for £20 within a month.

Whatever you do, don't commit yourself in writing to Grant Richards. As you can understand, it would make it impossible for me to negotiate freely. And we're in the happy position of having two competing publishers.

As I said in my other letter it would help a great deal if you could tell me what you have written to Richards.

I got a very belated letter from [the] Casetta to-day telling me of [the] change of yr attitude to L.M. Don't worry about me – I must say I hated your picture of me being thin-lipped & angry over it: your idea of me seems to get a long way from the reality. Whatever you feel towards L.M., I feel & there's an end of it. All I say is I should like it much better if you could get on with her again – she has done very much for *us* in her way.

I wake up with a sore throat this morning – I suppose I got a chill in the train. However it's bound to be slight as my last one was. I've also insured my life for £1000 in case I break my neck home-hunting.

    Your own Boge.

        [2 Portland Villas,
        Hampstead]
        [3 February 1920]
        Tuesday Evening

My darling,

Your Saturday letter has come – the one saying Please read this all through – at least it explains your silence, which had bewildered me.

That I have hurt you terribly I know; you would never say that unless it were true. The fact that I sent you £20 the moment I had it makes no difference. Feb. 1 came too late.

But there is something to be said for me. I couldn't send what I had not got. I hadn't got £20 when you arrived in Mentone. I was cleaned out. Paying £60 for income-tax finished me. I had just enough to get to the end of the month. The moment I had my monthly cheque – I sent you the £20.

Of course, I could, I suppose, have borrowed it. I would have if I had known it was so urgent. But God above haven't we known each other long enough for you to *wire* '*send £20*'. I understood you were very hard up, but I thought you could manage till my next cheque came in. I thought you would have said: I must have £20 or £40 immediately – if it was so urgent.

However, the hurt is done. I was stupid & clumsy. But in order that you may feel quite safe, in addition to the £20 already sent, I am paying in £20 direct into your bank to-night. I shall have enough to get through the month. I shall send you a wire saying that to-morrow.

Still, however brutal I have been, I think that you should have written to me before. You know at any rate that I'm not brutal at heart; so that you might have guessed that I had misunderstood instead of leaving yourself tormented & me with no news so long.

Well, Wig – darling heart, you say you won't write again. All I ask is that when you get this if you feel that the hurt is less, or if you feel that I love you still, you will wire me just the one word 'Love'. I shall understand. But don't, for God's sake, wire it if you don't feel it.

There are things in your letter that I just don't understand. One is what you say about the letter I sent you to Italy telling you 'to remember as you grew more lonely so I was loving you more'. I realise that is awkwardly put. But *if* I read it in a novel, I should know what the man meant, I'm sure. I would know that what he meant was that when his lover felt lonely, then she must think of him as loving her more deeply than ever – loving her with a love that tried to break through, that might break through *if she would let it*, the ghastly terror of her loneliness. I feel that you must suspect me somehow, otherwise you could not have so failed to feel the intention behind the clumsy words. I'm not ashamed of them, even now

> Your loving
> Boge.

This is written before your II card and telegram. I have opened this and replied on pages III and IV

> [L'Hermitage,
> Menton]
> [? 4 February 1920]
> Wednesday

Dear Bogey,

A slip was enclosed in a letter card but I have received no letter which explains itself. However I will tell you the situation between myself and G[rant] R[ichards].

I wrote him asking if he would consider an MS.

He replied delighted.

I replied saying I would send him one.

He replied the sooner the better.

Money has not been mentioned, but I think he ought most certainly to have the first look. If he wants it I must ask for an advance & if he refuses the advance the affair is off. Please send me the note you refer to – will you?

As regards the advance money I would rather wait and receive it for my book than that you should lend it to me. I MUST have it for my overcoat, fare home etc., and I certainly do not want to borrow it from you. Perhaps I did not make clear that I BOTHER you for the £10 a month – I mean, NOT as a loan. I am afraid from this note you may advance it for me & then take the book money. But I am afraid that will not do.

Will you please tell me *why* money is tight? I cannot understand – If it is necessary to say [these] things why do you buy a mirror? I feel, as I felt when you referred before to your heavy debts that you are keeping something from me all the time. You have expenses, you *must* have, that I don't know of. Oh, if only you would be frank about this: it would make things so different. Can't you confide in me? Are you helping somebody! I know you are saving up for the house but you ... don't put the house FIRST, do you, Bogey? Yet you find it necessary to again write *money is tight* – I don't want – God forbid to know your private affairs but if you can tell me a little it would be a great relief.

Wig

Bogey dear,

Your telegram came this afternoon and your second card enclosing the cheque but STILL not enclosing the letter came this evening. First, about the £20. You will doubtless adhere to your intention in the letter card that it shall be an advance on my book – but you will see why I do not want that. If you can agree to allowing me £10 a month for my expenses while I am here I shall look upon this cheque as the first 2 months instalment. I would perfectly understand your *money is tight* had I NOT consumption, a weak heart & chronic neuritis in my lower limbs.

About the overcoat you will doubtless explain how you want it paid for. So I can't write about these things neither will I touch the cheque till I hear from you.

My darling, I can't write every day – I love you but something has gone dead in me – rather – no, I can't explain it. Explanations are so futile – you NEVER listen to them, you know – I shrink from trying any more – Give me *time* will you? I'll get over this – I get over everything but it takes time. But darling, darling, that doesn't make me love you less – I love you – that's the whole infernal trouble!

Bogey, I cannot have the *German Pension* republished under any circumstances. It is far too *immature* & I don't even acknowledge it today. I mean I don't 'hold' by it. I can't go foisting that kind of stuff on the public – *it's not good enough* – But if you'll send me the note that refers to it I will reply & offer a new book by May 1st. But I could not for a moment entertain republishing the *Pension*. It's positively *juvenile* and besides that it's not what I mean: it's a lie. Oh no, never. But please give me the chance of replying to whoever wants to do so & offering another book.

      Wig

The Athenaeum,
10 Adelphi Terrace

Wednesday: Press Day   [4 February 1920]

Wig darling.

This afternoon I sent you an overcoat. It will be forwarded to Paris in the diplomatic bag. I hope you will like it. It's a terrible business hunting for an overcoat that's even approximately decent. Still, after a long hunt I found it, and I shall be disappointed if you don't like it. Don't be scared by the name of the maker. I tried better places in vain.

I'm afraid I shan't be able to do what I said yesterday, pay £20 into yr. bank here. I can only manage £10 which I will send to Kay to-night. But please don't go to the other extreme and think I am crippling myself – I shall be able to get through the month on what remains of my monthly cheque.

There was something which I left altogether out of my letter last night. When you said I had shown no sympathy, no joy at [your] being comfortable and getting better – I simply didn't know what to make of it. Either my first letter to you at Mentone went the way of my telegram, or I must be becoming absolutely incapable of expressing my feelings. I don't know. Perhaps the whole mystery of the strikes my getting no letters & never knowing where you were was partly responsible.

However, what's done is done. I can't believe you will continue to think as hardly of me as you do, even though I'm a failure as husband & lover. But I don't want to plead for anything.

At all events I have done one good practical thing. I have fixed up with Constable that they will publish your book on a 15% royalty, and pay you £40 in advance on delivery of manuscript, which I have promised within three weeks. Sadler has asked whether you would like the book to appear with some little drawings by Anne Rice. I took it on me to say you would – because I felt that it would in any case hurt Anne's feelings if you refused.

I'm terribly glad about the book. Don't think I've done the dirty on Richards. As soon as I had fixed the offer from Constable I sent a note to him by hand telling him I had an offer and asking him to say what would be his terms. Two days after I had a note (this morning) to say that they could of course do nothing without seeing the MS, that they would be pleased to give it to their reader, that Mr. Richards would be back *in three or four weeks* and would then come to a decision. I closed with Constable on the spot & sent a letter to Richards saying I had done so. I think Richards thoroughly deserves what he's got. After all his talk it appears that all he meant was that you might submit your book to him, just as you did to Heinemann. Well, he's learnt now that you're a much too important person to be treated in that way. Constables are evidently very keen to have anything of yours. Well it's one gleam of sunshine, anyhow.

                    Boge.

[L'Hermitage,
Menton]

Thursday in bed,   [5 February 1920]

Bogey darling

I have just received your Monday letter written on the back of the Constable note and hasten to reply. In the first place *your throat* – How is it? I cannot know. I must just wait then – and that remark flung at me about insuring your life. I beg of you not to say these things. They are just like the most terrible frightful earthquake – much worse. My day breaks up into terrified pieces. You *know* that you know it *quite well* – Oh how CAN you. I don't understand. But one must be very careful and say nothing one would regret. I have no right to reproach you and I don't want to appeal to your pity – but my Bogey you make it very hard when you say such things – that's all. (Everything I thought at the Casetta got 'a long way from reality'.)

Now about Constable. If they will give £40 in advance & Richards won't, it must be Constable of course. I have explained my relations with Richards. A book including 'Prelude', 'Je ne Parle pas' and so on would be interesting. But I must make very sure of what they collect from *Rhythm*. The story 'The Wind Blows' from *The Signature* is in the collection. It's the only one worth re-printing. The book had certainly better include 'Prelude': it makes a longer book. I am afraid this is adding to your great press of work. Sadler says even if an arrangement is come to nothing can be published for several months. In that case the final decision as to *which* stories could perhaps be left for my return in the first week of May.

But this is all rubbish beside your sore throat and your remark about breaking your neck househunting. I must wire you and somehow *stamp down* my anxiety until I have your reply –

Yours Wig

Forgive me for saying this.

Will you remember when you write that I don't go out or walk or see anybody to *talk* to – that you are my ALL. I lie in a chair all day. I am not strong enough yet to walk at all – and so when you say things like – that about insuring your life and breaking your neck – you have me at your complete mercy. Can you understand? Try to imagine it!! It is terrific torture – terrific. Don't you care about me at all? If I must bear it I *must* but I'm nearly at the end of my tether when you say such things.

[2 Portland Villas,
Hampstead]
[5 February 1920]
Thursday

Wig darling,

I'm sorry you kept your promise of not writing to me any more. I had nothing yesterday or to-day. I can't help thinking it's a bit unfair.

Your reviews arrived just in time for the number, at the very end of the eleventh hour, that is by the afternoon post on Wednesday. One little thing in them gave me a thrill of pleasure, namely when you said in brackets 'A herald against all the rules carrying a trumpet'. I immediately remembered the afternoon in July when we found that out for the first time, and for the moment at least it made up for the letter I didn't get.

I have had since Saturday a bad cold, which I must have caught in

272 Letters Between Katherine Mansfield and John Middleton Murry

the train coming back from Rye last week. However, it's like all my colds – only annoying by the amount of nose-blowing and dirty handkerchiefs it involves. Still, I wish they didn't get hold of me quite so violently.

This evening unfortunately is the evening I pledged to myself to take Jeanne out. I thought better of the theatre plan however, & thought it might be a good idea to take her to Ottoline's evening. It might have the advantage of impressing your family with the idea that we are rather distinguished.

Violet told me she had a letter from you yesterday – and I rather fancied I saw that one came for Mrs. Jones, who is away to-day, in your handwriting; but I can't be sure. But I was rather upset by their having letters, while I had nothing.

The only thing I can do is wait.

I do hope the coat reaches you safely. Sydney was called away to Paris last night, but he promised to make arrangements for it to go in the diplomatic bag. But I feel rather nervous all the same, particularly because I thought the coat really charming and distinguished.

Well, Wig, don't give me up entirely.

Your own
Boge.

Friday Morning

Before I could send this off, I received the letter which you sent on Monday. You still say I don't read your letters.

I hope I haven't done wrong in fixing up with Constable. Your letter seems to imply that you had settled with Richards – if that was so, I cannot understand that Richards' manager or partner should have sent me the letter he did, which I enclose and ask you carefully to keep. At all events I feel that the Constable arrangement is an extremely good one.

Don't worry about getting the 'Second helping' typed. I can do that, if you send the story to me.

You shall without fail see the proofs of the story which Rutter has. I promise faithfully. I also promise you that I will go through the typed copy with your MS, with special attention to the spaces.

[Menton]
[6 February 1920]

HOW IS YOUR CHILL ANXIOUS TAKE GREATEST CARE
REPLY
       TIG.

                                        [L'Hermitage,
                                         Menton]
In reply to your Tuesday letter   [? 7 February 1920]

My dear Bogey,
     I have your Tuesday evening letter. That you took my letter as
being primarily concerned with money is horrible. However, I'll
answer that first. I send you back the cheque for £20. As you have
paid £20 into my bank, I shall use that at the rate of £10 a month
and by the time it is finished, that is at the end of March, I hope that
my book will be paid for and I shan't have to ask you for any more
money. You ask me if we haven't known each other long enough
for me to wire for £20. But Bogey haven't we known each other
long enough for you to have said to me: '*I realise* you must need
money. But I'm cleaned out this month. I'll send some next'? If only
you'd thought for me – or imagined for me: it was *that* that hurt.
     You say I ought to have guessed you misunderstood – Curse
money! It's not really a question of money. It was the question of
sympathy, of understanding, of being in the least *interested* of
asking JUST ONCE how I was – What I thought about & felt – what I
did – if I was 'alright'? I can't get over the fact that it never occurred
to you and it makes me feel you don't want my love – not my living
love – you only want an 'idea'. When that strike was on – fool that I
was – my first thoughts always were 'What *I* feel doesn't matter so
much. Jack must be in such agony. When he doesn't hear he'll try &
wire and the P.O. will tell him no wires are delivered & he knows
I'm ill.' But your letter came 'drunk with the magnificence of the
Downs' a 'day's sheer joy' – the 'note of hysteria would go out of
my work' 'very fit'. And when you *did* hear – good – your anxiety
was over & you never referred to me again. So I *must* face the fact
that you have put *me* away for the time – you are withdrawn –
self-contained and you don't want in the deepest widest sense of the
word to be disturbed. As long as I'm on a suitable shelf – and ∴

YOU'RE not worried – ça va! Of course I still love you. I love you as much as ever. But to know this is torture until I get it in hand.

'A love that might break through *if she would let it* the ghastly terror of her loneliness.' Does not that show it up? Who could write such unspeakably cruel words if he loved at the moment? You suggest that my suffering was self-imposed, in so far as it was really a failure to love enough. If I had loved you enough I need not have suffered as I did. Bogey, you must believe me that is a DEADLY false view. A living, loving, warm being could not believe that or say it. It's a vile intellectual idea and it simply appals me. I can't wire the word Love because of it. (Of course I can, of course I will. You do *love* me; it's only you don't love me just now –) To make out my agony was my failure to love – that is really too much.

I want to mention something else. Lawrence sent me a letter today – he spat in my face & threw filth at me and said 'I loathe you you revolt me stewing in your consumption'.... 'The Italians were quite right to have nothing to do with you' and a great deal more. Now I do beseech you if you are my man to stop defending him after that & never to crack him up in the paper. *Be proud.* In the same letter he said his final opinion of you was that you were a dirty little worm. Well, *be proud.* Don't forgive him for that, please.

Goodbye, I am bitterly disappointed with the answer to my letter but I *must* bear it. You say you are not ashamed. I don't want you to be ashamed. And then you say you sent the £20 the moment you had it. February 1 came too late. *Damn* the £20. I suppose from that you look upon yourself as a man who is being bled – *you* did all in your power but FATE and your wife would not wait. It's UTTERLY false. I wanted love & sympathy and understanding. Were you cleaned out of those until February 1st? It is [a] nightmare that you won't understand.

> Your own
> Wig

Of course you love me, of course you do. It's only since I've been away you have withdrawn yourself from me & ever since I broke down at the Casetta and appealed to you things have never been the same. It [is] only that you don't love me NOW. Oh, darling – do do break through. DO care. It's so hard – Wait till I'm strong before you run away for a bit – it's so awful. Bogey you must love me. Fancy writing so coolly to me & asking me to wire if I think you do.

Would I be *here* if I thought you didn't – somewhere – deep down love me?

[Menton]
[7 February 1920]

OF COURSE YOU LOVE ME
TIG

[2 Portland Villas,
Hampstead]
[7 February 1920]
Saturday

My own darling,

This seems to be the first evening since I came back from Italy when I have been able to sit down & write to you calmly – not dashing off a few lines in time to catch a train, or to write a review. I feel that I have allowed myself to become an appalling machine, and that You have felt it [in] my letters, as you could not fail to feel it; & so you have been left without the sympathy I should have given.

There is, Wig, a certain amount of real insensibility in me. I think that has been proved now. I must just accept it: I hate it, and try to kill it. But the fact remains that I never realised how much you were suffering in Ospedaletti, nor how great would be your anxiety about money in Menton. Both those things you had a right to expect of me as your lover – and, there's no doubt in my own mind that I failed in them both.

Certainly, to be quite fair to myself, I have found it hard to keep going. My power of concentration has weakened, & it now takes me a good deal more energy than it did two or three years ago to do the same amount of work. But I don't believe very much in the argument. I feel, on the contrary, that there have been times when I have, not consciously or deliberately, turned my sympathy away from you. Something of the kind you must have felt.

Perhaps it all comes back to the fact that I am able to do nothing without an effort, neither to work, nor to love. It's what I mean when I say I'm no good as a lover – our old quarrel of years ago about the enamel spoon. I think that at bottom it's no worse, & no better than that. You managed to bear with it when you were well –

that was your generosity – and now when you are ill it becomes intolerable.

Don't let it become intolerable, Wig. Believe at least that my thoughts are not as cold & brutal as my words sometimes seem to be. That in fact I do give you my all, and if it's a poor one, it's because I have no more to give. You have the whole of me, darling, and when it fails, as it has failed so often I know, just remember that I would have given more if I had had it. It's not much consolation – it's certainly not the rich comfort I should be giving you, but it may be some. I mean that though I am a jagged, flowerless, & inhospitable rock, I am a rock. If I'm not beautiful or life-giving, I'm also not treacherous.

I don't suppose I have explained what I mean. I do try to give, Wig darling, try desperately sometimes because I know how much you need it, and from me. But the spring whence richness comes seems to dry up. I become a barren & dry land where no water is. I feel like a tree must feel in the winter. It knows it is not dead, yet it cannot show that it is alive – it has neither voice nor leaves. The only thing to do would be cut it open. But you can't cut me open. Things that You, being you, might read in a movement of my hand or a glance of my eyes when we are together are lost altogether in my bald letters. The more I try to make my letters live, the less I seem able to.

You see, my darling, it's wrong for us to be apart. That is what it comes to at the last. You can understand my harshness, blackness, my habit of silence when you are near me, and make allowances: but when we are so far away that is impossible, yet it is more necessary than ever.

The only thing is for you to get well – to make up your mind that I am the same Boge all the while – not the Boge I ought to be, but a better Boge than I look at the distance. Get well my darling, and let's put an end to this time of torture. Your voice is sweet, but mine is harsh when we call from so far away.

Well, my darling Worm, I'll tell you what news there is in my next letter. This one is all explanation, of something which cannot be explained. But as your telegram to-day said, *of course I love you* and love you for all I am worth, with all that I have.

Your own Boge.

[L'Hermitage,
Menton]
[8 February 1920]

Dear Darling,
I received a letter from you yesterday saying (1) you had bought me an overcoat. I wish you hadn't. It is obvious that you *raced* to buy it & that you bought it with your little brains and nerves. You are the man in the Daudet story you know – the man with the golden brain ... But there. When it comes I'll see. I'll cherish it.
(2) You have paid £10 into my Bank. Now I'm going to ask you if you can put in another £10 in March. After that I shall need no more of your money.
(3) You've sold my book. With the £40 I shall spend £10 for living expenses in the mois d'Avril & the £30 for fares and travelling home. Do you mind asking them to send the cheque to me. Pure childishness – but I want to see it with my own eyes & send it with my own hand to Kay. I feel the Bank will *close*. It is fearfully good of you to have done this for me & I feel it has been *no* end of a nuisance. Re the matter of the book – I suppose I have final say, I couldn't have 'The Woman at the Store' reprinted par exemple – If it's left to Sadler only Sadler has a say in what he [prints]. Anne's drawings don't matter. I do want the story called 'Second Helping' that I'm at now to be included. Enough. Richards is coming here you know to see me. That will be orkid.
Another change in the near future. I have not mentioned it, but this place is *intolerably* noisy. I am so sensitive to noise-oh-so sensitive. It *hurts* me really. They bang my door, other doors shout shriek crash – I can't endure it & really can't work OR sleep. The doctor suggested *une forte dose de Véronal.* Merci. But really it's *bad.* I just mentioned this to Jinnie. She came one day when I was feeling it a bit badly – Today she arrived with a carriage & fur rugs & silk cushions. Took me to their Villa – it is really superb – *exquisite* outside & in. They had a *chaise longue* in the garden – a tiny tray with black coffee out of a silver pot, Grand Marnier – cigarettes, little bunch of violets all ready – Then we went in to tea. Their villa is really – Boge – it's a dream. I mean even the furnishing is *perfect* – Spanish silk bed coverlets, Italian china – the tea appointments perfect – stillness – maids in tiny muslin aprons flitting over *carpets* ... & so on. Then they showed me into a room, grey & silver facing south with a balcony – the only touch of colour a little rose brocade couch with gilt legs & Jinnie said, 'Now my

dear we want you to come here, and live here. It's *dead* quiet. You can be alone all day if you like. There is the garden – We are here. First I must arrange that you see Doctor Rendall for him to sign that you are no longer infectious. If he does this, we want you here until May. You're going to get well. You can't afford to fight or see ugly people or have ugly trays.' And then she laughed & said, 'The Lord has delivered you into our hands & please God we'll cure you.' What do you think of that? They want me to stay there till May 4 then travel home together Bogey this is really very important; it's one of the most important things that ever happened to me – These women are *right*; they are what we mean to be in our life. They are wise & at rest & deeply happy – & they are very exquisite. It all depends on Rendall. Subject to Rendall's signing I shall go but I don't know when. Not for a week at least: I will let you know. And I shall pay what I pay here – but of course no extras. I go as a patient – & Jinnie couldn't afford to leave the room empty. Also it's right I should do that. But no money on earth can ever repay what I shall get there. You see I'll have that *Life* to share too – the meals & the room with great wood fires & the darling baby peke and the garden & the gardener – the orange trees, the lemons – their maid to look after my clothes. You know what I mean? And my work always arranged for & thought of. A table in the garden & a bath chair with rug & cushions that I can lie in & write.

WHY should they do that? WHY should Jinnie say, 'Then I'll be at rest about you, darling. I shall know you're safe'. It's as though my *Mother* were here again. I miss her so. I often long to lean against Mother & know she understands things ... that can't be told – that would fade at a breath – *delicate needs* – a feeling of great fineness & gentleness. But what Mother hadn't is an *understanding* of WORK.

The Villa is in style like Garsington. I mean that is the tone. It is very large – a huge hall lighted from above – a great double salon – It has delicate balconies and a tower. I want you to see it. I can't make you see it – I want you to see the garden & the potting-shed where I can walk & look at the little plants. Huge spring palms – great branches of orange against the sky – no, I can't draw them. As soon as I've seen Rendall I shall know when I go. Have you read so far? That's all, dearest, but that explains why I can't work here as I thought I could: the infernal noise – especially in the morning. You remember when I managed to ask you not to go on scraping your porridge saucer? It was so hard to say & I tried to say it nicely but I see now how you pushed the plate away & rumpled your hair & wouldn't eat or look at me – just *went blind*. It wasn't fair – you know, Bogey – really it wasn't. You know how hard it was for me to say – Why did you take offence? You know I think & think of those things sometimes and I *can't* account for them! It's hereditary but I wish you didn't – *pay me out* for having to say: 'I say old boy I'm *so* sorry – but my nerves are so awful in the morning – <u>DO</u> you mind – I hate having to say it?' And oh, he shows her how he does mind! Do you 'understand that in a novel'? I suppose you do: I wish I did. No, darling, at times you are very dark to me. Your devoted Wife

[2 Portland Villas,
Hampstead]
[9 February 1920]
Monday Evening

Violet wanted to catch the post so I broke off my letter abruptly. This little bit will go to-morrow morning. It's about the book.

(1) You mustn't think that because Constables can't get it out till the Autumn, that they don't want the MS. immediately (i.e. within 3 weeks). Conditions in the printing trade are so bad that you have to begin 6 months ahead. The very best time for your book to appear is the early autumn. (Mine was wrecked through coming out just before Xmas.) So make up your mind what exactly you want in it.

(2) I have read yr new story. The copy came this morning. Of course it's amazingly good. No-one can write like you – but it's also extraordinarily beautiful. That is the abiding impression. I'll give you a detailed criticism later. But it's a beauty.

(3) About the *German Pension*. You're getting hyper-sensitive about yr. work. By all means let the new book be as perfect as you can make it. But remember you are a *big* writer. You are as classic as Tchehov in your way. What you have written, you have written. And it's simply ridiculous to pretend there's anything to be ashamed of in the G.P. It was a splendid piece of work for 1911–12. Early work if you like. Write an introduction saying so if you like. But have it republished. Do listen to me on this point. I am advising you for the very best. I could understand if you had not a new book coming – but since you have, it's admirable that there shd. be a new edition of G.P. And I'm leaving utterly out of account the mere

business advantage of one publisher having both your books – the additional solidity it gives you – YOU MUST TAKE MY ADVICE IN THIS. By all means say in your introduction that I forced you to it.

Finally you don't seem to understand the *kudos* that an entirely new edition of a book published nine years ago gives you. Why, I don't believe there's a single writer of under 35 who has had such a thing.

(4) Another cheque for £10 will be paid into your bank as soon as I get my pay at the beginning of March. The £20 cheque was £10 for Jan & £10 for Feb.

Finally forgive these hurried scrawls. You will see I've written a lot – and I have to finish an article for the *Nation* to-night.

> Je t'aime mais sois persuadée par moi.
> Boge

> [Menton]
> [9 February 1920]

THURSDAY LETTER CAME. TELL WING WIRE IMMEDI-ATELY YOUR COLDNESS KILLING ME

> TIG.

> [London]
> [10 February 1920]

WIRE RECEIVED ALL WELL HE LOVES YOU DESPERATELY HE CAN'T DO MORE

> WING

> [The Athenaeum,
> 10 Adelphi Terrace, W.C.2]
> [10 February 1920]
> Tuesday Morning

My darling heart,

I have just had the wire from you saying my coldness is killing you. Wing has replied for me, because I don't know how to reply.

How can I say in a telegram that I am not cold, that I love you passionately, that you are my all. How can I convince you, when I don't even know what it is in my letters that makes you think I am cold. I feel as though I were lost in a mist.

What have I said – what have I not said. One day you say I don't read your letters, & that is why you won't write. So I answer everything in them to show at least that I read them.

Why do you say I am cold? I have got myself into a condition in which I am almost afraid to write except about definite things. I am terrified of hurting you any more.

Oh, Wig, do bear with me. Believe that I am at any rate just what I used to be. How could I change? Anxiety has made me fearful – and the awful feeling that all that I may write may have an effect utterly different from what I meant preys upon me.

Wig, you *must* believe what I say: you must trust me. After all I have [not] deserved this, no matter what I have done. Don't suspect me. That terrifies me, and makes the bad worse.

Don't close your heart against me. I've nowhere else to turn. Cold! Cold!

Well I love you, love you, love you I can do no more.

Your Boge.

> [2 Portland Villas,
> Hampstead]
> [10 February 1920]
> Tuesday Night.

Worm, Worm,

To-day I have had your wire – your coldness is killing me – and to-night a letter (in answer to my Tuesday letter) telling me the same thing more plainly.

Now, Mouse, I've waited a minute, lit a cigarette. I must be calm. For somehow in spite of myself our destiny has come to tremble on a razor's edge. Hitherto I have written desperately, and made the wounds I have inflicted on you worse. I must be calm.

Darling – my own heart – the very me. I feel to-night at the end of my tether. Some blind force is crushing the hope out of me. For I swear to you as my lover and my wife that all I have done since I came back has been with a single thought – love of you. Instead of bringing us nearer it has driven us apart.

Why, why! Why do you think I have withdrawn? My letters, you say, show it. But Wig if I write with my blood they won't be different from this. I can't explain. Somehow I have come to fear every word I write. Do you think the anguish of your letters doesn't tear my heart in bits? Do you really think I don't feel? Do you really think I had no sympathy for you in that ghastly time when I heard nothing? Don't you understand that a time like that beats even me down? That I have to grip at anything – the country – even drink – to prevent myself from collapse altogether? And I cling above all to our things – working for our house – buying our mirror. Silly things, God knows – but things that you & I don't think silly, because we know all they mean.

Do you think I wasn't hurt when you referred to my buying the mirror as a kind of extravagance, proving that I had money to burn? Above all when we talked about the mirror together at Xmas. Don't you understand that in buying it, for a moment I had you on my arm at my side, so light, so lovely, so my own, whispering: Yes, let's buy it, Boge. We can afford it. I'll save on the flowers – all those beautiful unforgettable things that you have whispered to me on my arm in the past.

Worm, Worm – you understand all this. I appeal to you, darling, do not judge me as something finer than I am – but just as the thing you have always known me to be. Remember my faults & manias – my madnesses – the way I fasten on material symbols of our being together – *our* chairs, *our* tables, *our* pillow-cases. Don't suddenly become deaf to all these things.

No, I'm not calm. Another cigarette.

Darling, do you realise that you *never* tell me how you are?

Another letter of defence & accusation. Forget it all.

Think that I love you. If you will think that, you can't go on believing that I withdrew from you.

Darling, listen to me in the quiet for one little moment. Hear my *voice*. I love you, love you, love you – and I am suffering as I never suffered before. Before I have been apart from you for a moment: but I have held you in my arms and we have known that we belonged to each other pour toujours. I can't do that, now. At least I can, only if you will listen to me.

Here am I – this is my voice – these are my lips, my eyes. Am I that stone? Answer me, Wig.

How can I speak with the great weight of your distrust, the anguish of the pain I cause you with every letter, bearing on me?

Throw it away. Oh, I beseech you Wig – who love me so much. Let me hold you in my arms. Let this ghastly nightmare go

      Boge

              [L'Hermitage,
              Menton]
              [11 February 1920]
              Wednesday – no – Yes –

My Precious,
    Your Saturday evening letter has come with the 'explanation'. Don't say another word about it. Let's after this put it quite away. Yes, I felt in Ospedaletti that you refused to understand and I have felt since I have been abroad this time that you have turned away from me. Withdrawn yourself utterly from me – I have felt like a person in an open boat, tossing about in frightful waves calling and crying to be saved & you have seen me from your ship & refused to see me or rescue me because you were not made of whipcord & steel. Yes, Boge, it has been a suffering such as I don't feel you ever could know. But it's over and it's taught me a lesson and I don't regret it. I could turn to it now, and kiss it. I can't enter into what it has taught me but the difference is there. It had to be. If I'm *dead* sincere I must say that I believe in the mystery: *out of evil good shall come*. But now – put it all away, my own. And you really must give up the word *desperate* with regard to our relations. Don't let it exist. Don't make an effort to love me – my silly darling – or to fly after enamel spoons. Just remember: *That From Now I am not ill.* Because that is the truth. So lean on me, give me your things to hold, confide in me, worry me, treat me as your wife. Just *rest* on the thought of me. You are absurd when you say you are no good as a lover. That is just nonsense and it's not fair to me. I don't want a slave and an admirer, my love, you would be a perfectly rotten slave & admirer – As a lover, you are – well simply you – just all my life and my joy and my *pride*. Call me your 'worm' – that is enough for me. But let's get over all this. What has been – has been. But, remember *no desperate* efforts are allowed. Not being an intellectual I always seem to have to learn things at the risk of my life – but I do learn. Let's be wise, true, *real lovers* from now on. Let's enter the Heron from today – from this very minute & I shall rejoice in you and if it's not too great an effort – dear love – try and rejoice in me. That's all.

I go to the Villa Flora on Sunday. All is arranged.

Heard from Mary Cannan this morning: she is at Capri & had heard from L. that I was a 'very sick woman' and you a 'great swell' – I thereupon wrote her an intimate letter & just put her right about US and just told her what you were really like & what your loyalty to L. had been and so on. I just felt I must do this. Heard from Grant Richards who's at Cap Martin – ½ an hour away – *very snuffy* but still wants to see me – He suggests bringing over a car & motoring me there. Well, I'd better see him. No he doesn't suggest a car just that I shall go – so I don't know.

It's lunch time. I'm in bed, I must fly up. My nib will not write – It must write that I love you & you only world without end amen – But you know it.

Yours Wigchik

Tell Wing to keep both eyes on you & when you disappear again he and Athy must just hunt you out and beat you – but not hard.

Are the snowdrops out?

The cuckoo has been heard at Hurstmonceux, Sussex.

Chaddie has a wide 'border of yellow crocuses'. It sounds like an Alice Prosser doesn't it?

C. and J. have given me the most exquisite fine woollen stuff for a dress & a dressmaker to go with it.

Your Mother wrote me such a nice letter today & I replied.

(1) *Tell Arthur* about my change of Address after Saturday. Please *be sure to do this* and give the old boy a loving hug from me.

(2) Mark the linen. (3) Whistle on the stairs. (4) Walk out of the steps & down the front on your hands please just to show all's well.

(5) Ask Violet when she's going to be married & tell her it's worth it. But do none of these things desperately.

[The Athenaeum,
10 Adelphi Terrace.]
[12 February 1920]
Thursday Afternoon

My darling

Last night I received a lovely letter from you telling me that you were probably going to Jinnie Fullerton's villa. How gorgeous that will be. I was overjoyed – not merely at the news – but at the letter itself, so sweet, so fragrant, perfumed with that bunch of black oranges. It was just going to my head when I remembered that your wire about my coldness must have been sent *after* the letter. That was a nasty shock.

But when I got to the office this morning I found yr. telegram saying you understood & sending me yr. love. So that now I am feeling that things are going well; that the cloud between us has been blown away. (Violet has just been in with my tea & to tell me that the first snow drop has shown its head in the garden. I am going to pick it & put [it] in this letter.) I do hope – most fervently that Dr. Rendall says you may go to the villa. You can imagine what I feel about that darling woman, Jinnie Fullerton. I must write to her – if it's only a word or two. Will you send me her address. I've sent a second £10 to yr. bank to-day. The cheque for £20 came back safely. Of course, darling, the Constable cheque for £40 will come straight to you. I'm merely acting as your agent. You will have to sign the agreement & receive the money.

You can hardly believe how profoundly glad I am about the fixing up of your book. It is one of my heart's desires; above all because I feel that it's going to have a great success. I don't mean that you'll sell as many as Elizabeth – your mind & your art are so much finer that we can't expect that – but I shall be really disappointed & surprised if you don't sell between 3 and 4 thousand. There's nothing like your work; and I am convinced it's the only real achievement of our generation in prose – outside *Sons & Lovers*. Lawrence has gone mad. You are the only person who is the real thing.

I've told you that before; but you might like to hear it again. While I'm on this subject – the choice of what is to go in the book rests *entirely* with you, except that *Prelude* must be included. That, I think, is necessary anyhow not only because of filling out the book, but because it shows a side of your work that is extremely important. In other words, it's necessary for the artistic balance.

I went to dinner with Beresford last night. Delamare, May Sinclair & Naomi Royde-Smith were there. I'm not telling you this to please you, but just as a fact. They were all very excited over my announcement that your book was really coming. May Sinclair turned to me & said that she admired your work more than any. And then Beresford & Delamare struck in together with: Your novel-reviews were the finest in England. There's nothing like them, said Delamare. Oh, it's silly, I know, darling, & they aren't great people (except in a way Delamare) but I thrilled with pleasure. After all you know they're the best we've got. And when Mrs. B took me aside as I was going & said 'May Sinclair told me just before you came that she had been terribly upset by K.M.'s review of her novel, because she thought that K.M. is the only person who really knows how to do it' – why, I thrilled even more.

I feel that all that you have deserved is coming to you, and it makes me so happy & excited.

To-morrow morning I'm going for the week end to East Grinstead. A man who used to work at Watergate House is putting me up – a poet chap called Locke Ellis, very nice, who has a motor-car in which he's going to take me round.

If everything's all right again, will you write about the paper. I miss your criticism so much. It seems to me that what the paper really wants is a page of literary *causerie*. People like that kind of thing; it costs them no effort; and I feel that at present the whole effect of the paper is perhaps a little too frigid & impersonal for the ordinary man. I am thinking of putting Aldous H. onto the job. I'm no good at it myself: I haven't a light touch.

I also incline to think that it might be an improvement if the first page were set solid with the contents on top – without that silly little pocket in the middle. And perhaps if instead of a leading article we had just a page of notes like the political weeklies – only editorial notes on literature & ideas. What do you think? It would have this advantage that we might gain a little space at the beginning of the paper to make room for the *causerie* in the middle.

> Your loving
> Boge.

> 2 Portland Villas,
> [Hampstead]
> [16 February 1920]
> Monday Evening 6.30.

My own darling,

I returned this afternoon. I could not stay at the office because I felt that there would be some letters from you. There were – four of them. Two were agonising; caused by a careless, brutal phrase of mine. God forgive me for it. Two were lovely, – undeserved perhaps, but oh, how thrilling!

I won't try to explain my brutal phrase. My explanations are so ghastly in their clumsiness that I am terrified of them, and of the pain they have concealed in them.

If you can forget the hideous suffering I have caused you through sheer selfish carelessness, I will. But believe me, Worm, never at any single moment have I conceived of our love coming to an end. I felt that I had wounded you so much that you could never forgive me, and I cried alone in my desolation & anguish.

In my last 2 letters I have talked about the house a lot. It is always in my mind. For, to me, it is the condition of our perfect existence together. You know I talked about you a lot down there at East Grinstead. My mind was continually off day-dreaming. You & I driving up in a little motor-car to their house – I half-handing, half-lifting you out. I always have to half-lift you, because you are so light and beautiful (you always have been the incarnation of these things to me since first I met you in your gauze scarf at the Georges'). I have a short fuzzy coat on & big gloves; you a superb blanket overcoat, chosen by me. And then I say with my heart bursting with pride: This is my wife. And they fall down & worship you.

Then there's another. It's Friday afternoon – tea-time. You are in the drawing room. I've come in from trundling a wheelbarrow about in the garden, making a rose-bed according to your directions. You can't see me. I'm in a cubby hole washing my hands. You call out Bog-ee Tea. Come now before it's cold. I trundle in and sit on the floor with my head against your knees. Silence & warmth by the wood-fire. The maids' steps die away into the kitchen. You say: Boge & stroke my hair. I say: Wig – this is what we dreamed. And then you bend over & turn my head round in your hands & say: Listen. And I listen. Do you know what you say? You say: It's all right, Boge darling. I'm going to have a baby. And I just kiss you. The room is so beautiful, you are so beautiful – even I am beautiful; and we know that our child will be more beautiful still, for all these things have entered into him.

Oh, Worm darling, I could go on giving you these pictures of my mind for hours & hours. Some funny. Hunting for eggs from our chickens; you scolding me & laughing for getting so oily from the motor-car.

If I seem to talk, or worry, too much about the house, Worm, remember that it means all these things to me. It's the place where we can be together; where all my hatred of life will depart from me & all the blackness you hate in me (& I hate too) will be dissolved away; where we can live as we were meant to live. All day long I think about it, simply because I can't help it. It brings me near you & holds us together. I shut the door & we are in each other's arms.

But I need you to talk it over with. I don't have time to write everything. I don't want you to think that I am going mad when I talk of buying a house. I'm grimly determined about it. If the real thing were being sold to-morrow, and it may be any to-morrow, I should bid up to £1500 for it. I should pay the 10% deposit with my war loan, & then hunt about for the rest of the money. Someone would have to give it me – I mean lend of course.

Of course, I wouldn't buy rashly. Besides the fact that I know what I want exactly, I should get a good surveyor to go down & overhaul it for the things I can't see. Moreover the man Locke Ellis has promised to go with me & give his opinion on anything I hit upon. I have a great respect for a man who has done what he has done with a house.

But I do want to know whether you agree with all my plans. As for finding the money – I must get that from friends – and I have no doubt that I shall be able to. But I want to buy the house first – then they'll have to help me out. I'm sure I can persuade Sydney to take a 7% mortgage for £1000 – and the rest I can borrow from the Bank. Milne has already promised to deposit securities for any amount I borrow up to £500. So I can see my way to £1500.

What I want to know is whether you think I'm getting very rash. My feeling is that we've only got one life, & that's yours. And that we must secure what we need.

Your own
Boge.

THE IMPORTANT LETTER

[Villa Flora,
Menton]
[26 February 1920]
[Thursday]

Darling Precious little Husband,

I want you to read this slowly and remember that I am loving you with my whole heart and putting you first in my thoughts, always. I know how terribly anxious you are to leave P.V., but what are you going to do if I go abroad in the winter? Rendall said today it would be madness for me to spend the next 2 winters in England because whatever the luxury I live in, the air is almost perpetually damp and there IS very little sun. It is not as though I were a simple consumptive who can walk, lie about and so on! I am handicapped very severely by my rheumatism which cannot be cured until my lungs are cured. It is that which prevents me from leading the normal life in a cold climate which another consumptive can do. He says that for the next two years I ought to be here from November till May. I must take this opinion into account; it is shared by these 2 women and I dare not face a prolongation of my illness. Now if I do come abroad L.M. must be with me. She would not let me come alone & she says she dare not. I think she is right. You remember I once was cruel enough to suggest that we put off establishing our house. *I still suggest it.* Yes, I still think it would be 1000 times better to wait for 2 years. Please don't get angry. Please read on. You could surely get a week-end place for yourself every week-end. I would spend May till October in P.V. I suggest offering Violet & Roger the basement floor & her bedroom – with a door at the top of the kitchen stairs for them so that they live there. I would get the whole house & the feeding arrangements and so on into *perfect order* before I left and arrange that you were never left without a servant even when she was out. In the meantime you take your time, you look; if you do see the perfect thing it's cheap you make it your week-end cottage – and for us when I'm there until I am well enough to live there. You'll say can't stand P.V. any longer. Not as it is now, of course, you can't. The house wants attention, care, organisation, the life of it wants changing; you must live like a gentleman and be served like one – But all that can be done when L.M. & I get back. I'll make it my job to see you are really comfortably and exquisitely housed. There's no reason why Sydney should not stay either. I KNOW you hate London but darling heart you MUST be in London, any way for a time and you certainly could get every week-end off & *when* the house is found perhaps you could spend every week-end there. P.V. when I've seen to it won't be in the least what it is now. And Bogey, you must realise that I want to give you your heart's desire *this moment* but I must consider well what is easiest and best for us. Life in the country without your wife would not do. It would make immense demands on your energy. It can't be done without L.M. and me there all the time – and I really think I *dare* not face this rheumatism for two years. You see what it amounts to is this: I come back thoroughly set you up – get all *really* exquisite – you find a country place or a pied à terre & go slow just for the present. Light a cigarette. Think it well well over. I wish you were here so that I might talk it out with you. I do so feel it's the right thing to do. Let Sydney know: ask him. Tell him how snug I mean to make P.V. & well kept in every way. And if you do agree please read this letter to Violet &

give it to her immediately & darling please please wire me either *agree* or *don't agree*. I shall wait for that wire. I'll go into all the details once I'm home – & I promise you great comfort – no domestic worries and L.M. shall establish your country comfort. That's all. Your devoted

Wife Wig

[Villa Flora,
Menton]
[7 March 1920]

My darling Bogey,
After two days and nights of misery trying to make bricks out of straw I was forced to give up. I can't write on novels unless I have some novels to write on. You see I have no intellectual stimulus here & my nerves are still so overstrained that they just fail me.
I am also exceedingly worried about you.
Except for that hurried note in reply to my important letter you have not referred to it: you have not talked it out at all. I tried my very best darling to make you realise how deeply I felt it for you but I am afraid I did not succeed at all. But try not to forget that we are *all in all* to each other and that you when you 'confess you are selfish' and talk of 'no compensations in London' you are saying things which I not only know just as deeply, just as finely, as you – we have talked of them all in the deepest intimacy – but you hurt my love in speaking as though I were a stranger. Must you? Try not to! It is like your other letter saying: 'My days are very laborious & I am none too pleased with life.' Can't you feel how those words strike another? Oh so strangely and sadly, dearest.
As soon as I get back (in 7 weeks) I shall arrange everything for you. I think the Cottage idea is the right one & we shall have a whole month, there in the summer. L.M. & I will make it perfect. I do not ask you to spend one penny on P.V. I never have. All that we buy will be for the Heron & P.V. is our storehouse. Remember this, Bogey dear. I have already spent 200 francs on most lovely things for us here. Cups, saucers, trays, boxes, exquisite oddments. I bought them with such deep joy but your letter makes me feel perhaps my joy was a little premature & you will not care so greatly. It's a great effort to love just now – isn't it? Ah, Bogey –
Darling – do not drink more wine than you need. It does you

great harm. Won't you get Sorapure to give you some injections as you are over-tired? May I write & ask him to come & see you?

And will you tell me in your very next letter whether you want Waterlow to stay on – As regards his money, I will pay the £13 a month. If you want him we must fit him in somehow. It is for you to say but please tell me, won't you?

I feel your fatigue is dreadful. Take care of yourself my precious boy & remember that in seven weeks please God you will be able to hand over many of your worries to your own devoted for ever – your very own

Wig.

Do confide in me if you possibly can – won't you?

[2 Portland Villas,
Hampstead]
[11 March 1920]
Thursday Night. 11.30 p.m.

My own precious Wig-wife.

There was a letter when I got home to-night. It was the one you wrote when you received my answer to your important letter. I'm sorry, darling, that I let the tinge of disappointment show through, but, believe me, I meant exactly what I said in my wire: that I agreed *absolutely*. I'm disappointed that we have to spend the next two winters apart – I can't help that – but at the same time I'm terribly glad at the thought that two more winters will make you perfectly well. I can't have everything as I want it.

But you shouldn't think that I wouldn't feel joy at the things you have bought. Good God, what should I do if I did not think that you would feel joy at the things I have bought? Don't be funny, Wig, you darling: if you go on in that way I shall begin to think of you as the little girl under the cabbage-leaf. And don't think I'm forgetting that we are all in all to each other because I make my little moan. You'll make me afraid of making any little moans; & that will be awful. Who can I moan to if not to you? You know me: take all my moans lightly: say there's that boy moaning again, drat him. But don't go wondering whether I love you.

I've just found a telegram asking me not to drink any more wine. I haven't, darling. Now that Ottoline's parties are over there's no need. The wire came addressed to Hurry. So Violet opened it and read it. So the cat's out of the bag.

About Sydney, I don't know what to say. The whole thing's rather complicated. If Violet & Roger come to live in the basement, and I live in this house alone next winter the expense will be pretty terrific. It would be far more sensible to let the house furnished during the winter & for me to go into rooms. If Sydney is here the expense is much less & I don't mind. And I don't quite see how we can turn him out in the Summer & ask him to come back in the winter. Besides, don't you remember that when you wrote your important letter you said Sydney can stay too if he likes perfectly well? I told him you said that.

Don't get things too tied up about this house, old girl. Think over it a bit. What about taking a furnished house in the country during the summer for instance? I feel it would be a great mistake for me to live alone here for 7 months during the winter. It would cost £8 a week; & that's far too much for me to spend on mere living. I'd far sooner go into rooms in the country & let the house furnished. We could get 4 guineas a week for it, & that would pay for me – a saving of £8 a week.

If you agreed to this notion it would be perfectly simple to tell Sydney that we had decided that the house was too expensive to keep on in the winter.

These things are easier to talk about than to write about. But I can't help thinking that the right thing to do is to let the house furnished while you are away – and live in it *alone together* while you are here, or live in a furnished house in the country. But to live in it alone together in the summer & then for me to live in it alone in the winter seems to me extravagant. It isn't as though I like this house when you aren't here. I don't. Every time I look at the shepherdess or Ribni or the wardrobe I feel a bit sad: & I would far sooner be out of it. Sydney is very nice indeed – but I would sooner live in rather dingy rooms alone provided I could have the cats. And as I say we could get at least 4 guineas a week for it in the winter, probably 5, which would more than pay for me.

It's probably impossible to decide these things until we talk them over together; but I just wanted to suggest various points. When you say you will pay Sydney's £13 a month, you funny Worm, what good will that do – the £13 comes out of our money. So why shouldn't I pay it myself? And for me to pay £13 a month to myself isn't worth while, is it?

Finally – I must go to bed, Wig – look at it like this. Letting the house furnished in the winter means saving about £8 a week if Sydney is not here, £5 if he is. Say I find the cottage, of the kind I hope to find, – one that with some enlargement would be the ultimate Heron. Think how much that £8 a week would pay towards it.

> Your own loving
> Boge.

Just got your telegram about Sydney. God bless you my darling. I don't know what to say. It was FEARFULLY IMPORTANT.

	[Villa Flora,
	Menton]
'House' letter	[14 March 1920]

My precious dear,
  I hasten to answer your letter (Thursday night) about the house. Look here, we can decide practically nothing while I am away but the main lines Bogey must be arranged....
  I don't see how we *can* have Waterlow. Where is he to sleep? I must have the South bedroom, Ida, the small room & you *must* have your dressing room with a little bed in it in case I have to sleep alone. But quite apart from that, oh Bogey the idea is *detestable* to me. Surely he'd understand that he can't be there in the summer. It seems to me so sensible. The house is *much* too small & the bathroom, lavatory & so on aren't a bit suitable. But the chief question is I cannot put to you too strongly my desire to be HOME and he is NOT part of my home. I want to dine 'en famille' – to be alone with you – to have all the rooms. I'll leave the winter scheme & Violet & Roger en l'air until I return. I can see you would rather I did. It's a poor look-out to let the house furnished I must say as I want it to be so lovely, but that must be as you wish. At any rate I cannot consider for one moment a furnished house in the country for the summer! Oh, you don't understand me a tiny bit. I'm in furnished houses all winter. P.V. is HOME. I want to be there with our things – our cats – our own little bits. I CAN'T GO ANYWHERE ELSE. Let's go to your cottage and we'll make that cottage perfect & have a month in it but I must have my own house. I can't be without it. You must decide what you like in the winter. If you would prefer rather dingy rooms & your cats – (who will look after *them*?) and who will look after you? No, we really had better not discuss all this till I return.

I'll write to Violet leaving all plans 'pending' – I rely on you to get rid of Waterlow and to let us be alone for those six months. If you would rather not – let me. I'll write at once. But it must be done at once. *Please wire me* if you would rather I wrote, or not – will you? But let us at least have our life together unspoiled by strangers for the little time we have together. Does that sound too 'queer' to you? Please at any rate try & leave it all till April 30th and DON'T unsettle Violet. I don't think you know how we depend on her – No, dearest love – the only thing is to wait but to get Waterlow out if you can or if not, let me explain to him at once.

Your own
'Wife

a *heart* flying to greet you & panting after the waterbrooks.

I'll have to add this. Marie has just brought your telegram about Waterlow. I am so happy I have turned a Katherine wheel & feel inclined to cheer. *Just wait till I get home* that's all the best. And we shall be alone & all the house ours and a perfect table & the new cups and saucers with their flowers & fluting. And the windows shall be open – you'll be in old clothes, I'll be in fair ones. Wing & Athy there – fruit in our Italian dish – HAPPINESS, happiness. We'll be really truly alone. I'll be able to pick up your hand – look at it – kiss it – give it back to you. I'll say Boge my own; you'll say yes Wiggiechik? We'll look at each other and laugh – Wing will wink at Athy and pretend to play the fiddle –

Oh I love you.

Je t'aime.

Wig

[Villa Flora
Menton]
[17 March 1920]

I am glad that Waterlow has been so decent Boge & I fully accept all you say. At the same time ...

Dearest Bogey

I have just received your Sunday letter answering my questions. Thank you darling. Now we'll cry PAX till I do come home – It's so soon now. At the same time I had a letter from Brett. I hesitated before opening. I felt it was not going to be pleasant … & it wasn't. She told me all about the 'orgies' and the 'drink' & the parties etc. I had known more or less before but I do wish she had left me with my 'less' I could never never be part of such a world, dear Bogey, however desperate I felt A great gulf separates me from it for ever. And then that precious Arthur writes that HE thinks the sun has risen over the Heron and will never set. Well, I hope it won't, for him. I shall do my very best to make him feel it is there and bright and warm when I come home. Don't ever let him see the 'orgies'or wine parties, will you Boge?

Poor Brett! She asks me to forgive her. Of course I forgive her – but she ought to take herself in hand. She can't afford to drift. And she can't fall drunk 'into a Lav' – then talk of the beauty of 'Cinnamon & Angelica'. I do feel so very deeply the need for dignity in this present Life. It's the only protest one can make – to be dignified and sincere and to – somehow keep love of human beings in one's heart. Really, it's no wonder people are so unhappy. Well, I cannot afford to judge any man. And after all I have lived another remote and different Life. My eight months are like eight years. The 'girl you left behind you' really did die after all in that Casetta and is buried there for ever.

My dearest little mate we shall have a month together in the summer all alone – and peaceful beyond words. We shall lie on the grass & look up at the clouds and play soldiers & you shall wear a daisy in your buttonhole & we'll blow some o'clocks & tell lady birds to fly away home. That is MY kind of gaierty, Bogey darling.

Take care of yourself and don't forget that I love you 'absolutely' and that I am

> Your own
> Wig

You see that combines a kiss ordinary and a heart with an arrow. It is a ∴ very powerful magick.

[2 Portland Villas,
Hampstead]
[22 March 1920]
Monday Evening

·My darling,

Two letters from you this morning – so I'm almost all square now. They were both lovely – so you are in reality several pegs up. I have a quaint feeling that Brett in her innocence gave you a queer account of 'orgies'. The word, at least, sounds to me unutterably odd as a description of any doings in which I have been concerned. I could understand it as applied say to our evening in Montmartre when I had the 2½ stamp on my forehead, or the famous Christmas party at Gilbert & Mary's, or the party at Brett's studio when Fergusson & Anne Rice & Beatrice Campbell were there – though even those I should say, being no expert, were very mild 'orgies'. But, Tig, you would have laughed if you had seen these 'orgies'; as far as I know, they consisted in me rather gloomy with rather too much to drink gradually getting gloomier & gloomier as I tried to talk to the impossible people whom Ottoline Morrell collected for her parties. I don't defend the drink, mind you; I think I'm better without it at all times; but on the other hand I do feel that it was the best way out of the difficulty of those parties. The last one I went to alone without a sniff of anything alcoholic; & my misery was abject. Why go at all, you say? Well, there was the blessed woman continually making cattish remarks about my not going to see her. And to tell the truth, I'm rather frightened of her; I can't afford to have her my active enemy; & I couldn't bear a soulful dinner-party with her. So I chose the less evil. That's my account of it, anyhow.

More dignity, you say. But so, Good god, do I. I pine for it. But I must honestly say it's not I who am undignified in the present pandemonium.

I am all for the New Forest. Yes, it must be an inn. How else shall we manage to do for ourselves. Ireland's very nice; but (1) the journey's a nuisance & (2) if we go to Ireland we shall be so deluged with invitations that we shan't have any enjoyment. There are about a dozen friends of Miss Vesey's who are apparently thirsting to put us up for unlimited periods if ever we set foot on the island. And it would be jolly difficult to refuse if we once got there.

No, for our purposes the New Forest seems the very thing. As for the time, I suggest July – the whole bang month of it. Will you write to Marie about it; it must be a decent place where we are really well looked after & well fed, & if possible near some bathing. I want a holiday *complet*; after all, it will be the first one I've had since I went in the W.O. – excepting always that six weeks' so-called breakdown at Garsington. No wonder I haven't any wool in the place where the wool ought to grow.

Wingley is becoming a desperate character; a willing [i.e. villain] of the deepest dye. You won't be a bit disappointed in him. He's got all the character he used to have, & he looks – to me – just the same. There's something essentially don't-care & kittenish about him, however much he grows – a strange contrast to poor old Athy, who's a sentimental idiot.

To-day came a letter signed Beatrice Hastings. 'Can you give me any work on your paper?' Not addressed to me by name. Editor – Dear Sir. What am I to do? She's no friend of mine, it's true; but you, I know, have memories of & feelings towards her. She must, I suppose, be hard up to apply to me even in the most formal way. I'd be willing to give her something; but, you see, I never thought anything of her work – and the paper isn't a charitable organisation; it has to remain a good paper. I wait for your suggestion.

Prelude I'll get & send to-morrow. As for B.C's Xmas card, Heaven alone knows where I've shoved it away.

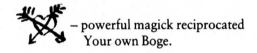 – powerful magick reciprocated
Your own Boge.

[Villa Flora,
Menton]
[about 25 March 1920]

My dearest Bogey,
I was reading your letter so happily this morning until suddenly I came across your remarks about Beatrice Hastings. Darling, your memory is very short lived. Yes, it is true, I *did* love B.H. but have you utterly forgotten what I told you of her behaviour in Paris – of the last time I saw her and how, because I refused to stay the night with her she bawled at me and called me a *femme publique* in front of those filthy Frenchmen? She is loathsome & corrupt & I remember very very well telling you I had done with her, explaining

why & recounting to you how she had insulted and abused me. I should have thought you could not have forgotten these things – Indeed I shall never forget your enemies – never forgive them – never forget if you tell me you have been insulted – London is a veritable sink of corruption if such mists gather & mislead your fine & pure understanding.

But darling, even though as you say you cannot cope with the world – don't for God's sake for that reason go to meet the world in any way. Withdraw. Be morose. Be silent. But oh Bogey Do be proud. What is our love worth if it hasn't taught us *pride*, if we don't defend each other and keep the shield bright for each other. Your honour is my honour; I'll not betray you – I'll defend you: I'll keep very very straight & good because I am a Heron. I will NOT be caught on their lime twigs. Even for one moment.

Love, you are too lenient. Is it much to ask you to be yourself & to condemn what you don't approve of? Those horrible parties of Ottoline when you were gloomy with wine. Oh how hot & ashamed I am that those sniggering fools could so egg you on! Wouldn't you rather it were said of us: 'Try as Lady O. did she could not persuade Middleton Murry to attend her parties or if he did his despair was manifest' than 'he came & was perhaps a trifle more gloomy than was natural' – Oh I am so deeply truly anxious that we shall be an example & in our small way hand on a torch. I could *never* – or I swear I never will – attend such functions unless I am my most sincere self. I'll keep away & make enemies by silence rather than by the words I wish I hadn't said. It is really a fault in your nature that you are not proud enough. Will you one day forget & forgive Lawrence – smile – give him your hand? Oh, that I should dare to write that – forgive me. But my own, do I beseech you keep clear of bad people until I return. Be fastidious. HURT bad people – rather than be hurt by them. Remember that B.H. is bad – has insulted us – insults us worse by thinking she has only to write to you for you to wag your tail.

I think I am too changed. Perhaps you will think I am too exacting altogether & that it can't be done. Well, if it can't, if we can't remain pure – let us not try & be artists. That's all. I have such a profound respect and reverence for our work & for *the universe* – for all that is being discovered, for all who really seek the truth that I want to belong to them *alone*. But if you muddle up Ottoline's parties – – no, no more of them. Brett should be ashamed of herself to tell me 'she fell into a Lav.' What does she expect me to say to that? Must I admire – pity – grin? I turn away in disgust. But will you, my gentle knight please defend me against my enemies – and I shall defend you and keep our name unspotted.

Let us be GREAT – FAMOUS Broomies through and through – I solemnly warn you that if you stir B.H. you will discover such a nest of serpents that you will repent it. Don't forget OUR PRIDE. Not that she's so important in herself; it's what she stands for. Don't you see?

Broomy II

[2 Portland Villas,
Hampstead]
Thursday.   [25 March 1920]

Darling,

I've just had your wire about Beatrice Hastings. I told you I was going to do nothing until I heard from you; and, of course, I haven't. I'm very sorry you were deeply hurt old girl, but I don't think you ought to have been. I had absolutely forgotten what she did in Paris; and I'm wondering whether I ever knew, really. I think you must be under the impression that you told me more than you actually did. Anyhow I have no definite recollection of her conduct. What I do know is that she was always an active & venomous enemy of mine, and that you told me she had gone completely to the dogs in Paris.

But in any case I was firmly determined not to do anything about it until I had heard from you. Now I shall simply send her an official letter saying that the Editor regrets. What I wanted to clear up was that I don't think you ought to have been deeply hurt; and that it's rather hard on me to wire those words. I always take such a thing from you very seriously indeed; it upsets me horribly.

Well, please Wig, forget all about it. I can't help thinking that you feared I would do something without consulting you: but of course I wouldn't & haven't. I'll wire that to you to-morrow morning.

I had a lovely letter from you last night – a perfect little beauty, offering me little heart-cakes of faery bread. The cannons were also being fired at Monaco. I feel they ought to be immense pop-guns; but I suppose they are the real thing. By the way that was a simply marvellously good little review of the Short Stories you sent the other day.

It was a very funny coincidence that in this letter you said 'Bunny Dunn is revealed a Beatrice Hastings of the worst kind'. I don't know about that Prince & Princess business. I can always see you as the Princess all right; but I seem to be a rather comic Prince, – not smart enough for my ideal, any how. But I shd. like to have been one all the same.

The weather even here is pretty astonishing. I haven't worn an overcoat for more than a week & it's still March. All the trees have tremendous great buds – real whoppers. M [arie]D [ahlerup] has got a job at £2.15 a week. She came & asked me whether she shd. take it. I said Yes, yes, yes! And she has. Now I suppose she'll expect me to get her salary doubled. Pas demi!

      Boge

You *are* not to be deeply hurt. You're always doing it – falling into ink pots I call it.

[2 Portland Villas,
Hampstead]
[7 April 1920]
Wednesday

Worm darling,

I wish those rotten old posts would behave better. I have nothing since the last batch of letters: as I've told you before they always come in batches nowadays. Postmen, especially foreign postmen, are beasts.

Sullivan came up from the country to-day. He did look ill; he must have had a pretty bad bout of influenza. So I forgive him for having let me down. And to-day I remembered about the copy of *Prelude*. I telephoned to the Woolves to get a copy; they had both gone away for the holiday. However the servant promised to send one by the night's post. I hope it arrives safely.

I have received a letter from Constables saying the excisions they want made in *Je ne p. p.* are these

(1) p. 5 last par. but 1 'and then after
   a soft growl.... back to our door'
(2) p. 6. last line but 2
   'If I find myself in need ....
   cake afterwards'
(3) p. 7. 1. 13 'Why should I be able ....
   I want.'

(4) p. 24. 5th. par from bottom
'And ... good-night my little cat....
I didn't give her time to reply'
(5) p. 25. line 13 from bottom 'And so on ... interested
in modern English
literature'
(6) p. 25. line 4 from bottom
'I'd rather like to dine with
her' to the end.

Now I can understand (1) easily (2) at a pinch (3) I can't really understand (4) not at all (5) I can only understand deleting the virgin (6) only 'sleeping with her'. What do you say? I should stick against cutting more than is absolutely necessary. On the other hand you don't get the £40 till the MS is satisfactory to them; and the true edition of *Je ne p. p.* is in existence.

Sadler – *how* I dislike him – suggests your substituting something for 'The Wind Blows' which his Majesty thinks is 'on [the] trivial side'. I can't remember which it is, myself. What do you think about that? The only MS of yours I have are '[The] Black Cap' – 'Something Childish But Very Natural' – or there's the 2 stories in the *Signature*. What about putting them in the book any how. I've just looked at them again. 'Autumns' & 'The Little Governess'. I should certainly put them in if I were you. If you think this a good idea just let me know

Surely the second of [the] 'Autumns' is 'The Wind Blows' – it's a superb little thing, superb. Oh! I'll smack that young fool's face.

But you must put 'The Little Governess' in. You've forgotten how good it is. I've just read it. Please do!

Your
Boge.

[2 Portland Villas,
Hampstead]
[8 April 1920]
Thursday

My own darling,
I saw Sadler to-day about the MS. He accepted my provisional suggestions with regard to
p. 5. line 6 from bottom. Only the one line to go
p. 6. last sentence. To stand altogether.

p.25. 'And so on & so on ... literature'. The whole par. to stand, with the exception of the word 'virgin'.

He would prefer

p. 7 l. 13 'Why should I be able to have any woman I want?' omitted

p. 24. last line but 11 'And good-night ... to reply' omitted

p. 25. last 2 lines omitted.

The ground he takes with regard to these is that they will do positive harm to the sale of the book; that by omitting them you will gain a good deal more than you will lose by retaining them.

Honestly, Worm, I think there's something in it. I mean in this way. Yours is essentially an exquisite talent, and one which, I am sure, will be appreciated by many more people than will appreciate the actual art. I mean people like my mother. She will love the stories, I know & I'm sure there are thousands like her.

Now these people will be shocked by the few things the omission of which is still suggested. I believe that it's bad policy to shock the people by whom, after all, you do desire to be read. And I think that if you compromise to this extent you will never regret it.

That's my honest opinion.

If you think you can accept these omissions will you just wire to me: 'Omissions accepted', when Constables will send you a cheque immediately.

I had a letter from Hardy to-day asking if I would like a poem for the *Athenaeum* of April 30. Wouldn't I! I wrote off immediately, of course, saying 'Please'. I wonder what it's going to be like. It's very mysterious, because he says it's quite essential that it should appear on *April 30* & no other day. He was going to send it to the *Times* when he suddenly realised that the *Athenaeum* came out on the 30th. I'm very excited. Also, an American publisher has taken 300 copies of my book, so that the first edition will certainly be sold out. I think that's all the good news; but nowadays there always seems to be a little bit.

Boge.

[Villa Flora,
Menton]
[?10 April 1920]

My darling Boge,

I've just got your note about 'Je ne parle pas'. No, I certainly won't agree to those excisions if there were 500,000,000 copies in existence. They can keep their old £40 & be hanged to them. Shall I pick the eyes out of a story for £40!! I'm *furious* with Sadler – No, I'll never agree. I'll supply another story but that is all. The *outline* would be all blurred – It must have those sharp lines. *The Times* didn't object. As to 'The Wind Blows' I put it in because so many people had admired it (Yes it's 'Autumn II' but a little different). Virginia, Lytton and queer people like Mary Hamilton & Bertie all spoke so strongly about it I felt I must put it in. But this had better be held over till I get back. I'll never consent. I'll take the book away first. Don't worry about it. Just tell Sadler he's a fool. As to 'The German Governess' it *was* on my list & I asked you to include it!! (Caught out!) But don't you worry love. It will have to wait. Of course I won't consent!

Wig

[Villa Flora,
Menton]
[20 April 1920]
Tuesday.

My precious darling,

All being well I shall be at the *Palais Lyon* on Wednesday until Thursday. Do you think L'Hôte would come and see me on Wednesday afternoon – or Valéry. If they'd leave a *'bleu'* letting me know when to expect them I'd be delighted. I want to see them for the firm – to have a chat – don't you know & hear what is happening. It's the most divine day. I am staying in bed until lunch as I had a heavy day yesterday buying small presents to bring back and so on. Exhausting work because one gets so frightfully excited as well. Connie went with me in the morning & bought *me* an antique brooch, very lovely; three stones set in silver. Then she bought me a pastel blue muslin frock with frills like panniers at the side. Ida who was by said she thought Connie had a very bad influence on me because she spoiled me so. And the poor old dear got pink just like Granma used to and said, 'Well, the child has had no fun, no life, no chance to wear pretty things for two years. I'm *sure* Jack would want to do what I'm doing....' You remember in Italy how I longed to return to Life with all kinds of lovely possessions. Funny it should have all come true. I also bought the most exquisite fruit plates with small white grapes & gold leaves on them pour la famille Murry, & a dish, high, to match, to take the breath. I've no money. I think I must be a little bit mad. Oh, could I bring the flowers, the *air* the whole heavenly climate as well: this darling little town, these mountains – It is simply a small jewel – Menton – and its *band* in the jardins publiques with the ruffled pansy beds – the white donkeys standing meek – tied to a pole, the donkey women in black pleated dresses with flat funny hats. All, all is so terribly attractive. I'd live years here with you. I'm immensely attached to it all & in the summer we'd go up to the Alpes Maritimes & live in the small spotless inns with milk hot from the cow & eggwegs from the hen – we'd live in those steep villages of pink & white houses with the pine forests round them – where your host serves your dinner wearing a clean white blouse & sabots. Yes, dearest darling, I'm in love with the Alpes Maritimes. I don't want to go any further. I'd like to live my life between Broomies and them. Your Sunday & Saturday letter has come. You are a darling to have made the garden so fair & had the grass cut. I've been thinking about that grass. You are having a worrying time about Arthur, dear love. Couldn't the decision be left till I talk it over with you. But after all there is nothing to talk over with me that you haven't mentioned. If Arthur is going to be a *real artist* he must have his chance & if I have the good fortune to make money you know I'll always help. As matters stand I spend every penny I have because you see I *can't* live except in a rather luxurious way & I can only get better by resting – taking carriages – living as though I had £800 a year of my own instead of £400. This journey home for L.M. & me, for instance has cost – I really can't say what – telegraphing to Paris – to the boat, to the other side – with *wagon lits* and so on – but I can't do it except like that. I've written Rutter 3 times for the money for my story & I've not had a penny nor have I had a cheque from the paper this month. But all the same we shall be alright I know & we shall take Arthur & when he is here with me he'll not cost you a sou.

I read your article on Negro Sculpture last night. It was *excellent*. I thought Fry most feeble in the *Athenaeum* – As usual he was afraid to say what he felt – he wanted – a small fry – to be in the cultured swim. Will you take me to see some pictures when I come home? I'm lunching with the Schiffs tomorrow. It will be our last meeting until they come back to London. Schiff – well, you'll see what he's like. I was at a big lunch the other day (about 10 people) at their house & you should have heard the talk against *The Nation* – & FOR the *A*. Massingham, according to some really rather intelligent men there, gets his facts hopelessly wrong about French affairs. But I learnt a great deal of interesting facts about the French – *not* to their credit. I'll tell you in about 3 years' time when the other things have been told. Darling, *don't* make my home-coming an effort – don't curse the upset of it all – I will try not to show how glad I am & so frighten my darling little mate. Don't feel you *have* to meet me even. It is very dreadful to know that even Love is an effort to you at times & I don't want you to make that effort. Feel – oh, well, she'll make things easy and L.M. will be on the spot and I shan't have to think of puddings. Years ago I wanted to change things in you – I wanted you to be less 'vague', less silent, more – almost – practical. But you must always remember that was years ago. Now I don't want you to be *anybody* but your natural self – free to wander away or to keep quiet just as it pleases you. I want you to feel that with me you can be absolutely FREE in spirit. If I find your hat's too awful I shall buy you other hats – or if your hair is too dreadful I shall seize the moment & brush it straight – but you must not *exert* yourself or pretend that you have to look after me. I'm very independent please altho' I am Your

Own little Wig.

September–December
1920

Katherine Mansfield's life had now slipped into the pattern of the consumptive who must keep travelling in search of better health. In September 1920 she again left London for Menton, accompanied by L.M. While Katherine's letters to Murry over the next few months have survived, his to her did not. Murry's one extant letter suggests that this was possibly the most difficult period in a relationship that became increasingly strained as her illness worsened and he pursued his career apart, in London.

What Katherine Mansfield's remarkable letters to Murry between September and December 1920 show is her coming to terms not only with her physical suffering, but also with her essential spiritual isolation, in a manner reminiscent of the great mystics. Her courage shines through these letters – as does her impatience with the husband who could not fully understand the lonely path she was following.

Isola Bella,
Garavan
Menton
[14 September 1920]

Darling Bogey,

What shall I tell you first? I have thought of you often & wondered if the beau temps is chez vous aussi, now that I've gone away. We had a good journey but a slight contretemps in Paris, Ida disappeared with the porter to find a taxi, and she forgot the door she's gone out – rushed off to another & lost me. After about ½ an hour I appealed to the police but they were helpless. The poor creature lost her head & when we *did* meet finally it was only because I saw her in the distance & simply *shouted*. This tired me & made my nose bleed and I had a v. bad night & had to do my review in bed next day, being fanned & bathed with eau de cologne. It's of no importance *to me* but I feel *all the time* I was betraying you and the paper. Forgive me once again. We arrived here yesterday at 4-50 after a day of terrific heat. Menton felt like home. It was really bliss to sit in the voiture and drive through those familiar streets & then up a queer little leafy 'way' and then another at right angles to a gate all hidden by green where la bonne Annette stood waving her apron and the peke leapt at her heels. This villa is – so far – perfect. It has been prepared inside and out to such an extent that I don't think it will ever need a hand's turn again. The path from the gate to the two doors has a big silver mimosa showering across it. The garden is twice as big as I imagined. One can live in it all day. The hall is black & white marble. The salon is on your right as you enter – a real little salon with velvet covered furniture and an immense dead clock and a gilt mirror & two *very* handsome crimson vases which remind me of fountains filled with blood. It has 2 windows one looks over the garden gate, the others open on to the terrace & look over the sea. I mustn't forget to mention the carpet with a design of small beetles which covers the whole floor. The dining room is equally charming in its way – & has French windows, too. It abounds in cupboards full of wessels & has a vrai buffet with silver teapot, coffee & milk jug which catch the flashing eye. All is delightful. There are even very lovely blue glass finger bowls.... On the other side of the passage is the garde-linge big enough for all our boxes as well – The linen is overwhelming. It is all in dozens – even to maids' aprons.... The kitchen premises are quite shut off with a heavy pair of doors. The kitchen gleams with copper. It's a charming room and there's a big larder & a scullery big enough for a workshop and outside there's a garden and three large caves & the lapinière. Upstairs are four bedrooms – the maid's on the entresol. The others have balconies & again are carpeted all over & sumptuous in a doll's house way.

Annette had prepared everything possible. The copper kettle boiled. Tea was laid. In the larder were eggs in a bowl & a cut of cheese on a leaf & butter swimming & milk, & on the table coffee, a long bread, jam, and so on. On the buffet a dish heaped with grapes & figs lying in the lap of fig leaves. She had thought of everything & moreover everything had a kind of chic – and she in her blue check dress & white apron sitting down telling the news was a most delightful spectacle.

The heat is almost as great as when we arrived last year. One can wear nothing but a wisp of silk, two bows of pink ribbon and a robe de mousseline. Moustiques and moucherons are in full blast; we are both bitten to death already. They are frightful. But so far I can accept them without a reproach the compensations are so great.

I must tell you a very big date palm grows outside my bedroom balcony window. At the end of the garden wall – (a yellow crumbling wall) there is a vast magnolia full of rich buds. There is a tap in the garden. In the vegetable garden the French artichokes are ready to eat and minute yellow and green marrows. A tangerine tree is covered in green balls.

I hope all this description doesn't bore you darling. But I content myself with thinking you are going to see it yourself one day & so my description is only 'in advance'.

The view is *surpassingly* beautiful. Late last night on the balcony I stood listening to the tiny cicadas & to the frogs and to someone playing a little chain of notes on a flute.

I do not know *what* it is about this place. But it is enough just to be here for everything to change – I think already of the poetry you would write if you lived such a life. I wish you were not tied. I have always at the bottom of my deep cup of happiness that dark spot, which is that you are not living as you would wish to live.

Here is Annette with a big dish of fresh lemons – broken off with the leaves remaining – And it's lunch time. The heat!

Goodbye darling. Take care of yourself. I hope you have good tennis & that all goes well. Yours ever

> Wig

Your Saturday night letter
[Villa Isola Bella,
Menton]
[6 October 1920]
Wednesday

Darling,

Forgive me my unworthiness and my failure these last days –

Your letter – surely the most wonderful letter a man ever wrote a woman – or a Boge ever wrote a Wig – almost made me cry out: 'Forgive me, forgive me.'

It is what my suffering has given to me – this letter – the reward of it. I seem to have just a glimpse of something I've never known before as I sit here thinking of you and me and our love.... it's as though, looking across the plains! What I had thought was cloud dissolves, lifts and behind it there are mountains. Always a new silence – a new mystery.

My precious love.

You HAVE come here. I mean – the ache of separation is over. I'm not alone. Of course, I long for you here, sharing my daily life, but I do not say 'come' – it's not only on account of the money, Bogey. If I believed at this moment that I was going to die of course I would say 'come' because it would be unbearable not – – to have you to see me off on the journey where you know the train drops into a great black hole.

(No, I believe even then I couldn't say 'come'.)

But what is it? I feel our 'salvation' – our 'future' – depends on our doing nothing desperate – but on holding on, keeping calm (this from *me*!) and leaving nothing in disorder, nothing undone. The 'paper' isn't really the paper, I suppose. It's the kind of battle that the knight has to wage, and the knight is you and me – he's our spirit. Also, my darling, I have got the queer feeling that 'holding on' we declare our faith in the future – our power to win through. *This* year is the important year for us. You ought, for your future freedom, to be where you are, you ought for THE FUTURE to keep the paper going one more year.

And there's this, too. But here I am speaking to myself. If I am to be what I wish to be I must not be rescued. That's *dead true*. Bogey and I have chosen each other for lovers in this world, and I believe absolutely in our choice. But I believe the reason beyond all other reasons why we chose each other is because we feel FREE together. I know that, at the last, I do not put the lightest chain on him, nor he on me. I feel, if he were here now, if I gave up and said 'come', there might be a danger – in fact the very cry is a denial of what I really really believe.

But it's all mysterious: it all seems to belong to another country. This speech will not explain it. There are signs, silences, a kind of flowing from light to shadow. I can only say – my love, we shall stay as we are.

I live for you. I will prepare myself for our life. Look into my heart. Believe in me. *Would I sooner have Bogey here now?* NO (what a funny looking no – a little bit gothic!) Oh dear, oh dear. Put your arms round me. Come at Christmas with candles in your hair – I want to hold you very tightly. I want to make you smile – I feel we are deathless when you write to me so. You HAVE come, Bogey; I say it again. You are here, and now I'm going to get up and work –

Let me not fail again. It is my dream to be here alone until Christmas and to do my work – to have a book ready by then. I shall begin my book today. It's just as though the ship has sailed into harbour.... Now, get off, my pilot, until next Christmas. I can manage rocks and shoals and storms – anything – (But even now your letter is unanswered. It is a GIFT. Time will show how I will use it). My darling love – you are happy? You understand?

I am your
Wig

[Villa Isola Bella
Menton]
[10 October 1920]

I think it was too sweet of the cats to have gone to the bathroom. Pathetic! Wonderful cat psychology, really. You ought to have a minute one installé with a mouse's tail for a plug.

My darling Bogey,
    It's Sunday and after awful storms fine again. My darling, I can't understand why my letters don't arrive. I know they are safely posted; I am sure they are stolen your end. My mind says Sydney egged on by Marge. But it is simply more than maddening to know the letters don't come. It makes me feel so helpless. And I know the feeling TOO well when they don't arrive.
    Thank you, my precious for sending me Brett's to you. As a matter of fact I do resent it most deeply – the peeping under your shirt and the threat to be severe with you – I can't say how hateful that was to me! I feel violently physically sick. And the *sickly barbed* letters she sends me. 'MURRY & I pick the bone fairly clean about so and so and so and so ... WE seem to do nothing but play tennis, dream tennis eat the balls and chew the racquet strings' ... I can't reply. I 'frisonne' – But Bogey don't let her come near. Forgive me – don't let her touch you. She [has] no earthly right to interfere and yet – there it is ... Is Gertler really ill? Do tell me. I always remember him swaggering up to me when I was just back from the South: 'Well, Katherine, I hear you've got it. Do you spit blood and so on? Do all the things in the books? Do they think you'll get over it' – And then he laughed out. It's like all Brett's friends having *spotty lungs*. I am very sorry, but I can't forgive these things. They may be ignorance and so on, but I not only can't forgive – I *do* condemn them. There's a kind of agitation in Brett's atmosphere that repels me.

Oh, if you knew what a joy your Shakespeare was. I straightway dipped in *The Tempest* and discovered Ariel riding on *curlèd clouds*. Isn't that adjective perfect? I'd missed it before. I do think *The Tempest* is the most radiant, delicate, exquisite play – The atmosphere is exactly the atmosphere of an island after a storm – an island reborn out of the sea with Caliban tossed up for sea wrack and Ariel blowing in a shell. Oh my divine Shakespeare!! Oh most blessed genius. Again I read of the love of Ferdinand & Miranda how they met & *recognised* each other and their hearts spake. Everything – everything – is new born and golden – God knows there are desert islands enough to go round – the difficulty is to sail *away* from them – but dream islands ... they are rare, rare. Yet, if I had not loved you I should never have understood Shakespeare as I do. His 'magic' is the same magic as our love. 'Where the bee sucks there lurk [sic] I: In a cowslip's bell I lie.' I believe this all sounds quite quite different to us than to all the rest of the world. I feel, if I lived with you where the climate was delicate the air most sweet fertile the isle, we should end by talking in a kind of blank verse. (I'm smiling as I write this, my true love, and yet I mean it.) Looking back at our time in the Villa Pauline when the almond tree was in flower remembering how I saw you come out of the cave in your soft leather boots carrying logs of wood ... it is *all* a dream.

Oh, Boge, I don't like the world. It's a horrid place. When I think of the Schiffs – Sunday lunch – Osbert Sitwell & he – I feel there is no place for us except Beyond the Blue Mountains. I want to wander through valleys with you drink out of leaves for cups, sit on warm hillsides & listen to bees in the heather. I want a house as small as possible and there to live & watch the clouds and mark the seasons – with you. There to work and *live* – no servants. Friends sometimes to see us, but all *jet simple*.... (I came to the back door then with a bowl of crumbs for some migratory birds that had come to rest on our hill-top after a storm and were still too weak to fly. They were quite tame – hopping about – rather large slender grey birds with silver breasts. You came walking from the field with a pail of milk. Our lovely little fawn cow was just wandering away – the pail glittered, you *strolled* along. I looked at the cow & the birds & thought all are enchanted) ...

Yes, I do understand how you must hate the idea of *dinners*. Carry me in your pocket. No, that won't do any good. I'd give my eyes to watch you dress. You'll look so lovely in your evening clothes & I've never seen you in them – But your *best dress* is that Jaeger jersey. That's the very Bogification of you.... I'm hoping for the paper tomorrow. The *D.N.* for October *1st* came today (Oct. 10th). Could I have the *Mercury*, please?

Now, I want if I can to finish a story today for you. I'll write it out here. I've got a HUGE umbrella lashed to the Terrace in place of that tente which was too expensive, of course – The umbrella does just as well. Oh, that you were here, just at this moment, sharing this sky and this gentle breeze. Your own

Wig

Just as I folded that, I had *callers*. M. et Madame showed on to the Terrace very gracious but OH DEAR! what a ghastly idea it is! What can one say? I can't play 'ladies' unless I know the children I'm playing with.

Now there's an asp come out of a hole – a slender creature, red, about 12 inches long. It lies moving its quick head. It is very evil looking but how much nicer than a caller! I was warned yesterday against attempting to kill them. (Do you see me trying to kill them, Boge?) But they *spring* at you – if you do. However darling, I'll catch this one for you at the risk of my life and put it in your Shakespeare for a marker at the scene where the old man carries in the basket of figs. You will have to hold your Shakespeare *very firmly* to prevent it wriggling, Anthony darling.

> Lovingly yours,
> EGYPT

[Villa Isola Bella,
Menton]
[18 October 1920]

My darling Bogue (Yes, that is right. It's your other name you know.)

I return De la Mare's letter. I long to hear of your time with him. It's very queer; he haunts me here – not a persistent or substantial ghost but as one who shares $\begin{cases} \text{our} \\ \text{my} \end{cases}$ joy in the *silent world* – joy is not the word. I only used it because it conveys a stillness – a remoteness – because there is a far-away sound in it.

You know, darling I have felt very often lately as though the silence had some meaning beyond these signs, these intimations. Isn't it possible that if one yielded there is a whole world into which one is received? It is so near and yet I am conscious that I hold back from giving myself up to it. What is this something mysterious that waits – that beckons?

And then suffering, bodily suffering such as I've known for three years. It has changed forever everything – even the *appearance* of the world is not the same – there is something added. *Everything has its shadow.* Is it right to resist such suffering? Do you know I feel it has been an immense privilege. Yes, in spite of all. How blind we little creatures are! Darling, it's only the fairy tales we *really* live by. If we set out upon a journey the more wonderful the treasure the greater the temptations and perils to be overcome. And if someone rebels and says, Life isn't good enough on those terms one can only say: 'it is!' Don't misunderstand me. I don't mean a 'thorn in the flesh, my dear' – it's a million times more mysterious. It has taken me three years to understand this – to come to see this. We resist – we are terribly frightened. The little boat enters the dark fearful gulf and our only cry is to escape – 'put me on land again'. But it's useless. Nobody listens. The shadowy figure rows on. One ought to sit still and uncover one's eyes.

I believe the greatest failing of all is *to be frightened.* Perfect Love casteth out Fear. When I look back on my life all my mistakes have been because I was afraid.... Was that why I had to look on death. Would nothing less cure me? You know, one can't help wondering, sometimes.... No, not a personal God or any such nonsense – Much more likely – the soul's desperate choice....

Am I right in thinking that you too have been ridden by Fear (of quite a different kind). And now it's gone from you – and you are whole – I feel that only now you have *all* your strength – a kind of *release.*

We are as different as can be, but I do believe we have the same devils as well as the same gods.

Here are your letters back again, love. They interested me deeply. Your Stendhal article ... seemed to fetch the French ducks off the water ... didn't it? I'm sorry about Knopf and the Yazpegs – but can't be helped.

Take care of yourself – my beloved child, with all the wild men about throwing stones and striking. Make yourself small – fold yourself up – I'm (privately it doesn't do to tell you these things) terrified that in your lunch hour you'll take your bisticks into the street & get caught in a crowd & march away. *Eat* – don't catch cold whatever you do – I want to put my hands on you – to touch you – anxiously & longingly. I *miss* you. Do you miss me? I miss your voice and your presence and all your darling ways.

> Your
> Wig

> P.S. – Can you bring Ribni at Xmas? There is a shop at Nice which cures Poupées cassées. When I read of it I almost telegraphed for Ribni. I want him to be made good as new again. He haunts me – Ah, I can see a story in this idea....

> [Villa Isola Bella,
> Menton]
> [24 October 1920]

Darling,
    The writing in this letter goes off. But I do awfully want you to read it if you've time.

> Wig.

le dimanche

My darling Bogūe,
    I got a letter from you today written on Thursday. I must answer a point or two. Schiff *entirely* mistook my intentions when I (most deliberately) lent him 'In a G.P.' What impertinence. I suppose he is angry with me (I know he is) because I didn't answer his last letter. Somehow I could not. He spoke of Couperus and himself as being co-equal co-eternal and altogether his letter was unpleasant. It seemed too hectic and arrogant. It frightens me, I mean I want to *sheer off*. His hour had struck you know the feeling? And *hers* struck in London when in saying goodbye to me she very nicely, a touch playfully, put her hand on my hair. *Finito.* These things are mysterious, but I can't help it. They now become to me a trifle grotesque, especially Schiff – overheated and (it seems now) overpoweringly *deaf* – deaf to everything! She I must write politely & get that book back. Will they make me pay £0000 for it. Hm! ...
    The paper has come. Your Baudelaire is *excellent*. I could not help comparing Eliot and you as I read. Your patient never dies under the operation – his are always dead before he makes an

incision. To be serious I thought it really remarkable because of the way in which you conveyed the *quality* of Baudelaire – I mean you produced Baudelaire, as it were. That's where Mat Arnold failed so lamentably. One never feels that Shelley or Keats or whoever it was sat on his bosom's throne & though I don't mean that your subject should occupy that position when you write about him he's got to have been there.

I am exceedingly glad you joined hands with the Oxford Professori. The *Daily Mail foamed* today on the subject. It almost went so far as to say the library at Liège and such acts of burning were by Professors only – It – but let it pass! In the *Times* I noted a book by a Doctor Schinz – not a good book, but the *Times* noticed it as though Schinz were kneeling on Podsnap's doormat. Faugh!

How long *can* it go on! You know whenever I go away I realise that it has happened – The change has *come*. Nothing *is* the same. I positively feel one has no right to run a paper without preaching a gospel. (I know you do, but I mean with all the force of one's soul.) I get an evangelist feeling, when I read Fashion News in the *D.N.* and then Strike News & Irish News and so many thousands out of work. But above & beyond that *when* I realise the 'spiritual temper' of the world, I feel as though the step *has* been taken – we *are* over the edge. Is it fantastic? Who is going to *pull us up*? I certainly had no end of an admiration for L[loyd] G[eorge] but then he's capable of that speech on reprisals – which really was a vile speech from a 'statesman'. It was perfectly obvious he had no intention of saying what he did when he got up to speak – he was carried away. It *is* all over really: That's why I shall be so thankful when you pack your rucksack & come over here – The only sort of paper for the time is an out and out *personal, dead true, dead sincere* paper in which we spoke our HEARTS and MINDS.

I want to say I was wrong about your book *The Intellectual*. I was right about the spirit (or so I think.) I was wrong about the aim.

You know there are moments when I want to make an appeal to all our generation who do believe that the war has changed everything to come forward and let's start a crusade. But I know darling I am not a crusader & it's my job to dwell apart & write my best for those that come after –

It *is* Sunday – Don't turn away if I talk. I have no one to speak to here – and I don't only want you to listen Bogue. I want you to reply.

Does your *soul* trouble you? Mine does. I feel that only now

(October 1920) do I really desire to be saved. I realise what salvation means and I long for it. Of course I am not speaking as a Christian or about a personal God. But the feeling is. ... I believe (and VERY MUCH) – help thou mine unbelief. But it's to myself I cry – to the spirit, the essence of me – that which lives in Beauty. Oh, these *words*. And yet I should be able to explain. But I'm impatient with you. I always 'know you understand & take it for granted'. But just very lately I seem to have seen my whole past – to have gone through it – to have emerged – very weak and very new – The soil (which wasn't at all fragrant) has at last produced something which isn't a weed but which I do believe (after Heaven knows how many false alarms) is from the seed which was sown. But Bogue it's taken 32 years in the dark....

Without our love it would never have come through at all.

And I *long* for goodness – to live by what is permanent in the soul.

It all sounds vague. You may wonder what induces me to write this. But as I walked up & down outside the house this evening the clouds heaped on the horizon – noble, shining clouds; the deep blue waves – they set me thinking again. I never felt the longing for you as I do this time – but for such other reasons.

Take care of yourself, my Beloved Boy – Ever your

      Wig

                    [Villa Isola Bella,
                      Menton]
Sunday,   [31 October 1920]

My dear Love,

Your Thursday letter & Hardy's letter have arrived. I shall keep Hardy's letter for you – unless you'd rather have it back. I'll put it in my Spenser.

In reply to your letter: I don't doubt for one instant that your feelings and mine have been alike: that we have been haunted again by our strange correspondences. Your letter might *be* my letter – if you know what I mean. You say just what I had meant to convey in my letter and I too, feel that I don't *want* a God to appeal to – that I only appeal to the spirit that is within me.

You say you [would] 'dearly love to know exactly what I feel' – I thought I had told you. But my writing is so bad, my expression so vague that I expect I didn't make myself clear. I'll try to.

What a
book is
hidden
here!

> 'Between the acting of a dreadful thing
> And the first motion, all the interim is
> Like a phantasma or a dreadful dream;
> The genius and the mortal instruments
> Are then in council; and the state of man
> Like to a little Kingdom suffers then
> The nature of an insurrection.'

The 'thing' was not always 'dreadful' neither was the 'dream', and you must substitute 'spirit' for genius – otherwise there you have my life as I see it up till now – complete with all the alarms, enthusiasms, terrors, excitements – in fact the nature of an insurrection. I've been dimly aware of it many times – I've had moments when it has seemed to me that this wasn't what my little Kingdom ought to be like – yes and longings and regrets. But only since I came away this time have I *fully realised* it – confronted myself as it were looked squarely at the extraordinary 'conditions' of my existence ...

It wasn't flattering or pleasant or easy. I expect your sins are of the subconscious; they are easier to forgive than mine. You are I *know* a far nobler and stronger nature. I've *acted* my sins, & then excused them or put them away with it 'doesn't do to think about these things' or (more often) it was all experience. But it hasn't ALL been experience. There IS waste – destruction, too. So, Bogey, – and my inspiration was our Love – I never should have done it otherwise – I confronted myself. As I write I falsify slightly. I can't help it; it's all so difficult. The whole thing was so much *deeper* and more *difficult* than I've described it – *subtler* – less conscious & more conscious if you know what I mean. I didn't walk up & down the room & groan, you know, darling. As I am talking to you I'll dare say it all took place on another plane, because then we can smile at the description & yet mean something by it.

But as I say my inspiration was Love. It was the final realisation that Life for me was intimacy with you. Other things attend this. But this *is* my life on this earth. I see the Fairy tale as our history really. It's a tremendous symbol. The Prince & the Princess do wed in the end and do live happy ever after as King & Queen in their own Kingdom. That's about as profound a Truth as any. But I want to talk to you rather than write to you. I feel – only *now* can we talk –

And I don't want to imply that the Battle is over and here I am victorious. I've escaped from my enemies – emerged – that is as far as I've got. But it is a different state of being to any I've known

before & if I were to 'sin' now – it would be mortal –
There. Forgive this rambling involved statement. But my
treasure, my life is ours. You know it.

A thousand thanks for managing the Constable affair. I am of
course more than satisfied.

The papers have come. I've not read the *A.* yet. The *D.N.*
astounds me. I believe they are making a dead set against us. Rose
Macaulay cracking up to the sky May Sinclair, Mary Hamilton &
Mrs. Scott. But really my quotations proved the idiocy of Mrs.
Scott – surely. Really, I CAN'T understand this world. Then did you
see their caricature of Prowse's novel? I'll send it you. It's almost
WORD FOR WORD. But Prowse wrote as seriously as Duhamel. AND
the *D.N.* reviewed his novel – gave it a 'good' review a week or two
ago. It's like each time one picks up a dish the crack seems more
evident. Each time I read the paper I get the same sharp little shock.
But it will be funny to see how they'll *rend* me.
    It's a very cold sea shell of a day. But *I am content.* That is what
this climate makes me feel.
    I will write about the *Athenaeum* tomorrow.

Goodbye my own love
Wig

[Villa Isola Bella,
Menton]
[2 November 1920]

My precious Bogey
    Your Saturday & Sunday letter have come – and I've read them
twice. I'll expect you then on the 20th of next month – on or about
– that's it, isn't it? Be sure to have your passport ready in time. I feel
we have such a tremendous lot to settle – We shall be talking nearly
all the time. But I expect it won't seem ½ so much once you are
here. Things will go easy. Yes, my calculation included rent. I think
it's more or less just. About this little house – I don't *think* I shall be
allowed to keep it after May – At any rate we ought not to stay the
summer through here. I should like to have this little house by the
year. It's extraordinarily satisfactory. In fact it's almost ideal –
quite ideal in its way. So small & yet not cramped – the position

perfect – the garden perfect. I love the little place *deeply*. It will be a great wrench to get away. But I've got my eye on another – quite near. At any rate we shall not have great difficulty I don't think. I should like to keep Marie if possible wherever we are in France. She saves enormously in time, worry, energy – Everything & looks after all one's interests – But indeed Marie is such a jewel that I expect to lose her any day. She's much 'too good to be true'. She's what one has always sought after.

We'd better keep all our plans *dead secret* until we have discussed them – hadn't we.

I'm not up to much today. Yesterday was dark and stormy; today is too. And in spite of my feelings the weather affects me physically. I fly so high that when I go down – it's a drop, Boge. Nothing serious; just a touch of cold, but with it to 'bear it company' a black mood – Don't pay any attention to it. I expect it will have lifted utterly by the time this reaches you. And it's really caused by a queer kind of *pressure* – which is work to be done. *I am writing.* Do you know the feeling & until this story is finished I am engulfed. It's not a tragic story either – but there you are. It seizes me – swallows me completely. I am Jonah in the whale & only you could charm that old whale to disgorge me. Your letters did for a minute but now I'm in again & we're thrashing through deep water. I fully realise it. It's the price we have to pay – we writers. I'm lost – gone – possessed & everybody who comes near is my enemy.

The very queer thing is tho' that I feel if you were here this wouldn't happen. Work wouldn't be then the *abnormal* but the normal. Just the knowledge that you knew would be enough. Here's egoism!! But it's to excuse a very faded old letter.

It's so *unfair* with these letters of yours. But you understand don't you love. Tomorrow I expect I shall be up in the clouds again with the story finished.

And my deep love – my new love – no breath could ever touch it. It abides. I am *your*

Wig

Floryan's letters came – thank you, darling – & a cheque for the books – 5/- too much. Take it off the next ones.

[Villa Isola Bella,
Menton]
8.35 Wednesday   [3 November 1920]

Darling Own
    Here it is under my hand – finished – another story about as long
as 'The Man Without a Temperament' – p'raps longer. It's called
'The Stranger'. It's a 'New Zealand' story. My depression has gone,
Boge; so it was just this. And now it's here – thank God – & the fire
burns and it's warm and tho' the wind is howling – it can howl.
What a QUEER business writing is! I don't know. I don't believe
other people are ever as foolishly excited as I am while I'm working.
How could they be? Writers would have to live in trees. I've *been*
this man, *been* this woman. I've stood for hours on the Auckland
Wharf – I've been out in the stream waiting to be berthed – I've
been a seagull hovering at the stern and a hotel porter whistling
through his teeth. It isn't as though one sits and watches the
spectacle. That would be thrilling enough, God knows. But one IS
the spectacle for the time. If one remained oneself all the time like
some writers can it would be a bit less exhausting. It's a lightning
change affair, tho'. But what does it matter. I'll keep this story for
you to read at Xmas. I only want to give it to you now. Accept my
new story – my own Love. Give it your blessing. It is the best I can
do and therefore it is yours. If it pleases you nobody else counts –
not one –

                    Your own
                    Wig

[Villa Isola Bella,
Menton]
Isola Bella *until* May 1922   [12 November 1920]

My darling Bogey
    Did I tell you yesterday that Jinnie has accepted my offer for this
villa! So it's mine until *May 1922*. I hope when you have seen it you
will be happy to think that it's our pied à terre. I can't expect you to
feel about it as I do. For me it's for some reason the place to work
in. Found at last. It's the writing table. But I only want to sit &
write here until May 1922. I've a horror of people or distractions –
the time is more than ripe. And here at long last Life seems to have

adjusted itself so that work is possible. Even if our finances went down & down we could live here more cheaply than anywhere else. I want you to plant veg. if you will at Christmas. Très important. Even if we had no maid we could live here (tho' God forbid) – we should just eat bread & lettuce on the Terrace & dust once a fortnight. I really feel it may not be notwendig even to go up into the Mountains. We'll have the whole garden of the Louise for ourselves after May (when Jinnie & Connie go) and as Jinnie points out the fruit & veg. That's bonzer cherries, oranges, tomates, pimentos, figs, grapes. The garden is simply divine with grass in it and trees. It's romantic, too, and very big, with lemon groves. Their villa and ours always seem to me to be an island. You see, we've no neighbours – only, out of sight up the hill a château which belongs to some Spaniards – & *that* garden we can wander in, too, for they never come & la gardienne is a friend of Marie's. It takes the ultimate biscuit.

But Isola Bella's the thing. Now, if you ever want to send anything over, dearest, like a bit of cretonne or – no, I'll get Ida to bring what I want after Christmas. For, of course the furniture isn't pretty. Still, it somehow, even as it *is*, looks ... to my doting eye.

You'll have a whole year here. Last night I walked about and saw the new moon with the old moon in her arms & the lights in the water and the hollow pools full of stars – and lamented there was no God. But I came in and wrote 'Miss Brill' instead; which is my insect Magnificat now & always.

Goodbye, my precious, for now. BE HAPPY. Your last letters have been so fearfully woeful. Such a fool I was to have told you about my head. I was *confiding*. And the worst of it is I felt so infinitely better till I got your sad, desolate, crushed reply – 'Not long now' as tho' we were waiting for *le dernier soupir*. Oh, Boge, Boge, Boge – Do let's try & not fall over! Or if we do – let's explain to each other (as I tried to) that we are falling.

Do please come back to me I feel you've gone away and are queerly *angry* – with life – *not* as you were.

Your true love
Wig

[Menton]
[14 November 1920]

ENTREAT YOU LET NO ONE HAVE HIDEOUS OLD
PHOTOGRAPH PUBLISHED IN SPHERE IMPORTANT
BURN IT

TIG.

[Villa Isola Bella,
Menton]
[17 November 1920]

Thank you for the flower. Yes, it *did* touch me.

No, darling. If I let this other letter go I shall repent it. For it is not all.

It's true I am hurt as I've never been. Perhaps it is your carelessness. But then carelessness in love is so dreadful. And what else can it be? Even after getting my present which I tried to make perfect for you in a case which I chose awfully carefully and you never even *gave one word to*, you didn't mention this other photograph. And to talk about too much fragility and so on – I hang my head. I feel timid and faint. I am not an ox. I *am* weak; I feel my hold on life is fainting-weak. But that is ME – the real real me. I can't help it. Didn't you know? And then when you toss off my letter about 'passports, kisses, O.B.E.' – oh, I am so *ashamed*. What anguish to have written as I did about kisses – Was that what I wrote about? Let me creep away and fold my wings. They quiver – you hurt me.

I must tell you; no one else will. I am not that other woman. I am not this great girl. Whether you did tell Sadler it was precious or not I don't know. I scarcely hear you saying that to him.

But I must tell you something else. I have been ill for nearly four years – and I'm changed changed – not the same – You gave twice to your work (which I couldn't see) to what you gave my story. I don't want dismissing as a masterpiece. Who is going to mention 'the first snow'? I haven't anything like as long to live as you have. I've *scarcely any time I feel*. Arthur will draw posters 100 years. Praise him when I'm dead – Talk to ME. I'm lonely. I haven't ONE single soul ...

[Villa Isola Bella,
Menton]
[18 November 1920]

Dear Bogey

For this one occasion I have the use of the Corona. It's an opportunity to write you a legible business letter. Will you regard it as such, as just the letter of one writer to another? That's to say – don't, I beg, think it is just my little joke. I am in dead earnest.

I have your letter saying you gave that picture to the press. Now I must ask you to see that it is destroyed at once! And in future please do not act on my behalf without sending me a wire. Nothing is so urgent it cannot wait twenty-four hours. No earthly publicity is worth such a price.

I am more or less helpless over here, as you know. But that has got to be changed. I beg you not to publish one single solitary thing that I may have left in England.

And I want to put my work and publicity into the hands of an agent with whom I shall communicate direct. Is Pinker the best man? I shall be doing a great deal of work from now on, and I want to free myself from journalism, which I hate, at the first possible moment. At the same time I must have money.

If you do not understand my feelings about that photograph – could you do this? Could you ACT as if you did?

And why on earth did you not go direct to Constable at once. Why write to Sadler's wife? That's not business, surely.

I am so bitterly ashamed of this affair that I'd pay for bookmarkers with my new photograph.

You do not understand. I cannot make you. But at least you did know – tho' you may have forgotten – that I hated this thing. And you did possess other photographs of mine that you knew I did not mind.

I can't write to you personally, to-night. The other face gets in the way! Is that the person you've been writing to for the last four years?

I am terribly sorry about it all. But please for my sake – I'll even stoop and mention my health – put me out of my anxiety and let me feel that you will always send me a wire – at my expense – before you act for me.

Don't misunderstand your
Wig

Until I do get an agent – you will act for me? I'm sending another story to-night. And I'd be immensely grateful if you'd suggest what I ought to do with it.

Wig

> [Villa Isola Bella,
> Menton]
> [end of November 1920]

My darling Bogey,

I have so much to say that I don't know what to start with. Yes, I do. First, foremost, most important, nearest is

Je t'aime

'cœur petit'

If only I could make that warm – or make a beam fly out of it into your heart. Your letters make me long to hold you tight and tell you that the golden thread never COULD be broken between us. Oh, don't you know that? The golden thread is always there. Bogey, you must believe that my little drawing of a heart IS a sign, a symbol. You know whom it comes from – don't you, darling? You are my Boge, my 'veen' (whoever he is: he's *very* important) you are also Basil-love and Jag-Boge. If you were here you would believe me. When you come – you will! You *are* coming at Xmas? I am preparing for you every single day. 'I should like it done before Xmas' is my one date when I give orders.

Darling, your letter enclosing the cover of *Bliss* came today. That's all right. Thank you for sending it to me. You must [not] be my dog any more tho'. Pinker must. He sounds a perfectly *horrid* dog, doesn't he: one that runs sideways. Do you know the kind?

I want to tell you I have had a chill. It's over now or rather it's turned the corner. Never was serious. But it took it out of me & I have been a farthing candle for light & warmth. I wouldn't bother to mention it except that I feel my novel review suffered so dreadfully in consequence – it took me 11 hours!! and the result was only that!! Is it too bad to print. I simply could not squeeze a review out of my head. But I'll make up for it this week & try & send you two bonzers.

About the punctuation in 'The Stranger'. Thank you, Bogey. No, my dash isn't quite a feminine dash. (Certainly when I was young it was). But it was intentional in that story. I was trying to do away with the three dots. They have been so abused by female & male writers that I fight shy of them – *much* tho' I need them. The truth is – punctuation is infernally difficult. If I had time I'd like to write an open letter to the *A.* on the subject. Its boundaries need to be enlarged. But I won't go into it now. I'll try, however, to remember *commas*. It's a fascinating subject, ça, one that I'd like to talk over with you. If only there was time I'd write all one wants to write. There seems less & less time. And more & more books arrive. That's not a complaint. But it *is* rather cursed that we should have to worry about Louis Goldring when we might be writing our own books – isn't it?

Oh, darling – Here's a Perfectly Dreadful Discovery of mine. Poor little Moult's book is the continuation of Opal Whiteley's Diary. He is in fact (this is for your ear alone) Opal Whiteley. Even the cat is called William Shakespeare & there are bits about roses in her cheeks & babies coming & horses having some tired feelings. In fact, if I didn't know poor Tom I should have said so in print.

And about 'Poison'. I could write about that for pages. But I'll try & condense what I've got to say. The story is told by (evidently) a worldly, rather cynical (not wholly cynical) man *against* himself (but not altogether) when he was so absurdly young. You know how young by his idea of what woman is. She has been up to now, only the *vision*, only she who passes. You realise that? And here he has put *all* his passion into this Beatrice. It's *promiscuous love* not understood as such by him; perfectly understood as such by her. But you realise the vie de luxe they are living – the very table – sweets, liqueurs, lilies, pearls. And you realise? she expects a letter from someone calling her away? *Fully* expects it? That accounts for her farewell AND her declaration. And when it doesn't come even her *commonness* peeps out – the newspaper touch of such a woman. She can't disguise her chagrin. She gives herself away.... He of course, laughs at it now, & laughs at her. Take what he says about her 'sense of order' & the crocodile. But he also regrets the self who dead privately would have been young enough to have actually wanted to *marry* such a woman. But I meant it to be light – tossed off – & yet through it – oh – subtly –

the lament for youthful belief. These are the rapid confessions one receives sometimes from a glove or a cigarette or a hat.

I suppose I haven't brought it off in 'Poison'. It wanted a light, light hand – and then with that newspaper a sudden ... let me see *lowering* of it all – just what happens in promiscuous love after passion. A glimpse of staleness. And the story is told by the man who gives himself away & hides his traces at the same moment.

I realise it's quite a different kind to 'Miss Brill' or 'The Young Girl'. (She's not 'little', Bogey; in fact, I saw her big, slender, like a colt.)

Will you tell me if you see my point at all? or do you still feel it's no go?

Here is an inside and outside photograph of me in and out of my Isola Bella. Would you like some more? I have more here if you'd like them. And shall I tell you the conversation which just went on between Marie & the carpet woman? Oh, no, it's not interesting really without the voices. Even old Marie *attend Monsieur* now. 'J'ai l'idée, Madame, d'acheter une belle tranche de veau – *alors* de faire une poch-e dedans et de la farcir avec un peu de jambon – *un* œuf –' and so on & on and on – the song becoming more & more triumphant & ending 'mais peut-être il vaudrait mieux que nous attendions l'arrivée de Monsieur pour *ça*. En effet un bon plat de nouilles est toujours un bon plat,' & then she puts her head on one side & says, 'Monsieur aime le veau?'

Pleased to tell you mice have made a nest in my old letters to Ida. Would that I could always be certain of such behaviour. The mice in this house are upstarts.

> Goodbye for now, darling
> I am your
> Tig

[Menton]
[27 November 1920]

BELIEVE THIS TELEGRAM ALL MY LOVE

TIG.

[Villa Isola Bella,
Menton]
[3 December 1920]

My darling Bogey,

I am so very sorry you had all that extry hard labour. And I hope your boat's out of the storm now, at any rate, & that it will sail in smoother waters until you've had a holiday. I 'note' you'll get here about the 22nd; you're very sensible to travel 1st class. It's madness to risk 2nd class anything, anywhere, for the next 50 years at least. I'll go through the paper today with a pencil & give you *my* views. Also your *Art & Morality* is come. I'll read that today, too. I sent off my reviews last night. Tomorrow I'm going to *wade* into my story. Oh – dear – curse this question of time! It's terrible here. I want to work all day – I shall never have the whole afternoon to spend looking at things or talking, darling, if you do come in Avrilo. I'm simply *rushing* to catch up & shall be for evermore – whatever evermore may mean. ...

You see, I was right about the dinner – after all. It was very nice of the Princess B. to give you a lift home. I hope you do meet Anthony, I heard from him again today. He's a very nice little friend to have out of the blue. Don't be suspicious about women. Are you really? Or is that *your way*? You're very attractive to women, as you know, but as long as they don't interfere – surely you like knowing them. And you always can escape – darling – for though you are so tender-hearted, you're ruthless too. I mean if it was a question of a woman or your work – there wouldn't *be* a question – would there? Otherwise, I think you ought to enjoy them – There is even a strong dash of the lady-killer in you! And think of the way you look at yourself in a glass if a glass is in the room – you return & return & return to it; it's like a woman to you – I have often noticed that. Don't forget you're only 31, Boge, and get all you can out of Life!! You see, Bogey, your position is difficult. I'm a writer first & a woman after ∴ I can't give you *all* you want – above all, a kind of easy relaxation which is essential to you – and which the glass (I don't mean that in the least scornfully) provides. A man with your kind of mind can't go on being strenuous and exerting himself the *whole* time, for your mental activity is, as it were, separate from your life. Mine is all one – so it's no effort to me. The story isn't always at a crisis – don't you know – but it is all part of the story. This is an essential difference. I was blind not to have understood it in the Brett affair – but no –

that *was* 'wrong', as we say – However – *do feel free*. I mean that. It's a lovely day – but by the time you come all the leaves will be gone. The last are falling. I don't know about mes roses; at present the whole garden is roses – where it's not violets. The different smells of different roses – I've only this year realised. There are 6 in my garden. I go from one to the other until I feel like a bee – Well, darling I must go out and sit in my tent with the A. & a pencil.

Take care of yourself

Tig

[Villa Isola Bella,
Menton]
[6 December 1920]

Darling Bogey

I've just finished a story called 'The Lady's Maid' which I'm sending for the paper. I do hope you will care to print it. It's what I meant when I said a Xmas story – Dear knows, Xmas doesn't come in it after all and you may think I'm a fraud. But I think, all the same, people might like to read it at Xmas time. The number of letters I've had about 'Miss Brill'! I think I am very fortunate to have people like my stories – don't you? But I must say it does surprise me – *This* one I'd like you and De la Mare to like – other people don't matter.

Curtis Brown's letter & your reply came today. I am deeply grateful to you. Yes, I feel I may make enough money in America to free myself to make money – It's *hell* to know one could do so much & be bound to journalism for bread. If I was a proper journalist I'd give the day to reviewing & so on – but no! Reviewing is on my chest – AND a sense of GUILT the whole week! However it can't be helped. I'll win out and then I don't want to read another novel for — But isn't it grim to be reviewing Benson when one might be writing one's own stories which one will never have time to write, on the best showing!

I've not written to Pinker yet, for the reason that I have not any reserve stock to offer him. I hope after Xmas to have at least 3 stories ready. But it only confuses things to get into touch with him & not have the goods. He's bound not to have any interest. So Brown had better go ahead with 'The Stranger' and I'll write promising him my 3 stories which will be ready at the end of this month. It was a nice letter.

Personally I want to make money by my stories *now* – I can't live poor – can't worry about butter and cabs and woollen dresses & the chemist's bill and work too. I don't want to *live rich* – God forbid – but I must be free – and ça coûte cher aujourd'hui. It's most awfully kind of you, darling, to have written to Brown.

Just while I'm on the subject I suppose you will think I am an egocentric to mind the way Constable has advertised my book & the paragraph that is on the paper cover. I'd like to say that I mind so terribly that there are no words for me – No – I'm DUMB!! I think it so insulting & disgusting and undignified that – well – there you are! It's no good suffering all over again. But the bit about – 'Women will learn by heart and not repeat' – Gods! Why didn't they have a photograph of me looking through a garter! But I was helpless here – too late to stop it – so now I *must* prove – no convince people ce n'est pas moi – At least if I'd known they were going to say that no power on earth would have made me cut a word. I wish I hadn't. I was wrong – very wrong –

The story will go to you Wednesday morning. A typist has been found at 7 francs a 1000. *I* think she is mad as well. But I can't afford not to send corrected copies.

What a horrible note this is. And there's the evening star – like an emerald hanging over the palm – Forgive me – evening star – Bogey, forgive me. These are only sparks on my coat – they are not my real fur – But the ancien couteau burns faintly in my left lung tonight – & that makes me wicked – Wicked – but loving – loving.

      Tig.

[Villa Isola Bella,
Menton]

I have sent back the books today.   [8 December 1920]

My dear Bogey,

It is with the most extreme reluctance that I am writing to tell you K.M. can't go on.

The fact is she ought to have given up months ago but money was so urgent that she dared not. I know you suggested a month's holiday – but a month's holiday doesn't fit the case. She won't be well in a month. The strain will begin all over again and I think she has told you fairly often *what* a strain it is.

She would not, however, have taken this step if Doctor Bouchage had not made her realise it was *absolutely necessary*. He has. It is not that her health is worse than it was in London. But it's no better. She has good days she didn't have then; but she has BAD ones she didn't either. And she is not improving, as they say.

In two words – and plain ones: it's a question of shortening her life, to keep on. And that she can't do.

But you must realise how deeply she 'appreciates' the awkwardness of this for you. She knows it all: feels it all.

One thing must be perfectly clear. She wants NO money from you and no sacrifice. She hates even discussing money affairs with you. She knows you have paid debts of hers; she hopes they will be the last you'll ever pay. *This is final*. You may smile at this and say: 'I haven't any money to give her, at any rate –' Right-o. But she just had to tell you.

And now I'll be personal, darling – Look here you ought to have sent me that Corona! You really ought to have. Can't you possibly imagine what all this writing out has been to a person as weak as I *damnably* am? You can't or a stone would have sent it. You knew what a help it was to me in London.

But oh dear I don't mean to accuse you – because I can't bear, as you know, to make you feel unhappy. But what you would have saved me – I can't say! Isn't it awful that I have not dared to *add to your burdens* by reminding you before? That's Mother in me. And you rather count on it, my darling.

But don't feel sad – or knocked over – or don't take any of this too seriously. Easy to say – isn't it. Yes. All the same it's not RIGHT to LIVE among mountains of gloom – or to sweat blood as one climbs them. One must just run on top and be careless. I don't mean that in putting you in this hole I'm laughing at the hole. But think of the hole that I might so easily trip into!! It's far bigger – far blacker – but I WON'T moan.

This is a very mixed letter – You ought just to love me – that's all the best – and you *must* understand.

> Your own
> Tig

[Villa Isola Bella
Menton]
[December 1920]

Darling Little Fellow,

I've just had the wire about the £30. Now this is just what I wanted to avoid. I presume it is my A. cheque augmenté to that sum by you.

Will you believe me or I shall be cross – I am in NO need of money. I'll pay you back every cent – il y a de plus. I'm as rich as Croesus (who *was* Croesus.) My kine are fat; my sheep are all jaeger – Stop now! Calmez-vous! What do you mean by jumping up – you Jack-in-the-Box? What can I do with you?

Doctor B. has just gone. We talked over the affair again. He was quite definite. I shall now tell you exactly so that you know where you are.

I *have* injured my heart for the moment by overwork – but not permanently. If I had persisted I should have endangered my life. It is difficult to explain to any one as wise as you the gigantic strain of one weekly article – to a person as 'weakly' (as Pa would say) as I am. It sounds fantastic. It hung over me like a cloud. But (1) money and (2) my feeling for the paper and you and so on made me cling. However it was (1) which kept me at it too long, I fear. At present, too, both my lungs are enflammés as a result of a chill. It's not serious or urgent but if I tried to exert myself it would be. My heart is however the trouble at the moment. It needs rest. So I have to lie low and rest the little *fiend*. It will then get better.

However, I am not forlorn. Je suis si bien ici. J'ai ma petite villa – ma bonne – un feu d'enfer flambe dans la chéminée & lying here I can do my own work when I'm not too tired, I can take it up & put it down à mon aise –

There. I only tell you all this because you're such a bad wicked Boge to worry. Stop! I'll tell you when to worry. Oh darling – take a long breath – *now*. Are you afraid of anything. I solemnly assure you I am afraid of NOTHING. I mean that – I do not want to die because I have done nothing to justify having lived yet. I mean to jolly well keep alive with the flag flying until there is a modest shelf of books with K.M. backs. Which reminds me I do think Constable might have sent me a copy of *Bliss* – don't you? But only vanity makes me want to see it. *Confession*: I want to leave it about for Marie to find and exclaim over.

Goodbye, darling. Help me to keep all fair – all serene and fine. Why should it be otherwise? No, you are not a Teddy Bear. You are a *Boge* and I am a *Wig*

[2 Portland Villas,
Hampstead]
[c. 10 December, 1920]

My darling Wig

Thinking about my lies this evening I discovered that if I had told you the whole truth from the beginning, I should not have been corrupt; there would not have been this perpetual struggle between the truth & the false in me, which has lately become so ghastly that you even suspect that the truth in me is false. So I determined to try to tell the whole truth.

The thing really began before I met or heard of E[lizabeth] B[ibesco]. When I wrote to you that my blunder over the photos & your letters had thrown me off balance – that was *true*. I suddenly felt naked & comfortless – utterly miserable.

One Monday evening I walked to Leicester Square Tube Station. I was acutely miserable. I saw a tart near the Express Dairy. I stopped and spoke to her. She wanted me to go home with her. I made, I suppose, two steps in that direction. Then I said: No, it's not my game. I want someone to talk to. Let's go to a restaurant. We went to Malzy's in Tottenham Court Road. I stood her a dinner. She was quite kind – a Lancashire girl. I said when we parted, and I had given her all the money I had 30/-, that I would give her dinner on Dec. 18. I didn't, and I didn't even write to tell her that I couldn't come. I don't know why. I have reproached myself bitterly for it.

This is in the wrong order. On Saturday before I had been to dinner at the Drey's. I was in the same state of misery. I went home with Mrs. Dobree who was there. As I left with her, I kissed Anne [Drey]: I felt that if she would take me in her arms, and comfort me, all would be well. I walked home with Mrs. Dobree, and listened to her talking rubbish through a kind of haze, then as I said goodbye

at her gate, I kissed her on the cheek. I never saw her again. I wrote
or began to write a letter explaining – but I tore it up.
The following Monday was the Leicester Square woman.
On Tuesday I had to see Brett's pictures. After I got home I
telephoned her and said I was coming to see her. I went down at
about 10 o'clock, and talked. Then I took her in my arms. I did not
kiss her but I caressed her. In a moment a great loathing of myself
& her came over me. I had an intense effort not to be downright
brutal when I left. I was more miserable than ever.
On Wednesday I went to Beresford's. That morning Mary
Hutch. rang me up asking me to dine with her & E[lizabeth]
B[ibesco] I said I couldn't because of Beresford. That night I felt
better – coming home with Hodgson I almost recovered my senses.
The next day was a bad one – miserable, as far as I remember.
On Friday I had a letter from Mary H. asking me to dinner for
the Monday with E.B. I have a vague recollection that the
intervening Sunday was a bad day.

I have given you a truthful description of the dinner – except for
the important thing that coming home in the car, as I left her – she
had just asked me to dine with her on the following Monday and I
had accepted – I kissed her on the cheek suddenly. I went home in
an agony of nerves.

On Tuesday or Wednesday she sent me her story to the office. I
replied very distantly that I would read it & give her my criticism
on Monday. Some time on Wednesday I wrote to her about it
criticising it in detail, as being 'clever' but, I said truthfully, I would
probably have accepted it with alterations for the *Athenaeum.*

On Thursday she rang me up thanking me & saying how much
she had enjoyed the dinner. She said it was a long time before
Monday – could she come & see me at the office on Friday. I said I
should be there. She came in on the Friday, & we talked about odd
things – I forget which. I felt very embarrassed. A queer feeling that
she didn't really belong to my world – and that she would resent my
having kissed her as I did. I felt very grateful for her having been so
nice & gentle as she was in the office. When she had gone I wrote
her a letter, beginning deliberately 'Dear Elizabeth' & saying that I
was terrified lest she should interpret my gesture as that of a man
making love. I said that I believed there was the chance of a true
friendship between us & that she had made me feel that
'somewhere on earth, wherever I was was Elizabeth Bibesco, with
whom I could feel safe & need not worry to defend myself'.

She answered this on Monday, saying that she rejoiced in the friendship, that the gesture I was looking for was kissing hands, & that my remark was one of the finest things she had ever had said about her.

I went to dinner on Monday. I was shown up to her bedroom; I said I was sorry she was ill. I ate at a little table at the foot of her bed and after dinner sat in a chair by her side. I smoked a great many cigarettes. I forget what we talked about. I remember that there was a great dog who made me very angry because she would not stop him from tearing things. At last I put him outside.

[incomplete]

[Menton]
[12 December 1920]

STOP TORMENTING ME WITH THESE FALSE DEPRESSING LETTERS AT ONCE BE A MAN OR DON'T WRITE ME

TIG.

[Villa Isola Bella,
Menton]
[12 December 1920]

This is much harsher than I feel, but you compel me to speak out. It isn't even *as* I feel; it's so crude. But I simply CAN'T ... bear your lack of a sense of proportion. It will be the ruin of us both.

Bogey,
   A letter has come from you in which you say you are 'annihilated' & tell me of Madame la Princesse because you think your ... what shall I call it ... meeting her may have had something to do with my illness. Well, Bogey – please let me speak.
   I told you to be free – because I meant it. What happens in your personal life does not affect me. I have of you what I want – a relationship which is unique but it is not what the world understands by *marriage*. That is to say I do not in any way *depend* on you, neither can you shake me.
   Nobody can. I do not know how it is, but I live *withdrawn* from my personal life. (This is hard to say.) I am a writer first. In the past, it is true, when I worked less, my writing self was merged in my

personal self. I felt conscious of you – to the exclusion of almost everything, at times. (All this is just outline).

But now I do not. You are dearer than anyone in the world to me – but more than anything else – more even than talking or laughing or being happy I want to write. This sounds so ugly, I wish I didn't have to say it. But your letter makes me feel you would be relieved if it were said.

Can't we stop this *horrible drama!* I hate explaining myself: it's so unnatural to me. It makes me feel indecent.

Let us quit ourselves like men.

      Tig

[Menton]
[14 December 1920]

PAY NO HEED MY LETTER ILLNESS EXASPERATED ME ARE YOU ARRIVING TUESDAY IF SO WON'T WRITE AGAIN FONDEST LOVE REPLY

      TIG.

January–June 1921

As he had done the previous year, Murry shared Christmas 1920 with Katherine at Menton. On this occasion, he made the momentous decision to give up his editorship of the *Athenaeum* so that he could remain with his sick wife. In January 1921 he went back to London to settle his affairs, intending to return for good in April. But a relapse in Katherine's health brought him to her side again in late January; and he returned permanently towards the end of February. In May 1921 Katherine and L.M. moved from Menton to the more bracing climate of Baugy in Switzerland. It was Murry's visit to England to deliver six lectures at Oxford University on 'The Problem of Style' that occasioned the correspondence between them at this time.

[Villa Isola Bella,
Menton]
[11 January 1921]

My own beautiful darling,
I've just got two minutes while you are getting up to say my secret word. I am going away with absolute peace in my heart, and the knowledge, certain & sure, like a warm thing curled up in side me, that I love you more, far more than ever. With all its horrors these three weeks have been a taste of our true serenity. I've no fears of anything – not one; but only a confidence that seems always on the point of breaking out into a smile deep down.

Trust me as though I were part of your own heart: I am part of your heart. I wanted you to have this [to] read after we've said good-bye. Know that all things are quite straight & plain in front of me – I am planted in 'the direct forthright'.

And now I have you in my arms my wonderful Wig-wife. You will be there always till I come in April.

> Good-bye
> Your
> Veen.

[Villa Isola Bella,
Menton]
[11 January 1921]
Tuesday

My precious darling,

I shall never forget your beautiful gesture in handing me that letter. I read it and I drove home with you and you are still here. You have been in every moment of the day; it is as though you had gone up to the mountains for a long afternoon. I have never loved you so. No, my precious, until now I did not know what it was to love *like this*. This peace and this wonderful certainty are quite new.

Take care of yourself. Depend on me. Tell me anything – and feel that I am with you. My one drop of 'sorrow' is that I am not helping you. But you *know* how I am with you. Oh, my Veen, how happy you have made me! I sit here on the striped couch & Rib does sentry-go up & down the back of it with the feather for a gun and I am still possessed by memories of my darling. On the red box there is the snail shell. It said to me this evening: 'Am I not one of your treasures, too?' Darling little snail shell – found by Boge – perfect little blue flowers brought by him. Oh, my Heart, how can I ever thank you for everything!

> Wig

This exquisite paper has just arrived. I must send a note to the Villa Louise – to impress them. ... Bogey, our photographs are very important ...

Sierre,
[14 May 1921]
Saturday

I am in the middle of one of my *Giant Coups*. Yesterday evening I decided to look no longer for doctors in Montreux. In fact I felt the hour had come for something quite extraordinary. So I phoned

Montana – asked Dr. Stephani to descend by funiculaire to Sierre and meet me here at the Château Bellevue at 3 o'clock today – then engaged a car and started off this morning shortly after 9 o'clock. It is years since I have done such things. It is like a dream.

[Hotel Beau Site,
Clarens-Montreux]
[15 May 1921]
Sunday

Sweethert myn

I got back from Sierre at about 7.30 last night. I rather wish I hadn't sent you that little note from there. It was so confuged. Tear it up, love ... While I write a man is playing the zither so sweetly and gaily that one's heart dances to hear. It's a very warm, still day.

Will you please look at this picture of the lake at Sierre? Do you like it? It's lovely – really it is. If we spend a year here in Switzerland I don't think you will regret it. I think you would be happy. Yesterday gave me such a wonderful idea of it all. I feel I have been through & through Switzerland. And up there, at Sierre & in the tiny mountain towns on the way to Sierre it is absolutely unspoilt. I mean it's so unlike – so remote from the Riviera in that sense. There are *no* tourists to be seen. It is a whole complete life. The only person I could think of meeting was Lawrence before the war. The only thing which is modern (and this makes me feel the Lord is on our side) is the postal service: it is excellent everywhere in Switzerland, even in the villages – There are two posts a day everywhere. As to telegrams they simply fly – and your letter posted 8.30 P.M. on May 12th arrived here 9.30 A.M. May 14th. All these remarks are, again of the carrot family. I heard there are any number of small chalêts to be had in Sierre and in Montana. We should take one – don't you think – darling! and have a Swiss bonne. As to cream-cows, they abound. And the whole country side is full of fruit and of vines. It's famous for its small grapes – and for a wine which the peasants make – The father brews for his sons – and the sons for their sons. It's drunk when it's about 20 years old & I believe it is superb.

Queer thing is that all the country near Sierre is like the Middle Ages. There are ancient tiny castles on small round wooded knolls, and the towns are solid, built round a square. Yesterday as we came to one part of the valley – it was a road with a *solid* avenue of poplars – a green wall on either side – little wooden carts came spanking towards us. The man sat on the shafts. The woman, in black, with a flat black hat, earrings & a white kerchief sat in front with the children. Nearly all the women carried huge bunches of crimson peonies – flashing bright. A stream of these little carts passed & then we came to a town & there was a huge fair going on in the market square. In the middle people were dancing – round the sides they were buying pigs and lemonade – in the cafés under the white & pink flowering chestnut trees there were more people & at the windows of the houses there were set pots of white narcissi and girls looked out – they had orange & cherry handkerchiefs on their heads. It was beyond words gay and delightful. Then further on we came to a village where some fête was being arranged. The square was hung with garlands & there were cherry-coloured masts with flags flying from them and each mast had a motto – framed in leaves – AMITIE – TRAVAIL – HONNEUR – DEVOIR. All the men of the village in white shirts & breeches were stringing more flags across & a very old man sat on a heap of logs plaiting green branches. He had a huge pipe with *brass fittings*.

Oh dear – in some parts of the Rhone valley there are deep, deep meadows. Little herd boys lie on their backs or their bellies & their tiny white goats spring about on the mountain slopes. These mountains have little lawns set with trees, little glades & miniature woods & torrents on the lower slopes & all kinds of different trees are there in their beauty. Then come the pines & the firs – then the undergrowth – then the rock & the snow. You meet tiny girls all alone with flocks of *black* sheep or herds of huge yellow cows. Perhaps they are sitting on the bank of a stream with their feet in the water or stripping a wand. And houses are so few, so remote. I don't know what it is, but I think you would feel as I did *deeply pleased* at all this. I like to imagine (am I right, my own?) that you will muse as you read: Yes, I could do with a year there.... And you must know that *from* Sierre we can go far and wide – in no time. I believe the flowers are in their perfection in June & July and again the *Alpine flora* in September and October.

I see a small chalet with a garden near the pine forests. I see it all very simple, with big white china stoves and a very pleasant woman with a tanned face & sun bleached hair bringing in the coffee. I see winter – snow and a load of wood arriving at our door. I see us going off in a little sleigh – with huge fur gloves on & having a picnic in the forest & eating ham & fur sandwiches. Then there is a lamp – *très important* – there are our books. It's very still. The frost is on the pane. You are in your room writing. I in mine. Outside the stars are shining & the pine trees are dark like velvet.

Farewell, Bogey, I love you dearly dearly

Wig

Thank you for Mrs. H[ardy]'s nice letter. I long to hear of your time there. I was not surprised at Sullivan. He's so *uncertain* at present I mean in his own being that it will come natural to him to pose. I don't know how far you realise that you *make* him what he is with you – or how different he is with others. Also at present he has no real self-respect and that makes him *boast*. Like all of us he wants to feel important & that's a *right* feeling – we *ought* to feel important – but while he remains undisciplined & dans le vague he *can't be* important. So he has to boast. I mustn't go on. You are calling me a schoolmistress....

Please give Mother & Richard my love.

c/o A.J. Jenkinson
Stanford House,
Oxford.
[16 May 1921]

Monday: after lunch.

My darling,

The first ordeal is over – an hour ago. Of course, it's Whit Monday, & I believe, impossible to send a telegram. However, I will go & see as soon as I have written this.

There was an enormous audience – I mean not less than 250 people. But I don't suppose there will be more than half that next time: for it was obviously above the heads of half the audience. It's not the fashion to applaud in Oxford; otherwise I should interpret the dead silence into which my conclusion fell as a bad omen. Roughly, I should say that half the audience enjoyed it, while to the other half it was double Dutch: and I imagine that one half the audience will persevere to the end.

In a sense I'm sorry that I wrote the lectures out; but I couldn't trust myself to work from notes alone. Otherwise it would probably have been better. Also, as I read, it seemed to me that the lecture was packed too full of material; it was, in fact, much more an essay than a lecture. However – it can't be helped; and if I can't call it a success, it certainly wasn't a failure.

Jenkinson has cordially invited me to stop on here till Monday next – therefore I shall. After next Monday I shall pay my visit to

Hardy and then return to London. I shall come up here to lecture on Friday 27th. & then go for the week-end to Sydney Waterlow. I feel in an odd way very much out of my element here. There's not very much in common between myself and Oxford, I'm afraid; but still the experience is worth having. Last night at dinner I met a ridiculous old tutor of mine – called Grundy – you may have heard Goodyear & me speaking of him. I had come to believe he was a legendary figure, and that we had invented all his absurdities; but not at all. He is just as richly and unconsciously comic as I remembered him. I could hardly avoid bursting into laughter when I saw him – and heard him.

Alas, there's no chance of a letter from you to-day, & not much to-morrow: on Whit-Monday the office will be closed so that nothing will be forwarded. That's a horrible long time to wait.

It's awful – I believe a kind of fatality attends me. The first night I slept in the nice clean bed here, I had a wet dream and there this morning were the two accusing splodges. It was enough to make me blush with shame.

I must somehow say how much I love you. Our lovely months together have made me feel the pain of separation much more keenly. Of course it can't be helped, but still. I want the weeks to pass quickly. I only feel a half of a being: and though it's wonderful to know that the other half is there waiting for me to join on again – I don't like the separation, Wig, I don't like it.

But, by the Holy Poker, what a time we will have together, working & talking. I hope I shan't be overworked any more, & that we shall really have time to breathe in unison.

> Goodbye darling
> Boge.

> at Stanford House
> Oxford.

Thursday   [19 May 1921]

My darling,
This morning came your letter with Stephani's report – and about Montana.

I simply long to spend a year – two years – a lifetime of years with you at Sierre. It sounds & looks divine. I know I shall be terribly happy there. I'm all for a little chalet.

I think you know all about me now; but perhaps you don't know *quite* how much I miss you – how deeply and quietly happy I have been with you this year. I find myself continually thinking of you. That has never happened before. Honestly I don't think an hour ever passes without my imagining that we are together again. When I do my exercises in the morning, it seems to me impossible that you shouldn't be seeing my feet waggling in the wardrobe glass.

However, the weeks are going quickly.

For some reason or other, I can't give you an account of my doings in Oxford. It's all so awfully unreal. Not that the people aren't very nice to me – and Jenkinson himself a perfect angel – but it's a world I left years & years ago. I love Oxford; but in the way I love my father. We're utterly strange to each other. Sometimes, when I'm dining at the high table the clock stops ticking and I hear everything from an incredible distance – and it's so strange.

Yesterday afternoon I went to see the cricket in the Parks – it was lovely. Great tall trees, smooth grass, bright sunshine, a slow clapping when a man came out to bat, the muffled click as he hit the ball. A dream game – so remote it was from me. And how I enjoyed my own remoteness!

How intimately I have *grown in* to you lately! With everyone else, everywhere else I am a kind of bemused spectator. Life seems like the slow dropping of water into a deep well. Fascinating and very far away. A curious deep happiness is hidden somewhere inside me.

Well, darling – we've had a strangely mixed time together – but if it had been a time of unmixed suffering it would still have been worth the price to get to the condition we're in now.

I can't really write anything: I should only be rhapsodical.

If you just feel how much, how deeply, how calmly & steadily, I love you – that's all I want

Boge.

My present plans are to leave Oxford on Tuesday 24 – stay at Wandsworth – return Oxford Friday 27 staying the night – 28–29 week end with Sydney Waterlow. 30 lecture, return London afternoon. Friday June 3 last lecture. Sat. 4 down to Hardy staying the night. Sunday return London. Monday–Tuesday 6–7 Broomies. 8th. depart for Clarens. Perhaps I may need 1 day more, but that's all.

[Pension du Lac,
Sierre]

Saturday evening,   [21 May 1921]

My precious Bogey,
  I am rather conscious that my letters have fallen off just these last days. Especially so, since this evening I have read yours written at Oxford on Thursday. You know how it is when just the letter you get is the letter you would love to get? That was my experience with this one of yours, my darling. I dipped into that remote Oxford & discovered you there; I heard that click of the cricket ball & I saw the trees & grass. I was with you, standing by you & – not saying anything – but happy.
  I love you with my whole heart, Bogey.
  The reason why I haven't written is I am fighting a kind of Swiss chill. It will go off. Don't please give it another thought. I've a tremendous equipment of weapons.
  All day, in the sun, the men have been working in the vineyards. They have been hoeing between the vines & then an old man has been dusting certain rows with powder out of a Giant pepper pot. The heat has been terrific. The men have worn nothing but cotton trousers. Their bodies are tanned almost red brown – a very beautiful colour. And every now & then they stop work, lean on their pick, breathe deeply – look round. I feel I have been watching them for hundreds of years – Now the day is over; the shadows are long on the grass. The new trees hold the light and wisps of white cloud move dreamily over the dreaming mountains. It is all very lovely .... How hot is it in England? Here it is really as Chaddie would say – almost tropical. The nights are hot too. One lies with both windows wide open and my toes as usual get thirsty – Yes, what you say about your exercises ... You know, the vision of you with naked foot stalking within my chamber is somehow most awfully *important* in the story of my love for you. And seeing you in the mirror & seeing you on the floor ... all so marvellously jewel clear! And you – a radiant – very free being – revealed in some way – in no need of the least 'protection' or 'covering'. I wonder if you see what I am getting at. It seems to me that my *false* idea of your helplessness was put absolutely, beautifully *right* by the sight of your nakedness. But here I spec you're smiling at Wig for making such a big bone about it. Nevertheless, I mean something 'very profound,' love.
  Thank you for Tchehov. Came tonight. I am simply captivated

by Chaucer just now. I have had to throw a bow window into my cœur petit to include him with Shakespeare – Oh dear! His *Troilus & Cressid*!!! And my joy at finding your remarks & your pencil notes.

I read today *The Tale of Chaunticleer & Madame Perlicote*: it's the Pardouner's tale. Perfect in its way. But the *personality* – the *reality* of the man. How his impatience, his pleasure, the very tone rings through – It's deep delight to read. Chaucer & Marlowe are my two at present. I don't mean there's any comparison between them. But I read *Hero & Leander* last night. That's incredibly lovely. But how extremely amusing Chapman's *finish* is! Taking up that magical poem & putting it into a body & skirt. It's v̲. funny. As I write there's a subdued roar from the salle à manger where Lunn's Lions are being fed. Fourteen arrived today for A Week by the Pearl of Lac Leman. It's nice to think I have this salon and don't need to go among them except when so dispoged.

I do hope you will be happy with Hardy. I feel it ought to be most awfully nice. I feel they are simple. There'll be no need to explain things. The kind of people who understand making jam, even – and would love to hear of others making it. I liked so what she said about their way of living – it was almost egg weggs for tea. I *look forward* to June. Be happy, dearest mine,

 Tig

 [Pension du Lac,
 Sierre]
Monday night, [23 May 1921]

Dearest Bogey darling,

 I have been trying to write out a long explanation of the reasons why I have felt out of touch with you. But I don't think such explanations are of the smallest good. If you were here I could tell you what I felt in a minute – but at a distance it's different – I don't think it's good.

 Do you know, darling what I think Love is? It is drawing out all that is noblest and finest in the soul of the other. Perhaps the other isn't conscious this is what is happening & yet he feels at peace – and that is why. That is I think, the *relationship* between lovers, and it is in this way that, because they give each other their freedom (for evil is slavery) they 'ought' (not in the moral sense) to *serve* each other. By service I mean what Chaucer means when he makes his true Knights wonder what they can do that will give joy to their love. (But the lady must, of course, serve equally.) And of course I do not mean anything in the least 'superficial'. Indeed I mean just what there was between us in the last months at the Isola Bella – that – and more perfect.

You ask me how I am, darling. I am much the same. This chill has been the worst I have ever had since I was ill, and so I feel weak and rather shadowy – physically. My heart is the trouble. But otherwise I feel ... well, Bogey, it's difficult to say. No, one can't believe in *God*. But I must believe in something more *nearly* than I do. As I was lying here today I suddenly remembered that: 'O ye of little faith!' Not faith in a God. No, that's impossible. But do I live as though I believed in *anything*? Don't I live *in glimpses* only? There is something wrong there is something small in such a life. One must live more fully and one must have more POWER of loving and feeling – One must be true to one's vision of life – in every single particular – And I am not. The only thing to do is to try again from tonight to be stronger and better – to be *whole*.

That's *how I am*, dear Love. Goodnight.

> Tig

[Stanford House],
Oxford
[23 May 1921]
Monday

My darling,

I am returning to London to-morrow morning for 3 days – coming back here on Friday, May 27, staying the night, then going (provisionally) to Sydney Waterlow's for the week-end. Here again on Monday, May 30 and leaving the same afternoon for London. There I stay May 31, June 1, June 2. Return Oxford Friday June 3, stay the night with Walter Raleigh, stay the night of June 4 with Hardy, return London June 5, Broomies June 7, start for Clarens June 8 or 9. These are my final arrangements. I thought you would like to know them.

Last night I dined in College with Walter Raleigh. He is, as his reputation goes – a good talker. Beside him I made a very silent Boge. However, it was quite enjoyable and we didn't quarrel. Perhaps even we got on fairly well.

You ask me in the last card I had from you – *ever* so long ago – am I happy? I reply, quite simply, only in thinking of you. I don't say I'm miserable here. The weather has been divine of late; but I feel a kind of malaise, compounded of many elements: the biggest is separation from you, which becomes more oppressive the longer it lasts: next comes the sense of not quite fitting my milieu: and after that the nervous strain of lecturing to an audience that – I am sure – doesn't really understand what I am driving at at all.

I'm afraid the truth is that you & I have carried our thoughts in literature ever so much farther than any of our contemporaries. It's not to be wondered at that I'm not particularly intelligible, I suppose. And at any rate the lectures will be a succès d'estime anyhow.

Goodbye, darling.

        Boge.

                                  [Hotel Beau Site,
                                    Baugy]
Monday   [23 May 1921]

My darling,

I feel certain this letter from father contains that Blow I am always expecting. Will you open it & read it & *wire* me the result? That sounds extravagent but you know the feeling? I've got it v. strong this morning. Perhaps I ought to cable Pa. I don't know. I suppose *you* couldn't write a line just to report? To say what old Stephani said

① There is still hope

provided I have no more fever *and*

provided I can get strong enough to stand treatment.

These are the unblushing facts.

I haven't heard from you today yet I expect I'll hear by the afternoon post. Don't know what it is Bogey but

I have never loved you as I love you now. This must be our Indian summer I think.

I send you my love. It is safe with you, you will send it back to me. I know it won't be lost. Keep it, dearest dearest heart

        Tig

Don't spare me any of Pa's letter. I can hear anything from you.

[2 Acris Street,
London]
[2 June 1921]
Thursday – Morning.

My darling,

I'm just going off to see about my passport. Sydney Waterlow has given me a letter which should make things fairly easy. If there's any time left to-day I shall try to do some shopping. Then to-morrow comes my last lecture, and I believe I am staying the night at Oxford with Raleigh. On Monday I shall finish up the shopping – on Tuesday go to Broomies: and I hope to start for Clarens on to-day week Thursday.

As soon as your cheque is cleared & the arrangement for cashing cheques in Switzerland completed, I should write to Kay and tell him what you think of him for sending your pass-book (or a copy of it) to your Father. It's an absolute breach not only of ordinary decency, but of the law. I asked the manager of Barclay's about it, and he said that if you wanted to you could bring an action for breach of contract against Kay. It makes me furious.

But I shouldn't worry about any possible effect on your father. He can't possibly cut off your allowance because you have a substantial balance: what on earth would you do without a substantial balance? Really, Wig, I think you're much too frightened of what your Father may do. I am perfectly certain he would never dream of cutting off your allowance for such a cause.

One other thing. If you find my letters scrappy and unsatisfactory, just think that I hardly ever have a moment's calm in which to write. Getting things done is a terrible curse to me at all times, but now with the coal-strike on and the trains & buses & tubes working at half-pressure, it's an awful business getting from one part of London to another. What used to take half an hour takes an hour – and so, it becomes a continual rush. The whole space between lunch-time and dinner is taken up with doing two things – then come these infernal journeys to Oxford – and a whole day goes in a mouthful. I toil after parting Time in vain. It's a silly, wearing life.

However, my oasis of calm is getting very near now. I feel that I shall come like Tartarin of Tarascon with my collapsible bath hung round my neck with a string. I have also bought a knickerbocker suit (quite nice & cheap) which will to some extent solve the problem of clothes. English knickerbockers – not Swiss ones – with bare knees.

But I feel you are worrying terribly about this money business. Don't darling: I'm absolutely convinced there's no cause for alarm – none at all.

Goodbye, you precious darling. Don't say you're out of touch with me. Then I feel you are that little girl who used to walk home from school to Karori in the ditch. You are completely hidden in the dock-leaves – I can't see you anywhere. I have to call: Wig – Wig! where are you?

Boge.

February 1922

In June 1921 Murry rejoined Katherine in Switzerland and they moved into the Chalet des Sapins at Montana. The months between June and December 1921, when they lived and worked together amid the peace and beauty of the Swiss alps, proved to be Katherine Mansfield's most productive. Here she wrote some of her most famous New Zealand stories and arranged for the publication of the book that firmly established her literary reputation, *The Garden Party and other Stories*.

This fruitful way of life was disrupted in January 1922. Influenced by the book *Cosmic Anatomy* and by reports of a cure for tuberculosis, Katherine sought out Dr Manoukhine in Paris. Her exchange of letters with Murry in February 1922 charts her last, desperate attempt to halt the disease that was killing her. After some initial indecision, Murry again packed up and followed Katherine, sharing hotel life with her in Paris until the first phase of her treatment ended in June.

[Victoria Palace Hotel,
Paris]
[1 February 1922]
Tuesday

Dearest,
I went to see M[anoukhine] tonight. I found him a tall formal rather dry man (not in the least an 'enthusiast') who speaks scarcely any French and has a lame Russian girl for his interpreter.

He read Bouchage's report & I brought him up to date. He then very thoroughly examined me and reported as follows:

I can promise to cure you – to make you as though you had never had this disease.

You have T.B. in the second degree – the right apex very lightly

349

engaged. All the left is full of rales (as usual).

It will take 15 séances – then a period of repose preferably in the mountains for 2–3–4 months just as you like. Then 10 more.

After the 15 you will feel *perfectly well*. The last 10 are to prevent any chance of recurrence. Fees as he stated.

I then explained our 'situation', exactly – what we wished to do, what would be more convenient in every sense, financially & otherwise. He said as follows:

It would be very much better for you to start now. Your condition is favourable. To begin now, to leave Paris in the 2nd week in May, to return in – even September if you liked for the last séances.

I do not insist on your beginning now. I do not say you will be greatly harmed by waiting.

I do say it is much better not to wait & especially as you have taken a journey not to take another or to have the re-effort of the altitude, again. Nothing is worse than travelling. He insisted on that and the great advantage in beginning now. At the same time he said of course he cannot really say anything if we prefer to wait until April. He asked me to write all this to you and to give the answer as soon as possible. His secretary told me that he had treated 8000 cases in Moscow, that here in Paris patients in the 3rd & 4th degree – far far worse than I – were now as well as possible. She also said of course do not wait. And especially they kept on speaking of the double journey again. I then left.

What do you think? Will you give me your opinion. The truth is it was a mistake that we did not see him together. It would have been far better. All my inclinations are to come back, not to 'upset' our life. All my wishes are for that. At the same time I must first put it all to you impartially. I said suppose I go for February & come back at the end of March. He said then you must be in Paris in June & July which is *not* good. It is very puzzling. The best thing of course would be for you to see him. But that's no good. Supposing you think I *ought* to take the treatment now I can of course send Ida back for as long as necessary. It is possible we might be able to sub let.

My desire is not to stay. Why? Because of our life. I feel I cannot break it again. I fear for it. If it were possible for you to come 3rd perhaps & just stay a couple of days. Is that a foolish idea? Consider well! Please darling think of this calmly. There is no hurry. I never felt less excited in my life. What do you think, my little King of Hearts? Shall I come *bang* back at the end of my fortnight? That is what I want to do. If I am leaving you to decide something hard, then just give me your 'advice'. But don't forget that above all I love you

Tig

Next day early.

I am going to send Ida out with this at once. I feel this morning perhaps we forget a little what a difference it's bound to make to us both if I was well. It would make our lives very wonderful. And to wait for that longer than we have waited is perhaps foolish. Two things remain. His opinion that I would do far better to start the treatment now – his remark that he did not insist on my starting before April.

Of course were I alone I should begin at once. But I am not alone and my life with you is nearly the whole of life. It is so precious that to endanger it by making you unhappy is – I find – equal to. endangering my own life. Remember Ida can do all that is necessary at Montana. And should you decide to come just tell Ernestine simply and leave stamped addressed envelopes with her for the post and some money for her food.

I have learnt my dear love that if we act calmly and do not forget our *aim* … it's not so hard. That's why I don't wire, or feel even excited. I refuse to. We must be superior to these things.

Forgive me if I am worrying you – my heart's dearest.

Chalet des Sapins,
Montana-sur-Sierre
Valais

Thursday Afternoon, [2 February 1922]

My darling,

I wired to you as soon as I got your letter. It seems to me that there aren't two choices, really. You must do what M. says, begin the treatment now, come back here for the summer in May and go back and finish the treatment in September. Quite honestly, I think it would be criminal for you to come back now. And we shouldn't really gain anything to set off the obvious loss. I can't see how we should be really happy while we were both thinking: She might be being cured now. The thing is as plain as a pikestaff in my mind as regards you. And what terrific news it js! And surely it's an omen that by the same post came this letter from Pinker saying Cassells have bought 'A Cup of Tea' for ten guineas and that's exactly the kind of story they want. Ever since you started for Manoukhin your luck seems really to have begun at last. That's how I feel.

Now there's the question of me – quite a minor affair really; but I want to keep my head about it. What I feel is – I want to stay here. If I come and try to live in a hotel in Paris, I shan't really be able to work. I can't have my books and I shan't be able to settle down to the regular grind of my novel. This place suits me, dead quiet & all. I've got masses of work to do and I want to get it done. Moreover, we've paid the rent here.

But I don't feel anything very definite about it. If you have a better idea don't hesitate. But if you think mine is the best, tell me. What I should then propose is that in about a week's time I should come 3rd. class to Paris, talk things over, & stay with you while Ida comes back here and gets all the things you are sure to want. Then I should come back and stay here the three months, and return to fetch you when the treatment is over. Then, perhaps, we would take the Oiseau Bleu for 4 months and then I would come back & stay with you in Paris in the autumn. I should have the bulk of my year's work done then. It would only be a matter of weekly articles.

I hope, darling, you won't think this very cold & calculating. But I feel that if I don't work now, I never shall; and that if I don't break the back of my year's work, it will drag on & on.

But as I say I'm not so much in love with my own idea that I can't believe in a better one.

Anyhow, speak to me as frankly as I have spoken to you. I mean, if you would rather I stayed in Paris now, say so straight out. Don't in any case let L.M. come back until I arrive in Paris. After all, there's not the faintest hurry to settle things here, and you have enough things for a fortnight. The main point – that you should stay & have the treatment now is quite clear. After all, this other thing is a flea-bite beside it.

> Your loving
> Boge

I shan't move from here, anyhow, till I get an answer to this letter. So please in reply quote Ref. No. Letter X.

> You are a darling:
> And it's plain

              You're beginning to be
              A great success.

I corrected the proof of 'The Garden Party' & sent it straight back
to Pinker; it was cleverly divided into 3 instalments.

                              [Victoria Palace Hotel,
                                    Paris]
                              [2 February 1922]
                                  Wednesday

My precious,
    I rested all day, but after sending your letter I wrote one to
Manoukhine, saying that before I decided anything I would like to
know all there was to know about this treatment, whether one ran
any risks, what its effects were on the heart, and so on. I told him
that I was very much in the dark, that I could not afford an
experiment; and in a word that I would be obliged if he would let
me see his French partner & talk it all over. His reply was to ask me
to meet them both at 5 o'clock at their cabinet médicale. So we took
a taxi and I went. The general impression was good – all in the
highest degree simple, scientific, professional, unlike anything I
have seen before. Manoukhin came & took me into Donat. He (D)
is an elderly man, rather like Anatole France in style, wearing a
white coat and skull cap. Quite unaffected, and *very* clever, I should
imagine. I told them my difficulties. It was a little bit awkward,
especially as Donat has evidently a great regard and admiration for
M. But there you were. This matter is serious & past pretending.
And they were awfully kind. Donat delivered an absolute lecture;
they drew diagrams, described the process, told me of its effects and
so on. There is no *risk*. It is, as you know, the application of X-rays
to the spleen. It produces a change of blood. It is a kind of
immensely *concentrated* sun action. What the sun does vaguely and
in a dissipated way this gently forces. He discovered it while
working at typhus & cholera and applied it to tuberculosis. Donat
spoke of it always as my 'colleague's discovery'. 'Dr. M. has taught
us ...' 'Doctor M. then experimented on so many animals and so on
and found such and such results.' The whole thing is *new*. That I
realised keenly. It is the latest thing in science. That was what one
felt. At the same time there was a very good responsible atmosphere
at this place. One felt in the presence of real *scientists* – not doctors.
And Donat never says a fantastic word. He is dead straight: one

does feel that. It's what I always imagined a Pasteur institute to be. Donat agreed I could be cured. He has healed an Englishman in the 3rd degree who after 12 applications has no more bacillus at all in his sputum.... He asked me about Montana. He & Manoukhine said that if I had been anywhere really healthy & led a quiet life free from worries I would have had the same amount of benefit. But in their united opinion Montana was too high for my heart in its present state. If I stayed absolutely still in bed there – *bien* – but to make a continual effort of that kind is not and cannot be good. One is living on *l'energie nerveuse.* He ended by saying, 'It is easy to see you are not a little ill. You have been ill for a long time. One has not an endless supply of force. You ought to get well. L'air de Paris et les rayons de docteur Manoukhine will make you well. Of that I am confident.' I then came away.

I am glad I saw this man as well as the other. But isn't it strange. Now all this is held out to me – now all is at last *hope*, real *hope* there is not a throb of gladness in my heart. I can think of nothing but how it will affect 'us'.

Dear love, don't worry about me though. The food in this hotel is excellent. I have such a nice airy room with a comfortable chair. It could not be better in all those ways and I rest, I take my evening meal in bed.

In all things though you are my first thought – you know it. Remember Ida asks for nothing but to manage everything for us – and at all times.

Your own Wig

[Victoria Palace Hotel,
Paris]
[4 February, 1922]
Friday

My precious Bogey,

Your telegram came yesterday as a complete surprise – a very very marvellous one – a kind of miracle. I shall never forget it. I read it, scrunched it up, then carefully unscrunched it and put it away 'for keeps'. It was a very wonderful thing to receive. I agree absolutely it is best that I start now & I telephoned the same moment to M. whose sole reply was: 'Deux heures'. (But before I speak of my time there I want to say your two letters my dear one are simply such perfect letters that one *feeds* on them! I **don't** know.

You have become such a wonderful person – well, you always were – but the beams are so awfully plain now – *on se chauffe* at every word you write. And there is a kind of calmness which I feel too. Indeed, I feel we are so changed since the days before Montana – different people. I do feel that I belong to you, that we live in our own world. This world simply passes by – it says nothing. I do not like it but that's no matter. It is not for long. do you realise that if the miracle happens we May Go to England This Summer Together? That's just an idear of what the future holds. May it make you a hundredth part as happy as it makes me!)

I went to the clinique today and there the French doctor with Manoukhine went over the battlefield – Really it was the first time I have ever been 'examined'. They agreed absolutely after a very prolonged examination that I had *no* cavities. *Absolument pas de cavernes*. They tested & tested my lungs & always said the same. This means I am *absolutely curable*. My heart, rheumatism, everything was gone into and into & finally I passed into another room & had a séance.

I want to ask you something. Do you really believe all this? There is something that pulls me back the whole time and which won't let me believe. I hear, I see. I feel a great confidence in Manoukhine – very great and yet.... I am absolutely divided. You know how, to do anything well, even to make a little jump, one must gather oneself together. Well, I am not gathered together. A dark secret unbelief holds me back. I see myself after 15 goes apologising to them for being not cured, so to speak. This is very bad. You realise I am in the mood now when I confess to you because I want to tell you my bad self – But it may be it's not me. For what is bad in me (i.e. to doubt) is not bad in you. It's your nature – If you do feel it, please tell me – please try and change – Try and believe – I know Manoukhine believes. I was sitting in the waiting room reading Eckermann when he came in, quickly, simply and took my hand and said 'Vous avez décidé de commencer. C'est très bien. Bonne santé!' But this was said beautifully, *gently*, (Oh, Boge, I do love *gentleness*!).... Now I have told you this I will get over it. It has been a marvellous day here, very soft, sunny and windy, with women selling les violettes de Parme in the streets. But I could not live in a city ever again. That's done, that's finished with. I read Shakespeare (I am with you as I read) and I am half way through a new story. I long for your letter which follows mine. Oh, those precious birds at the coconut. How I see and hear them! And it's fig pudding. You write the word 'fig' in such a nice way that all your precious darling self walks in the word. Goodbye for now, my blessed one. I feel a bit mysterious, full of blue rays, like a deep sea fishchik.

> YOUR
> Wig

> Chalet des Sapins,
> Montana-sur-Sierre
> Valais
> [5 February 1922]

Sunday morning,

No letter came yesterday; but then all that did come was this p.c. from Brett and a letter of acknowledgement from my bank. I couldn't tell whether it was a real post or not. However, the snow has stopped snowing, and this morning there's actually some sun. In the last 3 days at least 1½ times as much snow as there was when you left has fallen; and I don't want to see any more. Neither does Wingley. He was very miserable about it; but he came into my bed early this morning and that cheered him up. He's still there.

I haven't said anything about Manoukhin's promise that he can cure you absolutely – simply because I'm afraid to. Life & the world would be so different, so marvellous, that I just have to put it out of my mind. That's all.

And I don't know at all about this plan of mine for staying here. It's all right when I'm immersed in work and there's a grain of sun. But when it snows and snows, and one can't get out, and there's nothing to do but glue one's nose onto the window pane and watch the incessant fall – it's not so pleasant. For the life of me I don't really know what's best. I do want to break the back of this novel; I do want to get some articles done. But at the same time just as sincerely I want to be with you if I'm any help – even if it's only as a cribbage partner. So I rely on you to tell me faithfully what your mind is. I'm going down to Elizabeth's to tea this afternoon and taking Shaw Page with me as I once promised

I hope I get a letter from you at the P.O. this morning. I haven't had one since Thursday.

> Your loving
> Boge.

In reply to your telegram.   [Victoria Palace Hotel,
                                     Paris]
                                  [8 February, 1922]
                                     Wednesday

My darling Bogey,
    I do not 'understand' why you have sent this telegram, so my
reply is rather in the dark. Still, I must send it. Please do not come
here to me. That is what I wish to say, and I say it deliberately. It is
not *easy* to write so to you. I will try and explain my reasons. I want
you to have your freedom as an artist. You asked for it at Menton. I
thought it was a mistake – that you did not mean it and only wrote
under influence. But then after I left Montana you asked for it
again. You were willing to join me *if I wanted you* – you were
prepared, like a shot, *to be of help to me.* (But that is exactly like
saying to a person if you want to borrow money – borrow from me
– or Father's telling me I could count on him up to £50 if the
necessity arose. It is not the gesture of people who deeply
understand each other.) On the other hand your own personal
feeling was not that at this most critical of all the moments in her
life I could not leave Wig. Golly – no! It was my work – May would
be too late – my novel – and so on. Reverse the positions, darling.
Hear me saying that to you!
    It is no good. I now know that I must grow a shell away from
you. I want – I 'ask' for my independence. At any moment in the
future you may suddenly leave me in the lurch if it pleases you. It is
a part of your nature. I thought that it was almost the condition of
your working that we were together. Not a bit of it! Well, darling
Boge, for various reasons I can't accept this. And now that I am
making a bid for health – my *final bid* – I want to grow strong in
another way, too. Ida is leaving here on Saturday. She will be with
you on Sunday. Tell her what you want her to do, if you intend
leaving Switzerland. And write to me about everything.
    But my very soul rebels against when it's fine you prefer your
work & your work is more urgent than this affair in Paris has been.
When it snows you might as well be playing cribbage with me! And
also that remark 'Moreover the rent is paid here!'
    No, darling, *please.* Let me be alone here. This queer strain in
you does not, for some extraordinary reason in the very least atom
lessen my love for you. I'd rather not discuss it. Let it be! And I
must work now until May. These 'affairs' are 1000 times more
disturbing than 1000 train journeys. Pax, darling. You will see Ida

on Sunday – But for the last time I ask you not to join me. I cannot see you until May.

Your loving
Wig

Please just accept this. It's awfully hard having '*it*' to fight as well as my other *not* dear Bogies!

Later.

Dearest Bogey,

I have just opened my letter to say your Sunday & Monday ones have come – about the snow, about Elizabeth, about your staying there. If the weather is fine by now I daresay your doubts will have taken wings, too. But for my part – I would rather stay here alone. I have seen the worst of it by myself i.e. going alone to Manoukhin, having no one to talk it over and so on. I want now intensely to be alone until May. Then IF I am better, we can talk things over and if I am not I shall make some other arrangement. There's no need to look ahead. But that is my very *calm collected* feeling. So if you do want to leave the chalet before May – let us still be independent of each other till then – shall we?

I hope that horrible weather is over. Don't we get dreadfully few letters! I am going to see a little flat tomorrow which I hope will be suitable. Here – I can't stay longer than necessary.

Your loving
Wig

P.S. We haven't read *The Schoolmaster*. Have we? Are you certing? Don't send the *D.N.* about Bibesco.

Chalet des Sapins,
Montana-sur-Sierre
Valais

Wednesday.   [8 February 1922]

My darling,

You are an upsetting soul. After I spent all the morning writing & posting letters with my new address, & tidying up, & the afternoon in going to Chalet Soleil to get E. to cash a cheque, the same old telegram awaits me on my return. I almost expected it; it's come so often before.

Well, I am coming, simply *because I don't want to stay here*, darling. But just as I'd arranged things comfortably so that I could get off on Friday to have your wire telling me Ida is arriving on Saturday is confusing, above all as I particularly asked you not to send L.M. before I came. I don't quite know what to do – whether to wait till she comes or start off on Friday as I had arranged. The only thing to do is to telegraph again, which I'll do first thing to-morrow morning.

But what I do want to make quite clear is that I have, of my own free will and in my right mind, calm as ever I hope to be, decided to come to Paris till your fifteen séances are over. I suppose you 'beg me not to come' because you imagine that I am doing something I don't want to do myself, for your sake. Well, I'm not. I have realised that I shall be intensely miserable here by myself so far from you, that I shan't be able to work, and as I explained that my first burst of feeling that I could be a hermit doing 8 hours a day was simply due to the fact that I hadn't yet realised that you were gone. That sounds mysterious, but I've noticed it many times before it takes me 3 or 4 days to get the full flavour of your absence.

All the same, I wish you hadn't sent that wire. I was trundling along so nicely: and now I'm suspended again. However, I recognise that the original fault was my own. I miscalculated my own feelings – not for the first time. However, that's enough of that.

To-day was the first fine day we've had since the Monday when you left. E. (i.e. Elizabeth, not Ernestine) has never been out of the house since.

Boge.

There's not much love in this letter, but there's plenty in my heart.

[Chalet des Sapins,
Montana-sur-Sierre]
Thursday evening February 9 1922.

My darling Worm,
I must write to you though the letter will never be posted. Your express letter has just arrived in answer to my telegram. I must somehow kill the time by thinking that I am near you.
I deserve the letter. It's the most awful one you've ever sent me.

I deserve the letter. I mean my action deserves the letter. But my soul doesn't. Darling, I'm a difficult person. I don't understand myself. I don't know myself. You know me better than I do, probably. But I'll try to explain.

I hadn't prepared myself at all for the possibility of your staying there. Subconsciously, I shirked it. When I knew you were going to stay there, I instinctively shirked it again – the change, the uprooting. And I was able to, simply because your presence was in the house with me. We weren't apart. (There's an enormous difference, darling, in feeling between the one who stays and the one who goes. The one who stays is in a familiar place – everything here told me of your presence.) The day after I sent that letter, I knew it was all wrong. It was meant to be true: it wasn't put up. But that was just because I wasn't yet free to feel your absence. The next day I knew it was impossible for us to be apart. I began to be anxious every hour of the day: I had lost my mate.

Don't say I was 'claiming my freedom as an artist' – such an idea never entered into my head. If you think that, you've got it all wrong. I wasn't claiming any freedom; I don't want, never have for a year now even dreamed of wanting 'freedom'. I was just shirking, shrinking from being uprooted. That was bad enough, I know; but it's better at any rate than claiming 'freedom as an artist'. If I pleaded my novel, I pleaded it (unconsciously) only as an excuse for my shrinking. As a matter of fact, it took me exactly four days to realise that I *couldn't work at all* without your presence. I worked just so long as your presence remained, not a moment longer.

I hate defending myself to you, my darling. I feel I'm not worth it; you're a so much finer being than I am. But yet I want you to know the truth about me. I'm not bad. I do believe in the last year most of the badness has gone out of me, and that I am in most ways your worthy Boge. But one thing, instead of growing better, grows worse & worse. I am more and more frightened of the world: more terrified of moving: of venturing a finger into the cogs. The last four years have taken away what little courage I had – and I never had any. That is a ghastly confession to make for a man who is well, to his wife who is ill. I am utterly ashamed. But what can I do? I fight against it. But when the moment comes I'm just petrified with fear. I *can't* move.

And I forsake you. It's terrible; it's even more terrible that I somehow deceive myself. If you had said to me, as you very nearly did, 'Bogey, why don't you come *with me* to Paris?' the only answer I could have made, if I'd been honest, was: 'I'm *afraid, afraid*'.

Well, I've confessed – there's nothing else to confess. It's my very soul. It's fear makes me a miser even. I'm terrified of what may happen.

There's only one thing greater than my fear – that is my love. My love will always conquer my fear – but it can't do it immediately. It needs the full force of my love to do it and it takes days for that to emerge out of its dark hiding places. And in these days you have despaired of me again.

Wig precious, I shall never write anything truer of myself than this. Don't lose faith in me; I couldn't live unless you believed in me. But remember my fear – help me to fight it.

    Your
    Boge.

August 1922–January 1923

The X-ray treatment of Dr Manoukhine wrought no miracle. By June 1922, when she left Paris with Murry for Sierre, Katherine's reserves of energy as well as money were depleted. Once more sickness took its toll of her relationships as well as of her body: Murry stayed alone at Randogne, while Katherine and L.M. went to the Hôtel Chateau Belle Vue in Sierre. In August all three made the return journey to London.

Sadly, the shared life of Katherine Mansfield and the man who had been her companion for the last ten years, in letters if not in person, had, in effect, ended. She stayed with Dorothy Brett in Hampstead while Murry, unable to support her enthusiasm for the semi-mystical teachings of Ouspensky, lived elsewhere. In September he joined his friend, Vivian Locke Ellis, at East Grinstead. A month later Katherine returned to Paris. Instead of resuming her treatment with Dr Manoukhine, however, she sought out Gurdjieff, the mentor of Ouspensky, at Fontainebleau.

On 16 October 1922, to the last courting new impressions, testing new ideas, Katherine Mansfield made her brave pilgrimage to Gurdjieff's Institute for the Harmonious Development of Man at Fontainebleau. Only four of Murry's letters between October 1922 and January 1923 remain. Katherine's to him, however, document the remarkable spiritual resilience with which she adapted to a dramatically different way of living as well as to the imminence of death. It is a testimony to their continuing love, 'in spite of all', that on New Year's Eve Katherine summoned Murry to her side one final time. A joyful reunion took place at Fontainebleau on 9 January 1923, and that night she died.

[Hôtel Chateau Belle Vue,
Sierre]
7 August 1922

Dearest Bogey
   I have been on the point of writing this letter for days. My heart
has been behaving in such a curious fashion that I can't imagine it
means nothing. So, as I should hate to leave you unprepared, I'll
just try & jot down what comes into my mind. All my manuscripts I
leave entirely to you to do what you like with. Go through them
one day, dear love, and destroy all you do not use. Please destroy all
letters you do not wish to keep & all papers. You know my love of
tidiness. Have a clean sweep, Bogey, and leave all fair – will you?
   Books are yours of course, & so are my personal possessions.
L.M. had better distribute my clothes. Give your Mother my fur
coat, will you? Chaddie & Jeanne must choose what they want. I
suppose Vera would like something. My small pearl ring – the
'daisy' one – I should like to wear – The other – give to Richard's
love when you know her – if you approve of the idea. I seem, after
all, to have nothing to leave and nobody to leave things to. De la
Mare I should like to remember and Richard. But you will give a
book or some small thing to who ever wishes ... Monies, of course,
are all yours. In fact, my dearest dear, I leave everything to you – to
the secret you whose lips I kissed this morning. In spite of
everything – how happy we have been. I feel no other lovers have
walked the earth together more joyfully – in spite of all.

Farewell – my precious love.
I am for ever and ever
Your
Wig.

[6 Pond Street,
Hampstead]
[20 September, 1922]
Wednesday

My dear Bogey,
   There seems to me little doubt that the wave of mysticism
prophesied by Dunning is upon us. Don't read these words other
than calmly! But after yesterday to read that little leader in *The
Times* this morning was quite a shock. We had a most interesting

after-lunch talk at Beresford's. Orage gave a short exposition of his ideas and we asked him questions and made objections. It seemed strange to be talking of those dark matters (with passionate interest) in a big sunny room with trees waving and London 1922 outside the windows. Ask Sullivan about it when you see him in the country. He liked Orage and he found a very great similarity between his ideas and Dunning's. In fact, the more we talked, the more apparent the resemblance. This pleased me for I felt that you would accept what Dunning believed and like that you and I would find ourselves interested equally in these things.

I came back & found Richard here. He had tea and we had a most *terrific* talk. Nice is not the word for your little brother. Richard does believe it is possible to 'imagine' an artist a much more complete being than he has been up till now – not that exactly. But more *conscious of his purpose*. But if I try to reproduce his youthful conversation I shall antagonise you. For I can't put in all the asides and all the implications. Sullivan came back for supper & he & I talked of all these ideas afterwards. It was, as he said, a 'simply stunning evening'. I do hope you see Sullivan for a longish time and that you see Dunning, too. Is this interference. It's hard not to interfere to the extent of wishing you found life as wonderful as it seems to me. Even the least idea – the fringe of the idea – of 'waking up' discovers a new world. And the mystery is that 'all' of us, in our unlikeness and individual ways, do seem to me to be moving towards the very same goal. Dear dear Bogey, I hope I don't sound like Mrs. Jellaby.

Give my dear love to Selsfield – to the stairs especially and the chimney room and oh dear! the late light coming in at the small window by the fireplace – *all* the garden. I love Selsfield.

I had a card from Lawrence today – just the one word 'Ricordi' – How like him. I was glad to get it though. Schiff continues his epistolary bombardment. I refuse to reply any more. He is a silly old man.

Do you want anything sent? anything bought? Command me; I'll command Ida. It's a warm still day with a huge spider looking in at my windy pane – Spider weather –

Greet Locke-Ellis for me. Accept my love

Yours Wig

Saturday

Dearest Bogey

I'm so glad to hear from you. Our goodbye reminded *me* of the goodbye of a brother and sister who aren't each other's favourites ... But it didn't matter a little bit.

L.M. has been to Pope's. I'll tell her about Turner's Hill in case she cares to telephone.

I don't think I can come to S[elsfield] until my treatment here is over. I regret, very much, missing autumn that I love so. But at the same time I am happy in London just now. Not because of people but because of 'ideas'. At last I begin to understand the meaning of 'Seek and ye shall find.' It sounds simple enough, but one seems to do anything *but* seek ... However, that sounds a little too airnest for a letter.

Darling, I'm too shy to write proposing myself to Will Rothenstein. If you care to send him a card saying I'm agreeable I'd be pleased to be in a book. But wouldn't that be the best way to do it? Richard came yesterday and did a drawing. It was extremely well done. He's been to the Aeolian Hall and chosen rolls for the pianola. So this little house sighs like a shell with Beethoven.

Ah, Bogey, I had such a sad letter today from Roma Webster. Goodbye Arco. She is afraid there will be no Arco for her. And goodbye Paris and the Manoukhin treatment. It cannot be for her. 'Every day I am getting worse.' Brave noble little soul shining behind those dark, lighted eyes! She has wanted so much, she has had so little! She wants so terribly just to be allowed to warm herself – to have a place at the fire. But she's not allowed. She's shut out. She must drive on into the dark. Why? Why can't I go to Rome? I should like to start for Rome today just to kiss her hands and lay my head on her pillow –

It is so terrible to be alone – Outside my window there are leaves falling. Here, in two days, it is autumn. Not late autumn but bright gold everywhere. Are the sunflowers out at the bottom of the vegetable garden? There are quantities of small Japanese sunflowers, too, aren't there? It's a mystery, Bogey, why the earth is so lovely.

God bless you
Wig

Later. Richard has just been in again to finish his drawing. Then we went downstairs and he played. But what am I telling you? Nothing! Yet much much happened. Don't you think it's queer how we have to talk 'little language' – to make one word clothe feed, and start in life one small thought.

[6 Pond Street,
Hampstead]
[27 September, 1922]

Dearest Bogey

I have changed my plans and am going to Paris on Monday for the treatment i.e. for 8–10 weeks. I am not a little bit satisfied with the purely experimental manner of it here – And as I realise more than ever these last foggy days how dreadful it would be, to go back and not go forward I would endure any hotel – any Paris surroundings for the sake of Manoukhin himself. I'm sure you'll understand. You see Webster is simply a radiologist. He doesn't examine one, or weigh one or watch the case as they did at the clinic. Everything was different. It's quite natural – he knows nothing. He is experimenting. And I don't feel I'm in the mood for experiments.

If I leave on Monday I'll get another treatment next Wednesday at 3 Rue Lyautey.

I shall leave my rooms here just as they are. If Brett cares to let them furnished – she may. I shall be only too pleased. But no harm will come to them. And in the spring when I am at Selsfield it will be nice to have them. (That's not sincere. Ugh! how I hate London and all its works! Perhaps I shan't then, though.) But there it is. It couldn't be helped. I suppose I was too quick. At any rate no harm has been done yet. I shall have to count on making money in Paris. I have over £80 in the bank. Money does not worry me. I'll go to the Victoria Palace for the first week or so, and Ida has a famous list of hotels. She will find another and a better one I hope, then – somewhere more *cosy*. It's a little pity you can't take these rooms and let your flat. They are so fearfully nice & self-contained, with hot baths, attendance, food, telephone and so on. Brett is a very good creature, too. This won't alter anything will it? It only means that instead of being in London I shall be in Paris. I really have a very great belief in Manoukhin. So have you, I know. Do you care to come up for Sunday night – say? There is no need to. Phone me if you don't, dear Bogey and write me anything you would like done before I go. I'm seeing Orage Saturday or Sunday evening but otherwise I am free. I don't expect you to come and don't even recommend the suggestion. It's so unsettling just as you are I hope beginning to settle down. I think I'd better say – it's fairer – that I am engaged on Saturday from 8 to 10.30 and on Sunday from 8 to 10.30 – even though the engagement is only provisional. All the rest of the time I am free.

Ever Wig

<table>
<tr><td></td><td>Select Hôtel</td></tr>
<tr><td></td><td>Place de la Sorbonne</td></tr>
<tr><td></td><td>Paris</td></tr>
<tr><td>Tuesday. 11.30 A.M.</td><td>[3 October 1922]</td></tr>
</table>

Dearest Bogey

After great grief and pain we have at last found a hotel. Ida has gone off for the bagage registré and I'm in one of those gaps, looking before and after, in a room that's not ready with luggage half unpacked ... You know? It's not bad, though – rather nice, in fact. My room is so pleasant after *all* the rooms I saw yesterday night! I even went back to the Victor-Pal[ace] and had a glimpse of the 'uncles', still there, and the Mlle at the Bureau – toujours la même camisole. Happily, it, too was full. It was a glorious soft brilliant night – very warm. Only man was vile ... This hotel is the one I stayed at during the war. My room is on the 6ième rather small and low but very possible. Shabby, but it gets the sun. Outside the window there's the Sorbonne roofs with tall grave signors in marble peignoirs holding up a finger. Also a coy, rather silly looking eagle poised over a plaque call Géologie.

I think you'd find a change in Paris even since we were here. The lower orders are much more disagreeable – down right horrid, in fact. One has to fight with them for everything, even the right of sitting in their taxis. There's a queer feeling that the war has come back. Even waiting in the Victoria Palace last night I noticed an immense advance in de-civilisation in the faces. I don't think it's just fancy.

Yesterday at Calais reminded me so of our first voyage to France together. It was so hot and the train didn't go. Outside the windows old women held up baskets of pears. The sun was positively fiery.

Oh, I meant to suggest to you to ask for Yeats's *Memoirs* to review. I think they are coming out this autumn. I believe you would find them very interesting. He's not a 'sympathetic' person, as far as I know but he's one of those men who reflect their time. Such men have a fascination for me. Haven't they for you? I wish we lived nearer to each other. I should like to talk more to you. But there is time. When this jungle of circumstances is cleared a little we shall be freer to enjoy each other. It is not the moment now. Tell me what you can about yourself. Not even you could wish for your happiness more than I do. Don't forget that dragons are only guardians of treasures and one fights them for what they keep – not for themselves.

Goodbye darling Bogey. I hope to see Manoukhin tomorrow. I'll tell you what he says. Ever yours lovingly

Wig

[Select Hôtel,
Paris]
[4 October, 1922]
Wednesday

Dearest Bogey,

I don't *feel* influenced by Ouspensky or Dunning. I merely feel I've heard ideas like my ideas, but bigger ones, far more definite ones. And that there really is Hope – real Hope – not half-Hope .... As for Tchehov being damned – why should he be? Can't you rope Tchehov in? I can. He's much nearer to me than he used to be.

It's nice to hear of Richard sawing off his table-legs and being moved by the greengrocer. Why is it greengrocers have such a passion for bedding people out? ... In my high little room for 10 francs a day with flowers in a glass and a quilted sateen bed-cover, I don't feel far from Richard either. Oh, it's awfully nice to have passed private suites and marble-tops and private bathrooms by! Gone! Gone for ever. I found a little restaurant last night where one dines ever so sumptuous for 6-7 francs, and the grapes are tied with red satin bows, and someone gives the cat a stewed prune and someone else cries 'le chat a mangé une compôte de pruneaux!'

True, one is no longer *of* people. But was one ever – This, looking on, understanding what one can is better....

I've just come from the clinic. Manoukhin is far and away nicer. Donat's beard is cut in a very chic way. Poor Madame who opens the door has had a terrible *grippe* and still her fringe is not curled.

She said she thought she was *filait de mauvais coton*. But Manoukhin is an old friend, you know. Language doesn't matter. One talks as Natasha in *War & Peace* says 'just so', and it's quite enough. He and Donat promise me complete and absolute health by Christmas. My heart is much better. Everything is better. The sparks, the dark room, the clock, the cigarettes, Donat's halting steps – all were so familiar one didn't know how to greet them with enough love! Dear, what wonderful people there are in this world. There's no denying *that*, Bogey.

Is it really warm in England. Here one wears thin stockings again and my window is wide open day [and] night. Today is especially lovely – the air just moves on fanning wings – the sky is like a pigeon's breast.

I'm sending you some copies of Manoukhin's and Donat's pamphlets. Do you feel inclined to send them to – Sorapure, say, and Massingham & any one you know? I told him you would do this for him.

Goodbye, dearest. I hope you see Elizabeth and she's nice. (Haunted by the word 'nice'.)

                    Wig

                              [Select Hôtel,
                              Paris]
                              [8 October, 1922]
                              Sunday

My darling Boge,
    Do not bother to write to me when you are not in the mood. I quite understand and don't expect too many letters.

Yes, this is where I stayed *pendant la guerre*. It's the quietest hotel I ever was in. I don't think tourists come at all. There are funny rules about not doing one's washing or fetching in one's cuisine from *dehors* which suggest a not rich an' grand clientèle. What is nice too is one can get a tray in the evening if one doesn't want to go out. Fearfully good what I imagine is provincial cooking – all in big bowls, piping hot, brought up by the garçon who is a v. nice fellow in a red veskit & white apron & a little grey cloth *cap*(!) I think some English traveller left it in a cupboard about 1879. The salt & pepper stand, by the way is a little glass motor car. Salt is driver & Pepper esquire is master in the back seat – the dark fiery one of the two so different to plain old Salt.... What a good fellow he is, though!

Yesterday the wind was nor' north by north by east by due east by due east-north-east. If you know a colder one, it was there, too. I had to thaw a one-franc piece to get the change out of it. (That is a joke for your Sunday paper only!)

Of course I should like to read your lecture. I've just read you on Bozzy [Boswell]. You awe me very much by your familiarity with simply all those people. You've always such a vast choice of sticks in the hall-stand for when you want to go walking, and even a vaster choice of umberellas – while I go all unprotected & exposed with only a fearful sense of the heavens lowering.

Lawrence has reached Mexico and feels ever so lively. Father has reached Port Said. He quoted a whole poem by Enid Bagnold to say so. 'I am a sailor sailing on summer seas.' All the same a marvellous wash of the blue crept up the page as I read his letter, which had nothing to do with E.B.

By the way do you read letters at Selsfield? Do you ever read letters? You never do. You only skate over them. 'Here's a letter,' and down you sit, clamp on your skates, do a dreamy kind of twirl over the pages and that's all. Or is that libelling you?

Mary! There's a most beautiful magpie on *my* roof. Are magpies still wild? Ah me, how little one knows.

I must go out to lunch. Goodbye, my darling Boge. I hope to send you some MSS to type this next week. Give my love to L.-E. Tell him of this hôtel in case he comes to Paris. I think he'll like it. My room is on the 6ème. Didn't I tell you? I felt *sure* I did.

I know that water music. It is lovely – so very watery reminds me too in bits of Spenser's Swans.

> Ever
> Wig

> [Select Hôtel,
> Paris]
Wednesday,   [11 October, 1922]

Dearest Bogey,

I have a letter and a card of yours to answer. How horrid your Father is – really horrid! I am so sorry for your Mother. Do you think your policy of keeping silent for her sake is a good one? I quite see quarrelling would be no use but I *do* feel a few *chosen words*, so that he can't preen himself upon 'having had the best of it', would be worth while. Give him something to think over.

J.M.M. (quite quietly) 'you know Dad you're a horrid bully.

Nobody loves you.'
I am afraid he'll live for ever, too – Why should he die? All his life is there coiled up, unused, in a horrid way *saved*. He is a very odd character. I feel you left your Mother thinking of her with real tender love, seeing her at Selsfield even, helping her out of the car. Or am I wrong?

That lecture must have been a queer little aside – wasn't it? A sort of short loop line.
It has got very cold here. I feel it. I am adjusting myself to it and it makes me feel rather dull – *distrait*, you know. I have had to leave my dear little *grenier au 6ème* for something less lofty more expensive but warmer. However, it's a very nice room – 'et vous avez un beau pendule' as the garçon said. *He* thoroughly approves of the change. All the same, you say 'tell me about yourself ' – I'll have a try – Here goes.
A new way of being is not an easy thing to *live*. Thinking about it preparing to meet the difficulties and so on is one thing, meeting those difficulties another. I have to die to so much; I have to make such *big* changes. I feel the only thing to do is to get the dying over – to court it, almost. (Fearfully hard that) and then all hands to the business of being reborn again – What do I mean exactly? Let me give you an instance. Looking back, my boat is almost swamped sometimes by seas of sentiment. 'Ah, what I have missed. How sweet it was, how dear how warm, how simple, how precious.' And I think of the garden at the Isola Bella and the furry bees and the house-wall so warm: But then I remember what we really felt there, the blanks, the silences, the anguish of continual misunderstanding. Were we positive, eager, real – alive? No, we were not. We were a nothingness shot with gleams of what might be. But no more. Well, I have to face everything as far as I can & see where I stand – what *remains*.
For with all my soul I do long for a real life, for truth, and for real strength. It's simply incredible, watching K.M., to see how little causes a panic. She's a perfect corker at toppling over.
I envy you Selsfield. How I should like to be there now, this morning. How beautiful it is – how gracious. I am so glad you are there, my darling Bogey. I feel it *is* the house of your dreams – isn't it? Do you have flowers on your writing table? Or only pipes in pots and feathers? *You won't forget the Tchekhov will you?* I'd like the *Lit. Sup.* with your review if it won't [be] too much of a bore to send it.

　　　Ever your
　　　Wig

[Paris]

[12 October 1922]

DEAR HOUSE DEAR FRIENDS ACCEPT MY LOVE

KATHERINE

[Select Hôtel,
Paris]
[13 October, 1922]
Friday

Don't mind if I don't talk about health – will you? .... It's a *useless* subject.

My dearest Bogey dear,

That was a massive 1st instalment from Newcassel. What an observer you are become. But I don't think the North is at all simpatico – do you? Those big bones make one feel like a small Jonah in a very large cold whale.

It's a divinely beautiful kind day – so was yesterday. I hope you are having the same weather at Selsfield. The sky is as blue as the sky can be. I shall go to the Luxembourg Gardens this afternoon and count dahlia and baby heads. The Paris gardens are simply a glorious sight with flowers – masses of beloved Japonica – enough Japonica at last. I *shall* have a garden one day and work in it, too. Plant, weed, tie up, throw over the wall. And the peony border really will be staggering. Oh, how I love flowers! I think of them with such longing. I go through them – one after another – remembering them from their first moments with love – oh with rapture as if they were babies! No it's what other women feel for babies – perhaps – Oh Earth! Lovely, unforgettable Earth. Yesterday I saw the leaves falling, so gently, so softly, raining down from little slender trees golden against the blue. Perhaps Autumn is loveliest. Lo! it is Autumn. What is the magic of that? It is magic to me.

At that very minute in came your letter with the rose – and the aspen tree, the two little birds the ring from the anvil and the far away rooster. You never gave me such a perfect birthday present before. A divine one. I love you for it. Beautiful Selsfield sounds. I hope you *do* care for de la Mare – warmly. I feel that he is different to the others, but he too is hidden. We are all hidden, looking out at each other; I mean even those of us who want not to hide. But I understand perfectly what you say of friendship. With you it is love or nothing, and that you are in love with Elizabeth when she loves you. A relationship which isn't what you call a *warm* one is nothing to me, either. Feel I must. But then darling, oughtn't you to express your feeling & risk losing those people who think you 'ridiculous' or who don't understand it? That's hard to decide. For instance, I feel you & Locke Ellis only touch the fringe of what your relationship might be if you both were 'free' with each other. But perhaps I'm quite wrong. Yes, I care for Lawrence. I have thought of writing to him and trying to arrange a meeting after I leave Paris – suggesting that I join them until the spring. Richard, too, I think of with love. That reminds me. Won't you ask Milne down for a week-end? But he is so shy perhaps he would refuse. Do you know what I think he is? A Dreamer. A real one. He chooses to dream.

I am going to Fontainebleau next week to see Gurdjieff. I will tell you about it. Why am I going? From all I hear he is the only man who understands there is no division between body and the spirit, who believes how they are related. You remember how I have always said doctors only treat *half*. And you have replied 'It's up to you to do the rest.' It is. That's true. But first I must learn how. I believe Gurdjieff can teach me. What other people say doesn't matter – other people matter not at all.

But you matter to me – more and more. I'd like to say I believe as never before in the possibility of real living relationship between us – a *true* one.

> Ever
> Wig

Again, my love, I thank you for the rose.

> Selsfield House,
> [East Grinstead, Sussex]
> [14 October 1922]
> Saturday

My darling Wig,
Your letter has disturbed me very much. Your going to Gurdjeff's institute may be everything that you think: I'm sure you know & I don't. But to give up Manoukhin, as you evidently are doing, though you don't say so, seems to me criminal. I really mean wrong, utterly wrong.

However, I feel it's quite hopeless for me to say anything: and perhaps useless of me to try to say anything. I simply don't understand what you are doing – but then I haven't understood very much ever since Uspensky began. I've trusted in it & you as something beyond me. Now I don't trust in it. The horrid thing is that I had a feeling that this was going to happen which I dismissed.

Oh, please don't imagine me as scolding. I'm terribly disappointed about Manoukhine.

But then I feel I don't *know* anything. You've passed clean out of my range & understanding: and so suddenly, Wig.

That's the only fact worth thinking about. I can't make head or tail of it. I haven't changed, you have: so probably you're right. But I feel our ships are sailing away from each other, & that we're just waving.

Be happy. You know whether you are right. I can let you have £20 a month if that wd. help.

[Select Hôtel,
Paris]
[14 October, 1922]
Saturday

My darling Bogey,

Your sweet telegram and letter are here. Thank you my angel. I do think Selsfield sounds perfect but it's no good my coming there while I am a creeping worm. When I can fly – I will come if you will have me – so very deeply gladly. I am more than happy to know you are there. Most blessed house! How it lives in my memory. Fancy the blackberries ripe – There are some, aren't there? along the fence on the way to the Hen Houses I seem to remember. Michaelmas daisies remind me of a solitary bush in Acacia Road. Do you remember? I like them. They have such delicate arrowy petals.

I send back Elizabeth's letter. If that is grist you have a very superior mill indeed. Why do you mind punching holes in me? If you punch holes in her? I do think *she* writes the most fascinating letters. If I were a man I should fall in love every time I had one. What qualities she has – and tenderness – real tenderness – hasn't she? I feel it, or perhaps I want to feel it.

About doing operations on yourself. I know just what you mean. It's as though one were the sport of circumstance – one *is*, indeed. Now happy – now unhappy, now fearful, now confident just as the pendulum swings. You see one can control nothing if one isn't conscious of a purpose – it's like a journey without a goal. There is nothing that makes you ignore some things, accept others, order others, submit to others. For there is no reason why A. should be more important than B. So there one is – involved beyond words – feeling the next minute I may be bowled over or struck all of a heap. I *know* nothing.

This is to me a very terrible state of affairs. Because it's the cause of all the unhappiness (the secret profound unhappiness) in my life. But I mean to escape and to try to live differently. It isn't easy. But is the other state easy? And I do believe with all my being that if one *can* break through the circle one finds 'my burden is light'.

I have met two awfully nice men here. One is Mr. Pinder – did I tell you about him? The other is a Doctor Young. He came up from Fontainebleau today to meet Orage who arrives tonight. And on his way to the station he spent a couple of hours with me, talking about Gurdjieff and the institute. If I were to write it all to you it sounds fabulous and other-worldly. I shall wait until I've *seen* it. I still hope to go on Monday & I'll take a toothbrush and *peigne* and come back on Wednesday morning, only.

I've had such a queer birthday. Ida brought me a *brin* of mimosa. And I had my poem and the telegrams. Wasn't it awfully nice of L.-E. and de la Mare to send one. It's been sunny, too. But all the same I'd rather not think about my birthday.

Oh, the little Tchekhov book has come. Do you think I might have the *Lit. Sup.* with your article in it? I see no papers here at all. That's not a complaint, though. For Paris flaps with papers as you know. I haven't seen a single newspaper since leaving London. There! Does that shock you?

My *darling* Bogey,

> I am your
> Wig

> [Select Hôtel,
> Paris]

Sunday,   [15 October, 1922]

I have opened my letter darling to add something. It's this. Darling Bogey in your spare time, however little that is, get nearer the growing earth than that wheelbarrow and spade. *Grow things.*

Plant – Dig up. Garden. I feel with all the force of my being that 'happiness' is in these things. If it's only cabbages let it be cabbages rather than chess. Sweep leaves. Make fires. Do anything to work with your hands in contact with the earth.

You see chess only feeds your already over developed intellectual centre. And that regular spade-and-barrow becomes a habit too soon, and is likely only to feed your moving centre – to exercise your machine. Does that sound awful rot to you?

Why don't you get some animals? I'm not joking. Two hours a day would be enough for them. Birds – rabbits – a goat – *anything* and live through it or them! I know you will say you haven't the time. But you'll find your work is 100 times easier if you come to it refreshed, renewed, rich, happy. Does this sound like preaching? Don't let it. I am trying to tell you what I feel deep down is your way of escape. It is to really throw yourself into life – not desperately but with the love you even don't feel yet. People won't do. We know too well that unless one has a background of reality in oneself people can't endure in us. When we have a table spread we can afford to open our door to guests, but not before. But enough of this. I am afraid of boring you.

Did you ask L[ocke] E[llis] about tulips? Has he got anemones in the garden? *You* ought to see to them; they are your flowers. Why don't you write to Sutton's and ask their advice.

Oh, if you knew how I believe in Life being the only cure for Life.

> Ever your own
> Wig

About being like Tchekhov and his letters. Don't forget he *died* at 43. That he spent – how much? of his life chasing about in a desperate search after health. And if one reads 'intuitively' the last letters they are terrible. What is left of him? 'The braid on German women's dresses – bad taste' – and all the rest is misery. Read the last! All hope is over for him. Letters are deceptive, at any rate. It's true he had occasional happy moments. But for the last 8 years he knew no *security* at all. We know he felt his stories were not half what they might be. It doesn't take much imagination to picture him on his death-bed thinking 'I have never had a real chance. Something has been all wrong ...'

[Le Prieuré,
Fontainebleau]
[18 October, 1922]

My dear darling Bogey,
I have been through a little revolution since my last letter. I suddenly made up my mind (for it was sudden, at the last) to try and learn to live by what I believed in, no less, and not as in all my life up till now to live one way and think another – – – I don't mean superficially of course, but in the deepest sense I've always been disunited. And this, which has been my 'secret sorrow' for years has become everything to me just now .... I really can't go on pretending to be one person and being another any more, Boge. It is a living death. So I have decided to make a clean sweep of all that was 'superficial' in my past life and start again to see if I can get into that real living simple truthful *full* life I dream of. I have been through a horrible deadly time coming to this. You know the kind of time. It doesn't show much, outwardly, but one is simply chaos within!

So my first Leap into the Dark was when I came here and decided to ask Mr. Gurdjieff if he would let me stay for a time. 'Here' is a very beautiful old château in glorious grounds. It was a Carmelite monastery, then one of Madame de Maintenon's 'seats'. Now it is modernised inside – I mean, *chauffage centrale*, electric light and so on. But it's a most wonderful old place in an amazingly lovely park. About 40 people, chiefly Russians, are here working, at every possible kind of thing. I mean, outdoor work, looking after animals, gardening, indoor work, music, dancing – it seems a bit of everything. Here the philosophy of the 'system' takes second place. Practice is first. You simply *have* to wake up instead of talking about it, in fact. You *have* to learn to do all the things you say you want to do.

I don't know whether Mr. Gurdjieff will let me stay. I am 'under observation' for a fortnight first. But if he does I'll stay here for the time I should have been abroad and get really cured – not half cured, not cured in my body only and all the rest still as ill as ever. I have a most lovely sumptuous room a kind of glorified Garsington for the fortnight. As for the food it is like a Gogol feast. Cream, butter – but what nonsense to talk about the food. Still, it's very important, and I want you to know that one is terribly well looked after, in every way. There are three doctors here – real ones – But these too seem details. The chief thing is that this is my Selsfield for the time, the house of *my dreams*. If Mr. Gurdjieff won't let me stay, I shall go to the South, take a little villa and try and learn to live on my own, growing things and looking after rabbits and so on, getting into touch with *Life* again. No treatment on earth is any good to me, really. It's all pretence. Manoukhine did make me heavier and a little stronger. But that was all if I really face the facts. The miracle never came near happening. It couldn't, Boge. And as for my spirit – well, as a result of that life at the Victoria Palace I stopped being a writer. I have only written long or short scraps since 'The Fly'. If I had gone on with my old life I never would have written again, for I was dying of poverty of life.

I wish, when one writes about things, one didn't dramatise them so. I feel awfully happy about all this, and it's all as simple as can be. It's just the same for us, darling, as though I had stayed on in Paris *except* that I hope I shall be well when you see me again, instead of knowing it would be a variation on the old theme.

Will you send me letters here for a fortnight? Ida will be at the Select Hotel for that time so if you prefer to send them there she'll post them on. At the end of that time I'll either stay on here or as I say, go off to some warm place where I can turn into a worker. But I hope it will be here.

Mr. Gurdjieff is not in the least like what I expected. He's what one wants to find him, really. But I do feel *absolutely confident* he can put me on the right track in every way, bodily and t' other governor.

I haven't talked money to Mr. Gurdjieff yet. But in any case I shan't write any stories for 3 months, and I'll not have a book ready before the Spring. It doesn't matter. When we have discussed finances I'll tell you. The fact is I've hardly talked with him at all. He's terribly busy just now and he only speaks a few words of English – all is through an interpreter. I can't say how 'good' some of the people seem to me here – it's just like another life.

I start Russian today, and my first jobs which are eat, walk in the garden, pick the flowers and rest *much*. That's a nice calm beginning, isn't it. But it's the eat much which is the job when it's Gurdjieff who serves the dish.

I must stop this letter, dearest. I'm awfully glad Delamare is a real person: I know just what you mean about Sullivan & Waterlow. It seems 'right', somehow, in a queer way –

I take back my words Betsy about your quarrying. It sounded very different when you told me about the sand.

Goodbye for now, darling Heart.
Ever your own
Wig

[Le Prieuré,
Fontainebleau]
[20 October, 1922]

My darling Bogey,
 I'll tell you what this life is more like than anything; it is like Gulliver's Travellers [sic]. One has, all the time, the feeling of having been in a wreck & by the mercy of Providence got ashore ... somewhere. Simply everything is different. Not only language, but food, ways, people, music, methods, hours – *all*. It's a real new life. At present this is my day. I get up 7.30 – light the fire, with kindling drying overnight, wash in ice cold water (I'd quite forgotten how good water is to wash in & to drink) & go down to breakfast – which is coffee, butter, bread, gorgonzola cheese & quince jam & eggs. After breakfast, make my bed, do my room, rest, & then go into the garden till dinner, which is 11 a.m. Which is a very large meal with things like beans minced with raw onions, vermicelli with icing sugar & butter, veal wrapped in lettuce leaves & cooked in cream. After dinner, in the garden again till 3 o'clock tea time. After tea, any light job that is going until dark. When all knock off work, wash, dress & make ready for dinner again at 7. After dinner most of the people gather in the salon round an enormous fire and there is music, tambourine, drums and piano dancing & perhaps a display of all kinds of queer dance exercises. At ten we go to bed. Doctor Young, a real friend of mine comes up and makes me up a good fire. In 'return' I am patching the knee of his trousers today.
 But it's all 'stranger' than that. For instance, I was looking for wood the other evening. All the boxes were empty. I found a door at the end of the passage went through & down some stone steps. Presently steps came up & a woman appeared, very simply dressed with her head bound in a white handkerchief. She had her arms full of logs. I spoke in French, but she didn't understand. English – no good. But her glance was so lovely – laughing & gentle, absolutely unlike people as I have known people. Then I patted a log & she gave it to me & we went our ways....
 At present the entire Institute is devoted to manual work, getting this place in order, out and inside. It's not, of course, work for the sake of work. Every single thing one does has a purpose, is part of a 'system'. Some of the English, 'arty' & theosophical people are very trying, too. But one can learn to use them, I am sure. Though I'm not much good at it yet. On the other hand some of the advanced men and women are truly wonderful. I am still on my fortnight's

probation, simply spending a fortnight here. Mr. Gurdjieff hardly speaks a word to me. He must know me pretty well.

But even if he won't let me stay here I am finished for the time being with *old circumstances*. They have just not killed me, and that's all there is to be said for them. All the people I have known don't really matter to me. Only you matter – more and more, if that is possible, for now that I am not so 'identified' with you I can see the real tie that holds us.

Ida, of course, was very tragic. She had got to the pitch of looking after me when she gave me a handkerchief without my asking for it. She *was* me.

However, I am sure Ida will recover. There is something rock-like in her under all that passion for helplessness.

Jeanne's wedding made me feel sad, Bogey. I too do like that man myself. I think the fat purple fellow was MacGavin, for some reason. Thank you for telling me about it. I must write to Marie in a day or two. Forgive this hasty writing. Do send *Lit. Sups*. They are so good for lighting fires. I wish you were here. It's such happiness.

> Ever my darling
> Your
> Wig Voyageuse

[Le Prieuré
Fontainebleau]
Tuesday,   [24 October, 1922]

My darling Bogey,

I was so glad to get your second letter today. Don't feel we are silently & swiftly moving away from each other! Do you *really*? And what do you mean by us meeting 'on the other side?' Where – Boge? You are much more mysterious than I!

I have managed this badly for this reason. I never let you know how much I have suffered in these five years. But that wasn't my fault. I could not. You would not receive it, either. And all all I am doing now is trying to put into practice the 'ideas' I have had for so long of another, and a *far more truthful* existence – I want to learn something that no books can teach me, and I want to try & escape from my terrible illness. That again you can't be expected to understand. You think I am like other people – I mean – *normal*. I'm not. I don't know which is the ill me or the well me. I am simply one pretence after another. Only now I recognise it.

I believe Mr. Gurdjieff is the only person who can help me. It is great happiness to be here. Some people are stranger than ever but the strangers I am at last feeling near & they are my own people at last. So I feel. Such beautiful understanding & sympathy I have never known in the outside world.

As for writing stories & being true to one's gift. I wouldn't write them if I were not here, even. I am at an end of my source for the time. Life has brought me no FLOW. I want to write but differently – far more steadily. I am writing this on a corner of the table against orders for the sun shines & I am supposed to be in the garden. I'll write again, my darling precious.

> Ever your own
> Wig

> [Le Prieuré,
> Fontainebleau]
> [27 October, 1922]

Darling Bogey,

I was so glad to hear of your Sullivan excursion. But doesn't his chess obsession bore you dreadfully? It did me. But Beethoven and the stars & the baby all sounded nice.

What are you going to do to the fruit trees? Please tell me. We have masses of quinces here. They are no joke when they fall *exprès* on your head.

I do hope you are having this glorious weather. Day after day of perfect sunshine. It's like Switzerland. An *intense* blue sky, a chill in the air, a wonderful clarity so that you see people far away, all sharp-cut and vivid.

I spend all the sunny time in the garden. Visit the carpenters, the trench diggers. (We are digging for a Turkish Bath) not to discover one, but to lay the pipes. The soil is very nice here, like sand with small whitey pinky pebbles in it. Then there are the sheep to inspect & the new pigs that have long golden hair very mystical pigs. A mass of cosmic rabbits & hens – and goats are on the way, likewise horses & mules to ride & drive. The Institute is not really started yet for another fortnight. A dancing hall is being built & the house is still being organised. But it has started really. If all this were to end in smoke tomorrow I should have had the very great wonderful adventure of my life. I have learnt more in a week than in years là-bas. As to habits. My wretched sense of order, for instance which rode me like a witch. It did not take long to cure that. Mr. Gurdjieff likes me to go into the kitchen in the late afternoon & 'watch'. I have a chair in a corner. It's a large kitchen with 6 helpers. Madame Ostrovsky the head, walks about like a queen exactly – She is extremely beautiful. She wears an old raincoat. Her chief helper, Nina, a big girl in a black apron – lovely, too – pounds things in mortars. The second cook chops at the table, bangs the saucepans, sings; another runs in and out with plates & pots, a man in the scullery cleans pots – the dog barks & lies on the floor worrying a hearthbrush. A little girl comes in with a bouquet of leaves for Olga Ivanovna. Mr. Gurdjieff strides in, takes up a handful of shredded cabbage and eats it ... there are at least 20 pots on the stove & it's so full of life and humour and ease that one wouldn't be anywhere else. It's just the same all through – *ease* after *rigidity* expresses it more than anything I know. And yet I realise that as I write this it's no use. An old personality is trying to get back to the outside & observe & it's not true to the present facts at all. What I write sounds so petty. In fact I cannot express myself in writing just now. The old mechanism isn't mine any longer & I can't control the new. I just have to talk this baby talk –

I would like you to see the dancing here. There again you see it's not to be described. One person sees one thing; one another. I have never really cared for dancing before but *this* – seems to be the key to the new world within me. To think that later on I shall do it is great happiness. There may be a demonstration in Paris in a month or two. If so I wish you could see it. But would it just look like dancing? I wonder! It's so hard to tell.

Oh, about money – I don't need any, thank you Bogey. If ever I do need money I shall ask you first but at present I don't.

I wish you'd ask Ouspensky out to dinner when you are in London. His address is at 28 Warwick Gardens. He is an extraordinarily sympathetic person –

There are masses of work going on in this garden – uprooting and digging and so on. I don't see why there isn't in yours. Or perhaps you are more forward.

Won't you send Ida a card to Paris 'Select Hotel' and ask her to spend a week-end with you if she returns to England? I don't know her plans.

Still got cramp in my thumb. Oh, I wish I could write to you from this self not the other.

Suppose you throw up every single job in England, realise your capital, & come over here to work for Gurdjieff. Burn every single boat for once! Do you like the idea? That's why I thought you might care to see Ouspensky. Do you like that old mechanical life at the mercy of everything? And just living with a little tiny corner of yourself?

You could learn the banjo here and if the worst came to the worst always make enough to keep you with playing it – or anything. But perhaps this sounds very wild talk. We are not really wild here, at all. Very serious, in fact.

My darling precious Bogey,
Yours ever
Wig

[Le Prieuré,
Fontainebleau]

Saturday,   [28 October, 1922]

Darling Bogey,
    Forgive me if I don't write often just now. I am so glad you are happy. I am happy, too. And our happiness does not depend on letters. I feel certain we shall move towards each other. But we shall do it in our several ways. If I write at present I 'falsify' my position and I don't in any way help yours. It's absurd to give you the news here. News there is none that can be so expressed. As to the people I have known I know nothing of them & they are out of sight just now. If I am sincere I can only say we *live* here – every moment of the day seems full of life. And yet I feel I can't enter into it as I shall be able to: I am only on the fringe. But write about it I can't.
    Dunning's phrase is ½ good, I feel – no more. He always seems to me ½ way in everything. He has insight but not direction. Can he really help?
    There is always this danger of deceiving oneself. I feel it, too. I only begin to get rid of it by trying and trying to relax – to give way – Here one *learns* how to do it. Life never would have taught me.
    But I am sure you will understand why it is so hard to write. We don't move in our letters. We say the same things over and over.
    As I tried to explain, I'm in such a state of transition. I could not if I would get back to the old life & I can't deal with the new.
    But *anxiety* I never feel. Perhaps I shall; I cannot tell. But I am so

busy and so many people are here – so much is happening.

Goodbye for now, darling
Wig

Let us speak the new truth. What present relationship have we?
None. We feel there is the possibility of one – that is deep-down
truth – don't you feel? But no more. It doesn't mean we are moving
away, though! It's a thousand times more subtle.

[Le Prieuré,
Fontainebleau]
[2 November, 1922]

My own Bogey,
Ever since my last letter to you I have been so enraged with
myself. It's so like me. I am ashamed of it. But you who know me
will perhaps understand. I always try to go too fast. I always think
all can be changed & renewed in the twinkling of an eye. It is most
fearfully hard for me, as it is for you, not to be 'intense'. And
whenever I am intense (really this is so) I am a little bit false. Take
my last letter & the one before. The tone was all wrong. As to any
new truth – oh, darling, I am really ashamed of myself. It's so very
wrong. Now I have to go back to the beginning & start again and
again tell you that I have been 'over-fanciful', and I seem to have
tried to force the strangeness. Do you know what I mean? Let me
try now to *face facts*. Of course it is true that life here is quite
different, but violent changes to one's individuality – of course they
do not occur. I have come here for a 'cure'. I know I shall never
grow strong anywhere in the world except here. This *is* the place,
and here at last one is understood entirely, mentally & physically. I
could never have regained my health by any other treatment and all
my friends accepted me as a frail half-creature who migrated
towards sofas. Oh, my dearest Bogey, just wait and see how you
and I will live one day – so happily – so splendidly – But in the
meantime, love, please never take what I say for 'absolute'. I do not
take what you say for 'final'. I try & see it as relative. Essentially,
you and I are together. I love you & I feel you are my man. It's that
I want to build on and realise and really live in one of these days.
So I shall write at least twice a week & tell you any odd things
that are happening. Will you tell me, too?
Last night, for instance in the salon we learnt to make rugs from

long pieces of corn. Very nice ones. Very easy to make, too. I have been in the carpenter's shop all the morning. The small forge is alight; Mr. Gurdjieff is planing, a Mr. Salzmann is making wheels. Later on I shall learn carpentry. We are going to learn as many trades as possible, also all kinds of farm work. The cows are being bought today. Gurdjieff is going to build a high couch in the stable where I can sit & inhale their breath! I know later on I shall be put in charge of those cows. Every one calls them already 'Mrs. Murry's cows'.

This letter must be posted, love. Do please forgive my two silly ones. I learn terribly slowly, my precious Veen, & I must not hurt you.

> Ever your own
> Wig

I am making a cure of goat's milk – 4 times a day!

	[Le Prieuré, Fontainebleau]
£5 note enclosed.	[7 November, 1922]

My darling Bogey,
    I had a letter from you today saying you had bought a pruning knife. I hope you succeed with the old trees. Here it is part of the 'work' to do a great many things, especially things which one does *not* like. I see the point of that. It's the same principle as facing people whom one shrinks from and so on. It is to develop a greater range in oneself. But what happens in practice is that no sooner do the people begin doing those things they don't like than the dislike changes. One feels it no longer. It's only that first step which is so terribly hard to take.
    Are you having really divine weather? It's marvellous here – like late spring today – really *warm*. The leaves are still falling. The park belonging to this château is incredibly beautiful, and with our livestock roaming about it begins to look like a little piece of virgin creation.
    I am fearfully busy. What do I do? Well, I learn Russian – which is a terrific job – have charge of the indoor carnations – no joke – & spend the rest of the day paying visits to places where people are working. Then every evening about 50 people meet in the salon and there is music and they are working at present at a tremendous

ancient Assyrian Group Dance. I have no words with which to describe it. To see it seems to change one's whole being for the time. Until I came here I did not realise with what a little bit of my mind, even, I lived. I was a little European with a liking for eastern carpets and music and for something that I vaguely called The East. But now I feel as though I am turned to that side far more than the other. The West seems so poor, so scattered. I cannot believe knowledge or wisdom are there. I expect this is a phase. I tell it you because I said I would tell you my reactions.... In three weeks here I feel I have spent years in India, Arabia, Afghanistan, Persia. That is very odd – isn't it. And oh, how one wanted to voyage like this – how bound one felt. Only now I know!

There is another thing here – Friendship. The real thing that you and I have dreamed of. Here it exists between women & women & men & women, & one feels it is unalterable, and living in a way it never can be anywhere else. I can't say I have friends yet. I am simply not fit for them. I don't know myself enough to be really trusted, and I am weak where these people are strong. But even the relationships I have are dear beyond any friendships I have known.

But I am giving the impression that we all live together in brotherly love & blissful happiness. Not at all. One suffers terribly – If you have been ill for 5 years you can't expect to be well in five weeks. If you have been ill for 20 years & according to Mr. Gurdjieff we all of us have our 'illness' it takes very severe measures to put one right. But the point is there is hope. One can & does believe that one will escape from living in circles & will live a CONSCIOUS life. One can through work, escape from falsity & be true to one's own self – not to what anyone else on earth thinks one is.

I wish you could meet some of the men here. You would like them very very much, especially a Mr. Salzmann, who speaks very little. I must stop this letter. Is it a rigmarole?

I don't know what you mean darling by seeing me as an angel with a sword. I don't feel at all like one. There is another thing. You can't *really* be happy in my happiness. No one ever is. The phrase is only a kind of buffer – don't you think? It's like people living through their children. Well, they may do it. But it's not life. Neither can I ever teach you how to live. How is it possible? You are you. I am I. We can only lead our own lives together.

But perhaps I am treating too seriously what you said.

Goodbye for now, my darling heart,

Ever your
Wig

I enclose a £5 note. Will you pay Heal's bill & keep the rest for any odd bills I may send you later. I know there are some. If you know anyone coming to Paris *do* give them 2 pairs of grey milanese stockings, (for size 5 shoes) to post on to me. I need them awfully. *Merci en avance.*

[Le Prieuré,
Fontainebleau]
[12 November 1922]

Darling Bogey,
I have 2 letters of yours to answer. What a queer situation with regard to Sylvia Sullivan. Poor L.E. that is what comes of trying to help people without knowing how to. It may aggravate their disorders. Don't you find Sylvia S. attractive at all? I feel there is a certain personality in you which would be greatly drawn to her. I am surprised that her relations with Sullivan are not good. He gave me to understand that Dunning had warned him completely of – not of *her* need of him but of his of her.

I am so sorry for you when you speak of your life as emerging from your study & disappearing into it again. Don't you *sicken* of shutting that door & sitting down to that table? One feels like a spider in an empty house. For whom this web. Why do I strain to spin and spin? Here, I confess, after only five weeks, there are things I *long* to write! Oh, how I long to! But I shall not for a long time. Nothing is ready. I must wait until la maison est *pleine*. I must say the dancing here has given me quite a different approach to writing. I mean some of the very ancient Oriental dances. There is one which takes about 7 minutes & it contains the whole life of woman – but everything! Nothing is left out. It taught me it gave me more of woman's life than any book or poem. There was even room for Flaubert's *Coeur Simple* in it & for Princess Marya.... Mysterious. By the way I have had a great talk about Shakespeare here with a man called Salzmann, who is by 'profession' a painter. He knows & understand the plays far better than anyone I have met except you. He happens, too (this is by the way) to be a great friend of Olga Knipper's. His wife is the chief dancer here – a very beautiful woman with a marvellous intelligence.

Dear Bogey I'm not 'hypnotised'. But it does seem to me there are certain people here who are far beyond any I have met – of a quite different order. Some – most of the English here don't even catch a glimpse of it. But I am sure. I remember I used to think – if there was one thing I could not bear in a community it would be the women. But now the women are nearer & far dearer than the men – of course I don't speak of Mr. Gurdjieff. I couldn't say he was *near* or *dear* to me! He is the embodiment of the life here, but at a remote distance – Since last I wrote to you I have changed my room. Now I am in another wing – another kind of existence altogether. Where all was so quiet outside the door all is noise & bustle. My other room was very rich & sumptuous. This is small & plain & very simple. When Olga Ivanovna & I had arranged it & she had hung her yellow dancing stockings to dry before the fire we sat together on the bed & felt like two quite poor young girls ... different beings altogether. I like being here very much. I hope Mr. Gurdjieff does not move us again too soon. But it is a favourite habit of his to set the whole house walking. Easy to see why when one saw the emotions it aroused.

About my stockings, darling. I heard from Ida today saying she goes to England tomorrow & would like to see you. She intends to return to France where she goes to work on some farm. Would you give the stockings to her? I'll ask her to write to you. I never think of Ida except when I get letters from her. Poor Ida! When I do, I am sorry for her.

I must finish this letter, darling. It is written on the arm of a chair, on a cushion, on my bed – as I try to escape from the heat of my fire. Oh, I have so much to do this afternoon! It's terrible how the days pass. I had a bath this morning the first since leaving England! There's a nice confession. But it's wonderful what can be done with a basin and a rough towel.

Have you read Elizabeth's new novel? What do you think of it? Please tell me! How is your gardening getting on? Have you learnt to drive the car?

Goodbye my dear darling

Ever your
Wig

[Le Prieuré
Fontainebleau]
Sunday 6.30   [19 November 1922]

Darling Bogey,
The affaire at Selsfield does so puzzle me. L-E is not at all the man we thought he was if he has made it or allowed it to be difficult for

you to be there any longer. Why is it? Is Sylvia to be a permanency? What are the arrangements. I would like to know, they seem so strange.

I am thankful you have your little flat, darling. Rob mine to make yours snug. Take all you can or care to, away. But do you keep warm enough? And what about food, I wonder? I have asked Ida to buy me a number of things while she is in England, & to bring them over to Paris with her. Bogey, I have not got a cheque book for the moment. Would you send her a cheque for £10.0.0 on my behalf? I'll let you have it back in a week or two. But would you send it at once? As Ida is going to stay such a short while in England. Thank you, dearest.

It is intensely cold here – quite as cold as Switzerland – But it does not matter in the same way. One has not the time to think about it. There is always something happening and people are a support. I spent the winter afternoon yesterday scraping carrots – masses of carrots – & halfway through I suddenly thought of my bed in the corner of that room at the Chalet des Sapins ... Oh how is it possible there is such a difference between that loneliness and isolation (just waiting for you to come in & you knowing I was waiting) and *this*. People were running in and out of the kitchen. Portions of the first pig we have killed were on the table and greatly admired. Coffee was roasting in the oven. Barker clattered through with his milk-pail. I must tell you, darling, my love of cows persists. We now have three. They are real beauties – immense – with short curly hair? fur? wool? between their horns. Geese, too, have been added to the establishment. They seem full of intelligence. I am becoming absorbed in animals, not to watch only, but to know how to care for them & to know *about* them. Why does one live so far away from all these things? Bees we shall have later. I am determined to know about bees.

Your idea of buying some land & building a little house *does* seem to me a bit premature, darling. You know so little. You have never tried your hand at such things. It's not quite easy to change from an intellectual life like yours to a life of hard physical work. But your remark made me wish you did care for my 'ideas' – I mean by my 'ideas' my desire to *learn to work in the right way* and to live as a conscious human being. They are not much more than that. There is certainly no other spot on this whole planet where one can be taught as one is taught here. But life is not easy. We have great 'difficulties' – painful moments – and Mr. Gurdjieff is there to do to us what we wish to do to ourselves and are afraid to do. Well, theoretically, that is very wonderful, but practically it must mean suffering, because one cannot always understand.

Ouspensky came over last week. I had a short talk with him. He is a very fine man. I wish you would just see him – out of – let's call it curiosity.

I must get dressed for dinner. I badly need a good *washing*. Remarkable how clothes fall into their proper place here. We dress in the evening, but during the day ... the men look like brigands. Nobody cares, nobody dreams of criticising.

Oh, Bogey how I love this place! It is like a dream – or a miracle. What do the 'silly' people matter & there are silly people who come from London, see nothing & go away again. There *is* something marvellous here if one can only attain it.

Goodbye for now, my dearest.

> Ever your own
> Wig

I will write Elizabeth.

> [Le Prieuré,
> Fontainebleau]
> [after 19 November 1922]

My darling Bogey

I have received your letter saying you will leave Selsfield & that LE and Sylvia are to join forces. It sounds a very bad arrangement to me – I mean for LE and Sylvia. They are nothing to each other as types – in fact they are so far apart as to be almost different kinds of beings. However – I don't suppose it matters.

I hope you and Sullivan do find a place together in the country somewhere near Dunning. I am glad you feel Selsfield is too luxurious. It is very very lovely but it is not living. There is too much 'dinner is served, sir' about it. Do you ever feel inclined to get into touch with Lawrence again? I wonder. I should like very much to know what he intends to do – how he intends to live now his *wanderjahre* are over. He and E.M. Forster are two men who *could* understand this place if they would. But I think Lawrence's pride would keep him back. No one person here is more important than another. That may not sound much of a statement, but practically it is very much –

I shall be interested to hear of your meeting with Ida. That reminds me again of the stockings which arrived in perfect order. What an extraordinary brain wave to hide them in *The Times*. They are very lovely stockings, too, just the shade I like in the evening. One's legs are like legs by moonlight.

It is intensely cold here – colder and colder. I have just been brought some small fat pine logs to mix with my *boulets* – Boulets are unsatisfactory; they are too passive. I simply live in my fur coat. I gird it on like my heavenly armour and wear it ever night and day – After this winter the Arctic even will have no terrors for me. Happily the sun *does* shine as well and we are thoroughly well nourished – But I shall be glad when the year has turned.

Darling I must sit down to a Russian lesson. I wish you knew Russian. I have also been learning mental arithmetic beginning 2×2=1 3×3=12 4×4=13 5×5=28 and so on at great speed to the accompaniment of music. It's not as easy as it looks especially when you start from the wrong end backwards. In fact at 34 I am beginning my education.

I can't write to E. about her book. I thought it so dreadfully tiresome and silly. It didn't seem to me like a fairy tale; I saw no fairies. In fact, I saw nobody. And jokes about husbands, double beds, God and trousers don't amuse me, I'm afraid. In fact it seemed to me a sad tinkle from an old music box.

Goodbye for now, my dearest Bogey

      Ever your own
      Wig

              [Le Prieuré,
               Fontainebleau]
              [late November]

My darling Bogey,

I understand affairs much better from your last letter. I am v. glad you are going to be near Dunning. Of course I do not feel that my way is 'the only way'. It is for me. But people have such hidden energy, such hidden strength that once they discover it in themselves why should they not do alone what we learn to do here? You were only joking – weren't you – when you said you might find Le Prieuré was your way too. For one can only come here *via* Ouspensky & *it is a serious step*. However, one can always go again if one finds it intolerable. That is true, too. But the strangeness of all that happens here has a meaning; and by strangeness I don't mean obvious strangeness – there's little of it – I mean spiritual.

Are you having really perfect weather (except for the cold). It is absolutely brilliantly sunny – a deep blue sky – dry air. Really it's better than Switzerland. But I must get some wool lined over boots. My footgear is ridiculous when I am where I was yesterday – round about the pigsty. It is noteworthy that the pigs have of themselves divided their sty into two. One – the clean part they keep clean & sleep in. This makes me look at pigs with a different eye. One must be impartial even about them, it seems. We have 2 more cows, about to calve in 3 weeks' time. Very thrilling. Also our white goat is about to have a little kid. I want to see it very much. They are so charming.

You know I told you a Turkish Bath was being built. It is finished & working. It was made from a cave used for vegetables & of course all labour including the plumbing, the lighting & so on was done by our people. Now one can have seven different kinds of baths in it & there is a little rest room hung with carpets which looks more like Bokhara than Avon. If you have seen this evolved it really is a miracle of ingenuity. Everything is designed by Mr. Gurdjieff. Now all hands are busy building the theatre which is to be ready in 2 weeks. I have to start making costumes next week. All the things I have avoided in life seem to find me out here. I shall have to sew for hours on end just as I have to puzzle over these problems in mathematics that we get sometimes in the evening.

But I wish I could tell you of the people I live with. There is not only my friend Olga Ivanovna. There are the Hartmanns, husband & wife. He was – is – a musician. She is a singer. They live in one smallish room, awfully cramped I suppose. But to go & sit there with them in the evening before dinner is one of my greatest pleasures. Dear precious people! She is very quick, beautiful, warm hearted. No, it's no good I can't describe her. He is small & quite bald, with a little pointed beard & he generally wears a loose blouse spotted with whitewash, very full trousers, wooden boots. He is a 'common workman' all day. But it is the life between them; the feeling one has in their nearness. But so many people come forward as I write. They are all very different; but they are the people I have wanted to find – *real* people – not people I make up or invent. Tell me about your new plans when you can, my darling – will you? Was L.M. just the same? It is a horrible thing; I have almost forgotten her. And only two months ago it seemed I could not have lived without her care. Do Dunning's children have lessons? Why don't you offer to teach them something – It's good to be in touch

with children; one learns very much. Goodbye for now, my darling
Bogey. I do feel we are nearer than we were. But there is so much –
so very much one cannot write. One can only feel. Ever your own

      Wig

                  [Le Prieuré,
{ Friday   Fontainebleau]
{ Piat nitse   [1 December, 1922]

My darling Bogey
    I seem to have snapped at that £10 like a dog with a bone, and
never even said merci in my last letter. I am most awfully grateful
for it. I accept it with joy, though I *did* mean – yes, truly – to send it
back to you. Did you see L.M. I wonder? Wayside Cottage
reminded me of Rose Tree Cottage. The name only. They are of the
same type. I hope you are snug in it. I suppose you couldn't (or
wouldn't care to) snare L.M. as working housekeeper & gardener. I
don't see Sullivan as a great help in such matters. But perhaps I
wrong him.
    About Christmas. I want to be quite frank. For many reasons I
would rather we did not meet till the Spring. Hear my reasons
before judging me for that – will you? For one the hotels at
Fontainebleau are closed – the decent ones. You could not come to
the Institute as a guest at present. It's not running smoothly enough.
You would simply *hate* it. No, let me be very careful. I have not
asked Mr. Gurdjieff if you could come. He might say 'Yes'. But I
can't [think] what on earth an outsider could do here just now. It's
winter. One can't be out of doors. One can't just stay in one's
room. Meals are at all hours. Sometimes lunch is at 4 p.m. & dinner
at 10 p.m. And so on.
    But the chief *reason that matters* is this. Physically there is very
little outward change in my condition so far. I am still breathless, I
still cough, still walk upstairs slowly, still have to stop and so on.
The difference is that here I make 'efforts' of a certain kind all day
& live an entirely different life. But I have absolutely no life to *share*
at present. You can't sit in the cowhouse with me at present or in
the kitchen with seven or eight people. We are not ready for that
yet. It would simply be a false position. Then when I first came here
I had a most sumptuous luxurious room and so on. Now I rough it
in a little, simple, but very warm room. But it's tiny. We couldn't sit

in it. Deeper still is the most sincere feeling I am capable of that I do not want to see you until I am better physically. I cannot see you until the old Wig has disappeared. Associations, recollections would be too much for me just now. I must get better alone. This will mean that we do not meet until the Spring. If this sounds selfish, it must sound selfish. I know it is not and I know it is necessary. If you do not understand it, please tell me, darling.

I don't feel the cold as much as I have in other winters. It's often sunny, too, & I have just bought for 23 francs very good *boots* lined with felt with felt uppers.

But I'll say no more just now. I hope you will understand & not be hurt by my letter, dearest heart.

> Ever your
> Wig

	[Le Prieuré,
	Fontainebleau]
Wednesday,	[6 December, 1922]

My darling Bogey,

Your Sunday letter arrived today. Until I have your answer to mine suggesting that we do not meet until the spring, I will not refer to the subject again.... I think that's best.

Your little house and way of life sounds so nice. I am very very glad that you feel Dunning is your friend. Do you have something of your Lawrence feeling for him? I imagine it is a little bit the same. And Mrs. Dunning – you like her? And do you play with the little boys? There are nine children here. They live in the children's house and have a different mother every week to look after them. But I remember now I have told you all that before. I'll tell you instead about that couch Mr. Gurdjieff has had built in the cowhouse. It's simply too lovely. There is a small steep staircase to a little railed-off gallery above the cows. On the little gallery are divans covered with Persian carpets (only two divans). But the white washed walls and ceiling have been decorated most exquisitely in what looks like a Persian pattern of yellow, red and blue by Mr. Salzmann. Flowers, little birds, butterflies, and a spreading tree with animals on the branches, even a hippopotamus. But Bogey all done with the most *reel art* – a little masterpiece. And all so gay, so simple, reminding one of summer grasses and the kind of flowers that smell like milk. There I go every day to lie and later I am going to sleep there. It's very warm. One has the most happy feelings listening to the beasts & looking. I know that one day I shall write a long long story about it. At about 5.30 the door opens and Mr. Ivanov comes in, lights the lantern and begins milking. I had quite forgotten the singing wiry silvery sound of milk falling into an empty pail & then heavier – plonk – plonk! 'Mr.' Ivanov is a very young man, he looks as though he had just finished his studies, rather shy, with a childlike beaming smile.

I don't know how you feel. But I still find it fearfully hard to cope with people I do not like or who are not sympathetic. With the others all goes well. But living here with all kinds I am simply appalled at my helplessness when I want to get rid of someone or to extricate myself from a conversation, even. But I *have* learnt how to do it, here. I have learnt that the only way is to court it, not to avoid it, to face it. Terribly difficult for me in practice. But until I really do master this I cannot get anywhere. There always comes the moment when I am uncovered, *so zu sagen*, and the other man gets in his knock out blow.

Oh, darling – I am always meaning to ask you this. I came away this time without a single photograph of you. This is *intolerable*. I really must have one, Bogey. Not only because I want it fearfully for myself but people keep on asking me. And I am proud of you. I want to show them what you look like. Do please send me one for Xmas. This is very important.

Goodbye for now, my own Bogey. I am

> Ever your loving
> Wig

Don't forget the photograph.	[Le Prieuré, Fontainebleau]
Saturday,	[9 December, 1922]

My darling Bogey,

I have never had a letter from you that I so 'understood' as your last about your house & how you are living & the wages you give to John & Nicholas. I can't say what a joy it is to know you are there. It seems to me very mysterious how so many of us nowadays refuse to be cave dwellers any longer but in our several ways are trying to learn to escape. The old London life, whatever it was, but even the life we have led recently wherever we have been, is no longer even *possible* to me. It is so far from me that it seems to exist in another world. This of course is a wrong feeling. For, after all, there are the seeds of what we long after in everybody and if one remembers that any surroundings are possible ... at least.

What do you read? Has Dunning any unfamiliar books? You have rather a horror of anything at all.... Eastern – haven't you? I read Ouspensky's *Tertium Organum* the other day. For some reason it didn't carry me away. I think it is extremely interesting but – perhaps I was not in the mood for books. I am not at present, though I know that in the future I shall want to write them more than anything else in the world. But different books. There is Mr. Hartmann here with whom I have great talks nearly every evening about *how* and *why* and *when*. I confess present day literature simply nauseates me, excepting always Hardy and the other few whose names I can't remember .... But the general trend of it seems to me quite without any value whatever.

Yesterday when I was in the stable Mr. Salzmann came up. He had just returned from his work – sawing logs in the far wood. And we began to talk about poverty. He was talking of the absolute need for us today to be *poor again*, but poor in the real sense. To be poor in ideas, in imagination, in impulses, in wishes, to be simple, in fact. To get rid of the immense collection with which our minds are crammed and to get back to our real needs. But I shall not try to transcribe what he said. It sounds banal; it was not. I hope you will meet this man one day. He looks a very surly, angry and even fierce workman. He is haggard, drawn, old looking with grey hair cut in a fringe on his forehead. He dresses like a very shabby forester and carries a large knife in his belt. I like him almost as much as I like his wife. Together they seem to be as near an ideal couple as I could imagine.

Bogey are you having fine weather? Today is perfectly glorious. There was a heavy frost last night but it's marvellously clear and fine. No, I don't want any money just now, thank you, darling heart. What nonsense to say those W.S. certificates are mine. Why? They are yours! And don't go building a 7-roomed house. 7 rooms for 2 people! I will write again in a day or two. Goodbye for now, dearest darling Bogey,

Ever your own
Wig

Wayside Cottage,
Ditchling Sussex

Sunday   [17 December 1922]

My precious darling,
Of course, the moment I'd posted my last, yours came. As a matter of fact I have begun to read something Eastern, or rather something odder than Eastern, which Bill Dunning (i.e. Mrs. Dunning) gave me for a present. And in a queer way I was *very much* impressed by it. Moreover I've promised Dunning that I will read an Indian book on, I think, Rama Yoga, which he's going to give me soon. But mostly I listen to Dunning. I sit in their kitchen-sitting room in the evenings, and we talk. I don't know how to describe it – it's so very simple. Sometimes it reminds me of the times when you & I used to sit with the Lawrences in their kitchen. But the differences are so tremendous that that is rather misleading than otherwise. There's no *agitation* at, [*sic*] it's all very calm & pure. And I too shall never be able to lead the old life again or anything like it. Mine will have to be some kind of going on from this life I lead now.

So you see, darling, if you have your Salzmanns, whom I should dearly love to know, I have my Dunnings, whom I would dearly love *you* to know. And every letter of yours that I get now makes me feel more than ever that we are marching along parallel paths – parallel paths which converge, and that the day is not so terribly far distant when we shall be ready for one another. And then, I know, life will be quite simple. There simply will not be any difficulties.

We're having some most amazing weather. The climate in this part of Sussex is really remarkable, though: I can never really believe that it *is* winter.

My only real regret is that I have no garden of my own. But then, just at present, I couldn't manage both my housework and my gardening – so it's probably as well. And I've never been happy like this before – that is certain.

I have to go to London on Thursday until Sunday, to finish up this Sickert essay, also to buy some Xmas presents for the Dunning children, – also to see Kot, with whom I have – also quite simply – become reconciled, & for whom I'm doing some work of late.

        With all my love, my darling,
        Your own Boge.

[Le Prieuré,
Fontainebleau]
[17 December, 1922]

My darling Bogey,

I am so delighted to hear of your ½ motor-car. I think it is a most excellent idea. What fun you and Sullivan will have with it. It is so pleasant to think of you two together and I like to know that Sullivan will now understand you from a real standpoint – after sharing your life & working with you in the real sense. Do you teach him to cook and to sew and to knit. The fairies in the keyholes must have a quiet laugh or two of a gentle kind. As to those four little wood gatherers I love them. I hope your tooth is better. Just the same thing has happened to me. My biggest and brightest stopping has come out. But I shall have to hang on until the Spring when I can get to Paris. So far all is well.

My fortunes have changed again. I have been moved back from my little bare servant's bedroom on the general corridor to my beautiful sumptuous first room overlooking the lovely park. It seems almost incredible grandeur. I suppose – I feel I have learnt the lesson that other room had to teach me. I have learnt that I can rough it in a way you & I have never done, that I can stand any amount of noise, that I can put up with untidiness, disorder, queer smells, even, without losing my head or *really* suffering more than superficially. But how did Mr. Gurdjieff know how much I needed that experience? And another mystery is that last week when it was intensely cold I felt that I had come to an end of all that room had to teach me. I was very depressed and longing beyond words for some real change and for beauty again. I almost decided to ask him to send me away until the weather got warmer. Then on Saturday afternoon when I was in the stable he came up to rest, too, and talked to me a little. First about cows and then about the monkey he has bought which is to be trained to clean the cows. Then he suddenly asked me how I was and said I looked better. 'Now', he said, 'you have two doctors you must obey. Doctor Stable and Doctor New Milk. Not to think, not to write.... Rest. Rest. Live in your body again.' I think he meant get back into your body. He speaks very little English but when one is with him one seems to understand all that he suggests. The next thing I heard was that I was to come into here for the rest of the winter. Sometimes I wonder if we 'make up' Mr. Gurdjieff's wonderful understanding. But one is always getting a fresh example of it. And he always acts at precisely the moment one needs it. That is what is so strange.... Dear Bogey darling I shall not have any Xmas present for you. But you know that £5 I sent you. How much did you spend. Would you buy a book each for Chaddie & Jeanne for me & keep the rest for yourself? Jeanne would like Delamare's new poems, *Down-a-Down-Derry*, I am sure (it's 7/6 – isn't it?) and Chaddie – h'm – that is difficult! Some book that looks pretty and tastes sweet – some love poems. Is that too vague? And may I ask you to execute these commissions for me? I hope there will be something left over for you darling. Buy it with my love. I'll tell you what I want for a present. Your photograph. The proof of the drawing of course I should simply treasure but why should you send me that. Keep it. Of course if you could have it copied .... There is a man here who is going to take a photograph of me one day. I have changed. I have no longer a fringe – very odd. We had a fire here the other night. A real one. Two beautiful rooms burnt out & a real fear the whole place would go. Cries of 'Vode! Vode!' (Water!), people rushing past all black & snatching at jugs & basins. Mr. Gurdjieff with a hammer, knocking down the wall. The real thing, in fact.

What is the weather like with you? It's so soft & spring like here that actually primroses are out. So are the Christmas roses under the espalier pear trees. I *love* Christmas; I shall always feel it is a holy time. I wonder if dear old Hardy will write a poem this year. God bless you my darling precious.

> Ever your Wig

> [Le Prieuré,
> Fontainebleau]
> [23 December, 1922]

Darling Bogey

Just a note to wish you a Happy Xmas. I am afraid it will not arrive in time for today is Saturday *not* Friday as I imagined. But there! Put the blame on the poor Xmas postman. No, even to think of such an unfair thing won't do at all.... A Happy Xmas, my dearest Bogey. I wonder very much how you who always say you hate Xmas so will spend it this year. Perhaps the Dunning children will make it seem real at last. Do tell me about them.

Here we are to have great doings. The Russian Christmas is not due for another fortnight. So Mr. Gurdjieff has decided the English shall have a real old-fashioned English Xmas on their own. There are so few of them but that makes no difference to his ideas of hospitality. We are to invite all the Russians as our guests – And he has given us a sheep, a pig, two turkeys, a goose, two barrels of wine, whiskey, gin, cognac etc., dessert of all kinds, an immense tree & carte blanche with which to decorate it. Tomorrow night we have our tree followed by the feast. We shall sit down to it about 60. Whoever gets the coin in the pudding is to be presented with our new-born calf – a perfect angel. Would that it were mine!

I do love to hear about your Dunnings. What a queer thing you should have found them just at this time – not really queer for it does seem to me to be a truth than when one is in real need one finds someone to help. Are you and 'Bill' friends. I mean more friends than you and Frieda were, for instance, for you had no separate relationship with her really did you. I would like to know them both. Darling precious Bogey this is not a letter this time only this note written on a table piled with paper chains, flowers, little bon bon cases, gold wire, gilded fir cones – you know the kind of thing.

I attended the obsequies of the pig this morning. I thought I had better go through with it for once & see for myself. One felt horribly sad.... And yesterday I watched Madame Ouspensky pluck singe & draw our birds. In fact these have been gory days balanced by the fairy like tree. There is so much life here that one feels no more than one little cell in a beefsteak – say. It is a good feeling – God bless you darling

Ever your
Wig

[Le Prieuré,
Fontainebleau]

Boxing Day (1922)   [26 December, 1922]

My darling Bogey,

I think the drawing of you is quite extraordinarily good – and in a very subtle way. I had no idea Rothenstein was that kind of artist. People will say it makes you look old. That is true. But you have that look. I am sure *c'est juste*. I am more than glad to have it & I shall keep it v. carefully. Thank you, my dearest. The photograph I don't like so well for some reason. But photographs always pale before good drawings. It's not fair on them.

How is the old Adam revived in you, I wonder? What aspects has he? There is nothing to be done when he rages except to remember that it's bound to be – it's the swing of the pendulum – and the only hope is when the bout is exhausted to get back to what you think you really care for, aim for wish to live by as soon as possible. It's the intervals of exhaustion that seem to waste so much energy. You see, my love, the question is always: '*Who am I?*' and until that is answered I don't see how one can really direct anything in oneself. '*Is there a Me.*' One must be certain of that before one has a real unshakeable leg to stand on. And I don't believe for one moment these questions can be settled by the head alone.

It is this life of the *head*, this formative intellectual life at the expense of all the rest of us which has got us into this state. How can it get us out of it? I see no hope of escape except by learning to live in our emotional & instinctive being as well and to balance all three.

You see Bogey if I were allowed one single cry to God that cry would be: *I want to be real.* Until I am that I don't see why I shouldn't be at the mercy of old Eve in her various manifestations for ever.

But this place has taught me so far how unreal I am. It has taken from me one thing after another (the things never were mine) until at this present moment all I know really really is that I am not annihilated and that I hope – more than hope – believe. It is hard to explain and I am always a bit afraid of boring you in letters.

I heard from Brett yesterday – She gave a very horrid picture of the present Sullivan and his views on life and women. I don't know how much of it is even vaguely true but it corresponds to Sullivan the Exhibitionist. The pity of it is life is so short and we waste about $\frac{9}{10}$ of it – simply throw it away. I always feel Sullivan refuses to face the fact of his wastefulness. And sometimes one feels he never will. All will pass like a dream, with mock comforts, mock consolations.

Our cowshed has become enriched with 2 goats and two love birds. The goats are very lovely as they lie in the straw or so delicately dance towards each other, butting gently with their heads. When I was there yesterday Mr. Gurdjieff came in and showed Lola and Nina who were milking the cows the way to milk a goat. He sat down on a stool seized the goat & swung its hind legs across his knees. So there the goat was on its two front legs, helpless. This is the way Arabs milk. He looked very like one. I had been talking before to a man here whose passion is astrology and he had just written the signs of the Zodiac on the whitewashed stable door. Then we went up to the little gallery & drank koumiss.

Goodbye for now, my darling. I feel this letter is flat dull. Forgive it. I am ever your own loving

Wig

Wayside Cottage
Ditchling [Sussex.]
9 p.m.   New Year's Eve. [1922]

My precious darling,
New Year's Eve. Sullivan is away. I've just come back from the Dunnings', where I've been having supper, to write this letter. Afterwards, I'm going back to see the New Year in. I can't help thinking of the New Year you & I saw in – so long ago – at Rose Tree Cottage, do you remember?

I'm so glad you liked the drawing. I liked it. And then someone said, just before I sent it off, – oh, yes, it was Mrs. Jones – that it wasn't like me: so I was afraid you wouldn't care for it.

The Old Adam didn't last very long, thank Goodness. I'd forgotten all about him by the time I got your letter – and I couldn't really remember what I'd been talking about. But now I do. I wrote at the end of a day when I had been tense and irritable: and such a thing hasn't happened to me for so long that I felt rather depressed about it. I discovered eventually that the cause was that I couldn't get away by myself at all, and that the continual interruption made it impossible for me to relax. It's very hard for me to relax at the best of times: but I do make some progress. On this day I just felt that everything was in league against me. But it passed away completely.

I agree absolutely with you that the question to answer is Who am I? And that it can't be settled by the head. And like you I'm learning *how* unreal I am. (By the way, Dunning has lent me a deeply interesting Eastern book on this, called *Raja Yoga*: it's absorbing and very exciting. It makes me feel that I want to lose no time, to go terribly fast to the goal. But that, I know, is all wrong. There's no way of going fast.) But for heaven's sake, Wig, don't think you bore me by writing about these things: they're the only things which really interest me.

I don't a bit like the glimpse of Sullivan's activities I got through your letter *viâ* Brett. In some way he's very restive. While he's down here, and towards me, he is *very nice indeed*. I'm not exaggerating. He makes a real effort to be considerate, and to try to get rid of the horrid, uncouth, masculine intellectual pride that is the worst thing in him: it's so utterly unworthy of himself at his best moments. But then it seems he rebels against his efforts, and when he goes up to London sometimes (not always) breaks out into a real unregenerate Adam. But you mustn't imagine those moments are typical of him. I know of them only by what comes round to me. In all our direct relations he's very different, believe me.

So you also have a man who's keen on Astrology. Dunning sometimes talks a good deal about that also. For a long while he has been asking me to find out the exact date of my birth so as to have my horoscope cast. And some destiny or other makes me always forget when I see my mother.

When Beresford came here the other day he inquired a great deal about you. He also said he had given up Uspensky: he said that Uspensky's wasn't true mysticism, it was occultism. I didn't understand that at all – it seemed by the way to me that Beresford was trying to understand it all with his *head* – and I asked him what he meant. He gave me a definition of the difference between mysticism & occultism: mysticism is an effort to get beyond the self and to come to union with a higher, outer reality: occultism is an attempt to penetrate into the self, inwardly, and involves a withdrawal & isolation from human life. Well, that didn't convince me at all. Of course, I don't know how far Le Prieuré is connected with Uspensky: but what I do know of your life there suggests the very opposite of a withdrawal & isolation. And, moreover, according to my ideas – or rather instincts – a true penetration of the self, a true realisation is quite essential to mysticism. Only by doing that can you come into union with a higher reality – that part of it which is manifested in you.

However, I took it along to Dunning & asked him what he thought of Beresford's definition. I was glad that he said it was all nonsense.

I suppose you couldn't tell me whether you do any exercises, & what they are.

I've had a letter from L.M. She's doing cows, & is enthusiastic about them.

The motor-car (a 10 H.P. Citroën – the make, I seem to remember, that L.M. wanted me to have) is coming to-morrow. I'm going to spend the morning (I hope) trying to drive it. I want to be an expert driver by the time you come back.

I *adore* Michael Dunning – the youngest – I'll tell you about him next time. Ever your own

Boge.

[Le Prieuré,
Fontainebleau]
[31 December, 1922]
Sunday

Darling Bogey,

My fountain pen is mislaid, so as I am in a hurry to write please forgive this pencil.

Would you care to come here on January 8 or 9 to stay until 14–15? Mr. Gurdjieff approves of my plan and says will you come as his guest. On the 13th our new theatre is to be opened. It will be a wonderful experience. But I won't say too much about it. Only on the chance that you do come I'll tell you what clothes to bring.

One sports suit with heavy shoes & stockings and a mackintosh & a hat that doesn't matter. One 'neat' suit with your soft collar or whatever collar you wear & tie (you see you are my husband & I can't help wanting you to look – what shall I say?) slippers and so on. That's all. If you have a cardigan of course bring it and a pair of flannel trousers in case you get soaking wet & want to change.

I am writing to ask Brett to go to Lewis' and get me a pair of shoes. Will you bring them. I may ask her to get me a jacket, too. But she will give you the parcel. Will you wire me your reply – just 'yes' or 'no' & the date, if yes of your arrival.

There is a London train that reaches Paris at 4 something. You could then come on to Fontainebleau the same day. Otherwise it's far better to stay the night in Paris as no cabs meet the late train.

You get out of the train at *Avon* and take a cab here which costs 8 francs *with* tip. Ring the bell at the porter's lodge and I'll open the gate.

I hope you will decide to come, my dearest. Let me know as soon as you can – won't you? I hope Tchekhov's wife will be here. I have gone back to my big lovely room, too, so we should have plenty of space to ourselves. We can also sit & drink *kiftir* in the cowshed.

I can't write of other things in this letter. I hope to hear from you soon. Your ever loving

Wig

Wayside Cottage,
Ditchling [Sussex]
Friday   [5 January 1923]

My precious darling,
    I'm overjoyed at the idea of coming over next week to see you &
Le Prieuré. I would have arrived on Monday had it not been that
I've promised a leader for *The Times Supplement*, and I'm not sure
that I should be able to finish it.
    I shall come by Newhaven. It saves my having to go back to
London. I shall take the night boat on Monday arrive in Paris early
on Tuesday, collect your things from Mrs. Nelson who is taking
them over for me, & come on I suppose about midday.
    Apparently it occurred to Brett – very sensibly – that if I were to
carry some new shoes & clothes among my things which obviously
belonged to a woman, I should or might be badly held up. At all
events the arrangement is that Mrs. Nelson is to take them, & I'm
to call for them at 16 rue de Seine on Tuesday morning.

            Au revoir my darling
            Your own
            Boge.

Endnotes

p.10 *Aleister Crowley*: (1875-1947), leader of an esoteric cult that dabbled in Satanism.

* *Leon Engers Kennedy*: a painter and early participant in Crowley's rites.

p.11 *W.L.G[eorge]*: 1882-1926), a novelist at whose house KM and Murry first met in 1911.

* *the country*: KM was planning to leave London for 'Cherry Tree Cottage' in the country. Murry's feeling that she was withdrawing from him led to his addressing her as M.K.M. and saying that he wanted to get drunk.

p.12 *New Age*: the weekly review edited by A.R. Orage that first published KM's stories in London.

* *Johnny F[ergusson]*: (1874-1961), a Scottish painter who was art editor of *Rhythm*.

* *Holbrook Jackson*: (1874-1948), editor and writer who contributed to the Winter 1911 issue of *Rhythm*. In March 1912 he commissioned an article from Murry for *T.P's Weekly*.

p.13 *Macqueen*: Willy Macqueen, a member of Frank Harris's circle.

p.14 *Sydney Waterlow*: (1878-1944), writer, diplomat and second cousin of KM.

* *these Woolff people*: Virginia and Leonard Woolf, writers and later publishers, were introduced to Murry by Sydney Waterlow.

* *Gordon and Beatrice Campbell*: (later Lord and Lady Glenavy), Irish friends of Murry who lived at 9 Selwood Terrace.

* *Marcel Boulestin*: a French writer who contributed to the *Blue Review*.

* *Martin Secker*: took over the publishing of *Rhythm* (later the *Blue Review*) after November 1912.

p.16 *Mrs Gom*: helped with housework.

* *I have begun the story*: probably 'Millie', which appeared in the *Blue Review* in June 1913.

* *Hugh Walpole*: (1884-1941), novelist who contributed to the *Blue Review* and had written critically of some drawings in the May issue.

* *George Banks*: a female cartoonist who had contributed to *Rhythm*.

* *Henri Gaudier-Brzeska*: (1884-1915), French sculptor who had contributed drawings to *Rhythm* before quarrelling bitterly with KM and Murry.

p.17 *Gilbert Cannan*: (1884-1955), novelist and friend of Murry who lived next door in Cholesbury.

* *Floryan Sobieniowski*: (1881-1964), Polish translator and critic with whom KM became involved at Wörishofen in 1909. He cadged help from KM and Murry in 1912. In 1920 he blackmailed KM, demanding money for her Wörishofen letters to him.

p.17   *Ida Baker* (L.M. or Leslie Moore): (1888-1978), met KM at Queen's College and remained her selflessly devoted friend.

*   *Mary Cannan*: former wife of playwright J.M. Barrie, now married to Gilbert Cannan.

*   *George Bowden*: (1877-1975), singing teacher whom KM married and immediately left in 1909. They were not divorced until 1918.

p.19   *Lascelles Abercrombie*: (1881-1938), poet, dramatist and critic who contributed to *Rhythm* and the *Blue Review*.

*   *Albert Rothenstein*: artist and designer who contributed to *Rhythm* and the *Blue Review*.

*   *the epilogue*: 'Epilogue: II', a short story later called 'Violet'.

p.20   *Frank Swinnerton*: (1884-1982), prominent young writer who contributed to *Rhythm*.

*   *Denis Browne*: the *Blue Review*'s music critic.

*   *Arthur Ransome*: (1884-1967), journalist and writer of children's books.

*   *W.H. Davies*: (1871-1940), Georgian poet who contributed to *Rhythm* and the *Blue Review*.

*   *the Royde-Smith*: Naomi Royde-Smith, literary editor of the *Saturday Westminster*.

*   *Thomas Hake*: a novelist and writer.

p.21   *Richard Curle*: (1883-1968), a writer and friend of Conrad's who contributed to *Rhythm* and frequented its office.

*   *Edward Dominic Spring-Rice*: (1889-1940), a writer on banking subjects.

p.22   *Rupert Brooke*: (1887-1915), war poet who contributed to *Rhythm* and the *Blue Review*.

*   *Charles Philippe*: (1874-1909), French realist novelist.

p.24   R.C.: Richard Curle.

p.25   *epilogue*: 'Epilogue III: Bains Turcs', published in the *Blue Review*, July 1913.

p.28   a *'bleu'*: a telegram.

p.30   *J.A. Spender*: (1862-1942), editor of the *Westminster Gazette*.

*   *Bruce Richmond*: (1871-1964), editor of the *Times Literary Supplement*.

p.36   *D.H. Lawrence* ('Lorenzo'): (1885-1930), and his wife Frieda, met KM and Murry in 1913. A close but difficult relationship developed between the two couples – especially between Lawrence and Murry – who lived near each other for periods between 1914 and 1916.

*   *Mary's mill*: the mill house of Gilbert and Mary Cannan at Cholesbury.

*   *Lady Cynthia Asquith*: (1887-1959), married to the Hon. Herbert Asquith, son of the Liberal Prime Minister.

*   *Francis Carco*: (1886-1958), bohemian French writer with whom KM imagined she was in love.

*   *Elgin Crescent*: 95 Elgin Crescent. Murry took rooms there in 1915.

p.37   *my novel*: The Voyage (Constable, 1924).

p.37   *H.F. Fox:* Murry's former classical tutor at Oxford.

p.38   *rooms:* at 95 Elgin Crescent.

p.39   *Chartier:* an inexpensive restaurant.

*   *George Moore:* (1852-1933), author of *The Confessions of a Young Man.*

p.41   *A.R. Orage:* (1873-1934), editor of the *New Age,* who first published KM's stories in England.

p.43   *Beatrice Hastings:* (1879-1943), South African-born journalist who had once lived with Orage and contributed malicious articles to the *New Age.* Now living in Paris and consorting with the painter Modigliani, she was nicknamed 'Biggy B' ('B.B.') by KM.

p.45   *Rebecca Wests:* the novelist Rebecca West took her pseudonym from the name of the liberated female protagonist of Ibsen's play *Rosmersholm.*

*   *Aspasia:* a famous courtesan of Ancient Greece whose beauty and wit so captivated Pericles that he made her his life-long companion.

*   *B.B.:* short for 'Biggy B', their nickname for Beatrice Hastings.

*   *Colette Vagabonde:* Colette was one of KM's favourite novelists. *La Vagabonde,* about her music hall life, appeared in 1910.

p.46   *my first novel: The Aloe,* the long first version of 'Prelude'.

p.48   *Kay:* Alexander Kay, manager of the London branch of the Bank of New Zealand, where KM's monthly advance from her father was paid.

p.49   *S.S. Koteliansky* ('Kot'): (1882-1955), a Russian Jewish friend of KM and D.H. Lawrence. He collaborated with them in translating Russian literature into English.

p.55   *Molly Muir:* an attractive friend of Gilbert Cannan's.

*   *J.B. Pinker:* (1864-1922), a leading London literary agent who represented D.H. Lawrence and later KM.

*   *Dugald MacColl:* (1859-1948), painter and art critic.

*   *Aitken:* probably Conrad Aitken (1889-1973), poet, novelist and critic.

*   *Muirhead Bone:* (1876-1953), a Scottish painter whose work Murry had reviewed.

p.56   *Jarvis:* Murry's landlord.

*   *Frank Harris:* (1856-1931), biographer of Oscar Wilde. He had published KM's story 'The House' in *Hearth and Home* in 1912.

p.57   *a Willy novel:* a novel by W.L. George.

p.60   *this German chasing:* Murry had written to K.M. on 13 May about anti-German riots in London: 'It's enough to make anyone believe that we deserve all we get.... There's a photo at the back of the *D.N.* I send you – showing four policemen *just looking on* while some poor unfortunate German's whole house is plundered.'

p.61   *O Hara San:* a favourite Japanese doll whose head had come off.

p.62   *Walter de la Mare:* (1873-1956), poet, former contributor to *Rhythm* and friend of KM's.

p.63   *Frederick Goodyear:* (1887-1917), Murry's Oxford friend, whom KM was particularly fond of. He was killed in the war.

p.64   *the Dreys:* KM's American-born friend, Anne Estelle Drey (née Rice), was a fauvist painter and illustrator, married to Raymond Drey, a journalist who had contributed to *Rhythm* and the *Blue Review*.

p.65 *Le Radical*: a daily republican paper published in Marseilles.

p.67 *Day's Bay*: near Wellington.

p.69 *Marie*: Charlotte Beauchamp (1887-1966), nicknamed both 'Marie' and 'Chaddie', was KM's elder sister who also lived in England.

*   *Clive Bell*: (1881-1964), writer on art who had married (and separated from) Virginia Woolf's sister, Vanessa.

p.71 *Florida*: Lawrence, who was unwell and becoming embittered with England, talked about emigrating to some better place. About this time, he was offered a cottage in Florida.

*   *Chummie's death*: Leslie Heron Beauchamp ('Chummie') (1894-1915), KM's much-loved only brother whose death in 1915 left her desolate.

p.77 *Garsington*: Garsington Manor, the country home near Oxford of Lady Ottoline Morrell and her husband, Phillip. The guests at their Christmas house-party in 1915 included Clive and Vanessa Bell, Lytton Strachey, Maynard Keynes and Murry.

p.82 *Pyotr Stepanovitch & Kirillov*: characters in Dostoevsky's novel, *The Possessed*.

p.83 *Peter Wilkins*: a kitten.

*   *May*: a servant.

p.84 *make an end to it in October*: i.e., move back to London.

*   *accept you provisionally*: Murry had been classified as medically unfit for active service and was in London looking for a job of 'national importance'.

p.85 *Magdeburgische Zeitung*: one of the many German newspapers Murry had to read for his job at the War Office.

p.86 *Leon Bloy*: (1846-1917), acerbic French writer.

p.87 *your poems*: Murry's *Poems 1917-18* were published privately in 1919.

p.89 *Miss Wright*: the owner of KM's studio flat who had sent two prospective tenants to look over it, to KM's indignation.

*   *L.M.*: short for Lesley Moore, the name KM gave to Ida Baker.

*   *Chaddie*: KM's sister Charlotte Perkins, now living in London.

p.90 *Belle*: KM's aunt, Belle Trinder.

*   *Milne*: a classical scholar and friend of Murry who worked at the British Museum.

*   *J.W.N. Sullivan*: (1886-1937) an Irish scientist and writer with whom Murry had become friendly while working at the War Office. He was later Murry's assistant editor (with Aldous Huxley) on the *Athenaeum*.

*   *Brettushka*: a playful name for The Hon. Dorothy Brett (1883-1977), an artist friend of Katherine and Murry who belonged to the Garsington set.

*   *H[er] L[adyship]*: a private name for Lady Ottoline Morrell (1873-1938), half-sister of the Duke of Portland who entertained KM and Murry, among others, at Garsington Manor.

p.92 *Ainger*: KM's doctor who advised her to leave England.

*   *Ribni*: a Japanese doll.

410 *Letters Between Katherine Mansfield and John Middleton Murry*

p.93   *Allen's remark*: Percival Allen was an old school friend of Murry who had been killed in the war.

*   *the P.L.M.*: a railway office.

*   *Duval*: a restaurant where KM and Murry had previously gone together. She was alone this time.

p.94   *the Terminus*: the Terminus Hotel at the Gare St. Lazare.

p.97   *the Meynets; Maam Gamel*: people whom KM had met previously in Bandol.

p.98   *Madame Geoffroi*: an acquaintance from their 1916 sojourn in Bandol who was married to a doctor.

p.101   *heron or heronette*: Heron was the name KM and Murry gave to the house they one day dreamed of owning.

p.102   *Bee's husband*: Laura Bright was a friend of KM's mother. In 1920 the widowed Harold Beauchamp married her.

*   *Arthur*: Murry's younger brother, who later changed his name to Richard.

p.109   *my new work*: 'Je ne parle pas français'.

*   *Mark Gertler*: (1892-1939), talented Jewish painter who was friendly with D.H. Lawrence and the Garsington set. He died of tuberculosis.

p.112   *Raoul Duquette*: a French pimp who was the central character in 'Je ne parle pas français'.

p.118   *Beaufort Mansions*: a flat in Beaufort Mansions, Chelsea, that was for rent.

p.120   *Mouse*: the helpless young English woman in 'Je ne parle pas français' who has eloped with Dick Harmon.

p.126   *'Le P'tit' and 'Nausicaa'*: in *Raffin Su-su* by the French writer Jean Ajalbert.

p.129   *Les Charmettes*: a country house near Chambéry where Rousseau lived from 1738-1740 with Mme de Warens.

p.133   *Pierre MacOrlan*: pseudonym of the French writer Pierre Dumarchais with whom Murry was acquainted.

p.134   *Elle et Lui*: by French novelist George Sand.

p.145   *she must never know*: that they were not already married.

p.152   *J.T. Sheppard*: a classical scholar, later Provost of King's College, Cambridge, whom Murry employed as a regular reviewer for the *Athenaeum*.

p.153   *prospectuses*: for 'Prelude', due for publication by the Hogarth Press in July.

*   *your story to Harrison*: the *English Review*, edited by Austin Harrison, published 'Bliss' in August.

p.155   *Gwyne*: KM had been enraged when L.M. passed on the advice of Mr Gwynne, the foreman of the factory where she worked. He had said that without the strict regime of a clinic KM would not get better. There would be too much emotional stress between individuals if she tried a home cure.

*   *Mrs Maufe* (later Lady Maufe): KM's neighbour in Church Street, Chelsea.

p.157   *about Hampstead*: they were negotiating to lease 2 Portland Villas, a house in Hampstead.

p.158   *the monster*: 2 Portland Villas in Hampstead, which they also referred to as 'The Elephant'.

p.159   *Dearly*: a prospective housekeeper.

p.160   *the Pageant*: *A Pageant of English Poetry*, edited by R.M. Leonard.

p.163   *whiffing for pollocks*: fishing.

*   *Pagello*: a doctor.

p.166   *the black monkeys*: KM is probably referring to her depression.

p.167   *the drawings*: drawings by J.D. Fergusson for 'Prelude', which the Woolfs were publishing.

*   *Roger Fry*: (1866-1934), Bloomsbury art critic and friend of Virginia Woolf.

p.168   *Pour Toi, Patrie*: by A. Laclef and E. Bergeron (1918).

*   *Georges Duhamel*: (1884-1966), French poet and novelist who wrote about the war in which he served as an army surgeon.

p.169   *'feltie'*: an old hat of Murry's that they shared.

p.170   *the Bailiff's cottage*: at Garsington.

p.172   *Gus Bofa*: pseudonym of Gustave Blanchet, artist and illustrator.

p.174   *recovery of last year's*: a tax refund.

p.176   *Arthur Croft-Hill* ('Crofty'): a doctor-friend.

p.178   *Colour*: an art magazine with an article on the work of J.D. Fergusson.

p.181   *bregglechik*: breakfast.

p.185   *Thomas Vince*: the owner of the Casetta Deerholm.

*   *Rendall*: a doctor.

*   *sheets of translation*: KM was one of those whom S.S. Koteliansky badgered to assist him with translations of Russian writers.

p.186   *Mackenzie and Gilly*: reviews of Compton Mackenzie's *Poor Relations* and Gilbert Cannan's *Time and Eternity*.

*   *Wing*: Wingley, a favourite cat.

*   *Violet (and Gertie)*: live-in maids at 2 Portland Villas.

*   *No.7*: On 5 October, Murry announced: 'I'm going to number my letters henceforward, so that you can tell me in yours that they have been received, and see whether any are missing. Will you do the same? Then every time I write I will say at the top of my letter 3 & 4 received, and I too will know whether any are missing.'

p.187   *that revolver*: KM had bought a revolver for self-protection.

*   *Tom Moult*: poet and journalist who had contributed to *Rhythm* and whose wife, Bessie, was also a writer.

*   *Mary Hutchinson*: although married to the barrister St John Hutchinson, she was the close companion of Clive Bell.

p.188   *Scott-James*: R.A. Scott-James (1878-1959), critic and later editor of the *London Mercury*.

*   *Ripmann*: KM's admired former language teacher at Queen's College.

p.189   *Chaddie and Jeanne*: KM's sisters who lived in England.

p.190   *H.M. Tomlinson* ('Tommy'): a close friend of Murry who was for a time literary editor of the *Nation*.

*   *196 days*: Murry was numbering his letters according to the number of days left until KM's return to England on 1 May 1920.

p.190   *announcement list*: a publishers' advertising supplement to the *Athenaeum*.

*   *James Strachey*: (1887-1967), younger brother of Lytton Strachey who wrote dramatic criticism for the *Athenaeum*.

p.191   *Still Life*: Murry's first novel, begun in 1913 and published in 1916.

*   *Cinnamon and Angelica*: Murry's verse play that was published in 1920.

*   *[[   ]]*: this indicates KM's use of square brackets for special emphasis. See also p. 220.

*   *Stanley Weyman and Stella Benson*: KM's review of *The Great House* by Stanley Weyman appeared on 7 November and of *Living Alone* by Stella Benson on 14 November.

p.193   *Sylvia Lynd*: a writer and friend of KM.

p.194   *Bonwick*: the business manager of Arnold Rowntree, the wealthy chocolate manufacturer who funded the *Athenaeum*.

p.197   *the Albatross*: KM's nickname for Ida Baker.

*   *Ansaldi*: an Italian doctor who proved untrustworthy.

p.200   *Connie & Jinny*: Connie Beauchamp and Jinnie Fullerton, KM's elderly cousin and her friend, who lived in Menton during the winter.

*   *the parcel*: containing medicine prescribed by Dr. Sorapure.

p.201   *Aldous Huxley*: (1894-1963), novelist who was second assistant editor of the *Athenaeum*.

p.202   *enclosing Butler*: Murry's review of *Samuel Butler, Author of Erewhon* by H. Festing Jones appeared in the *Athenaeum* on 24 October.

*   *Dosty*: KM's review of Dostoevsky's *An Honest Thief and other Stories*, translated by Constance Garnett.

*   *Porter*: KM's dentist.

p.204   *Who said that?*: KM was quoting a line from one of Murry's poems.

*   *I am doing Virginia*: KM's review of Virginia Woolf's *Night and Day* appeared in the *Athenaeum* on 21 November 1919.

p.205   *Athy*: (short for 'Athenaeum') one of the Murrys' two pet cats.

*   *Frank Rutter*: editor of *Art and Letters* who had asked KM to review some novels.

p.207   *Richard Kurt*: by Stephen Hudson (pseudonym of Sydney Schiff).

p.209   *Bertrand Russell*: (1872-1970), the Cambridge philosopher, writer and close friend of Lady Ottoline Morrell. He and KM had corresponded in 1916.

p.210   *Wyndham Lewis*: (1884-1957), had been employed at the Omega (craft) Workshops, set up by Roger Fry, in 1913. After quarrelling with Fry he publicly vilified him.

*   *his book*: Wyndham Lewis's *The Caliph's Design: Architects! Where is your Vortex?* was one of the principal Vorticist manifestos.

p.215   *Dent's note*: Murry had written earlier that the writer, Edward Dent, was one of KM's admirers and had offered to contact on her behalf his elderly aunts who lived at Nice.

p.217   *Mr Salteena*: a central character in Daisy Ashford's *The Young Visiters*.

p.218   *Eric-or-little-by-little*: a moralistic child's story about school life by Frederic William Farrar, published 1858.

p.220 *Grant Richards*: a publisher with whom KM had been negotiating.

* *T.J. Cobden-Sanderson*: a printer and publisher who published Murry's *Cinnamon and Angelica*.

p.222 *Monkhouse & Stern*: KM's reviews of *True Love* by Allan Monkhouse and of *Children of No Man's Land* by G.B. Stern appeared on 28 November.

* *Edward (Eddie) Marsh*: (1872-1953), patron of writers and poets who edited five volumes of Georgian poetry between 1912-1922.

* *J.C. Squire*: (1884-1958), a Georgian poet who founded the *London Mercury* in October 1919.

p.227 *Duncan Grant*: (1885-1978), painter and member of the Bloomsbury Group with whom Vanessa Bell (née Stephen) lived after 1915.

* *John Drinkwater*: (1882-1937), poet and dramatist who had contributed to *Rhythm*.

p.228 *Edmund Gosse*: (1849-1928), critic and man of letters.

* *Thomas Hardy*: (1840-1928), poet and novelist whom Murry greatly admired.

p.229 *Couperus and Kuprin*: KM's reviews of *Old People and the Things that Pass* by Louis Couperus and of *The Garnet Bracelet* by Alexander Kuprin appeared in December.

p.231 *Dora's Gyp*: Gyp was the lap-dog of Dora, the sentimental wife of David in Dickens' *David Copperfield*.

* *an ad of my story*: 'Je ne parle pas français'.

p.240 *Bonwick*: the business manager of Arnold Rowntree (below).

p.241 *Arnold Rowntree*: (1861-1949), the chocolate manufacturer and philanthropist who financed the *Athenaeum*.

p.246 *the article*: Frank Rutter published 'The Man Without a Temperament' in *Art and Letters*, Spring 1920, but no review or article by KM.

p.247 *the story*: 'Je ne parle pas français', published by the Heron Press.

* *my book*: *The Critic in Judgement; or Belshazzar of Baron's Court* (Hogarth Press, 1919).

* *my poems*: *Poems 1917-1918* (Heron Press).

p.248 *Edith Sitwell*: poet and critic who edited *Wheels*, an annual anthology of modern verse, from 1916-1921.

* *Goldsworthy Lowes Dickinson* ('Goldy'): (1862-1932), Cambridge historian, philosophical writer and friend of E.M. Forster.

p.249 *Lev Shestov*: (1866-1938), Russian philosopher who wrote on Dostoevsky, Tolstoy and Nietzsche.

p.250 *Desmond McCarthy*: (1878-1952), writer and close friend of the Woolfs.

* *Mr Clough*: the rich and eccentric owner of a country house Murry was considering buying.

* *H.G. Wells*: (1866-1946), the novelist whom Murry had known since 1914.

p.251 *Nevinson*: either H.W. Nevinson (1856-1941), the war correspondent and journalist, or his son, C.R. Nevinson, the painter and war artist.

* *Marie Dahlerup*: an acquaintance who was being considered for the post of companion-help to KM.

p.253 *Foster*: a doctor.

p.254 *Lord Henry Bentinck*: half-brother of Lady Ottoline Morrell.

p.254   *Horatio Bottomley*: (1860-1933), editor of *John Bull*.

p.258   *How's money – let me know please*: Murry subsequently added a note to the head of his letter: 'This is the letter that *hurt* K. so much. Well, it doesn't seem very bad to me. June 30, 1948.'

p.259   *Mary Hamilton*: KM's review of *Full Circle* by Mary Hamilton appeared on 6 February 1920.

*   *a book of mine: Bliss and Other Stories* was published by Constable in December 1920.

*   *Old Boiled Egg*: Murry told KM on 17 January that he had been awarded the O.B.E. (for his war service as Chief Censor).

p.260   *Coggins and Limpidus*: KM's review of *Sir Limpidus* by Marmaduke Pickthall and *Coggin* by Ernest Oldmeadow appeared on 30 January.

p.263   *the letter*: From Michael Sadleir of Constable publishers.

*   *The Times Lit Sup. Review*: of 'Prelude' and 'Je ne parle pas français'.

p.264   *my copy of 'Je ne parle pas français'*: the story was published privately by Murry and his brother on their press at 2 Portland Villas in February 1920.

*   *that story Rutter has*: 'The Man Without a Temperament'.

p.265   *the enclosed letter*: from Michael Sadleir.

*   *though things are tight*: KM later underlined 'though things are tight' and 'if you will repay me when you get the money for your book'.

*   *Michael Sadler* (Sadleir): Murry's former Oxford friend who had helped him found *Rhythm* and now worked for Constable publishers.

p.270   *just as you did to Heinemann*: Heinemann had rejected a book of KM's short stories in April 1919.

p.272   *Jeanne*: KM's sister.

p.275   *enamel spoon*: a reference to a story by Anatole France.

p.277   *the Daudet story*: from Alphonse Daudet's *Lettres de Mon Moulin*.

p.279   *your new story*: Murry later added a marginal note: ' "Man Without a Temperament"?'

p.284   *Alice Prosser*: according to Murry, KM refers to the excessively refined wife of a New Zealand clergyman she had known.

p.285   *Elizabeth von Arnim*: KM's cousin and author of the best-selling novel *Elizabeth and her German Garden* (1898).

*   *J.D. Beresford*: novelist and senior reviewer for the *Westminster*. In 1922 he was one of the Ouspensky-Gurdjieff circle that KM joined.

*   *May Sinclair*: KM had reviewed her novel *Mary Olivier: A Life*, in June 1919.

p.286   *Vivian Locke Ellis*: a poet who lived in a seventeenth-century mansion near East Grinstead and who became a good friend of Murry's.

p.294   *Waterlow has been so decent*: Murry wrote to KM on 16 March, 'I gave Sydney notice to clear out by the end of the third week in April to-day at breakfast.'

p.296   *the New Forest*: KM suggested on 19 March that she ask her sister 'Marie' (Chaddie) to find them suitable holiday accommodation in the New Forest.

p.299   *Broomies*: a cottage in Chailey, Sussex, that Murry bought on 9 April for £480, in KM's name since he was an undischarged bankrupt. They never lived in it.

*   *Monaco*: writing of the celebrations for a royal wedding in Monaco, KM had said: 'You would have made a good prince ... but I wouldn't have been up to much.'

*   *Short Stories*: KM's review of collections of short stories by Archibald Marshall, Mary Gaunt and Dion Clayton Calthrop appeared on 2 April.

p.300   *Bunny Dunn*: a society woman whom KM saw something of in Menton. KM told Murry on 22 March that 'she is frightfully jealous of me and has been telling disgusting lies behind my back ...'

p.302   *Hardy ... poem*: 'The maid of Keinton Mandeville', Hardy's tribute to Sir Henry Bishop on the sixty-fifth anniversary of his death, appeared in the *Athenaeum* on 30 April.

*   *my book*: probably *The Evolution of an Intellectual*.

p.303   *I won't consent*: the next day KM changed her mind, telling Murry: 'I feel I was too undisciplined about my story and Constable. I leave it to you.'

*   *André L'Hôte*: French Cubist painter and writer.

*   *Paul Valéry*: (1871-1945), French poet and man of letters with whom Murry was acquainted.

p.304   *a worrying time about Arthur*: Murry's brother wanted to study art at the Slade and needed financial help to do so.

p.305   *the Schiffs*: Sydney and Violet Schiff were wealthy patrons of the arts whom KM met in Menton. Sydney Schiff wrote novels under the pseudonym 'Stephen Hudson'.

*   *H.W. Massingham*: (1860-1924), political journalist and editor of the *Nation*.

p.311   *Osbert Sitwell*: (1892-1969), writer, brother of Edith and Sacheverell and contributor to *Wheels*.

p.313   *Knopf and the Yazpegs*: Murry's book *Aspects of Literature* which Knopf had declined.

p.315   *Podsnap*: a character in Dickens' novel *Our Mutual Friend*.

p.318   *Rose Macaulay* (later Dame): (1881-1958) novelist and critic.

*   *Prowse's novel*: KM's review of R.O. Prowse's *A Gift of the Dusk*, a novel whose protagonist has tuberculosis, appeared on 29 October 1920.

p.319   *Floryan's letters*: blackmailed by Floryan Sobieniowski, KM had paid him £40 – Constable's advance on *Bliss and Other Stories* – for return of the letters she had written him in her early, bohemian years.

p.323   *gave that picture to the press*: (taken about 1913) to be used as publicity for *Bliss*.

p.325   *Louis Goldring*: KM's review of *The Black Curtain* by Louis Goldring had appeared on 16 April 1920.

p.327   *my story*: 'Daughters of the Late Colonel'.

*   *the Princess B.*: Princess Elizabeth Bibesco (1897-1945), daughter of the former Liberal Prime Minister, Herbert Asquith and his wife Margot, had married Prince Antoine Bibesco in 1919. She fancied she had fallen in love with Murry.

p.327   *Anthony Asquith*: (1902-1968), brother of Elizabeth Bibesco and youngest son of Margot and Herbert Asquith.

p.328   *Curtis Brown*: An American literary agent.

p.329   *K.M. can't go on*: writing weekly fiction reviews for the *Athenaeum*.

p.331   *Croesus*: the last king of Lydia (c.560-546 B.C.) whose wealth was proverbial.

*   *kine*: A biblical reference: kine = cattle.

p.332   *Mrs Valentine Dobrée*: a painter, married to the writer and critic Bonamy Dobrée.

p.340   *I wrote the lectures out*: Murry's first of six lectures on 'The Problem of Style' was on 'The Meaning of Style'. His book, *The Problem of Style*, appeared in March 1922.

*   *A.J. Jenkinson*: an Oxford don and friend of Murry's.

p.341   *Stephani's report*: the report has not survived.

p.345   *Walter Raleigh*: (1861-1922), Professor of English Literature at Oxford since 1904. He had invited Murry to deliver the lectures on style.

p.347   *substantial balance*: due to the success of *Bliss and Other Stories*, for which Murry had negotiated a 15 per cent royalty.

*   *Tartarin de Tarascon*: the boastful hero of Alphonse Daudet's novel *Tartarin de Tarascon*.

p.349   *Manoukhine*: a Russian doctor living in Paris who claimed to be able to cure tuberculosis by irradiating the spleen with X-rays. KM heard of him from Koteliansky.

p.350   *we might be able to sub let*: the Chalet des Sapins, which the Murrys had taken on a twelve-month lease.

p.351   *Ernestine Rey*: a Swiss woman who did the cooking.

p.352   *my novel*: The Voyage (Constable, 1924).

*   *the Oiseau Bleu*: a chalet in the neighbouring village which they were thinking of taking when the lease of the Chalet des Sapins expired.

p.353   *'The Garden Party'*: was published in the *Westminster Gazette* in February 1922 in three instalments.

*   *Anatole France*: (1844-1924), French novelist, critic and man of letters.

p.355   *J.P. Eckermann*: (1792-1854), German writer who recorded and published his conversations with Goethe.

p.356   *Elizabeth's*: Elizabeth von Arnim, who owned the Chalet de Soleil in nearby Randogne, and with whom Murry got on well.

p.358   *The Schoolmaster and other Stories*: by Anton Chekhov.

p.360   *the day after I sent that letter*: of 2 February.

p.363   *Dunning*: a practising Yogi whom Murry had met in 1920.

p.364   *Mrs Jellaby*: a character in Charles Dickens' *Bleak House*.

*   *Selsfield House*: the home of Vivian Locke Ellis at East Grinstead.

*   *a card from Lawrence*: sent from Wellington where he was en route from Australia to New Mexico.

p.365 *proposing myself to Will Rothenstein*: Rothenstein had suggested to
Murry that KM should sit for a drawing.

p.367 *our first voyage to France together*: according to Murry, in May 1912.

p.368 *P.D. Ouspensky*: a Russian mathematician and disciple of Gurdjieff who
gave lectures in London based on his book *Tertium Organum* (1920).

p.370 *Spenser's Swans*: in 'Prothalamion', by the sixteenth-century poet, Edmund
Spenser.

p.373 *Fontainebleau*: Gurdjieff had acquired as his headquarters The Prieuré, a
former Carmelite monastery, set in parkland at Avon near
Fontainebleau.

 * *George Gurdjieff*: (1872-1949), a widely travelled mystic of Russian origin
who established his Institute for the Harmonious Development of Man
(opened in Moscow in 1910) at Fontainebleau in 1922. His followers
were mostly well-to-do Russian and English 'intellectuals'.

p.374 *a very superior mill*: Murry had a letter file which required holes to be
punched.

p.375 *Doctor J.C. Young*: an English psychiatrist who, with A.R. Orage, was one
of the first to go to Fontainebleau.

p.380 *Jeanne's wedding*: KM's youngest sister married Charles Renshaw on 17
October 1922 at St Margaret's, Westminster.

p.385 *Alexander Salzmann*: a painter and friend of Chekov's widow who
decorated the gallery assigned to KM in the cow-house.

p.387 *Sylvia Sullivan*: the estranged wife of Murry's friend J.W.N. Sullivan.
 * *Princess Marya*: a character in Mikhael Lermontov's *Hero of Our Times*.
 * *Olga Knipper*: Chekhov's widow.

p.388 *Olga Ivanovna*: later the wife of the American architect, Frank Lloyd
Wright, she was one of KM's best friends at Fontainebleau.

 * *goes to work on some farm*: grieving for the loss of KM from her life, L.M.
took a job on a farm at Lisieux, which was on the estate of Madame van
Schunberger, a feminist.

 * *Elizabeth's new novel*: Elizabeth von Arnim's *The Enchanted April*
(London, 1922).

p.390 *E.M. Forster*: (1879-1970), novelist and member of the Bloomsbury group.

p.391 *near Dunning*: in November Murry moved from Selsfield to Wayside
Cottage, next door to the Dunnings and their four young sons at
Ditchling in Sussex. He was joined by Sullivan, whose wife had left him.

p.397 *this Sickert essay*: 'The Etchings of Walter Sickert' appeared in *Print
Collectors' Quarterly* in February 1923.

 * *'Bill'*: i.e., Dunning's wife.

p.399 *the proof of the drawing*: Sir William Rothenstein's portrait of Murry
appeared in *Twenty-four Portraits*, 2nd series (Chatto & Windus, 1923).

Index